Welcome To...

THE INTERNET

2ND EDITION

Tom Badgett

A Subsidiary of
Henry Holt and Co., Inc.

a subsidiary of Henry Holt and Company, Inc.
115 West 18th Street
New York, NY 10011

First Edition—1993

Printed in the United States of America.

Library of Congress Cataloging-in-Publication Data

Badgett, Tom.
Welcome to-- the Internet / Tom Badgett. -- 2nd ed.
p. cm.
ISBN 1-55828-424-9
1.Internet (Computer network) I. Title.
TK5105.875.I57B33 1995
0004.6'7--dc20 95-16007
CIP

10 9 8 7 6 5 4 3 2

MIS:Press books are available at special discounts for bulk purchases for sales promotions, premiums, fund-raising, or educational use. Special editions or book excerpts can also be created to specification.

For details contact: Special Sales Director
MIS:Press
a subsidiary of Henry Holt and Company, Inc.
115 West 18th Street
New York, New York 10011

Editor-in-Chief: Paul Farrell
Copy Edit Manager Shari Chappell
Development Editor: Debra Williams Cauley
Production Editor: Maya Riddick
Managing Editor: Cary Sullivan
Copy Editor: Annette Devlin
Technical Editor Elissa Keeler

ACKNOWLEDGEMENTS

No book is the work of the authors alone. This book on Internet, perhaps more than many, required the work of many people.

I can't mention everyone who helped with this book, but I'd like to extend special thanks to these:

Niels Jonker, President, and other staff at United states Internet, Inc. for answering questions, helping with research and for providing excellent, general support during this project. Niels read this book as it evolved, offered regular and valuable suggestions, and put me in touch with numerous other resources.

Holly Towne, computer skills teacher at Vine middle school in Knoxville, TN, and driving force behind Operation Uplink, an international education and community project on Internet. Holly first introduced me to the Internet and to her students, whose school lives are changing because of their Internet activities. I learned a lot from the students while they learned about the Internet.

Jack Lail, Metro Editor of Knoxville News Sentinel, and dozens of others around the world who answered questions, found resources, put me in touch with other people, and in general helped to make my travels fun and interesting.

Debra Williams Cauley, Editor at MIS:Press, who struggled with me to fine tune the book design, edit the manuscript, and do all the hundreds of other jobs that have to be done before a book can get to you.

Elissa Keeler, Annette Sroka Devlin, and Maya Riddick, whose combined editorial talents made a valuable contribution to the book.

I'd also like to thank The WELL, an on-line conferencing service, who arranged for me to experience their services and the Internet from a different perspective. And, there are countless other people on the Internet and at MIS:Press who worked behind the scenes to bring this book to you.

Table of Contents

INTRODUCTION

The Internet is a telecommunications superhighway, picking up information from corporations, government institutions, private individuals, and universities over branch roads leading into nearly every corner of the globe.

Like a superhighway, it beckons potential travelers with its promise of faraway places, exotic destinations, and interesting people. Like a superhighway, the Internet can take you from one major destination to another quickly, then introduce quiet back roads and quaint locales for leisurely exploration. Like a superhighway, the Internet carries holiday and family traffic, people who know precisely where they are going or those who are wandering, government and educational traffic as well as business and commercial traffic. In short, the Internet is there for anyone interested in short journeys or lengthy treks, for users who need a quick shortcut across town or across the country.

Unlike a regular superhighway, the Internet does all this electronically—you need never leave the comfort of your home, office, or classroom.

A few years ago the concept of sitting in front of a computer terminal and reaching out to other people across the country or around the world would have seemed impossible or at least foreign to most of us. Businesses were doing it, of course, using the expensive resources at their disposal to connect workers around the world. And a relatively small cadre of individuals—computer gurus or engineers, mostly—were doing it. But for the average person, accessing a global electronic network such as the Internet was out of the question. Most of us didn't know about the Internet, for one thing, and the cost was more than most individuals were willing to pay. No, global networking was for the big companies.

That has changed, of course. The Internet is only one of a group of fascinating and useful networks that are linking people in all walks of life into a giant, global community without walls:

- A group of middle school students from underprivileged neighborhoods in Knoxville, TN, log on to the Internet daily to chat interactively with other students in California, Kentucky, New York, and Canada. They also are on a first name basis with company presidents and college professors from Chicago, The Netherlands, and England.
- A college professor in Gettysburg, PA, logs on to the Internet several times a week to update colleagues on his latest discoveries working with computer-based testing of hand-eye coordination timing. He finds out what others in his field are doing and gets suggestions directly from other experts.
- A West Coast software developer uses the Internet during the final stages of writing a custom application to upload programs to his client in England and to get progress reports and early implementation suggestions.
- A range of users from executives and managers to salespersons and secretaries at companies such as J.P. Morgan, IBM, Coca-Cola, and Walt Disney check Internet electronic mailboxes several times a day to keep in touch with far-flung members of their corporate community, to send proposals and quotes to clients, or to confirm travel schedules.

- The curious and the expert, the young and the old, male and female, keep Internet wires humming well into the night from the darkened corners of bedrooms, dens, and offices at home. What are they doing? Talking with each other, working late, finding recipes, reading poetry, searching for news, playing games, and more.

The Internet is like a diverse community of millions of people, divided and subdivided into close groups of intimate strangers where everybody knows your name. Little wonder that as computer technology drops in price and moves onto nearly every corporate and home desk that we naturally seek a way to come together even as we sit apart in the privacy of our own logical worlds.

In this book I'll show you how to tap into the captivating world of the Internet, giving you "news you can use," whether you already are using the Internet or are merely fascinated by the prospect. I'll take you along the Internet superhighway in a travel guide that shows you how to get on board, how to explore the opportunities it presents, and how to bring back souvenirs from your journeys.

You'll find information that addresses your business and educational needs, as well as how to enjoy and benefit from the Internet as an individual user. There's also a survey of available databases and services along with easy-to-use information on how to search them fruitfully. And, I'll introduce you to the hundreds of conferences and libraries available online.

This is a hands-on book that you can use to learn about the Internet from scratch, to establish your own personal or business account, to find software to help you access the system, and most importantly to navigate this electronic maze on your own. But this book goes beyond the how of Internet access. I want you to know the what and the why. Why use one database or the other, why travel down this road or that one, what can you expect from this conference or the other one?

The idea is to take you as far as you need to go but to travel only along comfortable roads. You are ready for this book if you know how to turn on your computer and type a little on the keyboard. Sure, some of the Internet is couched in technical terms, and the procedures for using some features seem esoteric and befuddling.

Don't worry. I don't expect you to be a computer expert or to have any real experience with computer communications as you read this book. I will take you through the steps and show you what's required at every crossroad. If you'll take this promise on faith—then be willing to read on, even when things seem complex—you can learn enough about the Internet to explore it on your own. And soon you'll be expert enough to venture off to go where you want, and as far as you want.

CONVENTIONS I USE

Before we get started, let's agree on some terms and some ways of doing things. I'll try to keep the format of this book as simple and as straightforward as possible while, at the same time, making clear the various commands, files, and structures we need to discuss.

NOTE

TRAVEL TIP

WARNING

First of all, in addition to plain text, you'll find throughout this book some icons (small pictures) designed to draw your attention to one section or another. When you see the Note icon, for example, you know I have some special information that applies to the main text in that area, but I feel it is important enough to point it out. Likewise, if you see the Travel Tip icon you'll know there is information that can save you time or trouble on your journey. Finally, if you see a Warning icon, I am telling you about something that is potentially confusing, could cause you to lose data, or information that is really significant for you to notice.

Beyond icons, I have other ways of presenting data in this book that will alert you to important ideas. These include:

- New terms are *italicized*. These are words I am introducing for the first time and likely will use later in the book. You probably will find them described in the glossary.
- Keystrokes, file names, commands, and specific options are presented in **boldface**. Information you enter from the keyboard is shown in boldface, but you won't enter everything you see in boldface. I'll show you specifically when to type something on the keyboard.

We also make some assumptions about you and your computer system. Although the Internet is for anyone using just about any kind of computer system, we assume you are using an MS DOS machine or a Macintosh rather than a UNIX computer. (UNIX or UNIX-derivatives are the most common operating system on the Internet as hosts. When you access the Internet you may be using one of these hosts—or a DEC VAX or another relatively large machine—but we assume your machine is not a UNIX machine.) You might be using an Amiga, Apple or other machine as well, but we'll describe procedures from a non-UNIX perspective.

As you begin reading this book, you should be familiar with the communications software and modem you're using with your machine. As I describe modem command procedures, I will use the Hayes-compatible convention. If your modem isn't compatible with the Hayes "AT" command set, you'll have to refer to your modem manual to learn how to conduct the same commands with your hardware.

WHAT'S IN THIS BOOK

I've already hinted at some of the things I'll cover in this book. Here's more detail on what you will find.

In Chapter 1, I take you on two guided tours of the Internet to get you started immediately. Then I give you a little Internet background and history. Don't worry. It's not much, but it will help you understand why the Internet is the way it is.

Chapter 2 shows you how to get onto the Internet. You have to find a pathway, a road, to take you where you want to go. Depending on where you work, how much money you have, and your level of computer experience, this part of the journey can be easy or difficult. Either way, I'll take you by the hand so you can take this step with as little hassle as possible. I also describe the hardware and software necessary to access the Internet. Your modem questions will be answered here.

In Chapter 3 I handle the housekeeping part of using the Internet. These include file, node, and addressing conventions that you need to be aware of. I also, cover the basics of the physical and logical structure of the Internet including Telnet, email conferences and news, and transferring files.

Chapter 4 introduces you to popular Internet tools—the software utilities you will use to find your way around the Internet. These tools include Archie, FTP, Gopher, WAIS, Whois, Finger, and World Wide Web browser. More information on some of these tools will appear throughout the book, but in Chapter 4 you will get a good summary of what is available and how to use it.

Chapter 5 explores the different ways of connecting to the Internet, including DOS-based communications, Windows packages, graphical interfaces such as Mosaic, and more. This chapter also includes step-by-step information on configuring many of the popular online software packages.

Chapter 6 delves into the newest aspect of the Internet: online business. In this chapter you'll learn what other companies are doing with this new communications tool, and how you can make use of the Internet for your own business or product.

Chapter 7 shows you how to reach out and talk with anyone anywhere across the Internet. You'll use the skills shown in this chapter to chat with a local user on your host and to reach around the world with IRC (Internet Relay Chat).

Chapter 8 is an annotated list of Internet resources and how to reach them. This is hands-on stuff that you can try once you have learned a few basic Internet concepts. Consider this chapter an encyclopedia or almanac of Internet services and features that you can browse and experiment with at any time.

In Appendix A I give you a quick reference for UNIX and some of the important UNIX commands you're going to need to make Internet travel a little easier. Even if you've never used a computer from an operating system prompt before, this reference will help you with the little bit of UNIX you need to know on the Internet.

Appendix B discusses an unsavory topic, but one you need to know about: computer viruses. As you attach to foreign systems and download files and programs, you need to be aware of the possibility of a virus infecting your system. This appendix shows you what viruses are, how to detect them, and how to rid your system of one should it get infected.

Appendix C, a short Emotions Reference, is a list to help you track those drawings people use to show you what they feel about a topic or a comment. Emotions help personalize your email or newsgroup postings. As you will see from this appendix, some Internet users can be quite creative in their use of these often amusing symbols.

Appendix D offers a useful file type reference to help you understand a more about the files you encounter on your Internet journey. I can't list everything you might come across, of course, because that list would be too long. But you'll find in this listing a useful resource.

Appendix E is an annotated reference of companies and resources for the Internet. I include companies that provide local access services as well as those with Internet software offerings and more. I apologize in advance for the fact that I am sure the list is already out of date as you read this, but it still is a solid grouping that will help you begin your Internet research.

Finally, I include a glossary to help you understand the terms I use in this book and other terms you may encounter on the Internet.

ON TO THE INTERNET!

OK. Enough preparation. If you've stayed this long, you're ready to start our journey of learning and exploration. Turn the page and take an exploratory trip on the Internet. Then we'll look at some Internet history and background—so you'll know why the Internet is what it is. Finally, we'll start traveling the Internet superhighway together.

Let's have some fun...

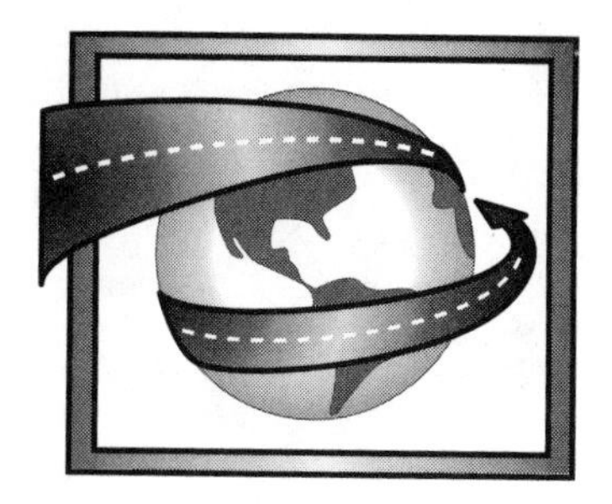

Chapter 1

Journey Into the Internet

You must have heard some of the excitement and read about the Internet, or you wouldn't be reading this book. However, the best way to begin learning about the Internet is to try it for yourself. Prepare to embark on a guided electronic exploration.

In this chapter you will quickly expand your understanding of the Internet—what it is, how it operates, and what it can do for you. Among the topics we'll cover are:

- Hands-on Internet practice
- An Internet definition
- Internet history and background
- Getting on the Internet
- Internet Resources
- Who is on the Internet?

Right now we're going to show you how to get a hands-on, brief introduction to the type of services you can find on the Internet. This is only a short excursion, but every long journey must start somewhere.

WHAT IS THE INTERNET?

The Internet is more than a network of computers—it is really a network of networks. Beyond that, the Internet is also a network of services and resources, a library, a database, a community of people from all walks of life ready to answer questions, listen, and share.

You can use the Internet to send and receive electronic mail. You write a message and post it on a host computer, where it is then routed to the proper destination a little later. You can participate in real-time, online discussions with people from all over the world, and you can conduct research by reading what other people have written about almost any topic.

To get a sense of the nature and personality of the Internet, you can log on to an Internet *node* (a computer connected directly to the Internet that offers at least some Internet features) and begin to explore some of its features. In fact, to help you get familiar with the Internet environment, I'll describe several ways for you to experience the Internet on your own.

A couple of years ago (when I first started working on this book) there were only a few limited choices for accessing the Internet. Today your choices are much more varied. However, you still must attach to the Internet through a computer or computer service that has direct access to the Internet. This can be through another online service such as America Online or CompuServe, through a university or work-related network, or by dialing into a local service provider.

Whatever method you use, you will need a valid account, including a user ID and password, that will let you sign on through one of these access points. If you already have an account that gives you access to the Internet, then you can skip the next section. However, if you don't have an account, and you'd like to explore the Internet for yourself, read on.

In the next section I will show you how to secure a free trial account from a private Internet provider and how to sample the Internet through a couple of other sources. If you explore these resources, you'll have a basic feeling about what the Internet is and will be well on your way toward having your own, full-time access account.

FREE TRIAL ACCOUNT

Many Internet service providers, understanding your lack of experience and understanding, provide free trial accounts so you can get a feel for their service before you have to commit to paying for it. One such provider is U.S. Internet, Inc., based in Knoxville, TN. U.S. Internet (USIT) is a full-service provider with 800 dial-in service from anywhere in the country and local access numbers in a growing number of cities. Receiving a free, five-hour trial account with USIT is a two-step process: 1) log in to the USIT server and enter your name, address, and telephone number; 2) call the USIT help desk with the authorization number the system displays after you fill out the form. Within a short time (typically an hour or less), you will have your own login ID and password on the U.S. Internet system.

U.S. Internet is typical of many service providers. While they offer 800-number access, you must pay for your use of this service. Using an 800 number usually costs in the neighborhood of $0.10–$0.15 per minute ($6.00–$9.00 per hour). These charges will be billed to your Internet account along with your hourly and monthly access fees.

Below are step-by-step instructions for getting your free trial account with U.S. Internet.

Reaching USIT

To reach USIT, and most other Internet service companies, you'll need a *modem* (MOdulator/DEModulator). A modem is a device that lets your computer talk to other computers over a telephone line. You'll also need communications software capable of emulating a VT-100 terminal. (See Chapter 2 if you need help setting up a modem.) The Internet started in the days before desktop computers, so a lot of the software is designed to use a "dumb" terminal such as the VT-100 standard. Most communications software, including Microsoft Windows Terminal, Procomm from DataStorm Technologies, Inc., and others, provide VT-100 terminal support. Use what you have. You don't need anything sophisticated for basic Internet access.

Set your software for 8 data bits, one stop bit, and no parity, specify a baud rate (communications speed) of at least 19,200, and choose VT-100 terminal emulation. These settings should be available from your software's setup, communications, or configuration screen.

From the main terminal screen of your communications software, type the following command:

```
atdt 1 800 270 5474
```

and press **Enter**. Your software should dial this number on your modem and after a few seconds the USIT host computer should answer. You will see an **Annex username:** prompt. At this prompt, type the user ID **guest** (all lowercase) and press **Enter**. The system then will ask for **Annex password:**. Type the password **guest** (all lowercase) and press **Enter**.

Then you should see the opening menu screen shown in Figure 1.1.

FIGURE 1.1

First USIT Logon menu screen

```
---------------------------------------------------------------------------
US Internet          !  Any Problems or Questions? Call our helpdesk!
1127 N. Broadway     !  Or send Email: helpdesk@use.usit.net.
Knoxville TN 37917   !
Phone (800)218-USIT  !  Thank you for choosing US Internet,
Fax (615)524-6313    !  Your Connection to the Information Super Highway!
---------------------------------------------------------------------------
 USE.USIT.NET has been Upgraded! If you run into trouble, Please Call!!

        T h e   U S I T   M a i n   M e n u

            1      Start a Dialup Session

            2      Resume a Dialup Session

            3      Start a SLIP Session

            4      Start a PPP Session

            0      Disconnect from US Internet

        Your Choice ?
```

Choose number 1, Start a Dialup Session, and you will be presented with the welcome screen shown in Figure 1.2.

FIGURE 1.2

U.S. Internet second screen

```
---------------------------------------------------------------------------
W e l c o m e   t o   t h e   I n t e r n e t !

UU      UU   SSSSSS   IIII  TTTTTTTT     We welcome you as a guest of
UU      UU  SS    SS   II      TT       United States Internet, Your
UU      UU  SS         II      TT       Connection to the Information
UU      UU   SSSSSS    II      TT       Super Highway!  If you have
UU      UU        SS   II      TT       ANY questions, call us! The
UU      UU  SS    SS   II      TT       number is (800)218-USIT.
 UUUUUUUU    SSSSSS   IIII     TT

Welcome as a Guest User of US Internet.  This guest account will allow
you to create your very own Internet Account, from which you may explore
the Internet for FREE for 5 full hours, no strings attached!

All we ask is that you fill out this application, and then call us during
regular business hours (8AM-Midnight EST) with your Account Number.  We
will then enable your account within 1 hour!

      *** Please press the <RETURN> or <ENTER> key to continue ***
```

Press **Enter** to move to the next screen where you can fill out a form to provide your name, address, and telephone number. Be sure to note the five-digit authorization number the system displays when you have finished filling out the information. Now, call the U.S. Internet voice number, **800-218-USIT** (8748), 24 hours a day, to have someone activate your guest account.

You will be asked to choose a login ID and a password. Then your guest account will be created, generally within an hour. Usually you will receive a call-back from someone at USIT to tell you the account is ready and, for security reasons, to verify that the telephone number you entered earlier is valid.

Once your account is created, you have five hours to explore the Internet through the U.S. Internet System. To try your account, dial **615-521-6117**. (The 800-number access isn't valid for activated guest accounts, only for filling out the request form. Once you have a regular, billable account, you can use the 800 number to access U.S. Internet facilities and have the charges for 800-number usage billed to your account.)

You will get the same **Annex username:** and **Annex password:** prompts as before, except this time you should enter your newly assigned ID and password. As before, choose number 1, Start a Dialup Session, at the first menu.

This time you should see the main U.S. Internet access menu, called Ciao! (see Figure 1.3).

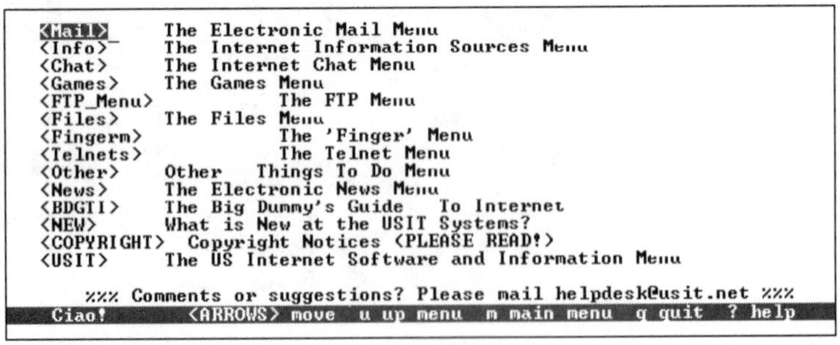

FIGURE 1.3

USIT Ciao! main menu

```
<Mail>        The Electronic Mail Menu
<Info>        The Internet Information Sources Menu
<Chat>        The Internet Chat Menu
<Games>       The Games Menu
<FTP_Menu>            The FTP Menu
<Files>       The Files Menu
<Fingerm>             The 'Finger' Menu
<Telnets>             The Telnet Menu
<Other>       Other   Things To Do Menu
<News>        The Electronic News Menu
<BDGTI>       The Big Dummy's Guide   To Internet
<NEW>         What is New at the USIT Systems?
<COPYRIGHT>   Copyright Notices <PLEASE READ!>
<USIT>        The US Internet Software and Information Menu

   %%% Comments or suggestions? Please mail helpdesk@usit.net %%%
  Ciao!        <ARROWS> move  u up menu  m main menu  q quit  ? help
```

This is a hypertext menu, which means that as you highlight entries on the left side of the screen by moving the cursor up and down with the arrow keys, you can jump to these areas of the system by pressing **Enter** or the **right arrow**. Use the **left arrow** to back up from deeper menus, returning to previous displays.

From here you can follow your nose, choosing menu items and places to explore. If you enter an area outside of the Ciao menu, you can usually press **q** to quit the subsystem and return to Ciao!. If you get into a subsystem that won't let you out, try pressing **Ctrl+]** or **Ctrl+C**. If all else fails, you can hang up the phone by issuing a hang-up command from your software or by turning off the modem. Then you can redial and start again from the beginning.

Since this is a menu-driven system, navigating around the Internet should be easy. However, I'd like to point out some specific places for you to try.

Sending email

Although the Internet is a valuable tool for research and other tasks, by far the most common single application is sending and receiving *electronic mail* (*email*). With an Internet connection like the one you can get through U.S. Internet, you can exchange electronic messages with other users in more than 150 countries. In most circumstances it takes only a few minutes (sometimes only a few seconds) for your message to reach someone on the other side of the world!

To try email for yourself with your trial USIT account, highlight the **Mail** menu item and press **Enter** or **right arrow**. Mail is the first item on the main Ciao! menu and is highlighted by default when you first enter the system. Choosing Mail from the main menu brings up a secondary Mail menu where you can choose from three mail readers. Again, take the default from this second menu to load the Pine mail reader. You will see the menu screen shown in Figure 1.4.

FIGURE 1.4

Main Pine mail reader menu

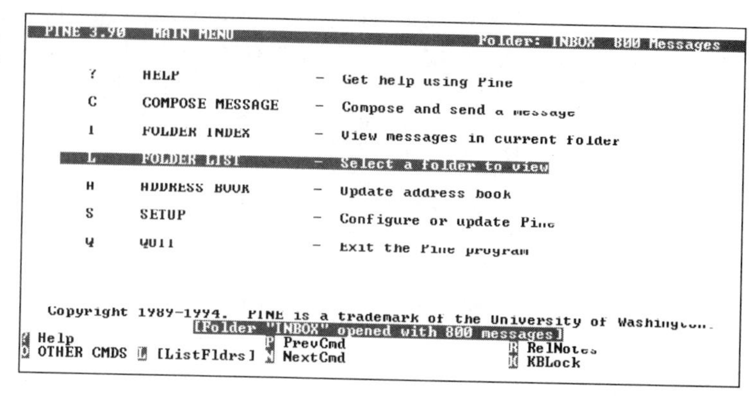

Press **C** (for Compose) to display the Compose screen shown in Figure 1.5.

FIGURE 1.5

Pine Compose screen

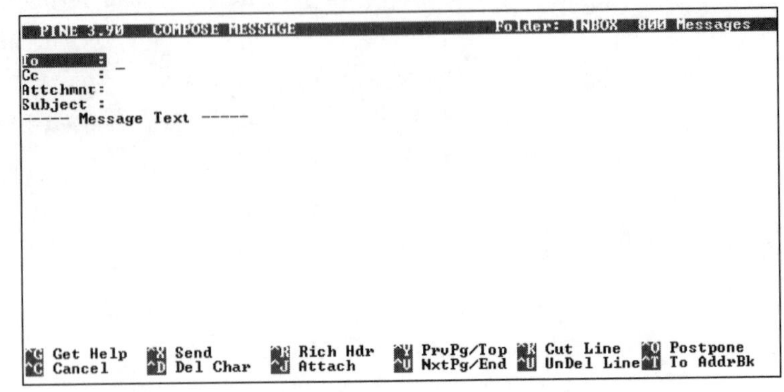

At the **To:** prompt you can enter any valid electronic mail address to send a message to someone else. I'll discuss network addressing again later in this book, but you can try sending a simple message to yourself right now.

When you signed up for service the vendor gave you an online name or user ID. Your email address is this ID, followed by the commercial "at" sign (@), then the system domain suffix. To send yourself an email message, type:

```
userid@usit.net
```

Replace **userid** with your own ID. My online name, for example, is **tbadgett**. So, my email address on U.S. Internet would be **tbadgett@usit.net**. Users on other systems have different email addresses. Just as you can send paper mail to anyone anywhere if you know the address, you can send email to anyone for whom you have the proper address information.

After you enter your email address (or the address of another user if you are sending mail to someone else), press **Tab** or **Enter** to move to the next line in the address. This is the **Cc** (carbon copy) line. Enter another address if you want to send a copy of the current message to someone else.

The next line provides for attaching a file (a spreadsheet, a word processing document, and so on). Just press **Tab** an extra time to skip this field for this first message.

Enter some text on the subject line. While you don't have to fill in the subject field, it makes things a lot easier for the mail recipient if the subject field contains meaningful data. After you have used email for a while you may have dozens or even hundreds of messages in your mail box at any given time. A meaningful subject field helps you sort things out as you process your mail.

Press **Tab** or **Enter** one more time to move the cursor into the message area. This is a full-screen text editor where you can enter the message you want to send. Use the arrow keys to position the cursor anywhere within the message to make changes. The backspace key will delete the character to the left of the cursor and you can enter new text by just typing it in. Existing text will bump to the right as you insert new information.

When the message is complete, hold down the **Ctrl** key and press the letter **x**. Pine will ask if you really want to send the message. Press **y** and your message will start moving through the Internet mail system.

The main Pine menu will be displayed. You can press **i** to display a list of any received messages or **q** to quit Pine and return to the Ciao! menu.

Since you are sending a message to yourself through the system to which you are logged in, it should take only a few seconds to receive this mail message. If you have Pine on the screen when the message arrives in your mail box, you will hear a beep and see a message at the bottom of the screen indicating that a new mail message has arrived.

If you send mail to someone on another system, it may take a little longer for the message to arrive, but the wait time is not long. I regularly exchange mail with a friend in Slovakia who, as I do, sits all day at a computer attached to the Internet. I can send him a question or comment and usually within ten minutes or so I receive a response. At different times of the day the delivery time may be longer, but you should be able to send email almost anywhere in the world within half an hour or so.

From the Mail menu within Ciao! you can return to the main menu screen by pressing **left arrow**. Now press **down arrow** once to highlight the Info menu and press **right arrow** to display the Info menu. From this screen you can choose gophers to browse gopher space (an Internet menu system) or Lynx to view a text version of the World Wide Web (a hypertext data system). Don't worry about the specifics of these terms. I will describe them fully later in this book.

Cursor down to the Gopher menu and press **Enter** or **right arrow** to display the gopher screen shown in Figure 1.6.

FIGURE 1.6

USIT main gopher screen

```
                    Internet Gopher Information Client 2.0 pl10

                         Root gopher server: use.usit.net

 -->  1.  USIT        United States Internet: Information and Software./
      2.  TOOLS       Internet Guides and Tools/
      3.  LOCAL       Tennessee News, Events, Weather, Info, Gophers.../
      4.  A&E         Arts and Entertainment/
      5.  MALL        US Internet Shopping Center/
      6.  SOFTWARE    The Internet Free Software Warehouse/
      7.  WEATHER     Weather Reports from Anywhere!/
      8.  BOOKS       Electronic Libraries, Books and Magazines/
      9.  MEDICAL     The Medical Corner        *** NOT OPEN YET ***/
      10. SCIENCE     The Science Corner        *** NOT OPEN YET ***/
      11. SOCIETY     The Society, Law & Politics Corner/
      12. GOV         The Government Corner/
      13. REFERNCE    The Reference Bookshelf./
      14. OTHER       Other Gopher and Information Services/
      15. INTERNET_QUEST


Press ? for Help, q to Quit                                         Page: 1/1
```

All Internet resources are dynamic. They change regularly. The screens in these examples will be similar to what you see during your tour, but they may not be identical.

Use the same cursor technique to step deeper into one or more of the gopher screens available from this menu. Everything should be easy to follow. It is a good idea to keep a note pad handy so you can track your progress, making it easier to return to areas of interest.

To exit the gopher, press **q** for quit. The Ciao! Info screen will be displayed. You can either continue your travels around the USIT menu system, or you can experiment with interacting directly with the UNIX operating system that underlies this and most other Internet host computers.

Experimenting with UNIX

Although the online world of the Internet is getting easier to use all the time, there still are systems you may use—and procedures you will want to try—that are based on the UNIX operating system. UNIX is a powerful and popular system for networking, and most Internet hosts use this operating system.

You may read that UNIX is very complex and difficult to learn and to use. This is not necessarily true. If you are reasonably comfortable with MS-DOS procedures such as copying files, creating directories, and so on, then the little bit of UNIX you need to know to comfortably navigate the Internet should be easy to learn.

If you'd like to experience UNIX, press **q** again at the Ciao! menu. You will see the **USIT%** prompt, indicating you are now interacting with a UNIX shell. (You now have a standard shell account. This type of interface is typical of many Internet service providers, which means you need to have a little UNIX experience to move around in these areas of the Internet.)

Interacting with a UNIX shell is a little like working with MS-DOS. The command structure is similar and, in fact, you will use many of the same commands. A short UNIX command reference is provided in Appendix A of this book. I'll just lead you through a few things to try here.

So what do you do when an Internet host just waits at a simple prompt until you type something? That depends on the type of host computer you're talking to. Among the common machines you'll encounter on the Internet are Digital Equipment Corporation VAXs, Sun and other UNIX workstations, and perhaps IBM mainframes. However, UNIX is a common operating system, even across multiple platforms, so you usually are safe trying UNIX commands at an Internet host prompt. The specific commands you can use also depend on which UNIX shell your provider uses, and whether certain commands have been bypassed or modified.

However, the commands in Table 1.1 should be available on most UNIX systems.

TABLE 1.1
Sample UNIX Commands

Command	Action
cd	Change Directory
ls	List Files
sz	Send ZMODEM
man	Display Manual Information

Notice the similarity of these commands to MS-DOS commands. Notice also that they are not the same as DOS. For example, when you enter a path in UNIX you use the forward slash (/) to separate elements instead of the backslash (\) you use with DOS.

These are UNIX commands that are available on many Internet nodes. One command, **man**, stands for manual. Use it to get more information from the online UNIX manual about any available commands. For example, try this command: **man ls**. You should see the display shown in Figure 1.7.

FIGURE 1.7
man ls command at UNIX prompt

```
Reformatting page.  Wait... done

ls(1)                     User Commands                     ls(1)

NAME
     ls - list contents of directory

SYNOPSIS
     ls [ -abcCdfFgilLmnopqrRstux1 ] [ names ]

AVAILABILITY
     SUNWcsu

DESCRIPTION
     For each directory argument, ls lists the  contents  of  the
     directory;  for  each file argument, ls repeats its name and
     any other  information  requested.  The  output  is  sorted
     alphabetically  by  default.  When no argument is given, the
     current directory is listed.  When  several  arguments  are
     given,  the  arguments  are  first sorted appropriately. but
     file arguments appear before directories and their contents

     There are three major listing formats.  The  default  format
--More--(5%)
```

Notice the—**more**—**(5%)** at the bottom of Figure 1.7. This indicates that only 5% of the information on **ls** has been displayed. The—**more**—prompt tells you that there is more information to follow. You can press any key to get to the next line; press the **space bar** to display the next screen.

Use the **man** command to explore other UNIX commands. This is a good method to learn your way around a system and to learn something about UNIX in general.

Now try this. At the **USIT%** prompt, type this command: **ls**. This is the UNIX list files command. It should produce a screen like the one in Figure 1.8.

FIGURE 1.8

List files (ls) command at USIT

```
usit% ls
Win32s115a.Zip  comp430s.zip  incoming   mtgexch  slip
avocat          cu            info       niae     tmp
bdgti.txt       fondue        lesjones   pc       tro
bookworm        hyperglot     mac        pfa      ttpm
comp430d.zip    ibm           macintosh  quest
usit% _
```

This is a list of files and directories located in your current directory on the USIT system. What is your current directory? Type **pwd** to find out. The system should tell you that yours is the **/homes/userid** directory, where userid is your assigned user name on the system.

You can change to another directory with the **cd** command. Just type **cd**, a space, and the name of the directory you want to make current: **cd /export/ftp/pub**. Now you are in a new directory, **pub**, with a whole new set of files and subdirectories at your disposal. Use the **ls** command again. Now you should see some files and directories. You can tell which is which by using the **ls** command again, but this time add the **-l** switch. In addition to the names of the files and directories in the current directory, you will see information about these files (see Figure 1.9).

NOTE

*When a listing takes up more than a single screen you can use the **Ctrl+S** key combination to stop the display and give you time to view the names. Use **Ctrl+Q** to start the display again. Alternately, you can use **|more** after the **ls** command to tell UNIX to pause the display as each screen is filled.*

FIGURE 1.9

UNIX directory display with -l

```
drwxrwxr-x  2 avocat        512 Jan 11 11:06 avocat
-rw-r--r--  1 root       394870 Oct  6 12:39 bdgti.txt
drwxrwxr-x  2 bookworm      512 Oct 19 17:17 bookworm
-rw-rw-r--  1 tbadgett    20241 Nov 15 20:46 comp430d.zip
-rw-rw-r--  1 tbadgett    70872 Nov 15 20:46 comp430s.zip
drwxr-xr-x  2 niels         512 Dec 15 08:56 cu
drwxrwxr-x  2 root          512 Oct  4 17:03 fondue
drwxrwxr-x  4 glot          512 Oct  6 16:26 hyperglot
drwxrwxr-x  3 root          512 Jan 22 14:23 ibm
lrwxrwxrwx  1 root           11 Jul 15  1994 incoming -> ../incoming
drwxrwxr-x  2 ftp           512 Jun  3  1994 info
drwxr-xr-x  2 lesjones      512 Jan 17 17:14 lesjones
lrwxrwxrwx  1 root            9 Sep 15 13:55 mac -> macintosh
drwxrwxr-x  2 root          512 Dec 25 20:37 macintosh
drwxrwxr-x  2 root          512 Oct 12 17:10 mtgexch
drwxrwxr-x  2 jutano        512 Nov 14 15:50 niae
lrwxrwxrwx  1 root            3 Sep 15 13:54 pc -> ibm
drwxr-xr-x  2 jutano        512 Jan 16 16:24 pfa
drwxrwxr-x  2 root          512 Jul 29 11:12 quest
drwxrwxr-x  4 root          512 Sep 15 13:56 slip
lrwxrwxrwx  1 root            6 Dec 15 12:16 tmp -> ../tmp
drwxrwxr-x  2 root          512 Oct 14 13:43 tro
drwxrwxr-x  5 root          512 Jan  5 16:22 ttpm
usit%
```

The 10-character section at the left of the directory display tells you what type of entry each one is, and what rights (permissions) each contains. Files with a **d** in the first position of this field are directories. A dash in the first position indicates a file. Other characters in this first position indicate a different type of entry (use **man ls** to learn more about this display).

The second through fourth positions show what rights the file or directory owner has. The characters **rw** in the second and third positions show that the owner has read and write permission, for example. The **x** in the fourth position indicates the owner has execute permission for this file as well. A dash in this third position would mean the owner does not have execute rights. The second group of three characters shows rights for the group to which the owner belongs and the final three-character group shows the rights enjoyed by everyone else on the system.

This display shows additional information as well. The size of the file in bytes is displayed, for example, as well as the name of the file or directory in the final position on each line.

NOTE

There are a number of additional switches (characters that modify command operation) available with the ***ls*** *command. Use* ***man ls*** *to learn more about these.*

You can use **cd** again to change to one of the displayed directories, then use **ls** to show what files and directories are there. As you list files, note which names end in **.Z**. These are archive files that have been compressed using a UNIX-based compression utility. Unless you have access to a UNIX system with the compression/decompression utility (or you download a compatible PC- or MAC-based utility), you can't use these files.

If you *do* have access to a UNIX system but you don't have the compression utility, you can download it. Ask your service provider for help. I'll show you later in this book how to download a number of files you may find useful as you tour the Internet. Right now I'll show you how to download one file in the current directory just so you'll understand the process for later. (Again, remember that Internet host systems are dynamic. If you don't see the file described below, pick another one from the directory to practice your download.)

Notice from your **ls** practice earlier that there is a file in the **pub** directory named **bdgti.txt**. This is the Big Dummy's Guide To the Internet (bdgti), and from the extension we can see it is a text file. Let's download this file so you can access it with a local editor or print it out on a local printer. Use this command: **sz bdgti.txt**.

This launches the *ZMODEM* transfer protocol and gets it ready to send the file **bdgti.txt** to your computer. If necessary, start the ZMODEM protocol on your local machine, specify a file name, and wait for the completion of the transfer. Notice that UNIX systems are case-sensitive, so if you specify **BDGTI.TXT** instead of **bdgti.txt**, the transfer won't work. Unlike *ls* and some other UNIX commands that are universal, the *sz* command depends on your system administrator installing an application. The U.S. Internet system uses *sz*, as do many Internet hosts. If you get an error message when you try to use *sz* it simply means that the particular host you are using has not implemented the ZMODEM protocol.

The suggested procedure in this section assumes your terminal emulator (communications) package supports the ZMODEM protocol. In fact, a communications package that does not support ZMODEM is very rare today. But if you discover that you can't complete the download, it may mean your software doesn't use ZMODEM. You probably can use kermit or XMODEM, however. The procedure is similar. Contact your service provider help desk or call technical support for the communications software you are using.

This is a *text file* (ASCII characters), so when the transfer is over, you can use the DOS EDIT utility or whatever text utility you have at your disposal to view text files. Most word processors, such as Microsoft Word or WordPerfect, can load, display, and edit text files. A text file is one composed only of 7-bit characters. You can display a text file at the operating system prompt and edit it with the simplest of text editors. It doesn't include any special characters beyond the alphabet, numbers, and some punctuation.

Want to try another download? Transfer to the **slip** directory under the **pub** directory (**cd slip**) and use **sz** again to download the file **download.doc**. This file offers hints on downloading files (what you're doing right now).

UNIX is a case sensitive operating system. In general, UNIX commands are entered in lower case. If you get an error message when trying any of these commands, make sure you have entered the command as shown, in all lower case characters.

With some ZMODEM systems, the local (destination) file is named automatically, based on the name of the source file. If you are transferring from a UNIX system to a DOS system, the file names may not be compatible. In this case, the destination file name won't be the same as the source file. If you have problems saving a file with a name incompatible with your system, use another protocol or turn off automatic naming in ZMODEM. Then you can specify a name for the destination file.

The *XMODEM* protocol, another popular file transfer method, usually does not launch on the receiving system automatically. For example, if you use XMODEM (the **sx** command on your UNIX host), USIT responds:

```
Sending download.doc, 25 XMODEM blocks. Give your
local XMODEM receive command now.
```

This gives you an opportunity to enable local XMODEM transfer and to specify a file name for your computer. You would use the same procedure for ZMODEM if automatic launch is disabled on your local system.

When you're through experimenting with USIT, type **lo** or **exit** at the **USIT%** prompt. You will be logged off of the system.

As you learn your way around these basic Internet features, take some notes on where you go and how you get there, so you can return if you wish.

Sometime before you have used up the five hours of free time, someone from U.S. Internet will call to see if you wish to convert the guest account. You are under no obligation to keep the service or to pay any fees beyond your long distance telephone charges. You can use this free five hour account as you read this book to experiment with the things I discuss here. Then you'll be ready to get the most out of a USIT or other service provider's account when you start paying the bills.

DELVING INTO THE WELL

The U.S. Internet experience shows you how a high-end service looks. This is a full-service provider that specializes in business accounts. However, the range of services you may encounter from Internet providers is very broad, each one specializing in a different area of Internet service.

In this next journey, you will try the local services of a popular West coast provider, *The WELL*. The WELL has made a name for itself in online conferencing, and it offers Internet access. It is one of the older, more established Internet vendors.

The WELL was started by the Whole Earth Catalog folk. (You *do* remember the Whole Earth Catalog, don't you?) WELL stands for Whole Earth 'Lectronic Link. The online information about The WELL describes it this way:

The first people on the WELL were an eclectic mixture of hackers, writers, ex-commune members from the Farm, telecom adventurers and many independently minded people.

The WELL is a computer conferencing system. This means that we have a computer here in Sausalito with a whole bunch of phone lines and a couple of networks connected to it. People connect to the WELL with their own computers and participate in discussions with each other, without having to be together at the same time and place.

The main thing that happens on the WELL is people using the Conferences as places to meet and discuss with one another.

You can access The WELL directly from the Internet if you have an account elsewhere in the country that lets you access other systems. You can also access The WELL directly through a telephone exchange in Sausalito, CA, or through the CompuServe Packet Network. Whatever method you use, as a member of The WELL you are charged a monthly fee ($15 per month as this book is written), plus an hourly access fee ($2.00 per hour or about 3.3 cents per minute, currently). However, I'm going to show you how to get a peek at The WELL for free (and get a flavor of the Internet in the bargain).

Remember you can access The WELL in three ways: via the Internet, by calling a Sausalito telephone number, or via *CompuServe Packet Network (CPN)*. For direct access, dial **415-332-6106** (I'll show you how to log on in a moment).

I'm assuming you aren't already on the Internet at this point, but if you are, you can access The WELL via Telnet at **well.sf.ca.us**. (If you don't know what that means, don't worry. I said I am assuming you aren't on the Internet yet anyway, remember?)

The third method of access is via CPN. If you're not already using CPN to access CompuServe or another online service, you can find the telephone number of your local node by dialing **800-848-8980**. That connects you with CompuServe network client support. Simply tell whoever answers that you're looking for a local access number for CPN. They'll ask you some questions, such as the area code from which you are calling and the modem speed you want to use, and then they'll give you a local phone number. This is the number you'll use to get onto The WELL.

If you are dialing directly into The WELL at the 415-332-6106 number, set your communications software for the highest speed your modem supports and specify eight data bits, one stop bit, and no parity. If you are using a CPN connection, specify seven data bits, one stop bit, and even parity. Enter your communications software's terminal mode where you can issue commands directly to the modem. If you are not sure whether you are in terminal mode, type **AT** on the keyboard (assuming your modem is Hayes or AT-command compatible). You should see the modem response, **OK**, on your screen.

Type **ATDT** (but *don't* press **Enter**) if your modem is an AT-compatible model and you are using a tone dial telephone line. If your modem uses another command set besides the AT command set, consult the modem manual for the proper command to dial a number on a tone dial line. If you are using a pulse dial line (you have a rotary dial telephone instead of push buttons), then use the **ATDP** command (but *don't* press **Enter** yet) instead of the **ATDT** (Again, if you are using a non-AT-compatible modem, substitute the proper command for dialing a number over a pulse tone line.)

To dial The WELL directly, enter the direct dial number after the dialing command and press **Enter**. At the **login:** prompt, type **guest** and press **Enter**. Your screen should look similar to the one in Figure 1.10.

FIGURE 1.10

First WELL login screen via direct dial

```
Type    guest      to learn about the WELL.

If you already have a WELL account, type your username.

login: guest
Last login: Sun Jan 22 23:17:48 from 204.97.9.200
Erase character is ^H


Welcome to The WELL Guest Account.

This account is designed to provide you with some information about The
WELL, and to let you read some samples of the discussion from some of the
conferences on The WELL.

Over the years The WELL has become known as something of a "virtual
community" - people come here to build and maintain relationships with
interesting people.

If you have any questions about what you find here, or about other aspects
of The WELL please let us know.  There is a menu choice to send us a note.


Press [Return] to continue...
```

Again, if you are using a pulse-dial line, then your dialing command would be **ATDP 415-332-6106** instead of the **ATDT 415-332-6106**. And, if yours is a non-AT-command modem, you will use a different dialing command on the first screen. After you have read this initial screen, press **Enter** again and you will see The WELL opening menu, shown in Figure 1.11.

FIGURE 1.11

WELL opening menu

```
                              WELL GUEST MENU

                 1 - What is The WELL? <4K>
                 2 - What is a WELL Conference?/
                 3 - READ SAMPLES FROM THE WELL CONFERENCES/
                 4 - AUGUST, 1994: WOODSTOCK Project/
                 5 - Access Information, Brochure, etc./
                 6 - Leave a note for The WELL staff*
                 7 - Register for The WELL*

q=Quit this menu              d=Download file               p=turn Pager OFF

Select one of the above items <1-7 or a letter> ==>
```

If you are using the CPN network, then use **ATDT** (or **ATDP**) and the local access number for CPN. When CPN answers, press **Enter**, and you will see this prompt:

```
Host Name:
```

Type **WELL** and press **Enter** at this prompt. You should see the screen shown in Figure 1.12 almost immediately.

FIGURE 1.12

First WELL logon screen via CPN

```
Host Name: WELL
    ============================================================
    You are reaching The WELL through CPN - There is usually a
    surcharge of between $4 and $12/hr for using this access method.
    For almost all people within the 48 contiguous United States
    the charge is $4/hr. Please call The WELL office for
    details (415) 332-4335 or e-mail (support)

    If you get a "Host WELL is inoperative" message you may wish to call
    our status report line: 1-800-326-8354 or 415-332-4627.

    Your communication software must be set to use 8 data bits,
    one stop bit and no parity when dialing into the WELL through CPN.
    If you have trouble logging in, use the strip or ignore high bit
    option in your software, or type a single + (plus sign) followed by
    RETURN at the first CPN "Host Name:" prompt.

Connected to 02WELL
SunLink X.29 Terminal Service - WELL
This is the WELL
Type   newuser   to sign up.
Type   trouble   if you are having trouble logging in.
Type   guest     to learn about the WELL.
If you already have a WELL account, type your username.
login:
```

At the **login:** prompt, type **guest** and press **Enter**. The WELL displays the menu shown in Figure 1.13.

FIGURE 1.13

The WELL main guest menu

```
                    WELL GUEST MENU

          1 - What is The WELL? (4K)

          2 - What is a WELL Conference?/

          3 - READ SAMPLES FROM THE WELL CONFERENCES/

          4 - Access Information, Brochure, etc./

          5 - Leave a Note for The WELL Staff*

          6 - Register for The WELL*

   q=Quit menus    d=Download file    m=Mail file    p=turn Pager OFF
   ---------------------------------------------------------------
   What do you want to do?
```

You may want to turn on a *capture file* or *log file* inside your communications software at this point to capture the screens you see as you browse. I'll suggest that you capture screens regularly throughout this book. If you aren't sure how to do this with your communications software, find out now. The ability to capture information to disk as it appears on your screen is an important part of using the Internet.

Now, just follow your fingertips around the guest area of The WELL. The entire procedure is menu-driven, so you should have no problems. To get out of The WELL, simply return to this main menu and type **Q** to quit.

Remember, accessing The WELL as a guest doesn't get you on the Internet, but it gets you on an Internet access node that is typical of some of the hosts you'll encounter in your Internet journeys. A *host* is a computer system attached to the Internet that you can use to access the Internet, to send and receive email, to converse with other users, and more. This WELL demo area is easy to use, with (mostly) menu access. It offers conferencing and other fun opportunities, as well as providing a gateway to the Internet if you want to use it. I'll discuss how to get you on the Internet in the next chapter, but remember The WELL. For many readers of this book, The WELL accessed through CPN is a low-cost, easy method for getting online with the Internet.

Other Online Opportunities

A lot has changed in the Internet world in the past couple of years, but the main change is the growth in the number of avenues you can follow to get connected on the Internet. Big-name companies such as IBM, Microsoft, MCI (the telephone company), and others are playing the game today.

For example, IBM is shipping OS/2 Warp with online tools, including a TCP/IP utility that lets you connect your computer directly to a remote network via a telephone line and a graphical World Wide Web browser. Microsoft is including some Internet utility software along with instructions for connecting to its own network with Windows 95. And there are Internet gateways showing up with major online providers such as CompuServe, Prodigy, Delphi, America Online, and so on.

If you are interested in getting on the Internet, you should be able to find a local provider or get enough information from one of the major players to get yourself connected. I'll provide more information on this in the next chapter.

INTERNET BACKGROUND AND HISTORY

By computer standards, the Internet is ancient, created in 1969 by a branch of the federal government's Department of Defense. This *ARPAnet*, as it was called (because it was started by the *Advanced Research Projects Agency*, or *ARPA*), was intended for use as a research vehicle for the military—a way to find out how to build *persistent networks* that could withstand the wages of war. (In computer jargon something "persistent" is able to withstand unusual conditions or unforeseen events and keep on working.)

This was the beginning of *peer-to-peer* computer communications. It helped to establish the concept of "error free" communications, where encapsulated *packets* of data are sent from a client to a host machine along with information about what should be in those packets. These packets of data don't necessarily have to follow the same route from source to destination. Therefore, even if a link goes down in the middle of a transmission, chances are that everything will arrive where it is supposed to be going. This communications process over the Internet was called the *Internet Protocol*, or *IP*.

This was a military project, remember, so the assumption during design of the IP was that the only known aspect of the network at any given moment is the fact that two computers, a client and a server, are communicating. If these two entities are exchanging data, then the link between them is sound. Beyond that, nothing about the integrity of the rest of the network is assured or assumed. In addition, even though client A is right now communicating successfully with host B, that link could be broken at any time.

Therefore, the IP and the physical structure of the network itself is such that temporary interruptions or even catastrophic destruction of some Internet facilities won't necessarily destroy the network itself. Moreover, the computers attached to the network are—and were—a disparate mix of different capabilities from different vendors. Standards had to be established that would allow this potentially confusing and incompatible mix of hardware and software to talk to each other.

As it evolved over the first few years, this electronic highway (it wasn't really a superhighway then) was aimed at providing a pipeline for electronic mail services and online libraries for universities and government agencies. These users could provide excellent tests for the network integrity the government wanted to establish, and the Internet could provide these agencies a useful vehicle for data exchange.

In the beginning, the Internet was like a strain of bacteria that was alive and healthy but which lacked the medium it needed to multiply. Twelve years after its establishment, in 1981, there were 213 computers registered on the Internet. Over the next ten years real growth started. But even in 1991, when there were 376,000 computers registered, the critical mass required for exponential growth had just barely been reached.

Then things began to happen. One year later, in 1992, the number of registered Internet computers had doubled to 727,000. Today there are millions of computers connected to the Internet, providing direct access for up to 40 million people.

From ARPAnet to Internet

In the early 1980s the original ARPAnet split into two networks, the ARPAnet and *Milnet*, but connections continued between the two networks as something originally called the *DARPA* Internet. (The original Advanced Research Projects Agency had now become the *Defense Advanced Research Projects Agency*.) Within a short time, common usage shortened the name to simply the Internet.

However, you can't really think of the Internet as a single entity that started small and grew. Actually, the Internet had multiple beginnings, like the tributaries of a great river that start small and alone in the recesses of a hidden mountain pass. As I mentioned, the Internet is really a network of networks, and that's how it got its start. As you might imagine, during the time ARPAnet was getting started, other groups outside the military and government establishment also were seeing the need for decentralized, reliable communications, and these groups started their own networks in parallel to ARPAnet.

Among them were *UUCP* (from UNIX to UNIX Copy Program protocol), an international UNIX communications protocol, and *USENET*, which stands for User Network. As with the Internet in the beginning, USENET started as a network for the university community and later branched into commercial services. USENET and UUCP came into being in the late 1970s. A few years later, early in the 1980s, we saw the rise of larger networks, including *CSNET* (Computer Science Network) and *BITNET*, both of which were targeted, again, at the university and research communities.

Changes in computer technology and networking technology came together in 1986 with the establishment of *NSFNET*, a National Science Foundation link that tied users together with five national supercomputer centers. The growing strength of this network, as it expanded to connect mid-level and statewide academic networks, began to replace ARPAnet for research networking until, in 1990, ARPAnet was dismantled. It didn't matter that ARPAnet ceased operations, however, because all of the interconnections growing out of other networks easily replaced it.

The backbone of the current network belongs to the National Science Foundation, but it is managed by Advanced Network and Services, Inc. (ANS), a partnership among IBM Corp., MCI Communications Corp., and a consortium of universities in Michigan. Since 1989, commercial Internet access providers have been able to lease *interchange points* from ANS and offer electronic mail, file transfer, and database services to individuals and corporations.

In addition, the regional networks connected to the Internet backbone are moving to become more independent of government funding by selling Internet connections. CompuServe, MCI Mail, and GEnie are among commercial online services that offer electronic mail gateways to the Internet, and Sprint Communications Co. launched SprintLink as an access to the Internet in 1992.

Today you have many choices for connecting to the Internet yourself, either as a corporation or as an individual. In the next section of this chapter we'll look at an overview of the Internet structure itself, and show you some of the ways you can access the power of the Internet.

Internet Road Map

From the hands-on trial at the beginning of this chapter you know what the Internet *looks* like, and you have learned about the history and background of the Internet. I'll provide more information about who and what are on the Internet later this chapter. In this section, I want to give you an overview of the Internet that shows what's there and how it all fits together. This is a road map, if you will, of the Internet structure and makeup.

Before you start a vacation trip you probably learn about your proposed destination by viewing a tape or reading an article about the area's history and background. Often you want to know more details of the area's attractions and what is the best way of getting to them. That's what I'll try to show you here about the Internet.

Surely you have guessed by now that the Internet is an extremely complex piece of physical and logical architecture. The Internet is made up of *Local Area Networks*, *Metropolitan Area Networks*, and huge *Wide Area Networks*. The systems are hooked together with everything from standard dial-up phone lines to high-speed dedicated leased lines and satellite, microwave, or *fiber-optic* links. The good news is you don't really have to understand it all to venture into its streets and highways, or to visit the vendors you find along the way. However, a high level view of this amorphous concept might help you find your way.

Look at the drawing in Figure 1.14. It shows a conceptual view of the Internet hardware. (There is a lot of software inherent with this hardware, of course, but for this view, we don't need to consider it.)

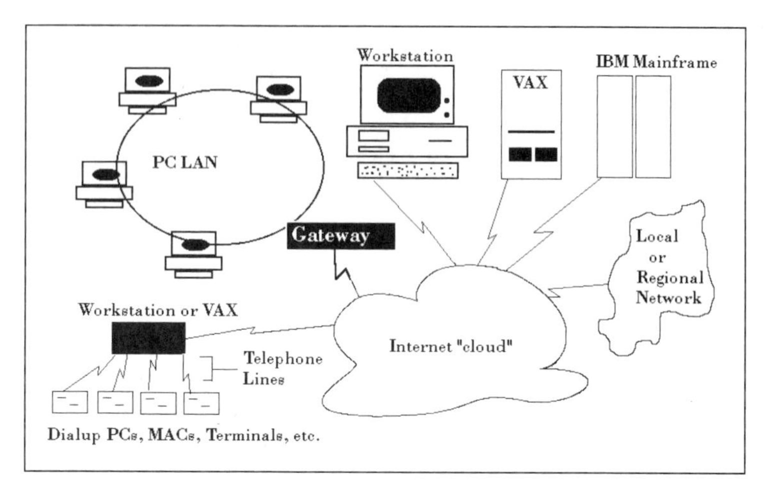

FIGURE 1.14 Internet hardware interconnection overview

This drawing shows the many types of hardware components that make up the Internet. Notice that there is no component marked "Central Server" or "Internet Headquarters." That's because there is no such entity on the Internet. Although mainframe computers certainly are on the network, these aren't necessarily any more powerful or strategic, from an Internet view, than the PC-based LANs or minicomputer nodes that also are part of the Internet.

The Internet itself is shown as a cloud because it is all but impossible to say what is there. Remember that the Internet itself is made up of other networks which include additional computer systems. In fact, the most accurate drawing of the Internet would be just one big cloud! Even the PC LAN, the Workstation, and other components we have shown here are, themselves, part of the Internet, so they are inside the cloud. Only the dial-up computers shown are actually outside the cloud.

That's the bad news—the Internet is a complex arrangement of LANs and individual computers. The good news is that to you, the traveler along this electronic superhighway, all this matters very little.

When you look at a map of, say, the Southern United States to plan a trip from Atlanta to Miami, do you concern yourself with all the little roads that connect to Interstate 75, or do you decide where to get on I75 and how to follow it to Miami? The important part of that map is how to get onto the main interstate, and where to get off at the other end.

The same is true of the Internet. We'll show you how to arrange to get on the Internet in your home town, and some of the main routes you can follow. The underlying technology and complexity don't need to concern you, until you are interested enough and have enough knowledge to start learning about it.

The Internet is a peer-to-peer network, which means that nearly all of the facilities that make up the network have equal importance and conduct themselves with respect to each other as equals. This isn't strictly true, because the type of connection being used to access the Internet just naturally gives more status to some hardware than to others, but basically Internet hardware is created equal.

Here are the basic types of Internet connections:

- **Dial-up:** This is the simplest and least expensive method for an individual user to access the Internet (unless you can get access for free through your company or someone else's company, of course). This is an indirect Internet connection because your computer isn't really part of the Internet, even when you are logged on to an Internet node. This is because a dial-up connection is handled through another computer that *is* a part of the Internet. You dial a phone number for the remote computer (this is a remote computer even if it is located in the same room with your machine; it is not your machine, so it is a remote machine). You answer a few questions, and then you can use that computer's Internet connection to get what you want from the Internet. This is the way you attached to the Internet at the beginning of this chapter, through a remote dial-up connection.
- **SLIP/PPP:** One step above dial-up is a telephone-line-based node connection that uses SLIP or PPP Internet software.

(Technically you dial up this connection as well, but the traffic carried over the link is different and, by convention, we don't usually use "dial-up" to refer to a SLIP/PPP connection.) You can use dedicated voice-grade telephone lines or a dial-up connection for this level of access (most frequently a dial-up connection is used rather than a dedicated connection). Either way you will use a conventional high speed modem for the attachment to the wire. This type of connection is like using dial-up Ethernet to your company host. It makes your computer a node on the network, but through a temporary telephone connection from a remote location rather than through a dedicated link onsite. This mode of connection is superior to conventional dial-up because your local computer actually becomes a part of the Internet; you aren't using another Internet node as an intermediary between your system and the network. That means you can transfer files from remote sites directly to your computer without saving them first on a host machine. Also, the network connection opens a variety of graphical interface software (such as Mosaic or Netscape) for your use.

- **Dedicated Connection:** This is top of the line Internet. Dedicated network access means you have a high speed communications line (such as a LAN connection within your company) attached directly to your computer. This is the way minicomputer, mainframe, and relatively large local area networks usually are connected. A dedicated link is always up. Your computer is part of the Internet all the time and anyone with access rights to the dedicated computer can reach the Internet. This level of connection is designed to service a large number of users with a relatively large amount of traffic. This type of link is relatively expensive, with sign-up fees of $1,000 or more and thousands of dollars a year in fees. When you use a dial-up link to an Internet provider, you're probably using that provider's dedicated link to access the Internet.
- **Remote Network Access:** If you are a member of CompuServe Information Service (CIS), GEnie, MCI Mail, or another online service, you can access the Internet to exchange electronic mail and perhaps use a few other limited

services. The process is similar (but different) for each network, so contact your network representative for information about exchanging electronic mail over the Internet.

You'll find more detailed information about arranging your own Internet connection in Chapter 2, and how to configure a SLIP or PPP connection in Chapter 5.

INTERNET RESOURCES

I've already talked about what the Internet is and who it is. In this section I'll give you a brief list and summary of Internet facilities just to give you a better idea of what you might find on this fascinating resource.

Computer Systems and Centers

Quietly sitting on the Internet are thousands of highly sophisticated computers that form the hub of various local and wide area networks. These systems are on dedicated lines, so they are always on the Internet. Part of their Internet offering is the wealth of information their users have in their heads and are willing to share with other Internet users. Such centers are repositories of research data waiting to be tapped. You can't get to everything on these machines, of course, because a lot of the information is proprietary to the company, government agency, or university that owns the machine. But you'd be surprised at how much information is available to Internet users.

Databases

In one sense, the entire Internet is one huge database. You can use the Internet to find out about almost anything you can imagine from a wide range of sources. However, in a more formal sense, you can access a variety of databases via the Internet—you just have to know where to go.

What's a database? It is a repository of similar or related data. One type of database is a list of databases, and you can find that on the Internet. You also can find databases you can search on such topics as:

- Legal information (The Columbia Law Library online catalogue, for example)
- Medical information (MEDLINE, for example)
- National education BBS
- Molecular biology
- Food and nutrition
- Alcoholism
- Miscellaneous data (Ham Radio Callbook, for example)
- Kidsnet, an international interchange for students
- ERIC, the educational database
- Periodicals
- Federal Information Exchange, a place for the higher education community to interact with various governmental agencies

That's just a sampling, but you get the idea. These databases are created and maintained by the people attached to full-time Internet nodes. In general they were conceived and created with another market in mind—perhaps an in-company project or the work of an organization—then made available to the Internet as an afterthought. Database access is one of the most fruitful aspects of the Internet and reason enough to avail yourself of the opportunity. However, once on the Internet, you get so much more, such as conferences....

Conferences and News

An Internet conference is just what the name implies. Like a conference held at a downtown convention center, Internet conferences attract experts, would-be experts, and the just plain curious to a central location to discuss and learn about a specified topic. There are Internet conferences on almost every conceivable topic.

If you have an interest for which there isn't already a conference (that's a little hard to believe), you and your group can start one. Conferences are usually called news or newsgroups. This is a store and forward system where participants make comments or ask questions, then wait for a response from one or hundreds of users a few hours or days later.

When you participate in a conference on the Internet you may or may not participate interactively, in real time. You can log on to a conference at any time and read the past discussions about a particular topic, add your own comments to a general audience or respond directly to one of the other participants, then log off. In this example, you haven't actually talked to anyone. Rather, you have read what other people had to say, posted your own comments for people to read later, then gone about your business. A few hours later or a few days later, you may log on again to see what has happened since you left.

There are also interactive conferences or discussions (or talks or chats) where you talk directly to other people as if you were on a party line or Citizen's Band channel. These conferences or discussion groups also can range across a wide list of topics and may include people from all over the world. See chapter 3 for a more detailed discussion of conferences and news.

Conferences frequently are accessed through a particular group, association, or service provider. One popular conference area is The WELL (did you try The WELL as I suggested at the beginning of this chapter?), which is really a conference of conferences. The WELL is an independent service provider that offers access to the Internet and can be accessed from the Internet, but it is known for its conferences. There are about 200 public conferences and 100 private ones going on through The WELL at any given time. Here's a brief sample of some of the topics:

Apple Library User's Group (ALUG) Conference
Biosphere II
Grateful Dead Conference
Internet Conference
Movies

Oakland Conference

Scientific Computing

Singles Conference

Spanish Conference

Telecommunications Conference

Veterans Conference

Virtual Communities

That's just a start, of course, and these are just the conferences available on a single resource. If you like to share ideas and learn from other people's expertise and experience, the Internet is a good place to do it.

In addition to conferences designed and supported by individual service providers, there are thousands of regular newsgroup topics available on most full-service Internet provider machines. These newsgroups are mostly universal, routed from place to place as they are created from the USENET system. (As this book is written, U.S. Internet is providing access to more than 12,000 newsgroups, for example.)

Electronic Mail

There are probably more users of Internet electronic mail than any other single Internet resource. You can send short letters or lengthy files via Internet email. One reason Internet email is so popular is that you can access it from a variety of non-Internet facilities through mail gateways. If you use CompuServe Information Service, for example, or MCI Mail, GEnie, Microsoft Network, America Online, or one of any number of online services, you have access to the Internet mail system through a gateway.

Mail is sent and received across the Internet in much the same way you send mail with the U.S. Postal Service across the country or around the world. Once you know the Internet address of the recipient, you simply prepare the message with a text editor (or use one of the available online editors) and send the message to the proper address.

One of the convenient features of electronic mail is that you can create mailing lists of individual recipients. You can send a letter to many people at the same time by sending it to everyone on the mailing list. There also are mailing lists used by various companies and organizations that you can join. Once your name is on one of these lists, you receive broadcast mail designed for a general audience within a specific topic area, and you also receive more specific information addressed to you or a subgroup within this interest area. Unlike a conventional postal mailing list, electronic mailing lists are two way: you can post information to other members of the list (like a conference).

Because electronic mail is usually posted within a few minutes anywhere in the world (though it sometimes takes several hours or even a few days), you can exchange information almost interactively, with very little delay in getting a response. In most cases your access to the Internet is through a local connection, so there are no long distance telephone charges associated with the email service. See Chapter 3 for more information about email.

Interoperability

Another key feature of the Internet is its *interoperability*, which means the ability of computer systems from a variety of vendors to participate in the network and to communicate with each other. Because the Internet uses a well-known and widely used communications protocol, you can communicate via the Internet with almost any kind of computer hardware. Thus, on the Internet, an IBM mainframe can talk to an Apple Macintosh which can talk to a DEC VAX, and they all are compatible with Intel-based PCs.

File Transfer

Although you may transfer files of information as you work with mailing lists and other Internet entities, there also are designated file areas where information files, computer program files, graphics images, and other diverse data are stored and available for download across the Internet. (I showed one such repository on USIT at the beginning of this chapter. If you haven't tried USIT's free five-hour trial account, go back to the beginning of this chapter and try it now. That's the type of facility we're talking about here.)

There are two types of file areas that you are likely to access: anonymous and specific. The specific files are ones you are allowed access to because you have a logon account and password on the repository system (the one where the file was generated or where it is stored). The anonymous files are made available to a general Internet audience, whether or not they are members of the company or computing group that created the file.

As you might imagine, there are thousands upon thousands of files available on the Internet at any given time. Luckily there are searching facilities that help you find and get what you need from the network. We'll discuss some of those in Chapter 3 and 4.

Shareable Software

The Internet began with technically oriented, computer-savvy people. And today, to access the Internet you have to use a computer. So it should not be surprising that among the common and popular resources on the Internet is a vast collection of shareable software. Distributed as shareware or freeware, Internet software offerings range from communications programs to routines that help you use the Internet to games.

To use shareable software, you simply have to find what is available and where it is, then download it across the network to your own computer.

Sounds and Video

It is not that widely used, yet, but sound and even photographs and motion video are becoming part of the Internet. As networking hardware gets faster and faster, and the facilities to attach to high-speed networks become more widely distributed, look for sound and other high-end information to become a regular part of nearly everything you do on the Internet. Many corporations and universities already are doing it within their own dedicated networks, and you can find sound and picture files already on the Internet. There are many archives that include interesting pictures and sounds such as music, movie dialog, personal comments, motion picture excerpts, and more. To access these facilities you generally download a file, then use a player on your local computer to view or hear the files.

It is only a matter of time before these facilities will be a common and expected part of public networks such as the Internet. With the growth of the World Wide Web (WWW), for example, you can click on icons that bring up sound or motion video enhancements to the onscreen image that is automatically displayed. As communications speeds improve, the images and sounds that are optional now will likely become an automatic part of email, advertising, online instructions, research, and nearly everything else.

One facility that is growing in popularity—but is definitely in the experimental stage—is CU See Me, a shareware video conferencing facility that lets you sit at your desktop Macintosh or PC and talk over a video link, real time, with users all over the world.

INTERNET TRAVELING COMPANIONS

The members of the Internet are about as diverse as any community you could choose. The individuals who make up the Internet family are doctors, lawyers, engineers, corporate executives, college teachers and students, elementary students, and kids of all ages.

But you also can categorize these companions into larger entities—groups that, because of their particular areas of interest or network usage, are segmented out for specific rate structures. In general these groups are:

- Educational
- Government

- Military
- Commercial
- Individual

Each of these groups receives a different rate structure, generally gravitates to different Internet facilities, and may operate under different guidelines.

For example, educational institutions are limited to providing access to students and faculty and they may not conduct commercial activities through their academic accounts. This restriction is made because educational institutions pay lower usage charges, and also because academic Internet traffic generally is routed over portions of the network that are subsidized by federal dollars earmarked for research and education.

If the site through which you access the Internet has a commercial license, on the other hand, usage is less restrictive, but the charges are higher. There is no federal subsidy for commercial routes.

As an individual user, you will have to abide by whatever standards are established by the access provider you use and by the general rules of the road, which include an awareness of copyright laws (you can't upload a commercial software package and share it around, for example), and international laws (you can't share certain technology such as computer encryption information with certain foreign countries). And, of course, you're expected to follow rules of common courtesy and politeness.

Although there are no network police monitoring your every conversation to make sure you comply with the rules, if you violate the rules and your license often enough, you will get caught because enough people will become aware of it. You likely will be reported to the appropriate local service provider who may terminate or limit your access. That's one way the network works, through people looking out for each other and for the integrity of the network itself. Truly, the Internet is a *community* of users, (mostly) all interested in the common good.

WHAT YOU LEARNED

There you have it, a general overview of the Internet. You have experienced some of the Internet through the hands-on tutorial at the beginning of this chapter. I've shown you who and what are on the Internet, and I've discussed some of the history of this interesting social and technical entity.

In addition, I discussed some of the types of information you can find on the Internet and the different kinds of Internet clients. I provided a brief discussion of how you can access the Internet yourself, and finally, I pointed out some of the rules of the road for traveling the Internet superhighway.

In the next chapter I'll show you how to arrange your own access to the Internet (if you don't already have it), and how to review what you're doing if you're already using the Internet.

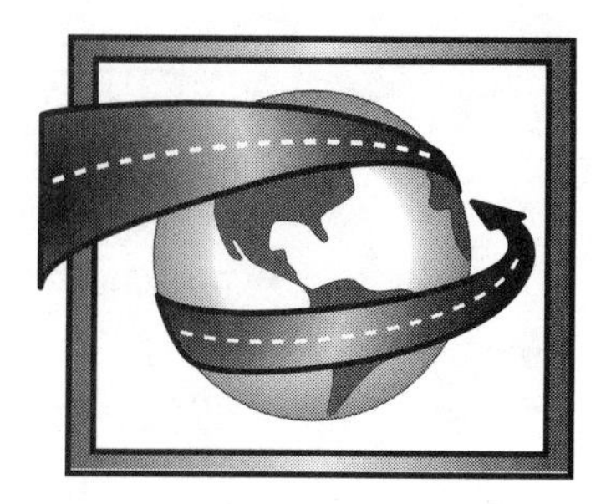

Chapter 2

MERGING ONTO THE INTERNET

Merging onto the Internet can present a complex array of choices. However, in this chapter I'll show you how to seek out the most economical and most functional Internet access method. And I'll give you more information about the Internet structure to make your travels easier. Finally, I'll provide a quick primer on modems and the communications software you'll need to connect to the Internet.

Here's a quick look at the major topics I'll cover in this chapter:

- What are the available Internet access points?
- How do you find Internet access for yourself?
- How can you get the most Internet "bang for your buck"?
- What software do you need to use the Internet?
- What hardware do you need to use the Internet?

I talked briefly in the last chapter about how you can become a part of the Internet. Depending on your present work or school situation, getting your own account for Internet access can range from simple to difficult. The easy part is if your company or school is already an Internet player and the people who control such things are open to adding new users. In this case, you'll simply have to make a telephone request, or perhaps fill out a simple form, and you're online. You'll probably access the Internet over your local area network through a server computer or gateway that is attached to the Internet.

The difficult part comes if you don't work for anyone already on the Internet or you aren't in school, and you want to (or must!) minimize the cost of your Internet travels. In this case the process becomes more like solving a mystery or playing a game, but don't despair, just keep reading.

As you move through this chapter, you will encounter some Internet terms and concepts that I may not explain right away. That's OK. If you don't know them, you'll pick them up in the next chapter. Or refer to the glossary at the end of the book.

Let's begin by discussing the various types of access points and how you might reach them yourself.

ACCESS POINTS: ROUTES TO THE NET

The concept of the Internet as a superhighway has become a little overworked, but one reason it has is that the analogy is a good one. Keep that concept in mind as I discuss access points to the Internet. An access point is like a highway interchange, a way to move from local streets and roads onto the interstate. Think about how you might use the interstate highway for a trip to the local shopping mall, for example:

- Get in the car.
- Drive out of the driveway onto your street.
- Follow the city street to a state highway.

- Take the state highway to an interstate interchange.
- Drive up the access ramp to the interstate.
- Follow the interstate to the proper exit for the shopping mall.
- Leave the interstate and follow a local road to the shopping mall.

The interstate highway is a good analogy for the Internet. Your journey along the Internet to find files or discussions of interest is a lot like the trip along the interstate to the local mall I just described. And, like the interstate, you can take the Internet not only to local or regional locations, but to places anywhere in the country. In fact, this is where the analogy breaks down, because you can take the Internet almost anywhere in the world—you aren't confined to the borders of the United States or even to the continent. As I write this book, the Internet is available to people in at least 150 countries!

To use any of the access methods I discuss, you'll need a way to connect your personal computer (IBM compatible, Macintosh, UNIX workstation, or whatever you have) to a computer that provides Internet access. You'll probably do this with a modem, communications software, and a dial-up telephone line. I'll discuss some of these hardware and software issues later in this chapter.

First, let's look at some basic hardware issues and definitions. How do you attach your desktop computer to the Internet? You will use an Internet node. A node is like the interstate entrance and exit ramps—it lets you move from a local or regional area toward some more distant place, using a general-purpose access route. In computer parlance a node is a computer system that is attached directly to a network. In fact, a node can be a single computer, or it can be a network of computers through which you access another, broader network. Ultimately you leave the local area through a port attached to a single computer, but precisely how this works or which computer you are using may not be immediately obvious. It doesn't matter. At this point all you need to know is that a node is what provides you access to the Internet.

As you might imagine, there are numerous, reasonably complicated hardware and software issues that surround attaching your computer or terminal to the Internet. As I explained in Chapter 1, you might connect through a dial-up connection to an Internet node, you might set up your computer as a node, you might be accessing the Internet through a local area network gateway, and so on. Luckily, we don't have to worry about these complex issues. What we are concerned with, however, is who builds and maintains these nodes, who is using them, and whether you can use them. You will learn more about nodes and gateways in our discussion of domains and addressing in Chapter 3.

That's the main concept. What I have to discuss here are the various routes you can use to merge onto the Internet, what you call them, and how to find them.

Academic and Freenet Access

For many Internet users, the academic route is the best, least expensive, and easiest road to follow to the Internet. That's because most educational institutions have some sort of Internet access for students and faculty. As a member of one of these groups at a college, university, technical school, or high school, you probably already have access rights to the Internet.

You're a member of the student body or a faculty member and you never heard anybody say "Internet"? That's not uncommon, but that doesn't mean you can't get on through your institution.

To learn more about access through an academic route, contact your local area network (LAN) administrator, local or regional MIS (Management of Information Systems) director, your supervisor, or coworkers. Somewhere along the line you'll find someone who knows the process for getting on the Internet from an internal or dial-up node.

Procedures vary at each institution, of course, but frequently the only requirement is that you are a student with one or more classes or a member of the faculty. Many institutions offer one- or two-session training classes to show you the various options for using the school's computer facilities in general, and for getting on the Internet specifically.

Even if you are not now a student but you can't find another viable option for accessing the Internet, you might consider taking up public speaking, photography, SCUBA diving, introduction to computers, or any class offered by a local school. Sometimes the cost of tuition—which incidentally gets you the right to use the school's computer facilities for Internet access—is lower than paying a commercial service. And of course, if you have no local service, this method can cost much less than paying long distance charges to access the Internet through a distant access provider.

Be aware, however, that accessing the Internet through a school can mean very limited access. Generally you will use a "dumb" terminal or a desktop computer emulating a dumb terminal and you may not even have access to a local gopher. With some schools all you get when you access the Internet is a UNIX prompt and from there you are on your own. Or, you may have a local gopher server that provides a menu for browsing the Internet, but you won't get your own email address, nor will you be able to access many programs and features of the Internet such as FTP or Lynx for World Wide Web browsing.

You may have another low-cost or no-cost access option in your community in the form of a freenet. Free or nearly free access sometimes is provided through a local library or other institution. A freenet is a community supported operation that may provide email services, online research, and Internet access. With some freenet services you may have to physically sit at the library or other institution that provides the service; with others you may be able to use dial-up access. Freenet access may require considerable research, so you shouldn't give up on freenet if your first pass at local facilities doesn't turn up anything. The number of institutions offering this type of Internet access is growing all the time. See the freenet list in Chapter 8 for more information.

Be aware that a freenet may provide less than full-featured access to the Internet, depending on what institution is offering the service, how it is funded, and so on. But it can get you on when other avenues aren't available or are too costly.

Government Access

Accessing the Internet through a governmental facility is like using a college or university. If you are a government employee or contractor, chances are there is Internet access somewhere within your facility. If you don't already know about it, you'll have to do some research. Simply start asking questions to learn where the Internet is being used and how you can access it.

Accessing the Internet through the government—especially a military or research facility—can be more complicated than from a university setting because of security issues. It is still possible; just ask lots of questions.

If yours is like most governmental facilities, there's probably a local network serving your department or workgroup, then a facility-wide or regional network tying some of these facilities together. If no one on your local network knows about or is using the Internet, you'll just have to branch out, broaden your sphere, and find out who is.

As with accessing the Internet through a university or other school, government access likely will be somewhat restricted. You may have only a limited menu system and you may not have your own email address.

Corporate Access

Guess what? Many large corporations also use the Internet regularly to conduct research, to use email, or to transfer information from one division to another. If your company has more than one office and you know that your computers are part of the regular hardware in use at your firm, chances are pretty good that somewhere, someone in your company already is using the Internet for something.

As with academic and government access, you'll simply have to find the right person who can tell you whether the Internet is being used and what you have to do to use existing facilities. At the very least you should be able to get email services. But you might also arrange full-featured Internet access through your existing company link.

Third-Party Access

If you can't get to the Internet through academic, governmental, commercial, or freenet channels, you may settle for partial access through what I call third-party channels (but see the discussion of commercial services—different from commercial access—that follows). Among these third-party channels are the CompuServe network, MCI Mail, America Online, BBS facilities such as FIDOnet, and a built-in facility of UNIX, UUCP. You can also find UUCP software for MS-DOS, Macintosh, and other platforms.

With these methods of access you can do little more than exchange electronic mail and perhaps read USENET News as it is distributed on the Internet (see Chapter 3). With MCI Mail, and some other commercial online services, you use Internet email facilities from inside the basic service simply by providing an appropriate Internet mail address. In fact, you can use the Internet to send messages to non-Internet addresses if both ends of the link have some way to attach to the Internet.

MCI Mail is an online commercial service dedicated to email while offering some research and other services. CompuServe is a commercial bulletin board, email and online service that provides Internet services. America Online is similar to CompuServe. With any of these services, you arrange access by signing up and paying a fee. Then you use a modem and communications software to dial an access telephone number to log on.

CompuServe

When CompuServe first began offering Internet access, all you could do was send and receive electronic mail. Today, the story is quite different. As this book is written, the CompuServe network is expanding to offer full Internet access using familiar, easy-to-use access tools. CompuServe's WinSim interface, for example, is being expanded to make full access to the Internet almost seamless. You can still use CompuServe to send and receive electronic mail, but you now can do a lot more.

The main difference between using CompuServe and other, Internet-only, commercial providers is that you first log on to

CompuServe, and then you access the Internet as a second step. You must follow a similar path with an Internet service provider in that you first log on to the provider's host machine, but with CompuServe you are in a completely different, non-UNIX, non-Internet environment before you step off into the Internet. In addition, CompuServe access to the Internet is somewhat more expensive than that of most Internet-only providers. (As this book is written, CompuServe charges $9.95 per month for basic access services and $4.00 per hour for Internet access.)

America Online (AOL)

America Online is among the largest online services and has undergone rapid growth in recent years. One feature that makes AOL particularly attractive is its easy-to-use user interface. The front-end software, available for both Microsoft Windows and the Apple Macintosh, is supplied as part of the service. As with CompuServe, Internet is not the fundamental use for AOL, but you can get to the Internet from within AOL. Users can access FTP, Gopher, WAIS databases and Usenet newsgroups. Telnet and World Wide Web services are planned for 1995.

Current prices for AOL online access are $2.95 per hour. The service also is stepping up its service offerings during 1995 with more local access numbers, more 14.4 k baud sites and some ISDN service.

America Online Inc., 8619 Westwood Center Dr.,
Vienna, VA 22182-2285; 800-827-6364, 703-448-8700;
email, postmaster@aol.com.

Prodigy

Prodigy is another popular online service that also offers access to the Internet. Prodigy Internet access, however, is not nearly as complete as CompuServe's or AOL's. You can send and receive Internet email, and you can read and respond to USENET news, but as this is written you don't have access to such Internet facilities as FTP or Gopher. Prodigy does, however, maintain a World

Wide Web site that showcases a number of business offerings, including its own.

Prodigy's AstraNet Web site (http://www.astranet.com) is basically a billboard for the service, plus a well-chosen selection of good links on various topics, including business and entertainment. Prodigy is not as popular for Internet access as some of the other services, but the company has promised some impressive enhancements, including a graphical World Wide Web browser. As with any online service in this fast-paced cyberspace world, Prodigy isn't standing still and you should keep abreast of the changes as you evaluate your current and future online access.

MCI Mail

Like CompuServe, MCI Mail has, in the past, offered only email access to the Internet. You can still use MCI Mail, an international electronic mail service, to exchange mail with Internet users. However, MCI Mail, through its parent company, MCI, is now part of a larger scheme. MCI is offering Internet access as a dedicated provider through local access numbers, similar to the way CompuServe provides access to its network in all major cities and towns around the country.

However, like CompuServe, MCI access to the Internet is considerably more expensive than that of some of the Internet-only service providers. As this book is written, for example, basic MCI Internet access costs $19.95 per month plus $4.00 per hour in access charges. Many Internet service providers around the country offer access in the neighborhood of $1.00 per hour.

UUCP

To use UUCP facilities to send and receive mail via the Internet, you need to make arrangements with a UNIX site that has access to the Internet. UUCP is a system built into most UNIX systems. (If it isn't included, you can get it as an option.) UUCP lets you transfer mail between your system and another automatically. You can also install UUCP functionality through software on non-UNIX systems. To get messages onto and off of the Internet, you want to UUCP to a system that is attached to the Internet. Again, you won't actually access the Internet directly, but you can send and receive messages. In addition, UUCP can dial out from a host system to another user to deliver mail directly.

With UUCP, Internet mail addressed to you arrives at the UUCP site you are using, and it waits there until you use UUCP on your system to dial up the remote site and download your messages. Likewise, you can send mail from your site via UUCP to the remote Internet node.

You'll frequently find UUCP access to Internet mail and newsgroups through a local bulletin board service. Most cities have dozens or even hundreds of BBS sites. They frequently work together to provide their users Internet mail and news. One BBS operator may actually connect to a UUCP host, then provide the data to other area BBS systems through a re-sell or sharing arrangement. Sometimes this service provides only Internet news (discussion groups), and sometimes UUCP data is a one-way path: you can read news but you can't respond to any of the comments. Where UUCP mail is available, however, you should be able to send and receive information.

If UUCP turns out to be the best solution for you, you can get details on using it from the service provider or from the UUCP software vendor. However, for most of us, UUCP is one of the last resort solutions. It doesn't give you full Internet access, for one thing, and for another, configuring your system for correct UUCP operation and finding a willing (and properly configured) site to work with can be a real problem. Again, unless you are a BBS owner, you'll probably get UUCP access indirectly rather than straight from an Internet service provider.

SLIP and PPP

A SLIP or PPP connection allows your computer to directly connect to the Internet through a service provider so that you can use graphical Web browser and other applications. As I have said, the most complete Internet access is from a dedicated machine, probably a UNIX computer, attached directly to a high-speed line on the Internet. There are solutions that are almost as good, though slower, and almost always cheaper. What you ultimately pay for SLIP/PPP connections depends on the arrangements you make with an individual service provider. This method uses SLIP (Serial Line Internet Protocol) or PPP (Point to Point Protocol) versions of Internet software designed to operate over standard telephone lines at 9,600 bps or faster. (You probably could run slower than that, but you wouldn't want to). You can use dedicated telephone line access, or use dial-up lines to save the cost of dedicated lines.

SLIP and PPP are designed for personal computer or very small network access to the Internet. With 9,600 bps or even 14,400 bps access, you don't have the bandwidth on the communications link to support very many users.

Today, with 28,800 bps becoming popular, a dial-in SLIP connection for more than one user is possible. If you have a small network you might be able to set up one computer as a modem gateway and provide SLIP or PPP access for multiple users.

Whatever link you use, SLIP and PPP access require that you access the actual Internet through a service provider who can accept your call (or dedicated link) and put you on the network. Because you are handling most of the overhead, including local data storage, addressing, and so on, at your local computer, the cost of access may be a lot less than attaching through a dumb terminal (or a computer acting like a dumb terminal). On the other hand, some service providers charge a premium for SLIP or PPP access because they may also provide software and detailed technical assistance, and because the quality of your Internet connection with SLIP or PPP is relatively high when compared to conventional shell or dial-up service.

NOTE

A dumb terminal is a device that includes a keyboard, display screen, and a communications port. It is used to communicate with a large, multiuser computer system, or as a modem-link to an online service. It contains no local storage or computing facilities.

As for the software, you probably can find SLIP or PPP software free for the asking if you can poke around the Internet or have someone do it for you. There is a lot of public domain software out there. Probably the most common for PC computers is the Trumpet Winsock package. The Trumpet Winsock (for Windows Sockets) suite includes a capable TCP/IP driver along with a relatively easy-to-use front end designed to run in the Microsoft Windows environment. The user interface includes a dialer and a script language to help you automate login. It is available for download from most Internet service providers.

Another available offering is KA9Q, a SLIP package that also supports packet radio (TCP/IP over a radio link) but is most commonly used for attaching a network to the Internet. In fact, this package, designed for amateur radio operators originally, is gaining popularity among technical Internet and networking users. It is a convenient way to build a bridge between local network segments and to provide Internet access for LAN users. If you are not among those technical types who enjoy a challenge, then KA9Q is not for you, but it is an interesting and quite functional package that you are sure to run across during your Internet travels.

If you are using a Macintosh machine, with the latest system software, MacTCP is included. TCP/IP software is also bundled with a number of books and with other software offerings.

PPP and SLIP offer comparable capabilities. PPP is the newer protocol and, according to some users, is somewhat faster than SLIP. I, myself, prefer SLIP because it usually is easier to configure, there is more software available to support it, and the people you turn to for help have more experience with SLIP than with PPP. However, packages such as Trumpet Winsock offer both. You select which protocol you want to use by clicking on a check box on a configuration screen. Many service providers market SLIP/PPP access together so that if you have access to one you also can use the other. Particularly since much of the consumer-level software available today offers a choice of either method, many users simply experiment until they find which method best suits their needs. See chapter 5 for more detail on configuring specific packages.

To use SLIP or PPP, you use communications software and a modem to log on to an Internet host, just as you would with any other access. This dial-up component may be offered as part of the TCP/IP package, or you may have to secure TCP/IP software from one source and the dialing/user front end from somewhere else. You normally can't use a standard communications package to establish the link before switching to SLIP. Once you have connected to the host computer, you start your SLIP software and the SLIP package on the host establishes communications with your local SLIP software. Once everything is working normally, your PC, Macintosh, or whatever computer you are using is set up with an IP address and is tied into the Internet almost as if it were on a direct link.

You can issue Internet commands such as FTP and have the requested file download directly to your local computer. With a conventional dial-up connection, the FTP command gets a file to your service provider's host computer, then you have to download it to your desktop using another protocol.

The only real advice I can offer in this regard is to call around and find out what your best options are. In the meantime, don't delay getting on the Internet. You can always use the services of a company such as The WELL (discussed in a later section), CompuServe, or another national provider to get on the Internet, then check around to see if there is a better and more economical choice for you.

Commercial Services

If you haven't already figured out a way to get onto the Internet through one of the other methods I have mentioned, you probably will have to turn to a commercial service. There are several companies offering pay-as-you-go Internet access. I'll discuss a few of them in this section.

U.S. Internet

U.S. Internet
1127 N. Broadway
Knoxville, TN 37917
800-218-8748 (USIT)

U.S. Internet is one of the hundreds of available local Internet service providers springing up around the country. This company began as a small, local provider in East Tennessee, but now is expanding to other parts of the country. You can access the Internet through U.S. Internet by using a local access number or through an 800 telephone number.

U.S. Internet offers a variety of access services, from its own hypertext menu system for shell or conventional dial-up users (I showed that menu in the previous chapter), to a custom SLIP software package that makes installing and using SLIP utilities quick and easy. Figure 2.1 shows the opening screen of this innovative package, TCP/Buffet.

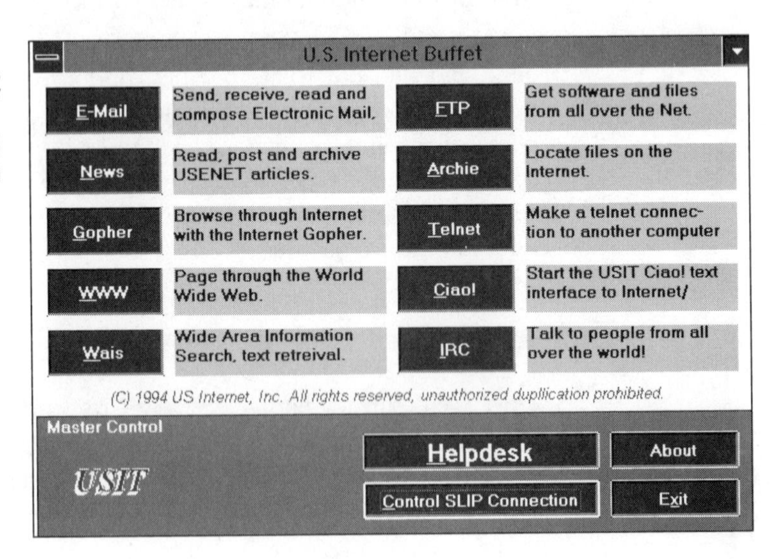

FIGURE 2.1
U.S. Internet/ Buffet opening screen

This firm offers dial-up at 28.8 Kbps, plus ISDN, T1 (1.54 Mbps), and other access options.

Current U.S. Internet pricing provides shell access for $19.95 per month (15 hours of online time and 10 Mbytes of storage included) and SLIP/PPP access for $25.95 per month with 15 hours included. If you go over the 15 hour allowance, you will pay $1.25 per hour for shell access and $1.50 per hour for SLIP/PPP access.

U.S. Internet will arrange larger blocks of pre-paid access, including unlimited dial-up time and dedicated (you have your own line) service. The company will register a domain name for you, sell you communications hardware (ISDN bridges, network routers, modems), train individuals or your whole staff, design and market advertising for your company on the Internet, and provide consulting services on the Internet or on other computer-related topics. U.S. Internet also offers 24-hour, seven-day-a-week telephone helpdesk support as well as online helpdesk support.

You can request information on the U.S. Internet service by sending email to **info@usit.net**. You can also sign up for a free, five-hour Internet account by dialing **800-270-5474**, logging in as **guest**, and entering the password **guest**. Fill out the questionnaire, then call one of the U.S. Internet sales or technical support staff to have your account approved. Then you can use the service—including full Internet access—for five hours with no obligation.

I will offer some service pricing throughout this chapter simply as a guideline to you as you attempt to get yourself online. However, the Internet service business is growing and changing rapidly. Use the prices and service descriptions I provide as a starting point only. For details, contact specific service providers.

The WELL

The WELL
27 Gate Five Road
Sausalito, CA 94965-1401
415-332-4335

The WELL is a conferencing system that Internet users can access for research and sharing. You also can use The WELL as a link to the Internet. You can't get to the Internet from The WELL guest account, but once you sign up as a WELL subscriber, you have the Internet at your fingertips right at The WELL OK prompt.

NOTE

If you have Internet access another way, you still may want to try The WELL. It is an excellent resource for conversation, research, and exchanging ideas on everything from using the Internet to cooking old-time recipes. To get to The WELL from anywhere on the Internet, telnet to well.sf.ca.us.

You don't have to do anything special to access the Internet from The WELL. As soon as you issue an Internet command—such as FTP, for example—you will be traveling the Internet. The first time you access the Internet from your WELL account, you will be asked to read and agree to a 160-line document that spells out usage guidelines and restrictions on your WELL Internet access.

Figure 2.2 shows you how the first part of this agreement looks.

FIGURE 2.2

The WELL Internet access agreement

```
OK (type a command or type  opt  for Options): ftp
Hello, you have reached the WELL's Internet Access Agreement.

The following text contains the rules and standards to which WELL users
must agree to abide by in order to obtain access to the WELL's Internet
connection.

** Please read this agreement carefully.  Intentional or repeated violation
** of this agreement will result in prompt termination of the user's WELL
** account.

This document is roughly 160 lines long.  Please read the entire text.

The WELL has set up a public conference for discussion of the Internet, how
to use it, what is available on it etc.  To get there type:

        g Internet

at an OK prompt.  The WELL support staff does not provide technical
assistance in using the Internet, beyond the information we have made
available for the public Internet conference (which includes a very basic
cheat-sheet for telnet, rlogin, and ftp).

We hope you have great time exploring out there and that you bring back
– <b> backup. <space> continue. <q> quit – wonderful stories of your adventures.
```

As this book is written you can use The WELL to get to the Internet for a $15.00 per month membership fee and $2.00 per hour of connect time.

You can request information on The WELL to be emailed to you by emailing a request through the Internet to **info@well.sf.ca.us**. You can send this message through other email services such as CompuServe or MCI Mail. As the Internet has grown in popularity, The WELL has enhanced its services. For example you can use PPP (Point to Point Protocol) to access The WELL. This opens the possibility of using graphical user interfaces such as Netscape or Mosaic, changing the face of The WELL's Internet component. Use The WELL menus during your guest tour to find out about the latest WELL facilities and services.

As this book is written you can use The WELL to get to the Internet for a $15.00 per month membership fee and $2.00 per hour of connect time.

The WELL prices are for basic access through The WELL's local number in California. If you access The WELL from an area that makes this a long distance phone call, you'll probably get a better rate by using the CompuServe Packet Network (CPN). This access will cost an additional $4.00 per hour. In addition, check with The WELL about local dialup from your area. The WELL, like many other strong service providers, is opening local points of presence in major areas across the country. Where local dialing access is available, there may be little or no surcharge.

a2i Communications

a2i Communications
1211 Park Avenue #202
San Jose, CA 95126-2924

a2i Communications is billed as a national Internet provider, yet they presently offer only limited national access. It is expected that this service will grow, offering local access from a broader area. As this book is written, you have two options for reaching a2i: a 415 area code direct number (local call in Campbell, Los Altos, Los Gatos, Mountain View, San Jose, Santa Clara, Saratoga, and Sunnyvale) and other area access numbers.

The cost is a $15 one-time fee, then monthly fees that range from $15 to $25 depending on the length of your service commitment. There are no hourly fees, only the basic membership charge. If you are accessing the service by dialing long distance, however, there are additional hourly charges.

A2i also offers SLIP/PPP access. The rate structure is different than for shell or dial-up access. You can get information online about the complete range of services and charges.

Figure 2.3 shows how a2i is described in an online document from a2i itself.

FIGURE 2.3

a2i online description

The a2i network is a professionally-run system based on a network of Sun machines. Our offerings include:

o Usenet news.
o Electronic mail.
o Internet access, including telnet and ftp.Our IP address is 192.160.13.1.
o A SunOS (Unix) software development environment. All the standard tools are available.
o A command-line-oriented MS-DOS environment which may be invoked from within SunOS. In this environment, you can execute most archiving/dearchiving programs, virus scanning utilities, compilers, and assemblers.
o News feeds and electronic mail via UUCP, for UUCP subscribers.
o A permanent electronic mail address for you.
o Other services to be added.

The a2i network is directly connected to the Internet via a 56 kbps leased line. As a result, we can provide you with 'real-time' access to the Internet. For example, as an a2i subscriber, you can interactively converse with other users on the Internet via commands such as 'talk' and 'irc', or exchange electronic mail with them in a matter of seconds.

Two types of subscriptions are available through a2i: interactive subscriptions and UUCP subscriptions. (See our discussion of UUCP earlier in this chapter.) An interactive subscription (or interactive account as it is sometimes called) is available through direct dial to a 415 area code number, as I mentioned earlier. Or, if you want some of the features of the a2i system such as conferencing, email, and so on, you can telnet to the a2i network on the Internet. (Telnet is an Internet command and software utility that lets you find specific Internet hosts and initiate the logon process with them). If your objective is to access the Internet, however, you'll have to use dial-up access, as just described.

With your subscription you get up to 5 megabytes of disk space as well. Not sure whether a2i is the link for you? The company offers a three- or six-month trial subscription. You pay the standard rate, but you can cancel at any time and get a proportional refund of the unused time. Note that there is a single rate structure for businesses and individuals. a2i states that each account is for the use of only one person. That means a business would need to arrange for a separate account for each user within the company. a2i also will register your own domain name for sending and receiving email. You would still use the facilities of a2i, but the people you correspond with would use your domain as if you had your own Internet connection. The current cost for setting up this type of addressing is $40 initially, then $5 per year for maintenance.

A UUCP account may be useful for companies that have local email or USENET News accounts, or that want to offer public UUCP access. Remember that UUCP is a function of UNIX that, when properly configured, lets two systems communicate to share email and USENET News. If you are an individual seeking Internet access, this is NOT the way to go. An individual account will let you send and receive email and will give you access to USENET News, so you don't need the headache and heavy hardware requirements of UUCP.

There is a dual rate structure for UUCP accounts—standard and low volume. The standard account offers unlimited services, while the low-volume account limits the user to a transfer of no more than 100 megabytes per month on the average. The UUCP account includes an interactive account and any required domain registration as well.

To receive subscription information on a2i by email, send a request to **info@rahul.net**. You can send this message through other email services such as CompuServe or MCI Mail. Also, you can log on directly to the a2i network to browse through a lot of information about a2i. Simply telnet to **rahul.net** (if you can borrow a connection) or use the direct dial numbers (408-293-9010 for v.32bis/v.32, or 408-293-9020 for PEP) and log in as **Guest**. A menu-driven system will answer your questions and show you how to sign up for a2i.

v.32bis and PEP are modem standards. v.32bis is the most common among high-speed modems. PEP stands for Packetized Ensemble Protocol, a design promoted by Telebit Corp. as the only multicarrier modem (one that makes use of the entire telephone line bandwidth instead of just a few frequencies as most modems do) that also is compatible with v.32bis. The reason for separate dial-in lines with these two technologies is that while "compatibility" may be designed into a PEP product, there can be delays in getting a reliable link because of the increased overhead while the two modems negotiate over protocol and speed. In addition, there are times when PEP modems simply won't link properly with v.32bis units.

PSI

Performance Systems International (PSI)
510 Huntmar Park Drive
Herndon, VA 22070
703-904-7187

PSI is another provider of dial-up Internet access, but with many access points around the country. The company offers access software for Windows, UNIX, and the Macintosh to help make your Internet travels easier. PSI offers a number of different services to address various access requirements. Contact PSI to find out how to fill your individual needs and to get current prices.

PSI's PSILink Global Messaging Service has two fundamental service options—lite and basic. Lite provides unlimited messaging and paging mailboxes. Basic adds anonymous FTP and USENET News facilities as well. This is a batch process supported through free PSILink software. You write email or news postings offline, then dial your selected PSINet node. The software takes over and checks your email, downloading any new mail and uploading mail you are sending. Then the software checks your chosen newsgroups for new postings and posts anything you have to add.

You can't use Telnet through PSILink (use PSI's Global Dialup Service—GDS—for this). However, PSINet can be accessed in over 175 North American cities and 40 foreign cities, and the list is growing all the time. Notice that while the PSILink service uses the Internet for messaging, you may not have access to all the Internet services available from other providers. On the other hand, you get free access software that makes the service extremely easy to use, and your charges are reasonable.

You can download the latest PSILink software by using FTP over the Internet. FTP to **FTP.psi.com** and download **psilink.zip** (or **psilinkw.zip** for a Microsoft Windows–based program) from the PSILink directory (type **cd /psilink** at the FTP prompt). (For more information about using FTP, see Chapter 4.) This will give you an early look at the software you get as part of the PSI service. Of course, if you're not already on the Internet you'll have to borrow a connection or have someone download the software for you.

UUNET

UUNET
Suite 570
3110 Fairview Park Drive, Suite 570
Falls Church, VA 22042
703-204-8000
800-488-6383

Like PSI, UUNET offers access to its own networking and mail services through 2,500 connections, as well as offering Internet mail access. The AlterNet public TCP/IP service from UUNET is for businesses that need direct, continuous links among multiple offices. AlterNet provides a 10 Mbps (million bits per second) national backbone. Because AlterNet is a commercial service, some of the restrictions that may apply to the Internet aren't applicable. Of course, you can send and receive mail from AlterNet to Internet.

As this book is written, it is unclear just how UUNET services may change in the near future. Microsoft Corporation has agreed to invest considerable money and resources into UUNET in an effort to boost the company into Microsoft's own national network. Call UUNET—and watch the popular computer press—to find out the current status of this growing company and to learn about precise services the firm offers.

You can have information on UUNET emailed to you by sending a request to **info@uunet.uu.net**. You can send this message through other email services such as CompuServe or MCI Mail.

ANS

Advanced Network & Services, Inc. (ANS)

ANS CO+RE Systems, Inc.

2901 Hubbard

Ann Arbor, Michigan 48105-2437

313-663-7610

ANS offers national leased line and 800-dial-up network services, including Internet access. The 800 service is called ANSRemote. Like UUNET, however, ANS is undergoing some transition as this book is written. The company was purchased by America Online, one of the more popular national bulletin board services that also provides Internet access. The purchase of ANS presumably will broaden the Internet services AOL is able to provide, but just what services will be available and how these offerings will be priced is not known.

The company offers a broad range of services for companies, research and government institutions, and individuals. However, you should contact AOL or ANS directly to find out about specific services and pricing.

Netcom

Netcom On-line Communications Services, Inc.

3031 Tisch Road (2nd Floor)

San Jose, CA 95128

Voice: 408-554-8649

Fax: 408-241-9145

Access Numbers: 800-488-2558 (National online number list)

Netcom claims to be the country's leading commercial Internet service provider. Indeed, Netcom gained a lot of attention during its first five years of operation, then really started to grow. This is a popular access point for the Internet among California users as well as users from other parts of the country. Currently Netcom access is available over the company's own digital network, which provides local-call services in more than 200 U.S. cities.

Netcom Internet access is priced as low as $17.50 per month with no online charges, if you pay by credit card. If you want a monthly bill, the price is $19.50 per month. In addition, there is a one-time $30 registration fee. You can use a direct dial connection to Netcom, or you can establish SLIP access if you wish. There may be other access options. Call the company directly—dial 800-488-2558 to find out the nearest local access number for you. Dial that number and log in as **guest**, or telnet **netcom.com** and log in as **guest**. If the system asks for a password, use **guest** again.

Netcom offers its own Netcruiser software to help make navigating the Internet easy. Netcruiser is a Microsoft Windows-based application providing SLIP-like access so that your PC acts like a member of the Internet. Netcruiser supports both Gopher and World Wide Web Internet access.

Other Dial-up Connections

The service providers I have mentioned to this point are pretty much countrywide or worldwide providers. In addition, there are a number of so-called regional or local providers. Actually, once you get onto the Internet it doesn't really matter where your node is. The important consideration is the route you have to take to get to the node, and, of course, the level of service, including technical support, your provider offers.

In other words, if you can access a node without paying long distance telephone charges but you have to pay more for the service, you may be ahead in the long run due to the savings on your communications costs. Likewise, if you can find a provider with a really low access fee, but you have to pay long distance fees to get there, you still may be better off if the long distance costs are reasonable and the access charges are competitive.

In this section I will list a few of the alternatives. If you live close by they are a good choice and, as I said, if you can use off-peak telephone times you may find these alternatives cost competitive over using CompuServe Packet Network, SprintLink, or other access methods to these nodes.

There are hundreds (at least) of local and regional providers, and new ones come online all the time. One way to find out about them is to get onto the Internet itself with your own account (or have someone conduct a search for you) and see what you can find. I'll show you, beginning in Chapter 4, how to browse the Internet for such information. Here's one source that supposedly is updated regularly and may have additional information for you. Send email with the subject **Send PDIAL** to **info-deli-server@netcom.com**. You will receive the PDIAL (Public Dial-up Internet Access List) document, which lists a lot of public access networks. Some of these may work for you.

In addition, I provide a quick reference list of service providers in Appendix E of this book. This list will give you additional options for finding your own way onto the Internet.

The PDIAL document is available through Netcom, but it is not maintained or supported by Netcom. It is shared by users on the network. As with any information you obtain on the Internet, use it skeptically and cross reference the information if possible.

Panix

Panix is a public access UNIX system in New York City that you can reach with a local call from anywhere in the city. The cost for Panix personal dial-up Internet access is $57 per quarter plus a $40 startup fee. This provides unlimited access time to the Internet without hourly fees. Notice that this pricing is for modem lines under 14,400 bps. To use the high-speed lines you must pay an additional $15 one-time fee; then the pricing is the same as for the low-speed lines. SLIP access is $35 per month. The company offers a free, two-week account to help you decide whether you want the service.

Panix is expanding regularly. Soon (if not already) there will be local access numbers in the 516 and 914 area codes and New Jersey locations, as well as to the existing 212 New York City area code. In addition to Internet access, when you use Panix you get a single-keystroke menu system to help with such functions as email and other Internet services. An optional learning mode helps you learn UNIX, and Pine mail and Pico editing are available along with other easy-to-use applications. Experienced users can choose a UNIX shell from several available.

Panix uses a T1 connection to the Internet, so once you get online things should go as rapidly as they can, given network traffic limitations that are built into any Internet access.

You can get more information by sending email to **Info@panix.com**, or by calling **212-787-3100** with your modem.

The World

Software Tool & Die
1330 Beacon Street
Brookline, MA 02146
617-739-0202

Another low-cost regional access point is Software Tool & Die's The World in Boston (Brookline). As this book was written, the basic charges were $5.00 per month plus an additional $2.00 per hour in connect time charges, or a flat fee of $20 per month for up to 20 hours of connect time. If you exceed your 20-hour allotment you will be charged $1.00 for each additional hour.

Call **617-739-0202** (voice) for information, or email **office@world.std.com**. You can register or get more information by dialing **617-739-9753** and logging in as **new**.

NovaLink

NovaLink Information Service
A division of Inner Circle Technologies, Inc.
800-274-2814 (Voice)
800-825-8852 (On-line information and registration)

NovaLink offers an interesting set of Internet services at reasonable prices. As you can see, there is an 800 number access for registration, or you can telnet to **novalink.com** and log in as **info** to get more information. Otherwise you access NovaLink through the CompuServe Packet Network (CPN).

Basic Novalink access is priced at $9.95 per month plus a connect fee of $1.80 per hour for usage over five hours. If you access NovaLink over the CPN network, there is an additional $1.80 per hour fee within the continental United States. Outside the U.S., CPN access fees range from $4.20 per hour in Canada, Alaska, Hawaii, and Puerto Rico to $30.20 per hour in Asia, Africa, and other areas of the world.

There are also discussion areas and the usual UNIX system services available once you get onto NovaLink. And, one of the main attractions (for some users, anyway) is NovaLink's intense role-playing fantasy game, Legends of Future Past. To get more information, dial the 800 number listed above with your modem and follow instructions on the screen.

VEHICLE CHECKPOINT: YOUR MODEM AND SOFTWARE

Whatever service or access method you use, in all likelihood you will need a modem and some communications software. The exception to this broad statement is if you are on a network that includes a communications server. In this case, you may be accessing the modem over the network and attaching to the Internet (or to a local host that gives you access to the Internet) through this remote modem. However, even if you are using a computer as part of a local area network, you may still have a local modem and your own communications phone line.

So, assuming you will be using a modem and some communications software, I will give you some information in the next section to make getting connected a little easier.

Modems

A modem provides an important hardware component of online communications. The word modem stands for modulator/demodulator, which describes the process of encrypting computer information for sending along a wire on one end (modulation) and decrypting it for receiving by the computer on the other end (demodulation).

Modulation is the process of superimposing one kind of signal on top of another. The signal that receives the modulated information is called the carrier because it carries the information. Radio transmitters and receivers work similarly to modems. A carrier wave—the powerful signal that lets you hear Fort Wayne's

WOWO broadcast station in Natchez, New York, or Knoxville—has superimposed on it an audio signal that consists of the words and music of the transmitted program. A receiver at the other end strips away the now unnecessary carrier wave, leaving the audio to send to the speaker.

A modem works in a similar way. A rising and falling audio tone is superimposed onto a carrier signal that transfers the information from the transmitting modem, along the telephone line, to the receiving modem. Although the actual process of generating and decoding this signal is complex, especially at the high rates supported by modern modems, the basic theory of operation is fairly simple.

You probably remember from studies elsewhere that computers work by storing and manipulating information in binary form—a series of ones and zeros. The ones and zeros are represented by the presence or absence of voltage in specific memory locations. WELL, that's how data is transmitted over a modem. A high-frequency tone represents the presence of voltage (a logical one), while a lower frequency tone represents the absence of voltage (a logical zero).

The transmitting modem converts the voltage levels sent from the originating computer into this tone series; the receiving modem listens to the tones and converts them back to voltage levels that the receiving computer can understand. This is done logically a bit at a time, with a high tone representing a "set" or positive bit, and a low tone representing a "clear" or negative bit.

That's the very basic theory. Today, of course, modem technology is much more advanced. In reality, there are many tone sequences sent together over a modem link, and the modem hardware at either end is encoding and decoding this information simultaneously. Although ultimately the computer must be made to understand a sequence of "highs" and "lows" to understand what is being transmitted, the actual process is highly technical and beyond the scope of this discussion (aren't you glad?).

When we first started using modems with computers, modems weren't very fast. That's because of the inherent bandwidth limitations built into the telephone system. Because a relatively narrow frequency range is needed to carry voice data (about 300 Hz to 3000 Hz or cycles per second), there isn't much range on the line for very high-speed data. As modem technology improved, however, engineers were able to cram more and more information into this bandwidth limit.

Whereas 110-baud modems were the norm when I started using them (I have been using computers a LONG time!), today 14,400 and 28,800 baud modems are very common and relatively inexpensive. Note that I used baud to rate the speed of modems. You'll also see bps (bits per second) used today. While the two terms aren't precisely equal, usage convention has made them so.

Remember that it takes eight bits to represent a single character and, depending on the protocol you are using, there may be one or two bits for error correction and other uses. So as a general rule of thumb, you can assume that it takes ten bits to transmit a single character. Therefore, at the very least, the actual throughput of your modem may be one tenth of its rating in bits per second. A 9,600-baud modem, then, could transfer 960 characters a second over a good connection, a 14,400-baud modem could send along about 1,440 characters per second, and a 28,800-baud modem should transmit 2,880 characters per second.

This is a good rule of thumb, and on the average probably won't be that far off. However, there are other considerations that affect the actual throughput of a modem-to-modem link. For one thing, you may be talking over a less-than-perfect telephone line. If there is noise on the line or other interference that degrades the signal, the receiving modem may have to ask the transmitting modem to repeat some information. This takes time and reduces the overall throughput.

In fact, throughput can be reduced significantly if the sending modem has to repeat data frequently. This is because high-speed modems don't send characters one at a time. They encapsulate data into packets or groups of characters, so the receiving modem doesn't ask for just the character or characters it missed; it must request a resend of the entire packet of data in which there was missing information.

At the same time, this grouping of information—and the fact that most modems today also compress the data they send—can sometimes make up for the time lost in requesting resends on missed data. For this reason, you can still guess that data transfer is about one tenth of the modem's rated speed. In fact, with a good line and efficient software, you may see transfer speeds greater than one tenth the modem's rated speed. On a couple of the links I use regularly, I see fairly consistent data transfer between 1,600 and 1,700 bps with a pair of 14,400-baud error-correcting modems.

What does this mean to you? At one level, not very much. It is doubtful that anyone reading this book is using a modem any slower than 2,400 baud, which has been the standard for general purpose communications for some time. And, when you are interacting with a menu system, entering commands at an Internet node, or chatting with another user across a communications link, 2,400 baud certainly is adequate. At 2,400 baud (about 240 characters per second, remember) the communications link will keep up with all but the fastest of typists, and screen updates (when the remote computer refreshes a menu or file list) will be fast enough.

Where you really notice the difference in speed is when you transfer files, either moving large amounts of information from your computer to an Internet host, or copying files from an Internet host to your machine. In this case, the faster the better. The faster modems—14,400 baud and above—not only transfer the files you want four to six times more quickly, they also reduce your online time, which is an important consideration if you are paying by the minute for your connection.

In addition, the increasingly popular graphical interfaces to gophers and the World Wide Web transmit a lot of information on each screen. Some pages contain multiple color pictures, graphics images, sound files, or even motion video. In this environment, 14,400 baud is about the slowest acceptable, and you would be a lot happier with 28,800. However, be sure to check with your service provider to find out what speeds are supported if you are considering a new modem purchase.

There is one additional consideration here: some packet switching networks and Internet gateways charge a premium for modem speeds of 9,600 bps or greater. On the other hand, if you are paying long distance telephone charges or packet switch charges for this access, using the high speed probably is worth the premium price at the other end. You should compute the relative merits of high speed versus low speed, especially if you use the service a lot or if you will be on for a long block of time to transfer files or participate in a conference.

Communications Software

A modem is a very important part of your communications link, but it can't work alone. You also need software that connects the computer to the modem and handles a lot of other important and useful chores as well.

You may have received communications software with your modem. A number of modem manufacturers routinely include their own or a third-party communications package with the hardware they sell. This will serve very nicely to get you started. You can learn your way around communications software and procedures, learn about your modem, and figure out whether this software fills all your needs or whether you need something more.

Communications packages can be rather Spartan, handling only the bare necessities, or they can include extensive features such as high-end terminal emulation (more on that in a moment), configuration and system testing utilities, auto answer and bulletin board features, dialing directories, programming languages, and more. For getting on the Internet, you just need the basics:

- Terminal emulation
- Serial port and modem communications support
- Information transfer protocol support

I'll offer a little more information on each of these communications software basics.

Terminal Emulation

When you communicate with a minicomputer or mainframe, that remote host expects you to be using a particular type of terminal that responds in a particular way to commands the computer sends. A *terminal* is a separate keyboard and screen that you use to talk to a large computer. The IBM PC and the early Apple machines were among the first computers to integrate the display electronics into the computer itself. Before that time, most computers were controlled through a serial line to a separate terminal.

The software in computers wants to be able to directly address the screen by placing characters and symbols at specific locations. The computer needs to be able to scroll the screen, clear the screen, and so on. Unfortunately, each manufacturer's terminal uses different codes. That's why your computer's communications software needs to know how to emulate, or act like, different kinds of terminals.

Fortunately, most online services today support a common terminal, the Digital Equipment Corporation VT100. If your software can emulate the VT100 or one of the later Digital terminals that includes the VT100 as a subset (VT200, VT320, and so on), then you'll have no problems navigating around the Internet. In fact, you can pretty much establish VT100 emulation as the default for your communications software, because almost anywhere you go online you'll find support for it. See chapter 5 for more detail on terminal emulation.

Besides, most online services actually use the addressable screen and other features very little. You don't need heavy terminal support—just the basics.

Serial Port and Modem Communications Support

Early computers—and many of today's larger machines—use serial ports to communicate with the user through a remote terminal. Similarly, you communicate through a serial port on your computer with the modem. Even if the modem is an internal device, it is using a serial port assignment. A *serial port* is an electronic doorway that sends and receives information into and out of your computer. It is called a serial port because data is sent through it in serial fashion, one bit after another. A *parallel port,* on the other hand, transfers data eight bits or more at a time over parallel wires. Therefore, your communications software must know about serial port addressing, communications speed setting, and keyboard support.

That's pretty basic. In addition to being able to talk to the keyboard and the serial port, communications software has to know something about modems, or for most applications, about one type of modem. Unless you are going to issue commands manually from the keyboard, the software has to be able to set line characteristics like speed and parity, store telephone numbers that you wish to dial, and automatically send initialization commands to the modem.

The majority of modems today adhere to the so-called "AT" or Hayes command structure. This comes from a popular design from Hayes Communications, maker of the SmartCom series. Their command structure, an "AT" (for attention) followed by one or more numbers or letters, became a de facto industry standard that is followed by a majority of modem manufacturers.

Information Transfer Protocol Support

An important software consideration for Internet travelers is the ability to download files and to capture text information displayed on the screen. Although some files you will want to download are in text format, most of them are likely to be in some binary form which you can't simply display on the screen and capture as they go by. (Most communications software will store text displayed on the screen in a memory buffer that you can then save to a disk file if you wish. This is a good way to capture menu sequences or text information you are reading on the Internet.) For binary files—program files or text files that have been compressed—you need a special file transfer protocol.

Remember I said that modems assemble data into blocks to transmit and receive over a telephone line? Well, a file transfer protocol takes this concept a step further. By assembling a data file or program into a series of packets and surrounding each packet with additional information about what is in the packet, data transfer programs can ship data around a network or across a telephone line with very little chance of making a mistake.

There are several methods commonly used to construct the actual error detection and correction part of this link. Each of these methods has a name. Among the common names are:

- XMODEM
- ZMODEM
- YMODEM
- KERMIT

In addition to these protocols, you should have some way to capture the text and graphic displays on your screen to disk. This allows you to store conversations, system information, and other interesting things you come across.

OTHER HARDWARE ISSUES

In addition to communications software and a modem, you also need some kind of hardware to complete the Internet link. You can access the Internet through a variety of computer hardware, from an old dumb terminal (not a very practical solution, but possible), to a really low-end eight-bit microcomputer such as a Commodore 64, to a PC Compatible (any flavor) or an Apple Macintosh. With any of this hardware you only need two things—a modem and communications software. In the case of a dumb terminal, you don't even need the software. You would just issue modem commands directly from the keyboard. Of course, with a dumb terminal you can't capture files and store information you find on the Internet unless the terminal is also attached to a computer. In today's environment, the dumb terminal is not a very practical solution as a stand-alone device, but if you don't have a computer, can't afford one, and you can find a cheap or free terminal, it works! Besides, a number of companies who have been using minicomputers and have upgraded to desktop machines have dozens or even hundreds of old terminals sitting around. In many cases they'll give them to you or your organization just so they don't have to throw them away. I personally know a number of users who access the Internet from school rooms and from home with nothing more than an old terminal and a modem. It is not a pretty sight, and it can be frustrating when you want to download information, but it gets you on the Internet!

Obviously, the type of traveling you will be doing on the Internet affects your hardware requirements. If you intend to locate and download a lot of files or programs, then you'll need a reasonably fast modem and a fair amount of disk storage. If you mainly want to send and receive short email messages and perhaps talk interactively with the folk you meet, then the dumb terminal or eight-bit micro will do fine.

Whatever hardware you have, if you are interested enough in the prospects of getting on the Internet to have read this far, don't wait. Find an access point and jump in. You'll learn more by doing than you can by reading and you also will discover quickly what kind of hardware upgrade you need, if any.

WHAT YOU LEARNED

This is a nuts-and-bolts chapter. You probably didn't need all of the information here, but you can come back and reference this material as you need it later.

I have shown you some of the many ways you can arrange Internet access for yourself, and have suggested which of these might be better for different situations. I have discussed communications software and modems, as well as the other hardware you need to use the Internet. Woven throughout this chapter are some obscure references to Internet locations and terms that may have you scratching your head right now. Don't worry. Work on getting yourself connected—you can pick up the additional knowledge you need through hands-on experience.

If you have worked through this chapter, following leads as I gave them, then you may have an Internet account by this time. You're ready to start poking around on the Internet. However, there's additional information in Chapter 3 that will help you understand some of the things you encounter in your travels. Keep practicing with your Internet account (or keep working to get one if you don't already have it), but turn the page for some useful information for Internet travelers, including naming conventions, network information transfer protocols, electronic mail, conferences, and more

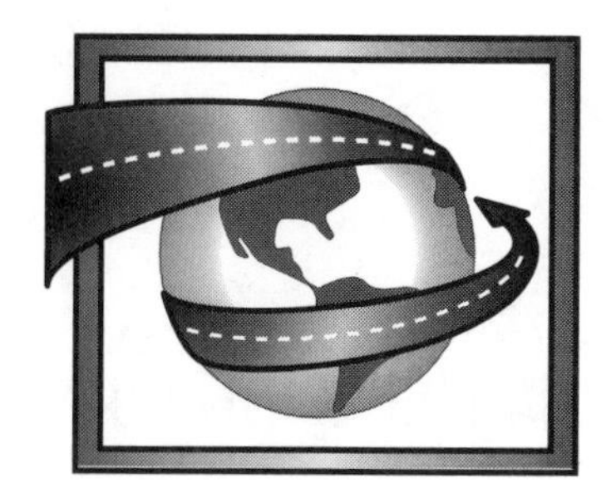

Chapter 3

TRAVELER'S AID: THE INTERNET BASICS

When traveling through cyberspace, it's important to keep your bearings. A guide to the Internet's basic services helps you quickly orient yourself as you arrive at any destination. This chapter describes the practicalities of how the Internet and its resources are organized. Among the topics I'll cover are:

- The Domain name system
- The IP address system
- Telnet
- Using Internet Mail
- Conferences and News
- Transferring data files

I offer miscellaneous hints, tips, and shortcuts along the way to help you get the most out of your travels. Scan this chapter so you'll become familiar with the terms and procedures of visiting on the Internet.

NAMING CONVENTIONS AND PROTOCOLS

To get anywhere in life—the grocery store, a better job, or even peace of mind—you have to know where you are going and how to get there. The same is true of the Internet. As I discussed in Chapter 2, to get access to the Internet you have to know the name of an Internet host and you have to know how to access that host to begin your Internet travels.

The Domain Name System (DNS)

Luckily, the Internet is actually easier to travel from point A to point B than an interstate highway. When you travel an interstate highway you have to be aware not only of where you are going, but of which routes to take and where to exit. With the Internet, on the other hand, all you really need to know is where to start your journey and where to end it. The Internet hosts that you use along the way will take care of getting you from one place to another.

When you drive the interstate highway system, you may go from Knoxville to Newark or from Philadelphia to Poughkeepsie. On the Internet you may go from **use.usit.net,** for example, to **nnsc.nsf.net,** or from **martha.utcc.utk.edu** to **archie.unl.edu.**

We are familiar with Newark and Philadelphia, Washington or New York, so these names seem OK. **nnsc.nsf.net,** on the other hand, probably looks a little strange. But what if we said "get on Interstate 75 and go to Ooltewah?" Would that sound any less strange than **"nnsc.nsf.net?"** For folk used to traveling between Knoxville and Chattanooga in East Tennessee, Ooltewah is just as familiar as Washington or New York for the rest of us. So it is with Internet place names. Once you understand how names are constructed and get an idea of where places are, using Internet names won't be any more difficult than using the names of cities and towns to help you get from one place to another on vacation.

One of the main differences in navigating the Internet as opposed to traveling an Interstate highway, however, is that on the Internet all you really need to know is the name. It isn't too important how you get to where you are going, or the route you travel to get there. When you enter the proper destination, built-in utilities take you there without your having to worry about the specifics of the travel.

Let's look more closely at one of the Internet names we have mentioned: **archie.unl.edu.** Look at the last three characters in this Internet address: **edu.** This is the location's domain. In regular English, a ***domain*** is a person's field, an area of influence, or an area bounded by defined limits. In Internet jargon, domain means about the same thing. An Internet domain specifies the type of organization or group that controls that specific Internet node.

You might guess correctly that the domain **.edu** is some kind of educational institution. Universities, colleges, secondary schools, and other educational institutions that provide Internet access and make information available to the network are identified with the **.edu** domain name.

Other types of organizations carry other domain designations. The common ones are shown in the following table:

TABLE 3.1
Domain Types

Domain	Name	Description
com	Commercial	A company or other commercial interest.
edu	Education	A college, university, or other educational institution.
gov	Government	A federal, state, or local government site.
mil	Military	A military site such as the U.S. Army.
net	Network	An Internet administrative organization or service provider.
org	Organization	A private organization such as a non-profit group, a foundation, or other association.

You may see some additional domains, sometimes called country codes, that signify the country of origin of the specified node or computer. This list is growing all the time, but below are some examples.

TABLE 3.2
Internet Country Abbreviations

Abbreviation	Country
au	Australia
ca	Canada
de	Germany
fi	Finland
fr	France
jp	Japan
kr	Korea
il	Israel
nl	Netherlands
nz	New Zealand
se	Sweden
tw	Taiwan
uk	United Kingdom
us	United States

The domain designation doesn't tell you everything about the host, but it does help you understand the type of users that may be at that local site, what general types of data might be stored there and offered to the Internet, and what types of rules and restrictions you might encounter at the site.

For example, you might guess that you would not be allowed to log in to a military site without prior authorization, but an educational site might well be a good choice for browsing and exploring. Ultimately you will have to try to do what you want to do and see what happens.

There is other information in a host designation, including the name of the institution or company, perhaps, as well as the name of the local computer. I'll discuss the rest of the Internet host name in the next section.

Host Names

Let's look again at the sample name we discussed in the previous section: **archie.unl.edu.** This is a very simple and mostly obvious host designation. It doesn't have as many components as some names and it includes one part that is easily interpreted: Archie. I'll discuss Archie in Chapter 4, but for now suffice it to say that Archie is a more or less universal online searching tool for the Internet. From this host name, we know it is an Archie server located at an educational institution. All that remains to decipher is the **unl** part of the host name.

We know the type of facility it is—an Archie server—and we know the type of organization that sponsors it—educational. So we might guess that **unl** stands for the name of the educational institution. That is a logical and accurate guess. There's no way for you to know which educational institution, but the **u** might logically stand for "university."

In fact, this address comes from a list of available Archie servers that we'll show you how to find in Chapter 4. If we refer to this list we learn that this server is located at the University of Nebraska in Lincoln. Now the **unl** part of the host name makes a lot of sense, doesn't it?

Almost any facility on the Internet carries a similar naming scheme. Although this naming structure isn't as easy to interpret or remember (at least not at first) as that of a company or person, there is method to this madness. In addition to the domain name and a possible location, Internet node names typically include the name of the local computer or computer group, a project designation, and other information. An Internet address can be relatively simple—such as the Archie server address I just showed you—or fairly complicated.

Consider this example:

```
martha.utcc.utk.edu
```

This is one of the nodes I sometimes use for Internet access. As you can see from the **edu** domain name, it is an educational institution. The next part of the address to the left shows that this is from **utk,** the University of Tennessee at Knoxville.

The **utcc** part of the name stands for University of Tennessee Computing Center, and **martha** is the name of the computer on this node. In this case "martha" is a Sun workstation, but you have no way of knowing that without some behind-the-scenes information. Ultimately, it doesn't matter what the hardware is.

Interpreting any Internet address works the same way. You work backwards, right to left, and try to understand the address based on what you know about the location of the node, what type of information it contains, the domain type, and so on.

IP Address (Internet Protocol Address)

The Internet domain system helps users access Internet facilities. Although these names aren't all that easy to remember, they are a lot easier to use than the computer's way of looking at the same location.

Computers on the Internet use a number-based system to address and access Internet nodes. The name-based system discussed above is first translated into the number-based form the computer prefers before the specified system can be accessed. It is a little like storing phone numbers in a telephone memory system by company name. When you want to dial someone at a specific company, you look up the company name on your phone's numerical readout and press dial. You don't know, and don't need to know, the actual number stored in that location. Once you identify the company, you can dial the phone number because you stored it there previously. You do have to remember the company name, but you don't need to know the telephone number that goes with it.

That's the way the *Internet Protocol* or IP address system works. You can use a series of numbers to access an Internet facility if you want to, but the name-based system is easier to remember.

Computer systems (called nameservers) on the Internet store the name-to-number lookup system, then use the numbers to send information to the proper location. Remember that the Internet is composed of many different types of components: corporate networks, educational networks, regional networks, dedicated workstations. All of these components are connected by Ethernet backbones, T1 links, and dedicated and dial-up telephone lines. You can see that without a sophisticated system of identifications and addresses it would be impossible to pass information where you want it. This is managed by computerized *routers* that sit on the Internet monitoring traffic and studying the addresses of each *packet*.

The Internet Protocol sends data from point to point by grouping information into packets. A packet is an assembly of characters—usually less than 1,500 or so—that may have originated at multiple sources. The link that ties these various characters together is that they all are going to the same destination. In other words, they all have the same Internet address.

Interestingly, all of the packets that make up a specific message don't necessarily arrive at the ultimate destination via the same route. This ability to move packets over different routes is part of what makes the Internet a persistent network. If part of a message is sent through one route and that route fails or becomes too crowded, the remaining packages in that message can be sent another way. Depending on conditions, this rerouting process may happen many times during the transmission of a message, or not at all.

The packets are sent through a series of computers, in stair step fashion, until the ultimate destination is reached. Like a letter addressed for delivery by the post office, Internet data is addressed hierarchically. In this scheme the address consists of up to four numbers separated by periods. Each number is less than 256. For example, the Archie server example we used earlier (*archie.unl.edu*) has the IP address 129.93.1.14. If you were telling someone about this IP address, you would say "129 dot 93 dot 1 dot 14."

Some of the numbers in this address specify which network on the Internet should receive the packet. Once the proper network has received the packet, it is up to another router to send the packet along to the next stop, and so on until the specified computer gets the packet. From there, the packetized data is broken apart and stored in a file, displayed on a terminal, or sent to a user.

The Internet Protocol address moves from general to specific, left to right. The first two or three groups of numbers represent the destination's network address. This is the network that includes the ultimate computer destination. For example, many of the networked computers at the University of Tennessee in Knoxville belong to the network 128.169. The two remaining sets of numbers denote other facilities within the network. Computers at U.S. Internet, the access provider I use for most of my Internet access, are in the network 199.1, as another example.

As I said earlier, this number-based system is necessary for computers to talk to each other without duplicating addresses and without getting lost in a labyrinth of network wires. For us, however, the system of names is easier to use and is all we need to know about accessing Internet resources. It is good to understand the basics of IP addressing, however, so you know how information gets where it is going.

Another reason to know a little about IP numbers is that the machine that runs BIND, the Berkeley Internet Name Daemon, is sometimes down. BIND is what makes the Domain Name System tick. If the BIND on your local host were down, you might be deferred to another system in your network. If that alternate system were down too, then you would not have a nameserver, and the computer would not have a clue about names. In this case you would either have to wait for the nameserver to come back online, or you would have to use the computer's number system.

Transmission Control Protocol (TCP)

The Internet Protocol handles sending prepackaged information around the network. However, that's only part of the story. Once the addressed packet is delivered, the data inside the packet has to be distributed properly. Remember that streams of packets may contain information from several sources. As the packets arrive, they have to be broken down and individual components need to be reassembled in the proper order.

This ability to share packets helps move data efficiently. Once the data gets where it is going, it is up to TCP software to open the packets and put the information together with data from previous packets in the proper order. Together the Internet Protocol and the Transmission Control Protocol form the familiar TCP/IP networking designation which you've probably seen many times as you have read about computer communications.

GETTING FROM HERE TO THERE: TELNET

How do you actually get from where you sit on a PC, Macintosh, or terminal out to somewhere else on the Internet? First, of course, you must attach your desktop machine to an Internet node. That is done by dialing a modem with a communications package and then logging on to the Internet node.

Generally when you dial the local access telephone number and the host answers, you are asked to enter a user identifier, then a password. The user ID is most commonly your first name and a few characters from your last name, or the first initial of your first name and the first seven characters of your last name. However, your user ID can be anything that is acceptable to the system administrator on the Internet node you are using, up to an eight-character maximum, in most cases.

Your password is an important part of your Internet identification. It identifies you uniquely and prevents unauthorized persons from using your account. Your password should be at least six characters (but no more than eight, for most systems), and should contain letters, numbers, and punctuation.

NOTE

Passwords and user IDs are case sensitive on most Internet nodes, so if you have problems logging in to your host, you may be using an incorrect combination of capital and lower-case letters.

Once you are logged on to an Internet node, how do you leave that node and search for information or exchange information with a node elsewhere on the Internet? One way is to send and receive electronic mail. I'll show you more about that in the next section.

Another common way to attach to a specific host on the Internet is to use a communications command called Telnet. This is software that automates the process of locating a specified host and initiating the log on process. Once you know the name of a remote host and you are logged on to a computer that has an Internet link, you can attach to that host with Telnet:

```
telnet ns.opup.org
```

or

```
telnet 128.169.92.86
```

Interestingly, the ns.opup.org address is, itself, an alias for mamaclaus.opup.org. An alias is a nickname or substitute name for an Internet entity. This sort of lookup or indirect reference is done frequently to simplify addresses.

You can also attach to a remote host with FTP (file transfer protocol) and with other utilities that I will discuss in Chapter 4. FTP is another software utility that lets you locate a specified host and initiate a file transfer session with it automatically. FTP works like a specialized Telnet command.

ELECTRONIC MAIL

I've talked about how information moves along the Internet from computer to computer, but how do individual users get information? That's all part of the Internet addressing scheme. By simply adding another level of address you can identify a particular individual, organization, or group to receive electronic mail, or email.

Electronic mail is one of the main uses for any network such as the Internet. Because the wires and computers are in place at locations all over the world, it is natural to want the ability to send messages to companies and individuals over this network. Most Internet users find email to be a useful and interesting part of the technology.

You can send short notes and messages or large files by simply providing the proper Internet address for the person or company you want to receive the information. You'll need a mail program, but once you know a person's Internet address you can swap electronic messages at will.

Electronic mail addresses look like the network addresses we discussed earlier, except that there is a person's name or the name of a company or organization at the front of the address. This name is that user's login name or user ID, which I discussed previously. This part of the address is separated from the rest of the network address by a commercial "at" sign (@).

For example, my current address is:

```
tbadgett@usit.net
```

You can read this easily enough, from left to right: "tbadgett at usit dot net." The **tbadgett,** of course, is the name. You can tell that not only because you knew the name before you started, but because it is set off from the rest of the address with the "at" sign.

The **usit** part of the address stands for U.S. Internet, and **net** signifies that this Internet entity is an Internet administrative organization or an access provider. The specific meaning of any of the components of an Internet address can't be interpreted precisely. There are just too many Internet entities from too many different areas. However, these general guidelines can point you in the right direction. The basic concept is pretty simple, if you know what a particular group is. However, you would have no way of knowing what **usit** stands for unless you found that information somewhere or knew someone from that company.

Other email addresses can get a little more complicated. For instance, if I were using another node within the University of Tennessee at Knoxville network, the address might be something like this:

```
tbadgett@martha.utcc.utk.edu
```

Even if you don't know anything about where this computer is located, you know two things as soon as you look at the address. You know that the addressee is tbadgett at some network on some computer system, and that this is an educational institution. (If you don't see this much of the address immediately, reread the section on domains earlier in this chapter.) I described part of this address earlier. **martha** is the name of a Sun workstation that is part of the **utcc** or University of Tennessee Computing Center, located at the University of Tennessee at Knoxville (**utk**).

Obviously it isn't necessary for you to know this level of detail about every address you use on the Internet. It is enough that you know the correct sequence of names and abbreviations. However, the more you use the Internet, the more you will find yourself interpreting each address—breaking it down so that it has an additional level of meaning for you. This makes Internet travel more fun, and helps you to remember the addresses you use frequently.

As with any Internet information, email is not passed directly from your machine to the destination machine. There may be one or several additional computers or networks that handle the message along the way. The message you send is given an address that includes the person or company name and the other routing information needed to get it to the proper computer. How it gets there depends on the source and destination systems and how they reach the Internet. There may be several stops along the way, and the time between sending the message and the message arriving at its destination may be several minutes or several hours.

Now let's discuss in more detail how you go about sending and receiving electronic mail over the Internet.

Sending Mail

For many users, electronic mail, or email, is one of the most important reasons for being on the Internet in the first place. The concept of being able to type a few lines, a page, or even thousands of words and then to send them off to someone in Atlanta, Alaska, or Almost Anywhere at the speed of light is impressive.

I've already discussed email addressing. Remember that to send someone an email message, you have to know their user ID or logon name, and the name of the system where their home account is located. The best way to get this information is to ask the person you want to write to. You can also send an email message to **Postmaster@Domain** if you know the person's Domain address. Or, try using the finger command (**finger name@Domain**) to discover what logon name the person uses. You could try the first initial and last name, for example, or the first name and last initial, etc. until you come across the person you are trying to reach. However, different systems use different user name conventions and this sort of name guessing can be extremely difficult. Universities, governmental organizations, and some large companies, for example, use user names that refer to a person's department rather than to their actual name. Again, the best way to find out how to address mail to someone on the Internet is to ask them for their address.

Once you have an address where you want to send mail, actually sending it is fairly easy. Depending on the Internet node you use, there may be one or several ways to send mail. I will discuss three of the most common here. You should ask your service provider for specifics on other systems.

UNIX Mail

Since the majority of the Internet nodes you are likely to access are UNIX-based, there is a very good bet that the UNIX Mail command is available. To access this facility, simply type **mail <recipient>** at the system prompt.

This procedure assumes you are using a node without a menu. The mail command is issued at the UNIX prompt. If your provider presents a menu when you log in, then you likely will step through a menu to access UNIX mail.

The <recipient> part of the mail command is the Internet address of the person or persons you want to receive the mail message. So, to compose a message to me, you could type:

```
mail tbadgett@usit.net
```

The mail system will respond by clearing the prompt and then waiting for you to type the text of the message you want to send to the recipient specified on the command line. Depending on how your local system is configured, you may also be asked for a subject at this time. If you are, enter the subject of the message, then press **Enter** or **Return** at the end of the line. Now simply enter the text of the message, placing a carriage return at the end of each line. This is a simple text editor—not as sophisticated as the word processor you're probably using, but enough to let you enter the text of a message.

After you have typed the message you want to send with mail, press **Ctrl-D** as the first character on a new line, or enter a period on a new line by itself and press **Enter.** The message will be sent to the user you specified on the command line when you started the mail application.

Notice that the mail system—if it is configured in the conventional way—is also monitoring the keyboard input for commands while it is in this mode.

While typing your message, you may be able to enter commands that let you do additional things. Standard mail uses a "tilde escape" sequence to issue commands to mail. For example, if you type **~e** on a line by itself while entering a mail message, you invoke an editor for the current message. Likewise, **~C** lets you specify a carbon copy address, **~S** lets you specify the subject, and **~H** prompts you for additional header information.

If these commands don't work as I've described, it means that you have a different version of mail or that your mail system has been configured differently. There are two things to try. At the main system prompt, enter this command:

```
man mail
```

This is a UNIX command that looks up the online manual for the mail command and displays it on the screen. Press the **Space bar** as each screen of data is presented to bring up the next screen. Turn on screen capture or a log file in your communications software so you can have a local copy of the document to help you with later mail activity.

If the commands and procedures described in the on-line manual don't work, you should send a message to the local system administrator or Internet service provider to find out how the mail system is configured.

There is a third thing to try when you are having problems with this or any other activity while using an Internet node: try using the UNIX **talk** command to discuss the situation with someone else online with you. I describe how to do this in Chapter 4.

Pine

If you are comfortable with a command-line interface, the mail command is all you need to send and receive messages to anyone on the Internet. However, most of us appreciate a user interface that is easy to understand and that anyone can use. There are several such interfaces on Internet systems, but one of the most common is Pine. To access this mail system, simply type **pine** at your local node's prompt. If Pine is on your system, you will see a screen similar to the one in Figure 3.1. If your provider does not support Pine, you will get an error message indicating that the command was not found. You could try elm, another mail reader preferred by many experienced Internet users. If neither of these is available, contact your service provider for instructions on using mail other than UNIX mail.

FIGURE 3.1

Sample Pine email screen

```
PINE 3.07          MAIN MENU          Folder:inbox  14 Messages

   ?   HELP           - Get help using Pine

   C   COMPOSE        - Compose and send a message

   I   MAIL INDEX     - Read mail in current folder

   F   FOLDERS        - Open a different mail folder

   A   ADDRESSES      - Update your address book

   O   OTHER          - Use other functions

   Q   QUIT           - Exit the Pine mail program

 Note: In Pine 3.0 we are encouraging folks to use the MAIL INDEX to read
       mail instead of VIEW MAIL, so it is no longer on the main menu. Once
       in the mail index, it is available as usual as the "V" command.

   [ * * This is a new version of Pine. To use old Pine run "pine.old". * * ]
? Help        Q Quit        F Folders      O Other
C Compose     I Mail Index A Addresses
ALT-Z FOR HELP | VT100   | FDX | 57600 N81 | LOG CLOSED | PRINT OFF | ON-LINE
```

As you can see, Pine—or any similar menu-oriented mail system—is much easier to use than the command-line mail system from inside UNIX. We won't spend a lot of time on using Pine here because everything is presented in the menu and with on-screen prompts. Besides, Pine frequently is modified at a local site, so it may not be exactly like my version. But don't be afraid to use it, even if nothing in the provider's literature or online help mentions Pine. It probably is out there somewhere. Just type **pine** at the system prompt and find out.

With a system such as Pine, you can compose messages in the editor and also attach files that reside on your host system to send with the letter.

If you select **C** for Compose from the main menu, Pine clears the screen and presents a screen similar to the one shown in Figure 3.2.

At this screen, enter the **To:** address and specify another address for the carbon copy on the next line, if you wish. Move the cursor to the **Attchmnt:** line, press **Ctrl-J**, and enter the name of a file stored on your local system. Provide the complete path if the file is not in your local home directory.

FIGURE 3.2

Pine Compose Message screen

```
     PINE 3.07      COMPOSE MESSAGE      Folder:inbox  73 Messages
To      :
Cc      :
Attchmnt:
Subject :
----- Message Text -----








^G Get Help ^C Cancel   ^R Rich Hdr              ^K Del Line ^O Postpone
^X Send      ^D Del Char ^J Attach               ^U UnDel Lin^T To AddrBk
 ALT-A FOR HELP | VT100   | FDX | 57600 N81 | LOG CLOSED | PRINT OFF | ON-LINE
```

Any files you save on a host system are probably stored in your home directory on the host. This is the disk area assigned for your use on the host. You will learn later in this book how to move information from other computers into your home directory.

Type a subject on the **Subject:** line, then press **Enter** or **Tab** to place the insertion point or cursor inside the editor area. Now you can type your message.

When the text of the message is complete, simply press **Ctrl-X** to close the editor screen and send the message to the addressee(s). If there was a file attached to the message, the recipient will be told and will be able to download the message using a file transfer protocol.

Eudora

With a network, SLIP, or PPP connection, Eudora is an available mail utility that is functional and easy to learn. A network connection means that you are accessing the Internet over a local area network (LAN). A SLIP connection is serial line Internet protocol—a network connection over a dial-up telephone line—and PPP stands for Point to Point Protocol, another way of making your local computer part of a remote network over a telephone line. You can't use Eudora with a standard dial-up or shell connection to your Internet host.

Eudora lets you create mail messages offline, then send them in a batch the next time you attach to your host. You can also download messages to your PC and read them offline. Eudora also makes it easy to attach other files such as word processing documents or spreadsheets to your mail messages for easy delivery to any Internet address. And, Eudora can automatically handle the conversion of binary files, including programs, spreadsheets, word processor documents and so on, for transmission over the Internet.

Eudora works in conjunction with an SMTP (Simple Mail Transfer Protocol) server, which must be a part of your service provider's hardware/software configuration (or a part of your local network if you are not using a SLIP or PPP connection), and a POP (Post Office Protocol) server. The POP server is where your electronic mail is delivered and stored until you log in to your host and move or copy it to your PC.

Unlike Pine and UNIX mail, discussed earlier in this chapter, Eudora runs on your PC or Macintosh and exchanges messages with your host. With Eudora, your sent and received mail is usually stored locally instead of on the host. And Eudora provides a graphical user interface and menu system.

Eudora is among the more popular email packages for desktop computers using a SLIP connection, yet the most common version is freeware, which means it is free for you to use in any non-commercial endeavor. You can't resell it, but you don't have to pay anything to use it.

Eudora was written by Jeff Beckley, Jeff Gehlhaar, and Mark Erikson. The design came from Steven Dorner, who offers this explanation of why this mail software is named Eudora:

When I was looking for a name for my new Post Office Protocol mail program, I thought immediately of the title of a short story I'd read years before: "Why I Live at the P.O." So I named the program after the author of the story, Eudora Welty.

A commercial version of the software also is available. If you want a mail client that includes enhanced features and comes with manufacturer support, contact Qualcomm, Inc. (**Info@qualcomm.com**). You can find additional information about this version of Eudora as well as the commercial version with FTP. Use FTP to connect to **ftp.qualcomm.com,** then choose the **/quest** directory. A readme file there will show you how to browse the rest of the system for additional information.

TRAVEL TIP

*A detailed user manual for Eudora 1.4 (**14manual.exe**) is available via FTP from **ftp.usit.net** in the directory **/pub/slip/ibm/eudora.** This is a self-extracting archive file that contains a Microsoft Word file in PC format, 14manual.doc.*

The first time you load Eudora you will see a screen like the one shown in Figure 3.3. The Inbox is displayed by default. Since you haven't received any mail to this point, you will have no messages displayed in the Inbox.

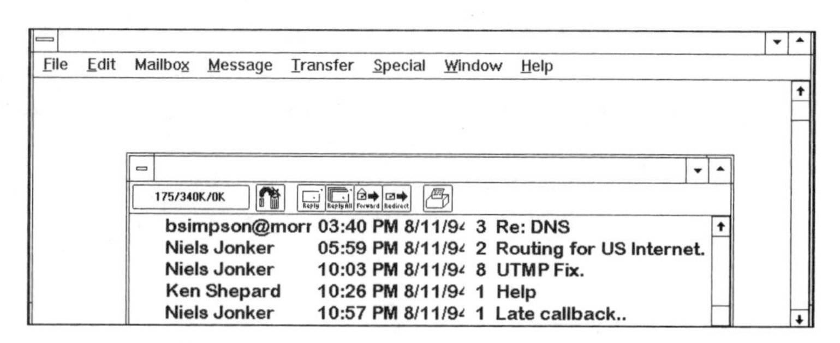

FIGURE 3.3
Eudora Main screen

This is a typical Windows application screen. At the top is the title bar that shows the name of the program, while below that is a familiar menu bar, which you will use to control Eudora's features.

The bar below the menu bar shows which mailbox folder is open. The Inbox is the default, but you also can display a folder with messages you have sent, messages you have trashed, or any other grouping you may want to create. The icon bar or toolbar is the final feature of the Eudora screen.

Sending a new message from within Eudora is extremely simple. From the main Eudora menu, select **Message** and choose **New Message** (**Ctrl-N**) from the pull-down menu.

Eudora displays a blank message screen with a new address header that includes your return address, but with the **To:** and **Cc:** fields blank. To send the new message, complete the address information, type the message, and click on **Send**.

This part of the process is very similar to using Pine, or any other screen-oriented mail handler. And, because Eudora is Microsoft Windows or Macintosh based, using the menus and other features should be familiar and easy. Remember, however, that Eudora is designed for use with a network connection to the Internet. This can be over a LAN (local area network), or via a SLIP dial-in connection.

Receiving Mail

When you get on the Internet and start poking around, you doubtless will start corresponding with other Internet users. You may leave your email address for someone to send you information, or you may send someone a message that will generate a response. After you have participated in a conference, someone may find your address and want to ask a question or follow up on the topic. Whatever the reason, you will start getting mail of your own if you make your presence known on the Internet.

The good news is that receiving mail on the Internet is even easier than sending it. In this section we'll look at the same three systems I discussed in the last section, UNIX Mail, Pine, and Eudora.

But first, lets look at ways of capturing the mail you receive to your desktop computer. With most communications software, you can turn on a capture file or a log file so that anything that scrolls across your screen will be captured to a file. Consult your software user documentation to find out exactly how to do this. Also, be aware that unless you are capturing screen data to a file, information will be lost when it scrolls off your screen. This may happen even when the software says it is capturing information, because some capture routines simply send the information into a RAM buffer instead of to a disk.

Another way to get mail and other Internet information onto your desktop is to save the information to a file on your host, then transfer the saved file to your desktop with XMODEM, ZMODEM, Kermit, or another file transfer protocol. You may want to use one or more of these techniques to store mail files to your desktop so that you can print the information or include it in other documents.

UNIX Mail

Usually when you log on to a system and you have mail waiting, you will get a message that says something like:

```
You have new mail
```

or

```
Mail waiting
```

When you see this message, you could simply type mail at the system prompt to see any unread mail messages. This accesses UNIX mail if you are interacting with a UNIX shell. Obviously, if your system uses a menu interface, you will have to locate the proper menu item to load UNIX mail or another mail reader.

The system will fill the screen, then wait for you to press the **Space bar** before presenting another screen of information. When the first message is completed, you will see the second one, and so on. If you want to capture these messages and read them or print them later offline, turn on a log file or a text capture utility inside your communications software before typing the **mail** command.

NOTE

*If you type **mail** without specifying an addressee for a new message and you don't have any new mail, you will get a message like:*

```
No new mail for tbadgett
```

and the mail software will terminate.

After you have read all of your new mail messages, you will be presented with the mail command prompt. This prompt may be a question mark (?), an ampersand (&), or whatever else the system administrator has specified. From this mail command prompt, you can issue certain mail commands, including the ones shown in Figure 3.4.

FIGURE 3.4
Typical UNIX Mail commands

q	quit
x	exit without changing mail
p	print
s[file]	save (default mbox)
w[file]	same without header
–	print previous
d	delete
+	next (no delete)
m	user mail to user
! cmd	execute cmd

To exit the command mode, simply press **Enter** or type **q,** for quit. You will be returned to the main system prompt for the system you are using. Turn off screen capture or file logging at this point and your mail is saved.

If a message is a simple one and you are sure you don't need it again, or if you have captured it to your local computer as it was being read, issue the **d** (delete) command after the message is displayed. This frees up disk space, and it keeps you from having to step through old messages each time you enter the mail system. On the other hand, it doesn't hurt to leave a few messages out there for reading later. Each message is presented in reverse order, so the newest messages are displayed first. When you have read the most recent ones, you can exit mail and go back to the system prompt, leaving previously read messages on the system.

When you receive mail over the Internet, the heading can appear a little complicated, but it really isn't. Figure 3.5 shows what is in a typical heading. Note that the heading shows the date and time of the message, who and where it is from, who it is to, and a message ID. Depending on the mail system, there may be other information there as well. Keep the heading when you save a message, because it helps you remember who it was from, and it makes it easier to respond later if you wish.

FIGURE 3.5

Sample mail header

```
From tbadgett Tue Aug 24 16:50:38 1993
Return-Path: <tbadgett>
Received: by MamaClaus.OPUP.ORG (4.1/SMI-4.1)
id AA05265; Tue, 24 Aug 93 16:50:37 EDT
Date: Tue, 24 Aug 1993 16:50:07 -0400 (EDT)
From: Tom Badgett <tbadgett@OpUp.ORG>
Subject: Mail Header Sample
To: tbadgett@OpUp.ORG
Message-Id: <Pine.3.05.9308241607.A5261-6100000@MamaClaus.OPUP.ORG>
Mime-Version: 1.0
Content-Type: TEXT/PLAIN; charset=US-ASCII
Status: RO
```

You can see that this message came from within Pine and that it was addressed to and from the same person.

TRAVEL TIP

Addressing a mail message to yourself is a good way to create reminders. Anytime you are online and you think of something that you need to remember later, simply send yourself a mail message. The next time you log on, you'll see that message reminder.

You can configure the Mail program to display different header information, so the version in use on your system may not produce messages that look exactly like the one in this example.

With some systems the heading may be a lot simpler. All that really matters is the name and address of the person who sent you the message. The rest of the header information usually isn't that important.

Pine

When you log on to a system and are told there is mail waiting, you can read the mail when it is convenient for you (you don't have to do it right away). Type **pine** to display the main screen shown in the previous section (or something close to it).

From the main screen, press **I** for Index to display a list of available mail. Pine displays a screen similar to the one shown in Figure 3.6.

FIGURE 3.6

Pine Index (List Mail) screen

```
   PINE 3.07        MAIL INDEX        Folder:inbox  Message 73 of 73

 58  Sep 16 Niels Jonker          (870) News Sentinel online.
 59  Sep 16 ...dreamer...       (1,467) Re: News Sentinel online.
 60  Sep 16 The Spectre         (1,194) Re: News Sentinel online.
 61  Sep 16 Bob Wilson           (188K) Mountain crest street map
 62  Sep 16 Niels Jonker        (1,810) Re: News Sentinel online.
 63  Sep 16 Niels Jonker        (1,314) Re: your mail
 64  Sep 17 Da Gorf             (1,431) Re: News Sentinel online.
 65  Sep 17 jack lail          (19,792) CC List (fwd)
 66  Sep 19 Niels Jonker        (3,409) Internet Access in East Tennessee.
 67  Sep 21 Niels Jonker          (620) The book? How're ya doing?
 68  Sep 21 Niels Jonker        (1,304) Data needed.
 69  Sep 22 jack lail           (3,812) Fw: Netter's Abbreviations (fwd)
 70  Sep 23 Bob Wilson          (5,383) ASC chichi rept
 71  Sep 24 Clay I. Spinuzzi    (1,735) Re: EMOTICON.TXT
 72  Sep 24 Holly H. Towne        (927) Re: Internet Video
 73  Sep 24 Holly H. Towne      (3,491) Re: Internet Video

? Help        M Main Menu  P Prev Msg      - Prev Page  F Forward     D Delete
O OTHER CMDS V View Mail  N Next Msg SPACE Next Page  R Reply       S Save
 ALT-Z FOR HELP | VT100 | FDX | 57600 N81 | LOG CLOSED | PRINT OFF | ON-LINE
```

You can use the up and down arrow keys to select the message you want to read, then press **Enter** or **Return.** The message will be displayed one screen at a time. Pine will wait for you to press the **Space bar** to view any subsequent screens.

There's a menu at the bottom of the screen to show you how to delete files, save files, and perform other functions. Pine, or whatever menu system your provider supplies, should make reading and managing mail a lot easier than with UNIX Mail.

Eudora

Eudora is a popular electronic mail reader that is designed to be used over a network connection. Whether you are accessing the Internet from an office with a direct network connection to a host, or using a dialup network connection from home or while you're traveling, Eudora is a capable and easy to use mail utility.

When you first open Eudora, the Inbox is opened to show received mail. Because Eudora is a desktop application, you will see listed mail you have previously downloaded. And, depending on how you have Eudora configured, you may see new mail as well. You can set a switch as part of the Eudora configuration to check automatically for any new mail as soon as Eudora is loaded, or you can elect to have the program check for new mail only when you choose **Check Mail** from the File menu.

From the Inbox display you can see the name of the person who sent each message, the date and time each message was sent, as well as the subject of each message (see sample Inbox display in Figure 3.7).

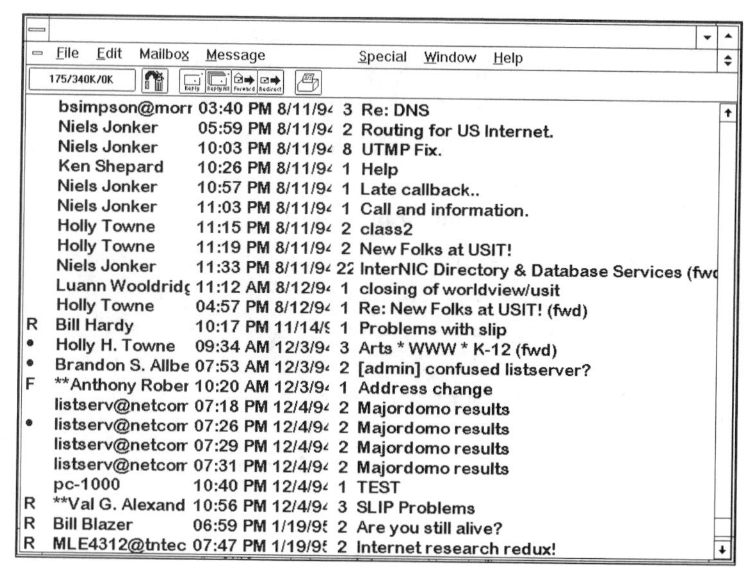

FIGURE 3.7
Eudora Inbox Message display

In addition, you can tell which messages you already have read, which have been answered or forwarded, and which are new, unread messages, by noting the character in the status field at the far left of the message line in the Inbox display. The status field displays the information shown in Table 3.3.

TABLE 3.3
Eudora Message Status Codes

Character	Description
•	New, unread message
R	Reply sent to person who sent the message to you
F	Message Forwarded to another recipient
D	Message re-directed to another recipient
	You have read this message

To read a specific message, simply double-click on the entry in the Inbox display, or use the cursor movement keys to highlight the entry, and then press **Enter** to display the message. Use the scroll bars at the right of this window to see the lower part of the message if the message is too large to fit inside the display window. Or, you can click anywhere inside the message window and use the cursor movement keys to move down lower in the message.

You can close the message and keep it in the Inbox by double-clicking on the control menu bar at the upper left corner of the message display window.

You can save the current message to a text file with the **File Save As...** command sequence. Simply provide Eudora a path and file name, and the current message will be saved to disk under the specified name. You may want to do this if you want to incorporate the message into a word processing document, for example. Note that saving a message to a file in this way does not remove it from the Eudora Inbox.

Using Eudora

Since this is a standard Windows product, using Eudora is fairly simple. To check your mail, for example, you click on the **File** menu and choose **Check Mail**. Eudora logs onto the host (perhaps asking for your password if you haven't entered it on the configuration screen), locates any mail you haven't read, and copies it to your desktop.

From the In box display, you can choose which messages you want to read and display them by double-clicking on the description.

To reply to a message you've read, click on **Message** and choose **Reply**. The email address of the person who sent you the message is automatically filled in on the **To:** line. You can edit other entries on the address header, if you wish, then type the message. When you are ready to send the reply, click on the **Send** button at the top of the message dialog box.

Creating a new message is just as simple. Click on **Message** and choose **New Message**. Fill in the address header with the recipient's email address and the other information you wish to include. Then type the message in the message area of the dialog box. When the message is complete, click on the **Send** button.

If you have set the Send switch to **Immediate Send**, your message will be sent immediately. Otherwise, the message will be added to the outbox queue to be sent the next time you log on.

Notice that you can attach a file to your message—a word processing file, spreadsheet, program, or other binary file—by clicking on **Message** and choosing **@@** after you have displayed the **To:** message header.

Exit Eudora by clicking on **File** and choosing **Exit**. Remember, you can get more information about using Eudora by downloading the user manual from the address noted earlier.

ONLINE COMMUNITIES

Downloading files and exchanging email are interesting and vital parts of the Internet experience. But once you've mastered these skills, you'll want something to give you more direct contact with other users. That's when you'll want to experiment with conferences, news, and real-time conversations.

I talked about conferences when I discussed The WELL in Chapter 1, but you can find conferences on many Internet nodes. Conferences are groups of people who come and go, reading each other's comments, offering an interesting or off-the-wall opinion of their own, and returning later to see what else has transpired.

A newsgroup—or simply news, Internet news, or network news—is a variation of a conference. Like a conference, a newsgroup discusses varied topics in a store-and-forward manner. You check into a group, read previous comments about a topic, add some of your own if you wish, and move on somewhere else. Later, you may come back to find out if anybody responded to your statement or question.

The main difference between conferences and news is that news is somewhat more organized, with a network-wide organization and software tools designed to help you find specific topics and comments. News topics are organized under broad subject headings and the discussions are pretty much network wide, whereas conferences are generally confined to a single node or private system.

Conversations, on the other hand, provide one-on-one or group discussions in real time about anything you can imagine. Conferences and news use store-and-forward procedures, but conversations, or chats as they are sometimes called, are exchanges among Internet users while they are online.

I'll introduce you to each of these interesting Internet features in this section. In later chapters I'll offer some hands-on hints on how to find and download information you need.

With any interactive exchange, anything can happen. Sometimes you may see a series of angry, rude, or profane responses to what appears to be a simple request. What you don't see is the exchange that took place between these individuals on another conference or in person. Be aware that such behavior—usually called flaming—sometimes comes at you unannounced and unexpected.

Conferences

Many Internet providers have active conferences or forums, and as you saw with The WELL, the topics cover a broad range of subjects. Usually if you want to join a conference you can issue a command (which, unfortunately, varies with the system you are using) to find out what conferences are available. The partial list in Figure 3.8 gives you an idea of how this exchange might take place. This sample is from The WELL.

FIGURE 3.8

Sample conference list—The WELL

```
OK (type a command or type opt for Options): browse

Topic - Number of responses - Header
100 87 Introductions – Me and the Net
104 23 What is the Internet (topic 4) Discussion
105 119 Acceptable Use of the Internet (topic 5) Discussion
106  0 Netiquette (topic 6) Discussion
107 131 About Telnet (topic 7) Discussion
108 162 About FTP (topic 8) Discussion
109 43 Tools for Finding Info on the Net (topic 9) Discussion
110 81 Libraries and Collections of Info (topic 10) Discussion
111 104 Frequently Asked Questions (topic 11) Discussion
112 247 Best Books & Articles on Internet (topic 12) Discussion
113 13 LISTSERVs (topic 13) Discussion
114 33 Zen and Articles on the Net Readable on the WELL (topic 14) Discussion
116 38 What Are Muds and Muses? (topic 16) Discussion
200 63 anonymous FTP into the WELL
  <topic is frozen>
201  4 topics to look at for linking here
202 157 Internet Access for the Masses
```

Notice these topics and the number of responses. Some have dozens of responses, and some have none. These conferences are started by someone who has a topic of interest they want to discuss. Sometimes the conferences are temporary—not designed to last very long once the question of the day is answered. Others are long-term topics.

Different systems have different types of conferences and topics. For most systems, an interactive session within something called a conference is conducted by selecting the conference you want to join, then viewing a series of messages. You will see where a user has asked a question about something he or she is interested in. Then you will see one or more answers to the query from other participants in the conference. All of this may, or may not, happen in real time. Usually a conference takes place over hours or days.

We can't show you actual conversations from a conference because the information placed on Internet systems is owned by the person who typed it or placed it there. However, the exchange in Figure 3.9 is typical of conference exchanges you will see on The WELL and other Internet systems.

FIGURE 3.9

Sample conference interchange

```
Topic 202: Internet Access for the Masses
By: Likado Tango (LTango) on Wed, Jul 29, '92
     157 responses so far

A place to report on Internet access for the masses. Looking for
a way to telnet to The WELL on the cheap? Maybe you'll find it
here.

157 responses total.
Topic 202: Internet Access for the Masses
# 2: Ben Franklyn (BeFrank)    Thu, Jul 30, '92 (04:21)    4 lines

You could try lobbying universities in your area that have Internet access.
Ask them for a dial-in login. My local university let me in after I showed them
I am working for a non-profit organization. Different schools have different
rules and regs. Doesn't hurt to ask!

Topic 202: Internet Access for the Masses
# 1: Likado Tango (LTango) Wed, Jul 29, '92 (18:23)    123 lines

I just learned about a new system in Podunk. They are offering 800 number
access at a reasonable price. Call (voice) at 800-555-1212 for information.
I understand there's a guest account for info, but I don't have the number (yet).
Topic 202: Internet Access for the Masses
# 3: Tillie Chutcha (TC)    Wed, Jul 29, '92 (19:24)    2 lines

Thanks, LTango. That was just the lead I needed. Looks like it'll work here. BTW, the
modem access number is 800-555-2121. Enjoy!

Topic 202: Internet Access for the Masses
# 4: Olive Branch (OBranch)    Thu, Jul 30, '92 (04:21)    2 lines
Maybe. But their price of $12 per connect hour is a little much for me. I'd like to find
something R E A L L Y cheap. Let's keep looking.
```

This sample is a sequence of responses to the primary question or statement, "A place to report on Internet access for the masses." This is a well-defined topic that generated a lot of response. With other topics it is more difficult to see the boundaries, and the conversation flows in a less-organized manner. Also, there may be a statement followed by two or three responses, then someone else may ask a question or make a statement. The next responses are in answer to the second query. Then someone new logs in to the conference, reads the first statement and makes a response to that one, way down in the file.

This may sound a little confusing—and sometimes it is—but it is also fascinating to log in to such a conference days or weeks after the fact and read through the progression of responses. The hindsight offered by a distance of time can put the discussion into a new light, offering perspective that is educational and/or interesting.

News

News is a variation of conferencing. Whereas a conference is usually designed and controlled by a single local system, news is of a more global nature. Internet nodes share with each other information about news topics, so when you log on to your service provider's computer you have news topics and location information at your fingertips. The discussions you find on news are not confined to a single system; rather, they come from Internet nodes all over the world.

As you might imagine, keeping track of topical discussions across a network as large as the Internet can be somewhat complicated. Luckily, programs called news readers take care of your part of this management. When you access a news reader, it seeks out a pre-determined news server, an Internet node that stores the news item exchanges. The news reader you use and how it is configured depends on the Internet service provider you are using.

News servers collect news items from a variety of sources, including USENET (where the majority of news items originate), local news sources, email, and other places. Mail files are stored on the server for a pre-determined period, then discarded. Many of them are updated by later versions; some go away forever once they become outdated.

As I mentioned, USENET is the source of a large amount of available news files on the Internet. USENET is not really a separate entity; rather, it is a set of rules or agreements for sharing news across the network. USENET consists of the messages and the people who write them and read them. System managers work with this data, following generally accepted (but rather loose) guidelines to present news items (files that contain comments and discussions) to the various news servers on the Internet.

In addition, there are some agreed upon major topics for news sessions in which exchanges on news take place. Originally news was more structured than it is today, and the seven topics shown in Table 3.4 offered news boundaries.

TABLE 3.4
The seven main newsgroup topics

Topic	Description
comp	Computer topics
news	News and news software
rec	Recreation
sci	Science
soc	Social
talk	General discussion
misc	Everything else

In addition to these standard topics, you will find many additional topics. (How many topics depends on the system you're using.) There are a dozen or so recognized alternative topics, but you'll find additional topic types as well. For example, in browsing around The WELL, a California-based conferencing system, you will find newsgroups with the ba. type (for Bay Area). These can be very specific topics, from where to eat, to houses offered for sale. The news system is well-designed and managed under guidelines that came from USENET, which again is a loose organization of users who agree on voluntary usage guidelines. However, you are bound to see local topics and usage conventions that don't follow the guidelines precisely.

Figure 3.10 is a sample listing of news within the news reader software **nn** from one Internet node. This illustration shows only a very small portion of available topics. As you can see on the second line, there were 1,021,121 articles when we captured this screen, 2,230 of which were new articles.

FIGURE 3.10

Sample news topics

```
Newsgroup: news.announce.newusers
Articles: 21 of 1021121/2230 NEW
a David C Lawrenc 667  List of Active Newsgroups, Part I
b David C Lawrenc 667  >List of Active Newsgroups, Part II
c David C Lawrenc 915  Alternative Newsgroup Hierarchies, Part I
d David C Lawrenc 735  >Alternative Newsgroup Hierarchies, Part II
e David C Lawrenc 834  List of Moderators for Usenet
f David C Lawrenc 152  How to Create a New Usenet Newsgroup
g Stephanie Silv 1476  >Publicly Accessible Mailing Lists, Part 5/5
h Jonathan Kamens 784  How to become a USENET site
i Jonathan Kamens 284  Introduction to the *.answers newsgroups
j Jonathan Kamen 1371  List of Periodic Informational Postings, Part 1/6
k Jonathan Kamen 1354  >List of Periodic Informational Postings, Part 2/6
l Jonathan Kamen 1096  Changes to List of Periodic Informational Postings
m Jonathan Kamen 1264  >List of Periodic Informational Postings, Part 3/6
n Jonathan Kamen 1239  >List of Periodic Informational Postings, Part 4/6
o Jonathan Kamen 1451  >List of Periodic Informational Postings, Part 5/6
p Jonathan Kamen 1443  >List of Periodic Informational Postings, Part 6/6
q Ron Dippold    715  Usenet Newsgroup Creation Companion
r Stephanie Silv 1024  Publicly Accessible Mailing Lists, Part 1/5
s Stephanie Silv 1395  >Publicly Accessible Mailing Lists, Part 2/5
```

This was just one of many screens I stepped through that day to find interesting topics. Once I found an area that looked promising, I selected the topic by moving the cursor to it and pressing the **period** key, or by pressing the letter displayed to the left of the entry. (Depending on your terminal configuration you may not be able to cursor to the entry.) Notice that the letters beside the entries are lower case letters. Upper case letters are used for the program's commands.

A topic area is displayed in Figure 3.11. I have reformatted this entry a little to make it easier to see, and I have changed the origin information to something nonexistent (or I think so!). But this gives you an idea of the kind of entry you can find within a news topic. The information you find in News is always varied, ranging from business hints to hobby discussions to household and education information. Consider another entry, shown in

Figure 3.12. Again, information has been changed, but this certainly is the type of entry you'll find throughout News.

FIGURE 3.11

News Article entry in nn program

```
Forsale:
486DX/33 w/64k cache
4MB Ram (60ns)
130 MB HD
101-key Maxiswitch keyboard
3-button mouse
Teac 1.44 disk drive
Teac 1.2 disk drive
1 meg SVGA video card
Non-Interlaced 14" SVGA Color Monitor
Medium Tower Case w/230 watt PS
9600/2400 baud fax/modem
Comes complete with all manuals and packaging.
$1295 and I'll pay for shipping costs. E-mail me if interested!

* Origin: ClipBoard BBS (415) 239-0454–
Andy Sellers - via FidoNet node 1:125/1UUCP:
...!uunet!shelter!415!Andy.Sellers
INTERNET: Andy.Sellers@f415.n125.z1.FIDONET.ORG

– 09:08 –.market.computers– 1 MORE –help:?–Top 66%–
```

FIGURE 3.12

Another news entry

```
From: UCISRCY@CIS.Unocal.Com
Organization: Unocal Corporation
Date: Wed, 25 Aug 1993 19:56:56 GMT
Newsgroups: sci.environment,sci.energy,ca.environment,rec.autos.tech,
sci.answers,rec.answers,news.answers
Subject: Electric Vehicles FAQ Part 1/3

  Here is a *partial* listing of electric vehicle clubs and alternative
  energy publications last updated 24-AUG-1993.  If you have any additions
  or corrections to this list, send them to me and I'll add them.  This list will
  be published monthly.  This file is available for FTP from HMCVAX.CLAREMONT.EDU
  in the  directory INFO-EV-ARCHIVE as RESOURCES.PARTn
  (There are 3 parts right now).  I try veryhard to keep this list up to
  date, but since I've gleaned this information from a number of sources,
  no guarantee is made for correctness.  (If you find anyerrors *PLEASE*
  let me know and I'll fix it!  :-) )

  Electric Vehicle discussions have occurred in the following usenet
  newsgroups: Sci.Environment Sci.Energy CA.Environment Rec.Autos.Tech

  Contents:
        1) Common questions and answers
        2) Electronic Lists
        3) Publications
        4) Books
        5) Governmental Agencies
        6) EV Associations
```

News is somewhat of a strange animal, as computer facilities go. It has been around since before the Internet became as popular as it is today, and it continues to grow. As you can see from the sample topics, you can find something on News that fills about any need. But it is hard for any book to describe adequately what News is and how to use it. The best learning experience is getting on the Internet, finding a service provider that has the nn program (or another of the many news reader facilities), and giving it a try. With the help of a news front end, you will learn your way around quickly and begin to find news items for yourself. (See the following section for more information on some available news readers.)

You probably have one of these reader programs right on your local host system. At the system prompt, type **nn,** for example, to see if the program is available. You can try **tin** or **rn** as well. One of these should be available. If you are using the Internet from a PC over a SLIP or PPP connection, you may be using the Trumpet News Reader, a graphical news reader.

There are other news reader utilities available as well. You may run across them—or references to them—as you browse the Internet. If the one you want to use is not available on your host, contact the system administrator. Chances are you can get the one you want installed for your use.

News Management Software

One of the advantages that a news conversation has over many conferences is the management software that helps you navigate through a topic. One common option is **rn,** an older utility that is quite popular but which lacks some of the features of **nn.** Both **rn** and **nn** are generally part of the UNIX system you're using. A popular third party option is **tin,** a program closer to **nn** than **rn,** and one that offers a number of desirable features. If none of these is available on the system you are using, try **trn,** a full-featured reader package similar to **tin.**

I'll discuss some of the main points of **tin** and **nn** in this section and leave you on your own for more information on **rn** and **trn.** I'll also introduce the PC Trumpet News Reader, a really easy to use utility that you can use with a PC over Ethernet or via a SLIP dial-in connection.

With some of these systems, you can get more information with the **man** command. Simply type **man** followed by the name of the program you want to study.

I've already shown you some sample output from the **nn** program and discussed how it works. Let's look next at **tin.** It is similar to **nn,** but, I think, has a better user interface. It is easier to see the levels of information you are viewing within **tin.** Figure 3.13 is a display of available newsgroups on The WELL during one session. Obviously, with over 12,000 groups available, this screen is only a small portion of the list. When you use **tin,** you can first look at the list of groups or topics, then display a summary of responses within any topic.

FIGURE 3.13

tin newsgroup topic list

```
         Group Selection (3039)                       h=help

   1   407  news.announce.conferences                        Calls for paper
   2        news.announce.important                          General announc
   3   132  news.announce.newgroups                          Calls for newgr
   4    70  alt.3d                                           Discussions of
   5  1052  alt.activism                                     Activities for
   6    75  alt.activism.d                                   A place to disc
   7     5  alt.aeffle.und.pferdle                           German TV carto
   8  1601  alt.alien.visitors                               Space creatures
   9  1150  alt.angst                                        Anxiety in the
  10   354  alt.aquaria                                      The aquarium &
  11    95  alt.archery                                      Discussion of a
  12    35  alt.artcom                                       Artistic Commun
  13  1014  alt.astrology                                    Twinkle, twinkl
  14  3240  alt.atheism                                      Discussions of
  15    66  alt.autos.antique                                Discussion of a
  16     6  alt.bacchus                                      A newsgroup for

    <n>=set current to n, TAB=next unread, /=search pattern, c)atchup,
  g)oto, j=line down, k=line up, h)elp, m)ove, q)uit, r=toggle all/unread,
   s)ubscribe, S)ub pattern, u)nsubscribe, U)nsub pattern, y)ank in/out

ALT-Z FOR HELP | VT100 | FDX | 57600 N81 | LOG CLOSED | PRINT OFF | ON-LINE
```

Figure 3.14 is a display of responses within a selected topic. You first select a topic from the list in Figure 3.13, then browse through the list of what people have to say about it in Figure 3.14. When you select a topic shown in the list in Figure 3.14, you can read a paragraph or several paragraphs of comments by that person about the selected topic.

FIGURE 3.14

Display of responses within a topic

```
   alt.alien.visitors (144T 405A 0K 0H R)                      h=help

    1  +    FactComm 1                                          Michael Parks Swai
    2  + 29 Strange Black Helicopters...                        Robert Dinse
    3  + 2  UFO Abduction Research PLEASE REAC                  Center for Psychol
    4  + 26 First the Canals, now the Face...                   Jason Haines
    5  +    Ufo sighting in AZ                                  Searchnet Zec
    6  + 8  Mothman Prophecies                                  Paul Milsom
    7  + 2  ****************   WEIRDOS   ****************       Ralph 'Hairy' Moon
    8  + 4  Jacques Vallee and Common Sense                     Evan M Corcoran
    9  +    Vallee email?                                       Evan M Corcoran
   10  + 12 X-Files 9/17/93 (#2)                                Don Nellesen
   11  +    Answer                                              John_-_Winston@cup
   12  + 3  Why I have great difficulty believing i             Marc Milanini
   13  +    * SpaceNews 20-Sep-93 *                             Robert Rouse
   14  + 3  This morning's JOHN SPRINGER show                   Superuser
   15  + 4  Jesus Christ coming back on a UFO                   alpha
   16  +    testit                                              Operator

   <n>=set current to n, TAB=next unread, /=search pattern, ^K)ill/select,
 a)uthor search, c)atchup, j=line down, k=line up, K=mark read, l)ist thread,
  |=pipe, m)ail, o=print, q)uit, r=toggle all/unread, s)ave, t)ag, w=post

ALT-Z FOR HELP | VT100  | FDX | 57600 N81 | LOG CLOSED | PRINT OFF | ON-LINE
```

As you can see, there's a lot of information on these screens, including the menu prompt. I find **tin** extremely easy to use. Just type **tin** at your system prompt and see what you find.

Let's look a little more closely at these screens. Figure 3.13 shows some available newsgroups. At the left side of the display is the newsgroup number, followed by the number of unread messages in that group. The third column is the name of the newsgroup, which is followed by a brief description. You can select a newsgroup by moving the highlight up and down the screen and pressing **Enter** or **Return** when the one you want is highlighted.

Notice the names of these groups. They all begin with an abbreviation. In the illustration you see two kinds of newsgroups, **news** and **alt.** The **news** type is one of the seven main groups we discussed earlier, and the **alt** group is one of the alternative newsgroups.

For more information on how **tin** works, use the **man tin** command at the system prompt. Note that **tin** and other newsreaders can be configured to display different information on the screen, so your **tin** screen may not look exactly like these examples. Don't worry about these differences; whatever the format, it should be obvious and relatively easy to use.

For network or SLIP (and PPP) users with PC hardware, the Trumpet News Reader is among the more popular options; it provides an even easier news format. Figure 3.15 shows a typical Trumpet News Reader screen for selecting newsgroups.

FIGURE 3.15

Trumpet News Reader Subscribe dialog

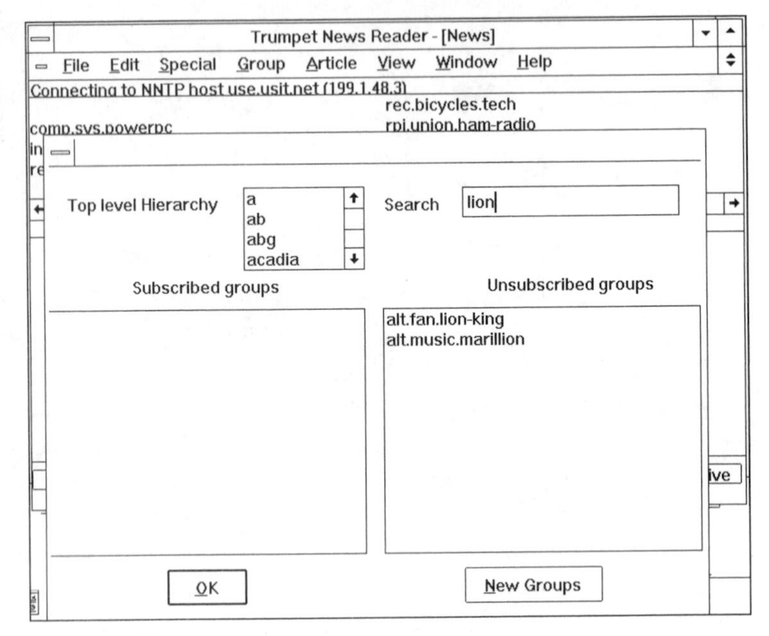

As you type a topic name, the Trumpet News Reader scans the list of available topics and inserts a list in the window below the topic field. This window will begin to fill as you type even two or three characters. As you type more characters, the program refines the list further.

If you click on one of these topics it is moved to a separate list to the left of the display, indicating that you have selected it to read. When you close the selection window, the reader copies the list to a window at the top of the screen, where the list remains until you change it. The next time you open the Trumpet News Reader, the same list of topics is available. You can open the latest versions of these newsgroups without having to select the topics again.

DATA TRANSFER

I've shown you a glimpse of what you may find on the Internet once you start traveling on your own. But how do you grab the information you find, and how do you share information of your own with other travelers? I'll talk about these concepts in this section.

Sending Files

I've demonstrated one way to send files over the Internet: the mail system. Especially if you are using Pine or another menu-driven mail utility, it is relatively easy to send text or program files along with a mail message. This is probably the most direct and easiest of all file sharing methods when you have a specific file that you want to send to one or more specific Internet travelers.

Why would you want to do this? Suppose you get into a discussion with someone about water quality problems in Tennessee Valley Authority lakes and streams. You happen to be an environmental expert who has conducted a recent study of the problem for TVA. Rather than try to reconstruct the information you have gathered painstakingly over weeks or months, you simply send the other traveler an email message and attach a spreadsheet or word processor file to it. Because these files are in the format created by the spreadsheet or word processor applications, not ASCII or text format, the user on the other end of the link can load them up and see fully-formatted documents (assuming they have a copy of the source program that created the original file).

Binary information transmitted over the Internet must be encoded to maintain data integrity. UU encoding is a common method and is frequently handled automatically by mail reader software. If you receive a word processing or spreadsheet file that is unusable, it probably means that the sending software encoded it, but your receiving software failed to decode it. Ask your system administrator what type of encoding/decoding your software can do. Also, your service provider probably has stand alone encode/decode utility software available for downloading.

You also might want to share a graphics image with someone else, ship a shareware program over the wire, or send someone a mailing list or other database file. Whatever the reason, you surely will want to send files across the Internet occasionally. You will also want to receive files, either from another Internet user or by downloading information from a remote host. *Downloading* is the process of copying a file from a remote system down to your system. When you send a file from your machine to a remote computer, you are *uploading* a file, copying it up from your machine to the Internet.

Addressing Files

The simplest method for addressing files is to use a mail facility that will let you attach a file. Note that some mail programs will insert or attach a text file, but won't handle binary information. A binary file is one that uses all eight data bits and that is saved in a format other than text. Program files are like this, as are spreadsheet files, database files, most word processor files, and anything you have compressed with PKZIP, COMPRESS, or other compression routines.

If you can't send a file via mail, then you'll have to upload it to some system available to the Internet, then send the recipient a mail message describing where the file is and how to get it. For example, you might upload a file to your local host into a public directory such as **incoming.** If you can't access a public directory directly, use ftp to attach to your host at a point that should provide public access.

Change to one of the public directories, probably **/pub/incoming** or something similar, then upload the file using whatever protocol is available on your host. (See the discussion of file transfer protocols later in this chapter.)

Here's a sample dialog with the local host to show you how to get the file into a public area. Change **ftp.usit.net** to the name of the system you want to use.

```
ftp ftp.usit.net
```

At the prompt asking for your login ID, enter **anonymous** (or **ftp**)

The host system will ask for a password. Enter your complete email address.

type: `cd /pub/incoming`
type: `bin`
type: `put <filename>`

This copies the specified file from your home directory on your host—or from a specified directory on your Macintosh or PC if you are using a SLIP, PPP, or network connection to the Internet—to the incoming directory on the remote host. Once the file is in place on the remote system, you can send the recipient mail telling them where the file is located.

Not all systems allow anonymous FTP. Or, they may not allow anonymous FTP into the main computer. You may have to ask someone at the remote host for an address to use for anonymous ftp. If you get an error message indicating that access is denied, it doesn't mean you did anything wrong. It simply means that this particular host doesn't allow anonymous FTP.

You could also send a file by establishing a link to the machine the recipient calls home, then uploading the file into his or her directory, where it will be available for downloading to that user's local computer. The precise process you use depends on a number of factors, including the size of the file, what rights you have on your own system, what rights you have on the remote system, personal preference, and so on. Having rights means you are authorized to copy files over to a specific system—you have "write" rights, in other words.

Receiving Files

You receive files in the same way that you send them—just reverse the process. Supply the other person with your mailing address and have them send you a mail message with a file attached. When you get the mail, the mail system will indicate that a file was sent with the text message. Note, however, that some older mail systems limit the size of the files you can transfer in this way to 64 kilobytes. In some cases you can download the file right from the mail system by selecting a download option from the menu. You will then be prompted to select a protocol and prepare your own system to receive the file. With other systems you save the attached file onto your Internet machine, and from there download it outside of the mail system to your local computer.

You can receive files with FTP as well. To get a file, enter this sequence:

```
ftp.usit.net
```

At the prompt asking for your login ID, enter anonymous (or ftp)

At the prompt asking for a password, enter your complete email address.

```
type: cd /pub/incoming

type: bin
type: get <filename>
```

The file transfer protocol utility, or FTP, lets you download files from remote systems to your own host machine (or directly to your desktop if you are using SLIP, PPP, or another network connection to the Internet). I will describe it fully in the next chapter.

Protocols for Uploading and Downloading Files

If you are using FTP you won't use file transfer protocols. FTP over a SLIP or PPP connection handles transfer of data from your desktop to a host. And, if you use FTP to move data between your local host and a remote host, the file transfer is handled for you.

To send and receive files with a terminal connection from your desktop, however, you will need some software to ensure that the data is transferred over the phone line without loss of information.

This is because you need error correction, for one thing. If you simply send a text file to a remote system as if it were being typed by a very fast typist, there are bound to be errors. There's a lot of traffic on the Internet, and data collides, telephone lines drop out, noise of one kind or another develops. You can't achieve reliable file transfer in this manner. Besides, as I mentioned earlier, much of the file data you want to transfer will be in the form of binary data: compressed files, program files, data files. A text-based link won't understand these files, so you couldn't get reliable data transfer anyway.

Enter *file transfer protocols*—program utilities that package data in specific ways, surrounding it with new information that helps the receiving computer know whether or not everything got transferred properly. As these packets of data arrive at their destination, the software on the other end checks what was received against what was sent. If data is lost, the receiving machine tells the originating computer to send that packet again. This send, check, resend process can go on until the packet arrives as it was sent.

There are dozens of these protocols, but the ones you are most likely to encounter on the Internet are ZMODEM, XMODEM, and Kermit. ZMODEM is among the most popular, newer protocols. XMODEM is an older protocol that is still used by many hosts and communications programs. Kermit is a universal protocol that should be on any machine you try. In its latest versions, Kermit is very fast and very reliable, and can handle file transfer situations that can choke some other protocols.

If you are sending data from one Internet host to another with FTP, you won't use the protocols discussed here. These protocols are used to download data to your desktop from a host or to upload files from your desktop to a host.

Protocol transmission of file data requires a sending and a receiving component. If you are using a PC or a Macintosh with communications software, chances are that you have the ability to send and receive files with several protocols. The other half of the link is on the remote host with which you are communicating. Whether this remote host is a Sun workstation or other UNIX machine, an IBM Mainframe, a Hewlett-Packard minicomputer, or a Digital Equipment Corporation VAX, there should be file transfer protocol software available.

With most host systems, the file transfer protocol software is started with the same set of commands:

TABLE 3.5 File transfer Command Summary

Command	Description
sz	Send a file via ZMODEM.
rz	Receive a file via ZMODEM.
sx	Send a file via XMODEM.
rx	Receive a file via XMODEM.
Kermit	Launch the Kermit application from which you can send or receive files.

To use protocols to send and receive data, simply enter the command at the host prompt. If you are sending files, specify the file name on the command line, like this:

```
sz int01.zip
```

When I say "send" a file, I mean that you want to send it FROM the host to which you are attached TO your own computer. This is how you download data to your machine over a terminal-type dial-in link. If you type sz without a file specification, you may be asked for a path and file name.

To use receive, simply type **rz** or **rx** at the remote system prompt. You will be told to start the file transfer on your local machine. When you see this message it means that you should issue whatever commands are required by your communications software to initiate the file transfer. This may include specifying a destination file name and path. When you use receive on a remote system, you are uploading data from your machine to the remote machine. Receive tells the remote computer to get ready to receive data.

Kermit is a little different. To use Kermit to send or receive files, simply type **kermit** at the command line. The prompt will change and the Kermit utility will wait for further commands. To send (download) a file, type **send** and the name of the file on the command line. The host probably will instruct you to start the file transfer from your local machine. Issue whatever commands are required to initiate the Kermit transfer on your machine.

To upload a file (send a file from your computer to the remote computer), type **receive** at the Kermit prompt, then start Kermit at your machine.

Unlike XMODEM and ZMODEM, Kermit is sensitive to the type of data you are sending. If you are transferring text files with Kermit, then you don't need to do anything special. To transfer a binary file such as a word processing file, a spreadsheet, or anything you have compressed with PKZIP, type ***set file type binary*** *at the Kermit prompt before starting the transfer.*

Note that on some systems you can enter any of these program commands (except Kermit), but you may get the default utility for which that system is configured. Also, if you use the **man** command to display information about protocol utilities, you may get information on all of these utilities—not just the one you asked for.

Be aware that transferring files with a protocol utility can become tricky at times. Remember that you are transferring program or other data that uses all eight bits to define a word. That's one reason you need the protocol in the first place. However, some hosts—especially when you go through more than one computer to actually get to the Internet link—are configured to strip off certain control codes. This means that if you try sending information over a 7-bit link (one that requires you to set your modem for 7 data bits), there is a chance that the protocol software on either end of the connection won't link up, or if it does, you may not get reliable data transfer.

An example of this problem is when you use the CompuServe Packet Network (CPN) to talk to The WELL. CPN uses a communications setting of E71 (Even parity, 7 data bits, one stop bit), but The WELL likes to see N81 (No parity, 8 data bits, and one stop bit). CPN talks to your machine with E71 and talks to The WELL over the Internet, so during file transfers you may lose some information.

If you initiate a data transfer and the system starts to transfer data but then hangs, you may have to hang up the modem and re-dial the connection. If you try this a couple of times with more than one protocol and still have trouble, then you probably have a problem somewhere in the route to your destination machine. As a last resort try Kermit, because it will work when some of the others won't. But if you can't even transfer data with Kermit, give up and try another way.

Here's what I do in those circumstances. I first look for a direct dial-up link into the destination system. That's the quickest and surest way of getting reliable data transfer. It probably means you'll have to pay for a long distance phone call, but if the destination machine is within the same country or even the same continent, the cost won't be prohibitive if you are using 9600 bps or above.

The next thing to try is to get on another Internet link, transfer the data up to that machine, then use FTP to get it over the Internet to the computer where you want it. You also can use a mail system from the second host to send the file to yourself at your service provider or to send it directly to the ultimate recipient if you wish.

This procedure requires that you have an account on more than one Internet host.

I'll talk more about using protocols and transferring data as I discuss some of the resources you will find on the Internet. This section at least gets you started. I'll bring up specific issues as you need to know about them. Use the index to locate a particular topic if you need more information now.

WHAT YOU LEARNED

I've covered a substantial amount of information in this chapter, from how Internet machines and the people who use them are named to how you transfer files across the Internet. I showed you how to use electronic mail, discussed file transfer protocols, and talked about conferences and newsgroups.

With this chapter you have gained a fairly solid background of information about some of the tools and facilities of the Internet. In the next chapter I will continue discussing Internet features, but ones that are more fun and directly useful. The information in this chapter is baseline and practical. In the next and following chapters you will start doing some hands-on searching for places to go and people to see.

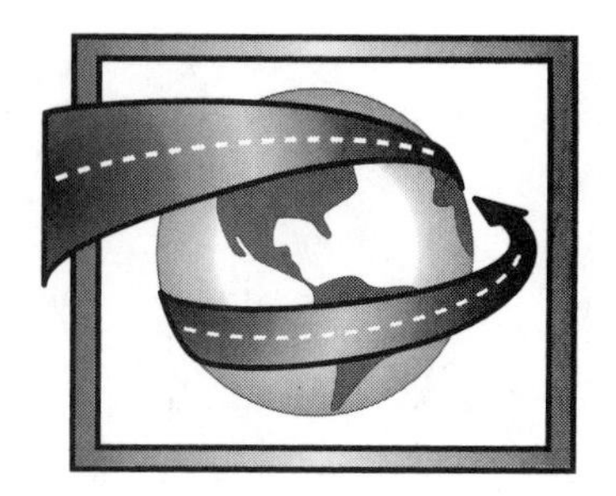

Chapter 4

Navigational Tools

In this chapter, I'll show you where to locate and how to use the following online tools that will help you find people and information on the Internet:

- Archie
- File Transfer Protocol (FTP)
- Gopher
- WAIS
- World Wide Web (WWW) browsers
- whois and Finger

Early users of the Internet were at a distinct disadvantage compared to those of us using the Internet today. For one thing, there weren't as many people or computers on the network, and there wasn't nearly as much useful information out there for them to access. But there was another disadvantage that continued even as the Internet grew—there weren't many tools to help them find who and what was out there.

In fact, probably the only reason so much useful work got done on the Internet in those days is that there was relatively less information to search. Today, with millions of users and an untold amount of information and other facilities, it would be extremely difficult to use more than a small percentage of the available information without tools to help.

Think about it. How do you know which road to take off the interstate highway to drive to a small town, and then how do you get around from town to town? You use maps, with varying levels of detail, drawn by people who have studied the system.

How do you find out what is in a book if you want to look for a specific topic? You use the index, the table of contents, and perhaps a list of illustrations. These tools help you narrow down your search for something specific from all of the data the author put into the book.

What about a computerized database? You may have thousands upon thousands of names and addresses or inventory records stored on a disk. How do you find a specific one out of the thousands of records? You use a database search utility that lets you specify certain criteria about the record or records you want, and the software handles the searching for you. These database tools might include forms, reports, queries, and other facilities specifically programmed for your database to help access the information.

The same is true of the Internet. It is a vast database of information—many databases, actually. Without some kind of software help you'd never be able to find even a portion of the resources available on the Internet, at least not within any reasonable time. In this chapter I will talk about several of the most common searching tools that you can use to find an almost unbelievable array of Internet information.

If you investigated the leads I suggested and you're still not using the Internet, go back to Chapter 1 and try your hand at The WELL or sign up for the U.S. Internet trial account. As long as you can afford the fee, anyone can use The WELL to get on the Internet and meet a lot of knowledgeable people. And with the free five-hour account at USIT, all you pay for is the long distance telephone charge, if any. Use The WELL or the USIT trial account to get started; from there you can learn about alternatives if you find you need some.

ARCHIE (ONLINE FILE-FINDING UTILITY)

The utility *Archie* is one way to find program or data files on the Internet. Archie is software that runs on a host computer and helps you search a database of directory listings from Internet computers willing to register their available files for general access. The list is updated automatically about once a month. When you want to find information on a particular topic, you run Archie and ask it to find files that contain certain groups of words or letters. Archie displays a list of files—sometimes more than you really want to see—that seem to deal with the topic you specified.

Accessing Archie

Before I discuss any specifics of how Archie works, let's talk about how you access it. As with many things on the Internet, the precise answer to this depends on which Internet server you are using. If your system administrator has set up a command file to attach you to an Archie server, all you need to do is type **archie** at the system prompt. Some systems have another command you use to attach automatically to one of the available Archie servers. Check with your service provider for the proper command for you.

Not every Internet node or service provider maintains the Archie program and database (though most probably do). You have to log in to a host that does and run the Archie program there before you can use it.

If there is a command file set up for you, it simply issues the proper command to attach to a specific Archie server where you can log on and go to work. If you type **archie** at your service provider prompt and nothing happens or you discover there is no Archie command file, then you should ask someone at your service provider to help you locate an Archie server. Once you know even one server location, you can use telnet to attach to an Archie server. And, having logged in to one Archie server, you can find out where other servers are located. To get the latest list of Archie servers, type **site** at the Archie prompt. Of course to do this you must run the Archie program once from somewhere! When you ask for the Archie site list, you should get the list shown in Figure 4.1, or one that resembles it. Remember that like everything else on the Internet, the list of Archie sites is changing all the time.

FIGURE 4.1

Archie Server List

archie.ans.net	147.225.1.10	(ANS server, NY (USA))
archie.au	139.130.4.6	(Austrailian Server)
archie.doc.ic.ac.uk	146.169.11.3	(United Kingdom Server)
archie.edvz.uni-linz.ac.at	140.78.3.8	(Austrian Server)
archie.funet.fi	128.214.6.102	(Finnish Server)
archie.internic.net	198.49.45.10	(AT&T server, NY (USA))
archie.kr	128.134.1.1	(Korean Server)
archie.kuis.kyoto-u.ac.jp	130.54.20.1	(Japanese Server)
archie.luth.se	130.240.18.4	(Swedish Server)
archie.ncu.edu.tw	140.115.19.24	(Taiwanese server)
archie.nz	130.195.9.4	(New Zeland server)
archie.rediris.es	130.206.1.2	(Spanish Server)
archie.rutgers.edu	128.6.18.15	(Rutgers University (USA))
archie.sogang.ac.kr	163.239.1.11	(Korean Server)
archie.sura.net	128.167.254.195	(SURAnet server MD (USA))
archie.sura.net(1526)	128.167.254.195	(SURAnet alt. MD (USA))
archie.switch.ch	130.59.1.40	(Swiss Server)
archie.th-darmstadt.de	130.83.22.60	(German Server)
archie.unipi.it	131.114.21.10	(Italian Server)
archie.univie.ac.at	131.130.1.23	(Austrian Server)
archie.unl.edu	129.93.1.14	(U. of Nebraska,Lincoln (USA))
archie.uqam.ca	132.208.250.10	(Canadian Server)
archie.cs.huji.ac.il	132.65.6.15	(Israel server)
archie.wide.ad.jp	133.4.3.6	(Japanese Server)

If you issue the command

```
telnet archie.unl.edu
```

at the system prompt, you should see this response:

```
Trying 129.93.1.14 ...
Connected to crcnis2.unl.edu.
Escape character is `^]'.
SunOS UNIX (crcnis2)
login:
```

At the **login:** prompt, type **archie** and press **Enter**. The system then asks for a password. At this prompt you should press **Enter** again (do not enter your email address for the password as is done with FTP sites). The system will respond with the screen shown in Figure 4.2.

FIGURE 4.2

Typical Archie Login Screen

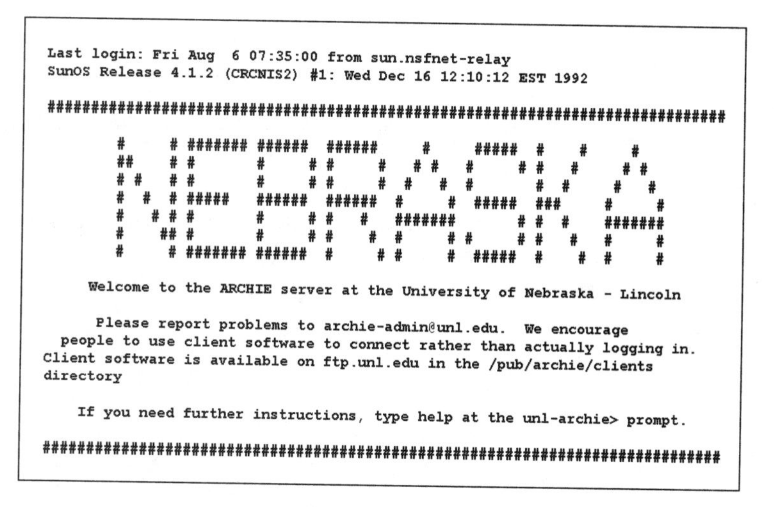

```
Last login: Fri Aug  6 07:35:00 from sun.nsfnet-relay
SunOS Release 4.1.2 (CRCNIS2) #1: Wed Dec 16 12:10:12 EST 1992

     Welcome to the ARCHIE server at the University of Nebraska - Lincoln

     Please report problems to archie-admin@unl.edu.  We encourage
  people to use client software to connect rather than actually logging in.
Client software is available on ftp.unl.edu in the /pub/archie/clients
directory

    If you need further instructions, type help at the unl-archie> prompt.
```

As the prompt suggests, you can type **help** at the command line to find out more about this particular Archie server and the commands you can use. If you type **help** at the **unl-archie>** prompt, you will see the display in Figure 4.3.

FIGURE 4.3

unl-archie Help Topics

```
Currently, the available help topics are:

   about   - a blurb about archie
   bugs    - known bugs and undesirable features
   bye     - same as "quit"
   email   - how to contact the archie email interface
   exit    - same as "quit"
   help    - this message
   list    - list the sites in the archie database
   mail    - mail output to a user
   nopager - *** use 'unset pager' instead
   pager   - *** use 'set pager' instead
   prog    - search the database for a file
   quit    - exit archie
   set     - set a variable
   show    - display the value of a variable
   site    - list the files at an archive site
   term    - *** use 'set term ...' instead
   unset   - unset a variable
   whatis  - search for keyword in the software description database

For information on one of these topics type:

  help <topic>
```

Also, depending on the Archie client installed at the site you are using, when you type **archie** alone on the command line, you may see another prompt asking you to supply additional information. Some clients, for example, expect to see the argument for search criteria on the same line with the Archie command. So to search for bicycle using an Archie client of this type, you would enter:

```
Archie bicycle
```

This type of Archie client may support a number of additional switches, or arguments, to make the command work in different ways. You might enter **-c** to specify a case-sensitive search, for example, or **-l** to list only one match per line.

Many utilities such as Archie have multiple implementations, each one slightly different. In general, you should be able to enter the command on a line by itself to receive a summary of available commands and syntax. In addition, you may be able to use the **man** command to display several pages of help on the local Archie command. If neither of these works, try using **/?** or **/help** after the command. And, of course, you can contact someone at your service provider to get additional help. The precise topics available under help depend to some degree on the Archie server you are using.

One other thing about accessing Archie is worth mentioning. Archie, as you might imagine, is an extremely popular service. Without Archie, or something like it, your ability to find files on the Internet would be severely limited. Archie is so popular, in fact, that you frequently see a message like the one in Figure 4.4.

FIGURE 4.4

Rutgers Archie Busy Message

```
> telnet archie.rutgers.edu
Trying 128.6.18.15 ...
Connected to dorm.Rutgers.EDU.
Escape character is '^]'.


SunOS UNIX (dorm.rutgers.edu) (ttyqa)

login: archie
Last login: Thu Aug  5 16:18:04 from gwusun.seas.gwu.
SunOS Release 4.1.3 (TDSERVER-SUN4C) #2: Mon Jul 19 18:37:02 EDT 1993
      Sorry, but there are too many concurrent archie users on this
machine right now. At this point, you have several options. First of
all, the most preferable alternative would be to use an archie client
such as xarchie (cs.rochester.edu:/pub) or the "archie" command line
client (ftp.std.com:/src/util). These clients reduce the load on the
server, as well as often providing additional functionality.  Another
alternative would be to contact one of the other archie servers. ( a
list of alternate servers is appended to this message ) If you aren't
in a rush, you could submit your request by email. Just send a message
to archie@archie.rutgers.edu with the subject line "HELP" to get
detailed instructions. Oh, and the final option is to try here again
later :)
                        - Archie Mgt
                        (archie-admin@archie.rutgers.edu)
```

The list of available Archie sites mentioned in this message is similar to the one shown in Figure 4.1. Simply use Telnet as I showed you earlier and try a different site. If you get an "Archie busy" message from one site, simply try another. Or you can do as the Rutgers Archie message suggests, and use an Archie client to conduct your search.

What is an Archie client? It is simply a local software package that handles some or all of the local user input/output and sends formatted requests to Archie. Using a client reduces the direct load on the Archie database software, because the client only attaches to Archie when it is ready to send or receive information. Use a client when you can. In fact, if you have an Archie, QArchie, or XArchie command on your local system or on your service provider, it probably is a client package of some kind.

Some clients offer a command line interface similar to Archie itself. Other clients are better, providing menu-driven access, and some clients force you to enter a command line that is complex and difficult to understand. Normally you can type **help** at the Archie or Archie client prompt and find out what commands are available.

Using Archie

Once you gain access to Archie, directly or through a client, you are ready to search for specific information. To understand how this works, consider the directory listing from a local PC for a moment. The listing of one directory might look something like the one in Figure 4.5. If you are using a Macintosh or other desktop machine, you have some kind of directory facility that is similar to this one. The files may be represented as icons, or you may see file names, but you will get a list of files and some additional information about each file.

FIGURE 4.5

Typical PC Directory Listing

```
 Volume in drive C is GATEWAY2000
 Volume Serial Number is 2950-15EB
 Directory of C:\WP\WINWORD\BOOKS\INTERNET

.            <DIR>       07-03-93  11:49a
..           <DIR>       07-03-93  11:49a
00INTNET DOC     138897  08-05-93   2:46p
01INTNET DOC     170876  08-05-93   2:26p
02INTNET DOC     417028  08-24-93   6:11p
03INTNET DOC    1599060  08-26-93   9:01p
04INTNET DOC       8804  08-30-93  10:49a
0GINTNET DOC       3211  08-30-93  10:44a
A2I      NTE      10416  08-22-93   8:00p
A2I_1    LOG      70370  08-22-93   8:01p
ARCHIE   LOG     128118  08-17-93   1:16p
CPN      LOG     157358  08-09-93  10:08a
DIRLIST  TXT          0  08-30-93  10:56a
IMA      LOG       5314  08-18-93  12:04p
INETLOG  802     262358  08-02-93   6:30p
INTENET  NT1       3012  08-02-93   4:09p
INTERNET MCI       4360  07-03-93  10:26a
INTERNET CI1        977  07-03-93   9:53p
INTERNET CIS      10722  07-03-93   1:40p
INTERNET INF      31101  07-03-93   3:05p
INTERNET CI2       4873  07-07-93   9:42a
INTERNET COR       4712  07-05-93   1:36p
INTERNET NTE      71394  07-16-93   2:59p
INTERNET NT1      16070  07-22-93  11:30a
INTERNET OUT      14682  08-02-93  11:31p
INTERNET LOG     251637  08-02-93   6:09p
IWELL    LOG      12470  08-21-93  10:00p
MAIL     LOG     171378  08-21-93   5:38p
MAIL_MAN DOC      53847  08-17-93   3:54p
MARTHA   LOG      10047  08-17-93   1:43p
```

This list of files looks slightly different from what you might find on an Internet UNIX system. The names of the files under MS-DOS usually must be shorter, for one thing. Under UNIX you can have much longer file names. This helps you to understand what might be in the file, but only if the person naming the file is creative and descriptive in their file-naming conventions. Figure 4.6 shows a file list from one UNIX system on the Internet. Some of the names are longer, and you could search a database of those names to come up with some topics, but they still don't tell the full story.

FIGURE 4.6

Typical UNIX System Directory

```
ls -l
total 41
drwxrwxr-x   5 jayr     pubdom       3072 Aug 28 23:39 amiga
drwxrwxr-x   4 root     pubdom        512 Jun 16  1988 appleII
drwxrwxr-x   3 jayr     pubdom        512 Mar 30  1990 atariST
drwxrwxr-x   2 root     pubdom       1024 Oct 10  1991 bmugsig
drwxrwxr-x   4 root     host          512 Mar 24  1988 c64
drwxrwxr-x   3 root     pubdom       1024 Dec 13  1991 cpsr
drwxrwxr-x   3 root     pubdom        512 Jul 18  1991 dtp
drwxrwxr-x   3 jayr     pubdom       1536 May 19 01:16 forth
drwxrwxr-x   3 jayr     pubdom       3072 May 24 19:49 hypercard
drwxrwxr-x   3 root     pubdom       4608 Aug 21 03:07 ibmpc
drwxrwxr-x   3 root     pubdom        512 Feb  5  1991 jewish
drwxrwxr-x   2 root     pubdom        512 Oct 15  1989 kermit
drwxrwxr-x   3 root     pubdom        512 Nov  6  1990 lan
drwxrwxr-x   3 root     pubdom       1024 Mar 30 08:55 mac7
drwxrwxr-x   3 jayr     pubdom       9728 Aug 27 08:18 macintosh
drwxrwxr-x   3 root     pubdom       2048 Dec 28  1992 midi
drwxrwxr-x   3 jayr     pubdom        512 Sep 27  1989 music
drwxrwxr-x   3 root     pubdom        512 Sep  9  1991 naplps
drwxrwxr-x   3 root     pubdom        512 Feb 15  1992 next
drwxrwxr-x   3 root     pubdom        512 Feb  4  1993 os2
drwxrwxr-x   3 root     pubdom        512 Aug 14  1990 wholeearth
drwxrwxr-x   2 root     pubdom        512 Oct 18  1991 windows
```

Most of the information stored in the Archie database is in the form of a series of directory names. The Archie database stores information from many Internet sites, and you can search the files through Archie to find out where they are. Do this with the **prog** command, the **find** command, or whatever command your particular Archie server uses. If you're not sure which command to use with the Archie client you are using, type **help** at the Archie prompt to find out. Or, if you use **prog**, for example, and receive an error, try **find**. You can't break anything by entering the wrong command.

NOTE

***prog** should be universal, but some servers implement additional commands to do the same thing, just to make things easier. After all, **find** is more intuitive than **prog** to look for information, right?*

Figure 4.7 shows one search in Archie using the **prog** command, along with the results.

FIGURE 4.7

prog Search in Archie

```
>prog pine
Processing Case Insensitive Substring Search for 'pine'

Host esel.cosy.sbg.ac.at

    Location: /pub/mirror/guitar/NEW.THIS.WEEK/m
      DIRECTORY drwxr-xr-x        512  Jul 13 00:50  Tony.MacAlpine
    Location: /pub/mirror/guitar/m
      DIRECTORY drwxr-xr-x        512  Jul 13 00:52  Tony.MacAlpine
    Location: /pub/mirror/guitar/w/Lucinda.Williams
           FILE -rw-r--r--       2133  May 20 14:01  Pineola.crd

Host knot.queensu.ca

    Location: /wuarchive/systems/linux/binaries/usr.bin
           FILE -r--r--r--     398604  Apr  6 04:43 pine3.05.1.bin.tar.z

Host hpcsos.col.hp.com

    Location: /mirrors/.hpib0/linux/binaries/usr.bin
           FILE -r--r--r--     398604  Apr  6 03:43 pine3.05.1.bin.tar.z

Host world.std.com

    Location: /obi/obi2/DARPA/drafts
 (?%)           FILE -r--r--r--        111  Dec 28 1992  happiness-for-all-01.txt%.Z
           FILE -r--r--r--        111  Dec 28 1992  happiness-for-all-01.txt.Z
```

Notice that on the Archie command line I entered the command **prog pine**, which told Archie to search the directory listing for any file name that includes the string **pine**. I was looking for information on the Pine mail system that I mentioned in Chapter 3. Notice what Archie found. (This is only a small part of the total list that this command produced. I cut it down so I could show you in general how such a search works.)

The first hit in this search doesn't have anything to do with the subject I hoped to find, but the directories listed do include the string "pine." The next two listings show the file **pine3.05.1.bin.tar.z**. This is more like it. Apparently this is version 3.05 of the Pine program, stored in a combined (**tar**) and compressed (**Z**) format. The final entry in this sample is not what

I wanted. The file name includes the word "happiness," which does include the string "pine," which is what I told Archie to find. Still, I got two correct hits, and a lot more information on Pine that I didn't show you in this figure. The search worked by locating the search text I specified within the file name database maintained through Archie.

I can then use FTP to download the files located in this Archie search that seem to be what I need. (See information on using FTP later in this chapter.)

If the list that **prog** (or **find**) generates about a specific topic is too long, you can narrow down the search by changing the search parameters. You can't use Boolean searches with AND and OR, but you can specify as much information as you know about the topic. For example, if I knew enough about my Pine search to know that I wanted information on version 3.0 and higher, I could use the search command:

```
prog pine3
```

This would eliminate all of the file names that include the word pine as an incidental part of the name. As you conduct searches with Archie, try to be creative and use search parameters that will produce as specific results as possible.

You can narrow the search by adding additional parameters to the search line. Three examples are shown in Table 4.1.

TABLE 4.1
Sample Archie Search Extensions

Command	Description
prog ^text	locates **text** only when text is at the beginning of word
prog text$	locates **text** only when text is at the end of the word
prog ^text$	locates **text** only when it is an exact match, with no additional characters at the beginning or end

Notice that Archie is capable of several kinds of search. The default is "case insensitive substring," but you can use the command **set search <type>** to change to one of these search types:

- regexp (regular expression)
- substring (the default)
- casesub (case sensitive substring)
- exact (exact match)

Use **help set** at the Archie prompt to get more information on these options. As with many features of the Internet, these specific types are subject to change. You should find search types similar to the ones I've listed, but different clients may call them different things.

Also, note that the information you find with Archie may be in one of several formats. It may be plain text, it may be a program binary for UNIX, MS DOS, Macintosh, and so on, and it may be a compressed text or program file. Compressed files are identified with a .z, .Z, .gz, or .zip suffix (among others). When you see a capital Z, it means the file was prepared using Compress. The lowercase z or the gz means the file was prepared with gzip. You need Uncompress for UNIX systems or a compatible utility for MS DOS or other operating system to restore a file that ends in Z. You need Gunzip to restore a file that ends in z or gz. A file that ends in .zip was probably compressed with the pkzip utility for MS-DOS. You need pkunzip (or the UNIX utility unzip) to extract the files from a .zip archive.

Suppose you issue a **prog** command and get nothing back? Archie may say something like "Nothing Appropriate," or "No Matches." Or, you may conduct a search that results in several files, but none of them is what you really wanted.

When this happens, you can use another Archie command that accesses another database. Try **whatis** followed by the information you want to find. This searches the file description database, an auxiliary file that contains descriptions of many of the files tracked by Archie. This data file may not be as complete as the main Archie file name database. However, it may help you find information you couldn't locate otherwise. **Whatis** is particularly useful for finding background information or descriptive information about basic Internet programs or facilities.

Here's an example. Suppose you wanted to search for files that reference UUCP. You conduct the search but don't find what you want. Try using **whatis**:

```
whatis uucp
```

With this search you may find a description of programs related to UUCP, such as utilities that support UUCP functionality. In short, you can try **prog** or **find** first, then try **whatis** to locate information that is not as easily spotted from the names of the files. Even after you get a list of programs with **whatis**, you may have to use a conventional Archie search to find out where these files are located.

Again, if you have problems using your particular Archie server or Archie client, you should be able to type **help** at the prompt to get more information on available commands.

Finally, here's a command that will show you just who participates in maintaining the Archie database. At the Archie prompt, type **list**. You should see a screen similar to the one in Figure 4.8. This figure shows only a small portion of the display generated by this command. As you can see, when this listing was prepared, 952 sites were offering information about their directories and files that can be downloaded via FTP. Sometimes there are more sites—1,200 or so—and sometimes fewer.

FIGURE 4.8

Archie list Command Results

```
unl-archie> list

952 sites are stored in the database

a.cs.uiuc.edu                  128.174.252.1     12:25 28 Jun 1993
abdallah.cd.chalmers.se          129.16.79.20    13:21  7 May 1993
accuvax.nwu.edu                  129.105.49.1    05:20 23 Mar 1993
acm.acm.rpi.edu                  128.213.5.10    21:30  1 Oct 1992
acsc.com                          143.127.0.2    04:48 18 Jan 1993
aelred-3.ie.org                 192.48.115.36    00:06 23 Jul 1993
aeneas.mit.edu                     18.71.0.38    01:07 23 Jul 1993
agate.berkeley.edu               128.32.155.1    01:32 23 Jul 1993
ahkcus.org                      192.55.187.25    01:11  9 Feb 1993
aisun1.ai.uga.edu                128.192.12.9    01:41 23 Jul 1993
aix.rpi.edu                     128.113.26.11    01:47 23 Jul 1993
aix1.segi.ulg.ac.be             139.165.32.13    01:53 23 Jul 1993
ajk.tele.fi                      131.177.5.20    02:17 23 Jul 1993
ajpo.sei.cmu.edu                128.237.2.253    02:23 23 Jul 1993
akiu.gw.tohoku.ac.jp               130.34.8.9    02:35 23 Jul 1993
alf.uib.no                       129.177.30.3    02:44 23 Jul 1993
alfred.ccs.carleton.ca            134.117.1.1    02:50 23 Jul 1993
```

When you have finished an Archie or Archie client session, type **quit** at the prompt to be returned to your local or service provider prompt.

FILE TRANSFER PROTOCOL (FTP)

Once you've found information files on the Internet that you want to move to your own machine, how do you do it? I described in the last chapter how you can use file transfer protocols such as XMODEM and ZMODEM to move data files from one machine to another. If the ultimate destination is your desktop computer, which you are using in terminal emulation mode to access an Internet service provider, then a protocol transfer may be the best choice.

However, there are probably lots of files out there on the Internet that reside on systems for which you have no access rights. Even if you know the domain name of the machine that has a file you want, when you Telnet to that machine it will ask you to log on. If you don't have an account on that machine with a valid password, you are going nowhere. You need the FTP facility to get you into the foreign host and to transfer the file for you.

In addition, you may be getting a file that is in compressed format, and you will need to use Uncompress, for example, on the host before you try to use it. The files may be bundled into tar packages and you will need the tar program (a tape archive utility that is part of UNIX) first. Or, you simply may have more available storage on your provider machine than you do on your own.

Besides, you may be attaching to the Internet through a direct connection or a low-cost or no-cost local dial-up machine. In this case, you may prefer to conduct the protocol transfer from your local service provider host to your desktop computer rather than across the network. This is particularly true if you are accessing a remote file on a system that charges for connect time, such as The WELL.

It is just such conditions that FTP is designed to address. The FTP utility has two ends—the one at your Internet node, and the one at the remote host where the file you want to download resides. The FTP utility accepts a command for an FTP connection at your local host, sends the appropriate commands to the remote host, and finally initiates the connection dialog.

Suppose, for example, you want to download to your Internet host the file **bicycles-faq**, which is located in the **/pub/usenet-by-group/news.answers** directory on host **rtfm.mit.edu**. This is a remote host and you don't have an account on this machine. (By the way, *FAQ* with a file like this means frequently asked questions.)

If this host supports anonymous FTP, then you can get the file quite easily. Remember, normally when you log on to a computer system you need a user account and a password to get in. With some facilities, however, service providers agree that they will let anybody in to conduct certain procedures. Among these common, anybody-can-do-it procedures is getting public archive files through FTP. In addition to setting up a login sequence for anonymous FTP login, these providers place files of general interest in a series of directories to which these anonymous users have access rights. It is a handy way to share information among Internet users. Here's what you need to do. Type the following at your service provider's UNIX command line:

```
ftp rtfm.mit.edu (or other host name you want to access)
```

You will see a screen similar to the one in Figure 4.9.

FIGURE 4.9

Sample FTP Login Screen

```
ftp charon.mit.edu
Connected to charon.mit.edu.
220 charon FTP server (Version 6.6 Wed Apr 14 21:00:27 EDT 1993) ready.
Name (charon.mit.edu:tbadgett):
```

At the **Name** prompt, type **anonymous** or **ftp**. You will be asked for a password. Enter your email address (e.g., **tbadgett@usit.net**). Then you will see an FTP prompt, usually something like **ftp>** .

If you are sure where the file you want is stored, simply issue a **get** command with the full path and file name of the file you want. In this example you would type the following at the **ftp>** prompt:

```
get /pub/usenet-by-group/news.answers/bicycles-faq
```

If you're not sure where the file or files you want are located, use the **cd** (change directory) command to view the files in different directories. The command **cd pub**, for example, makes the pub directory current. Once there you can use the **ls** command to list the files. Use **cd** again to move to a lower directory, and so on until you have found the file you want to retrieve.

If you are retrieving files from the current directory, then you can copy a file to your system with the **get** command, like this:

```
get bicycles-faq
```

Since this is a frequently asked questions file I assume it is a text file. FTP file transfers usually default to text format. If you want to transfer a program or other binary file (such as a compressed file, for example), you should issue the **binary** command prior to initiating the transfer. Simply type **binary** at the **ftp>** prompt. If you have specified binary, then want to transfer a text file, issue the **ascii** command prior to initiating the transfer.

The FTP software will automatically transfer the specified file from the remote system to your host system.

The file or files you transfer with the ***get*** *command are copied to your home directory at your Internet host computer, not to your desktop computer. FTP is used to transfer files between computer systems that are actually part of the Internet. Your desktop machine attached to a host through terminal emulation is not actually part of the Internet.*

When you have copied the files you want from the remote computer to your Internet host, you can type **quit** at the **ftp>** prompt to close the FTP connection and return to your local host prompt. Then you can use the list files command (**ls**) to see if the files arrived in your home directory. You can use another protocol (ZMODEM, XMODEM, etc.) to download the file to your desktop machine, or you can manipulate it with a resident editor or viewing program on your local host.

Notice that the file name and directory information for this sample came from an Archie search conducted earlier. However, when I attempted to download the file, I got an error message. If this happens it may mean that you have typed the path or file name incorrectly, or that the file in the list is actually a directory. Remember that UNIX commands and file names are case-sensitive. If the name shows up as all lowercase, it must be entered that way. On the other hand, if there is even one uppercase letter in the name, you must include it or the system won't be able to find it.

If the name and path are entered as you found them in Archie, it probably means that someone has changed the file name or moved the files since the Archie listing was updated. Check out the directory with the **ls** command to find out what files are in that directory. (You can use **ls** at the **ftp>** prompt as well as at a UNIX shell prompt.) If you get a very long list (which you probably will, since this is a public archive directory), you can narrow down the directory list by including the file name you found in Archie. In our example, you would issue the command like this:

```
ls bicycles-faq
```

When I tried that, I got a listing that looked like this:

```
bicycles-faq/part1
bicycles-faq/part2
bicycles-faq/part3
bicycles-faq/part4
bicycles-faq/part5
```

There are five files, part1 through part5, all stored in the bicycles-faq subdirectory that is located within the **/pub/usenet-by-group/news.answers** directory I started with.

Now I can get the files with the following command sequence:

```
cd bicycles-faq
get part1
```

If you want all five files, then issue the **get** command four more times with **part2**, **part3**, **part4**, and **part5** arguments.

*When downloading multiple files in a directory, use **mget** instead of **get** and use a wildcard file specification (use * to fill out the rest of a file name, for example, or a ? to replace any single character in a specification). This tells FTP to "message" you on each file, asking if you want it. Answer **y** or press **Enter** to get the listed file. Answer **n** or anything else to skip it. In this example, you could use **mget part?** at the **ftp>** prompt to start a download of all files in the current directory that are named **part** plus any other single character. **mget part*** would get all files that start with **part** and include any other characters in the remainder of the file name.*

When you have transferred the files you want, type **quit** at the **ftp>** prompt to be returned to your home system.

That's anonymous FTP. Many systems support it, and it is an excellent way to get copies of files from other systems that you ordinarily couldn't access. You can also use FTP to move files very rapidly across the network between systems you do have an account on. If you use FTP to log on to a system where you have an account and you use your logon name and password, you will be placed in your home directory. From there you have whatever access rights you normally have on that system. If you log on as **ftp** or **anonymous**, however, you will be presented with another directory structure and will not be able to access files in your home directory.

For example, if you log in with your authorized user ID, you may be placed in the directory **/home/username**, or whatever your host system uses as a directory structure to the home directories.

If you log in as **ftp** or **anonymous**, on the other hand, the default directory likely will be shown as /, the root. However, it is doubtful that you actually are using the true root directory. You are most probably accessing the top-level FTP directory, from which you can access additional directories that this particular system makes available to anonymous users.

TRAVEL TIP

*If you can't access FTP from your local host, you can use email to retrieve public files from FTP sites. To get more information on how to do that, send an email message to **mail-server@rtfm.mit.edu** with "send usenet/news.answers/finding-sources" in the body of the message.*

You can also use FTP to upload information to a remote host. Employ a process similar to the one for getting a file, but instead of using **get**, use the **put** command. **Get** copies a file or files from the remote system to your home system; **put** copies a file or files from your home system to the remote system.

You can upload information to make it available to FTP on your own and perhaps other machines. Look for the **incoming** directory (probably in the **/pub/incoming** path when you use anonymous FTP) and place files you want to share there. You could send an email message to other persons telling them what you made available.

Note, however, that some access providers monitor what you upload to make available to other users. You may be able to upload a file to the **incoming** directory, but neither you nor another user can see what is there. The system administrator will scan this directory regularly, then make the data available in some other public directory to which users have only read rights. (If you have only read rights you can look at data in a directory, but you can't write anything to it.) This is done for security reasons and to make sure the system complies with copyright laws. You can't upload your copy of Microsoft Word to share it with other Internet users, for example. If the **incoming** directory is not accessible for reading, check with your service provider to find out what directory will be used to post your uploaded files.

NOTE

Remember—you can't share anything you don't own, so don't upload copyrighted material unless you own the copyright.

There are a number of other FTP commands. You can get a list on screen by typing **help** at the FTP prompt. A typical help screen for FTP is shown in Figure 4.10.

FIGURE 4.10

FTP Help Display

```
ftp> help
Commands may be abbreviated.  Commands are:

!           cr            macdef      proxy       send
$           delete        mdelete     sendport    status
account     debug         mdir        put         struct
append      dir           mget        pwd         sunique
ascii       disconnect    mkdir       quit        tenex
bell        form          mls         quote       trace
binary      get           mode        recv        type
bye         glob          mput        remotehelp  user
case        hash          nmap        rename      verbose
cd          help          ntrans      reset       ?
cdup        lcd           open        rmdir
close       ls            prompt      runique
```

Here are some additional useful things to know about using FTP. When in FTP, you can list the files in your local directory by preceding the **ls** command with an exclamation. **ls** shows files in the remote FTP directory; **!ls** shows the files in the current directory on your local host.

When listing files in a directory, you can format the display so it is easier to read with **ls -C** (this provides columnar output instead of scrolling output). Use **ls -l** for additional detail about the files (such as size). And you may be able to use **dir** instead of **ls -l**, since some providers map **dir** to **ls** in recognition of the fact that most of us aren't UNIX users.

Most FTP commands can be issued with only three letters. To change the file format to binary instead of ASCII, you need only say **bin** instead of **binary** at the **ftp** prompt. You can also use **mge** instead of **mget** and so on.

After downloading a file in FTP, you can view the contents of text files in your current local host directory with the **cat** command or perhaps the **more** command: **!cat filename**, **!more filename**. The exclamation point sends the command back to your local host so you don't have to exit FTP to use the command. If the file is binary, you'll see meaningless garbage on the screen and may even break your link with the remote system because of some code that scrolls across your screen.

GOPHER (MENU SYSTEM)

Gopher is another useful tool on the Internet to help you find the information you want. Instead of looking for specific information like Archie, Gopher lets you browse through Internet resources using a menu system. As with the Archie **whatis** command, your success in using Gopher depends to a fairly large degree on how information was catalogued or tagged when it was put into the Gopher database you are using. Sometimes it is creative and complete. Then again, you will find information about the same topic stored under different headings, depending on who made the decision. Overall, however, you'll find Gopher a useful and interesting tool to help you find your way around the Internet.

The name Gopher, by the way, comes from a description of its function—it goes for things. Someone who serves a low level function in a company or on a project is sometimes called a "go fer" or "go for," so the name Gopher stuck. Besides, this Internet menu tool was developed at the University of Minnesota, which uses a gopher as its football team mascot.

To use Gopher, you need client software installed on your local machine or at your Internet service provider. To use this client—a software package that automatically connects to one Gopher server over the Internet then provides you a menu—simply type gopher at the service provider prompt. As with Archie, there are other implementations of the Gopher client, including **xgopher**. Which one you use depends on your site. If the **gopher** command doesn't work, check with your service provider to find out how to access Gopher.

Once the local client software logs on to the previously specified Gopher host (this specification is part of the client software—in all likelihood you don't have any control over where you attach to Gopher), you should see a screen similar to the one in Figure 4.11. The screen you see depends on the type of Gopher server you are using. There are versions that have graphical user interfaces that support a mouse. The one I am showing here is a very common text-based client and was accessed from The WELL. There are other clients on other Internet servers. Just type **gopher** at the system prompt and see what you get.

FIGURE 4.11

Typical Gopher Menu Screen

```
--> 1.  Information About Gopher/
    2.  Computer Information/
    3.  Discussion Groups/
    4.  Fun & Games/
    5.  Internet file server (ftp) sites/
    6.  Libraries/
    7.  News/
    8.  Other Gopher and Information Servers/
    9.  Phone Books/
    10. Search Gopher Titles at the University of Minnesota <?>
    11. Search lots of places at the University of Minnesota<?>
    12. University of Minnesota Campus Information/

    Press ? for Help, q to Quit, u to go up a menuPage:
```

As you see, you can learn about Gopher by stepping through the menu. For example, select number **1** from the menu for "Information About Gopher." After that, you can narrow down your search by selecting one of the general topic areas, such as Discussion Groups, Fun & Games, Libraries, or Phone Books.

With a menu system such as this, the best way to learn about it is to put your hands on it. Type **gopher** at your service provider or local prompt. When you have the main Gopher menu up, select a menu choice that tells you more about this Gopher. You may see a screen like the one in Figure 4.12.

FIGURE 4.12

Typical Gopher Information Screen

```
--> 1.  About Gopher.
    2.  Search Gopher News <?>
    3.  Gopher News Archive/
    4.  comp.infosystems.gopher (USENET newsgroup)/
    5.  Gopher Software Distribution/
    6.  Gopher Protocol Information/
    7.  University of Minnesota Gopher software licensing policy.
    8.  Frequently Asked Questions about Gopher.
    9.  Gopher+ example server/
    10. How to get your information into Gopher.
    11. New Stuff in Gopher.
    12. Reporting Problems or Feedback.
    13. big Ann Arbor gopher conference picture.gif <Picture>

Press ? for Help, q to Quit, u to go up a menuPage:
```

Just step through the menu selections on this screen until you have learned all you want for the moment, then return to the main screen by pressing **u** on the keyboard.

TRAVEL TIP

It might be a good idea to turn on screen capture or file logging within your communications package when you use this menu system. Save the information to a GOPHER.LOG file—then you can refer to it at any time without retrieving it online again.

A gopher is really a utility software application that runs on many Internet hosts. Your local information provider probably has designed a local gopher to provide information about the local system and to point to Internet data the provider wants to make available to its users. In addition, the local gopher probably has links to gophers on other systems, so as you step through a gopher menu you are accessing information from a variety of Internet sources. Where each system is located may or may not be obvious, but in most cases it doesn't matter where the application actually resides. You simply choose menu items that display the data you want to see without particular regard to where the data comes from.

For example, suppose you select **Phone Books/** from the main Gopher menu shown in Figure 4.11. You will see a screen like the one shown in Figure 4.13.

FIGURE 4.13

Phone Books/ Selection in Gopher

```
Internet Gopher Information Client v1.11     Phone Books

 --> 1.  University of Minnesota <CSO>
     2.  About changing information in the U of M directory.
     3.  Phone books at other institutions/
     4.  Internet-wide e-mail address searches/
     5.  X.500 Gateway/
     6.  WHOIS Searches/
Press ? for Help, q to Quit, u to go up a menuPage: 1/1
```

From this screen you can choose **Internet-wide e-mail address searches/** to present the display shown in Figure 4.14.

FIGURE 4.14

Internet-wide email Address Searches in Gopher

```
Internet Gopher Information Client v1.11
Internet-wide e-mail address searches

 -->  1.  Gopher to Netfind Gateway/
      2.  Netfind search for Internet e-mail addresses overview.
      3.  Netfind server at AARNet (Melbourne, Australia) <TEL>
      4.  Netfind server at Catholic University, Santiago, Chile <TEL>
      5.  Netfind server at OpenConnect Systems, Dallas, Texas <TEL>
      6.  Netfind server at Slovak Academy of Sciences, Czech and Slova..<TEL>
      7.  Netfind server at University of Alabama, Birmingham <TEL>
      8.  Netfind server at the University of Colorado, Boulder <TEL>
      9.  USENET contributor e-mail addresses <?>
      10. USENET contributor e-mail addresses overview.
      11. X.500 directory <TEL>12. X.500 directory overview.
```

And so on. You simply step through the levels of the menu until you locate the resource you want. Note that you are prompted at the bottom of each menu screen to press **?** for Help, **q** to Quit, or **u** to go up one menu level.

Menu entries that end with a forward slash (/) will show another menu or a file. If the menu entry ends in a question mark (?), that item is searchable; this means it contains an index of key words which you can search for specific entries. When you select an indexed item, you will see a search input screen similar to the one shown in Figure 4.15.

FIGURE 4.15

Gopher "Words to search for" Screen

```
                    Internet Gopher Information Client v1.11

                                   Movies

--> 1.  Search Movie Archive <?>
    2.  Current USENET Movie Reviews/
    3.  1987/
    4.  1988/
+--------------------------Search Movie Archive--------------------------+
|                                                                        |
| Words to search for  lucas                                             |
|                                                                        |
|                                 [Cancel ^G] [Accept - Enter]           |
|                                                                        |
+------------------------------------------------------------------------+

Press ? for Help, q to Quit, u to go up a menu                  Page: 1/1
 Alt-Z FOR HELP | VT100 |  FDX | 57600 E71 | LOG CLOSED | PRINT OFF | ON-LINE
```

For example, suppose I wanted to see a list of movie-related files that contain the word Lucas (for the director). Select **Fun & Games/** from the main Gopher menu (on the University of Minnesota server I used), then choose **Movies/** from the Fun & Games list. Finally, choose **Search Movie Archive <?>** to display the search screen. Enter **Lucas** in the search field. The result I got from this search was as you see in Figure 4.16.

FIGURE 4.16

Gopher Menu Search for Lucas

```
Internet Gopher Information Client v1.11
Search Movie Archive: lucas

 --> 1.  fun/Movies/1987/Jun/KOYAANISQATSI : From: cracraft@ccicpg.UUCP (St.
     2.  fun/Movies/1987/Jun/RETROSPECTIVE: STAR WARS : From: leeper@mtgzz..
     3.  fun/Movies/1987/Jun/THE UNTOUCHABLES-2 : From: moriarty@tc.fluke.C.
     4.  fun/Movies/1987/Jul/RETROSPECTIVE: LABYRINTH : From: reid@decwrl.d.
     5.  fun/Movies/1988/May/LADY IN WHITE : From: leeper@mtgzz.att.com (Ma.
     6.  fun/Movies/1988/May/WILLOW : From: jfreund@dasys1.UUCP (Jim Freund.
     7.  fun/Movies/1988/Jun/MISC: 12th Annual SF Lesbian & Gay Film Festi .
     8.  fun/Movies/1988/Jul/OUT COLD : From: moriarty@tc.fluke.com (Jeff M.
     9.  fun/Movies/1988/Aug/SOMEONE TO LOVE : From: thakur@eddie.MIT.EDU (.
     10. fun/Movies/1988/Sep/PUpcoming Films : From: leeper@mtgzz.att.com (.
     11. fun/Movies/1989/May/INDIANA JONES AND THE LAST CRUSADE : From: mor.
     12. fun/Movies/1989/May/INDIANA JONES AND THE LAST CRUSADE-1 : From: l.
     13. fun/Movies/1989/Aug/THE ABYSS-1 : From: leeper@mtgzx.att.com (Mark.
     14. fun/Movies/1990/Jan/SPY SMASHER RETURNS : From: teb@stat.Berkeley..
     15. fun/Movies/1990/Jan/MISC: TOP TEN of 1989 : From: ecl@mtgzy.att.co.
     16. fun/Movies/1990/Mar/HENRY: PORTRAIT OF A SERIAL KILLER : From: bau.
     17. fun/Movies/1990/Apr/DERSU UZALA : From: watson@ames.arc.nasa.gov (.
     18. fun/Movies/1990/May/LONGTIME COMPANION : From: Hoffman.es@XEROX.CO.
     19. fun/Movies/1990/Jun/LONGTIME COMPANION : From: leeper@mtgzx.att.co.
     20. fun/Movies/1991/May/BACKDRAFT : From: butterworth@a1.mscf.upenn.ed.
     21. fun/Movies/1991/Aug/DEAD AGAIN : From: leeper@mtgzy.att.com (Mark .
     22. fun/Movies/1991/Oct/RAMBLING ROSE : From: leeper@mtgzy.att.com (Ma.
     23. fun/Movies/1992/Jan/HEARTS OF DARKNESS : From: eugene@nas.nasa.gov.
     24. fun/Movies/1992/Apr/MISCELLANEOUS: Academy Award Winners (1992) .
     25. fun/Movies/1992/May/K2 : From: eugene@nas.nasa.gov (Eugene N. Miya.
     26. fun/Movies/1992/Jul/PRELUDE TO A KISS : From: leeper@mtgzy.att.com.
     27. fun/Movies/1992/Jul/MISC: Siskel & Ebert Ten Best Lists (1979-199 .
     28. fun/Movies/1992/Jul/PRELUDE TO A KISS-1 : From: frankm@microsoft.c.
     29. fun/Movies/1992/Aug/COOL WORLD : From: lon@edsi.plexus.COM (Lon Po.
```

As with most Gopher searches, you take pot luck; you may or may not get precisely what you had in mind. Suppose I select the third entry in the movie list: The Untouchables. This was not a George Lucas film, of course, but Gopher found Lucas in the index. When the file is displayed, I see that the reviewer mentions George Lucas films by way of introducing the review, but this is not an article about a George Lucas film.

If any of the entries from a Gopher search seem strange, you can display the associated information and find out why it was selected. The server will highlight the key word you were searching for inside the file. Simply display screen after screen until the key word you specified appears. It may or may not relate to the topic you wanted to find. If you entered more than one word on the Search For line, try entering only the main word you're really interested in. This will drop the files that have the modifier word you specified, leaving only the files with the main entry.

It will take a little practice to learn to get the most out of Gopher searches, but that is one of the fun aspects of the Internet.

WIDE AREA INFORMATION SERVERS

The Internet Wide Area Information Servers, or WAIS, is another information locating tool. WAIS (pronounced "ways") doesn't replace Archie or Gopher, but is used in conjunction with them.

WAIS is an indexed database of Internet information. This is significant because, when you conduct a WAIS search, you aren't looking at the source files. You are searching an index file that points to the information in the database. That database information can be text files, program files, graphics, or anything else you can store on a computer. I've shown a crude representation of an index and its related data in Figure 4.17.

FIGURE 4.17

Drawing of Index and Related Data

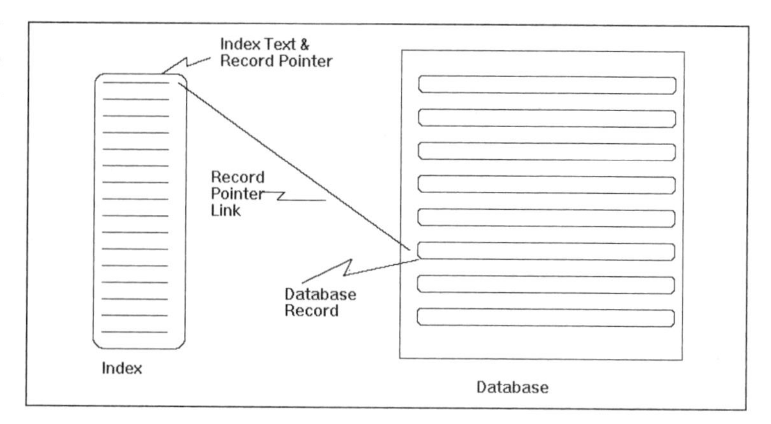

The difference between Gopher and WAIS is that WAIS includes a searching tool, so that instead of stepping through menus and lists until you come across something you want, you can specify what you're looking for and WAIS finds it.

WAIS is a *distributed application*, which means that both data and the software that searches the data are stored in multiple locations. When you submit a search to WAIS, the program steps through a series of checks, decides where the search should be conducted, and then hands off the search criteria to the host that contains the database you need to search.

This distributed search scheme is pretty sophisticated, but the actual searching you can do with WAIS isn't much different from Archie and Gopher. You can't conduct Boolean searches or narrow searches with any of these tools. The best you can expect is to get into the right ball park; locating the correct section of bleachers and then a particular person is a little more difficult.

Arriving on the scene are WAIS clients that have some expanded search capabilities. Investigate the Boolean WAIS—a Booleanized version of WAIS from ***ftp.bio.indiana.edu****—or get the new free WAIS.*

Accessing WAIS

To conduct a WAIS search you first have to get access to a WAIS client, just as you do with Archie and Gopher. Where do you find a WAIS client? You could use Archie and conduct a **prog** search for WAIS. That will show you where there are files on the Internet with WAIS in the name. In fact, I tried that and got the results shown in Figure 4.18. (Only a part of the search is shown.)

FIGURE 4.18

Archie Search for WAIS

```
Host syr.edu

    Location: /novell
      DIRECTORY drwxrwxr-x        512  May 13 1992  wais

Host uceng.uc.edu

    Location: /pub/wuarchive/systems/mac/info-mac/card
      FILE -r--r--r--     261026  Mar  9 10:13  hyper-wais-14.hqx

Host ruby.ils.unc.edu

    Location: /pub/internet_software
      FILE -rw-r--r--     162526  Apr 13 15:28  wais

Host sunsite.unc.edu

    Location: /pub/.cap
      FILE -rw-r--r--         71  Jul  6 23:28  wais
    Location: /pub/Z39.50/Standards_documents
      FILE -rw-r--r--      37911  Nov  7 1992  wais
    Location: /pub
      DIRECTORY drwxr-xr-x       1024  Aug 17 15:21  wais

Host cac.washington.edu

    Location: /msdos/lwp
      DIRECTORY drwxr-xr-x        512  Aug 20 12:45  wais

Host nic.wisc.edu

    Location: /userinfo
      DIRECTORY drwxrwxr-x        512  May 14 1992  wais
    Location: /
      DIRECTORY drwxr-xr-x        512  May 18 20:16  wais
```

From this partial list (a search for WAIS produces a LONG listing) you can see that there are several sites that seem to have WAIS access. I arbitrarily selected **sunsite.unc.edu** and used Telnet to access this host. The result is shown in Figure 4.19.

FIGURE 4.19

Sunsite.unc.edu WAIS Telnet Access

```
telnet sunsite.unc.edu
Trying 152.2.22.81 ...
Connected to sunsite.unc.edu.
Escape character is '^]'.
**************** Welcome to SunSITE.unc.edu ****************
SunSITE offers several public services via login. These include:

For a simple gopher client,                          login as gopher
For a simple WAIS client (over 500 databases),       login as swais
For WAIS search of political databases,              login as politics
For WAIS search of LINUX databases,                  login as linux

For a FTP session, ftp to sunsite.unc.edu. Then login as anonymous

For more information about SunSITE, send mail to info@sunsite.unc.edu


SunOS UNIX (calypso)



     login:
```

This site—as many sites do—tells you how to log on to WAIS. (At this site you use the SWAIS client.) Once in WAIS, you get the screen shown in Figure 4.20.

FIGURE 4.20

First WAIS Screen with Topic List

```
login: swais
Last login: Tue Aug 31 07:54:48 from AULA.RZ.Uni-Augs
SunOS Release 4.1.3 (SHOOP) #5: Tue Jun 29 15:56:38 EDT 1993

University of North Carolina Office For Information Technology

You could be running this code on your own machine.
You'll find it and other WAIS stuff available via anonymous ftp
from SunSITE.unc.edu in the pub/wais directory.

These databases are also available via gopher.
Just point your gopher client to sunsite.unc.edu 70
and enjoy using these databases from your gopher interface.

you're probably a vt100 or should be
TERM = (unknown) vt100
It takes a minute to load all the database information
SWAISSource Selection    Sources: 540
#Server     Source                                               Cost
001:    [   archie.au]          aarnet-resource-guide            Free
002:    [weeds.mgh.harvard.ed]  AAtDB                            Free
003:    [munin.ub2.lu.se]       academic_email_conf              Free
004:    [wraith.cs.uow.edu.au]  acronymsFree
005:    [    archive.orst.edu]  aeronautics                      Free
006:    [ bloat.media.mit.edu]  Aesop-Fables                     Free
007:    [ bloat.media.mit.edu]  aesopFree
008:    [ ftp.cs.colorado.edu]  aftp-cs-colorado-edu             Free
009:    [nostromo.oes.orst.ed]  agricultural-market-news         Free
010:    [sunsite.unc.edu]       alt-sys-sun                      Free
011:    [    archive.orst.edu]  alt.drugs                        Free
012:    [    wais.oit.unc.edu]  alt.gopher                       Free
013:    [sun-wais.oit.unc.edu]  alt.sys.sun                      Free
014:    [    wais.oit.unc.edu]  alt.wais                         Free
015:    [alfred.ccs.carleton.]  amiga-slip                       Free
016:    [munin.ub2.lu.se]       amiga fish contents              Free
```

With this site—and many others on the Internet that provide public access—you leave the password field blank. The host asks for a password, but you are expected to press **Enter** *without typing anything else in that field.*

You are prompted at the bottom of the screen to press **w** for a key word search or **s** for sources. I wanted to search the Internet for information about young people and amateur radio. From this list of topics (you can't see all of it in Figure 4.20) I chose two indexes: **kidsnet** and **k-12-software**. You select topics by moving the highlight down the screen to a topic and then pressing the **Space bar**. An asterisk appears beside the items you have selected. Then you enter the key words you want to search for—in this case **ham radio**. As you can see in Figure 4.21, I got 21 hits on the topic Ham Radio from these two databases.

FIGURE 4.21

Ham Radio Search for Kids

```
SWAIS              Search Results                               Items: 21

 #      Score              Source        Title                                 Lines
001:   [1000] (          kidsnet)        Scott Loft Re: KIDSNET & Ham Radio      22
002:   [ 940] (          kidsnet)        Mark Halla Re: RE: KIDSNET & Ham Radio  10
003:   [ 910] (          kidsnet)        V076GZHB@U Re: RE: KIDSNET & Ham Radio  11
004:   [ 728] (          kidsnet)        Scott Loft Re: More on Amateur Packet Ra 32
005:   [ 576] (          kidsnet)        phil@bts.c Re: Nixpub Posting (Long)    978
006:   [ 546] (          kidsnet)        aftp-list@ Re: Anonymous FTP List - Site 2788
007:   [ 455] (          kidsnet)        Mark Halla Re: RE: More on Amateur Packe 6
008:   [ 455] (          kidsnet)        Scott Loft Re: RE: More on Amateur Packe 14
009:   [ 455] (          kidsnet)        Mark Halla Re: RE: More on Amateur Packe 7
010:   [ 424] (          kidsnet)        LVRON@SATU Re: An article I got from a N 166
011:   [ 394] (          kidsnet)        opresno@ex Re: kids-93 newsletter #3    422
012:   [ 364] (          kidsnet)        mjk11@po.C Re: School Shuttle simulation 137
013:   [ 364] (          kidsnet)        yanoff@csd Re: Internet Services List   47
014:   [ 364] (          kidsnet)        yanoff@csd Re: UPDATED Internet Services 61
015:   [ 364] (          kidsnet)        Tom Grundn Re: Ammunition for K-12 Netwo 268
016:   [ 364] (          kidsnet)        yanoff@csd Re: Updated Internet Services 113
017:   [ 364] (          kidsnet)        yanoff@csd Re: Internet Services Listing 164
018:   [ 364] (          kidsnet)        yanoff@CSD Re: Updated Internet Services 201
019:   [ 364] (          kidsnet)        yanoff@csd Re: Updated Internet Services
     238
020    [ 364] (          kidsnet)        Rhonda ChInternet Resources for Sc      494
021    [   0] (    k-12-software)        Search produced no result. Here's the Ca 4204
```

Notice that some of these references obviously have to do with amateur radio and, since they were found on indexes that were targeted at kids, are probably a good match. Others don't seem to have titles that show a relationship between kids and ham radio. They may or may not be appropriate, but Figure 4.21 gives you a clue.

Notice the numbers in brackets just to the right of the entry numbers. These are the result of calculations performed during the WAIS search to show how close to your specified search criteria each article appears to be. A 1000 means that that file matched better than any of the others. Any file with less than 1000 didn't match as well. This points you in the right direction, at least, toward finding the information you were looking for. The only way to know for sure is to use the cursor movement keys to highlight the articles you want to view and then press the **Space bar**.

As with the other resources I have discussed in this chapter, WAIS software is mostly self-instructing. You read instructions on the screen and do what they say. The best way to learn about WAIS is to put your hands on it and try it out.

WORLD WIDE WEB (WWW)

Internet users, designers, and programmers are never satisfied, and thank goodness. That's how we have established all the tools and utilities that make using the Internet so much easier than it once was. One of these is the World Wide Web. WWW is much more than a tool—it is a complete system for storing, finding, and presenting information over the Internet. WWW, and the programming and user tools associated with it, moves the Internet toward the next generation of computer tools with a feature called *hypermedia*.

What is hypermedia? It means slightly different things on different systems and with different searching software, but in general hypermedia is a database that includes links among documents and files. These links are based on key words found inside each document.

For example, if you are reading a document about exotic animals and see a reference to Saber Toothed Tiger, you can select **Saber Toothed Tiger** with your mouse or cursor keys and open a document specific to that topic. While you are reading about Saber Toothed Tigers, you see a reference to the Pleistocene Epoch. By selecting that topic, you open a document dedicated to it, and so on. Depending on how the particular groupings are organized, you may be able to continue this process indefinitely, getting deeper and deeper into a topic, or jumping across topics as new ones present themselves.

Initially, hypermedia systems were all text, letting you browse document files by moving from link to link. Today—especially with the World Wide Web—hypermedia uses various multimedia data types such as color graphics, photographs, sound files, and motion video. Not only can you view these data types, but some of these (pictures and drawings, specifically) are used as the hyperlink itself. Instead of pressing **Enter** on a highlighted word, you can now use a mouse to click on a drawing or photograph that serves as an icon to represent the next block of data. Such features make browsing the Internet a very different experience from what it was in the beginning.

The concept of hypermedia is an important one for computer-based research and education. As we learn to code files and build more sophisticated search tools, look for hypermedia to become a natural part of most database front ends, word processors, and other search and data management tools.

In WWW, hypermedia is read and accessed with a software tool called a *browser*. A browser is simply a utility that lets you read text and select additional references based on that text. A browser may include a menu system that points you toward the general topics you want to study. Then you can access additional information in two ways—with a graphics browser and with a text-based browser. In our example with saber toothed tigers, a text-based browser might show that this is a linked term by placing a number in brackets beside it:

```
In addition, saber toothed tigers [22] were
common during very early periods, when. . .
```

By entering **22** at the bottom of the page that includes this reference and then pressing **Enter**, you can open a separate document about saber toothed tigers. This sort of number-based hypermedia is designed to support the lowest common denominator of terminal—line-oriented terminals or terminal emulators that don't support full-screen addressing. Luckily, this type of terminal is becoming increasingly rare.

Today, text-based browsers generally let you move through a document with the cursor keys, jumping from link to link. These browsers are designed for terminals or terminal emulators that do support full-screen addressing. The most common of these is the VT-100 terminal. Each link is highlighted with a reverse video or colored highlight as you move through the document. You need only press **Enter** or the **right arrow** on your cursor movement keypad to access linked information.

If you are using a graphics-based browser, on the other hand, icons, pictures, drawings, and colored text are used to represent the links. With a graphics browser you use a mouse or other pointer to select additional hyperlinked information. (See Chapter 5 for detailed information on some of these WWW browser tools and on the WWW itself. These browsers require additional software and a special account from your service provider.)

Where do you get browsers? Several are in use or under development. Many are distributed as freeware or shareware, such as NCSA Mosaic, and, increasingly, you can purchase browsers from a number of commercial companies. You can access a text browser via Telnet (I'll show you how in a moment), and you can download graphics-based browsers for MS-DOS, Macintosh, X-Window, and other implementations by browsing around inside WWW documents. Let's look at some examples.

To access a basic WWW text-based browser, enter this command at your Internet service provider prompt:

```
telnet telnet.w3.org
```

NOTE

*You may come across an earlier address for WWW info, **telnet info.cern.ch**. That site is no longer valid. You can try to access it, but you will get instructions telling you to use the **telnet.w3.org** instead.*

This connects you to a WWW server managed by the World Wide Web Organization. WWW was primarily developed at the European Particle Physics Laboratory, but as usage grew with its rise in popularity, a separate organization was required to provide information and to support users. This is a good place to start with WWW—the "head shed," so to speak. The first screen you see will look similar to the one in Figure 4.22.

FIGURE 4.22

Initial WWW Screen at WWW Organization

```
THE WORLD-WIDE WEB

  This is just one of many access points to the web, the universe of
  information available over networks. To follow references, just type the
  number then hit the return (enter) key.

  The features you have by connecting to this telnet server are very primitive
  compared to the features you have when you run a W3 "client" program on your
  own computer.  If you possibly can, please pick up a client for your
  platform to reduce the load on this service and experience the web in its
  full splendor.

  For more information, select by number:

    A list of available W3 client programs[1]

    Everything about the W3 project[2]

    Places to start exploring[3]

  Have fun!

1-3, Up, <RETURN> for more, Quit, or Help:
```

Notice that the screen in Figure 4.22 is a hypermedia browser. The numbers after certain words and phrases show that you can get additional information on these topics by entering the proper number at the end-of-screen prompt. The prompt tells you there are three possible choices on this screen. For example, if you enter **1** at the prompt, you get a list of available web browser client programs, shown in Figure 4.23.

FIGURE 4.23

WWW Browser Client Program List

```
W3 CLIENTS

  These programs allow you to access the WWW[1] from your own computer. See
  also: other W3 software[2] .

Email based browsers

  Agora[3]            Based on the line-mode browser. If you cannot have
                 full access to the Internet. (beta)

Terminal based browsers

  Line Mode Browser[4]  This program gives W3 readership to anyone with a dumb
                 terminal. A general purpose information retrieval
                 tool.

  "Lynx" full screen browser[5]
                 This is a hypertext browser for vt100s using full
                 screen, arrow keys, highlighting, etc.

  Tom Fine's perlWWW[6]  A tty-based browser written in perl.

1-35, Back, Up, <RETURN> for more, Quit, or Help:

_
```

This is as good a way as any to get a feel for hypermedia and its implementation in WWW. Simply Telnet to the WWW Organization site and poke around for a few minutes. You can do this with a computer and a simple terminal emulator, or even a dumb terminal. That's one of the benefits of a text-based system.

Text-based systems are the mainstay of the Internet, though very simple systems like this one are becoming increasingly rare. It is unusual for anyone to access the Internet today without at least a screen-addressable terminal, and graphics interfaces—Microsoft Windows, Apple Macintosh, X-Window Systems—are on the rise. For example, you can download software from a number of sites to give you a graphics interface to the WWW.

You will need different software for each platform. There are versions of graphical World Wide Web browsers for Macintosh, Amiga, PC, and UNIX platforms.

Figure 4.24 shows you just one sample graphics browser. This is a Netscape screen, captured from an IBM-PC compatible computer. There are similar software packages available from a variety of vendors.

FIGURE 4.24

PC Netscape Sample Screen

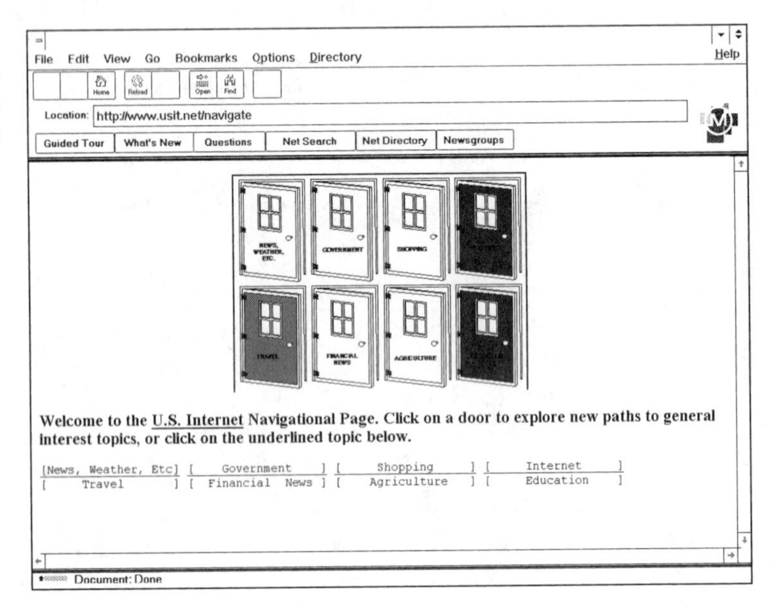

As you can see from Figure 4.24, navigating the World Wide Web with a graphical interface such as Netscape is an easy and enjoyable task. As you consider securing an Internet account, you should look into a SLIP account to allow access with one of the available graphics WWW browsers.

Web Searching

You can frequently jump directly to information on the World Wide Web, thanks to a growing trend toward standardized addressing (See Chapter 6 for more information on this technique). Suppose you try a couple of addresses that seem reasonable for a specific company, but don't locate anything. All is not lost. You can try a WWW search for a product or company.

Just enter the following URL (Universal Resource Locater) address in the proper place for your Web browser:

```
http://home.mcom.com/home/internet-search.html
```

This takes you to a Web search screen maintained by Netscape Communications. There are several Web search programs available on this page, along with some general information about web searching. As you might imagine, such tools are used heavily and you may have to wait your turn to access the one you want, but it can be worth the wait.

Choose the **Lycos** option to see the search screen shown in Figure 4.25.

FIGURE 4.25

Lycos opening search screen

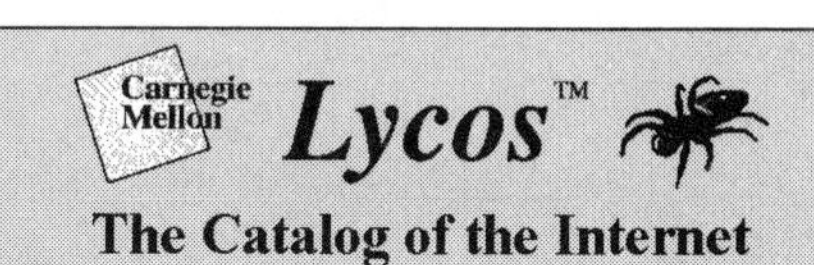

If you choose the WebCrawler from this screen, for example, you will see the screen shown in Figure 4.26.

FIGURE 4.26

WebCrawler opening search screen

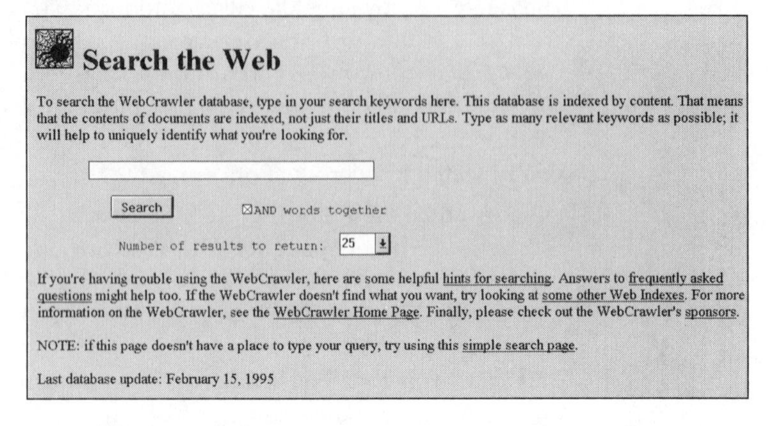

Type the search string **printers** in the search field and click on the **Search** button. By default, the WebCrawler returns a maximum of 35 hits on a specific search request. There may be many more possible pages that match your search request. Use the pull-down menu to change the number of hits you want to display if 35 is not enough. After a few seconds you should see the screen in Figure 4.27.

FIGURE 4.27

WebCrawler printers search results

WebCrawler Search Results

The WebCrawler is sponsored by DealerNet and Starwave. Please see the sponsor page for more details.

The query "printers" found 1032 documents and returned 25:

1000 Postscript Printer Status
0341 THE PRINTER WORKS -- Printers, Service, & Parts
0200 Color Printers
0184 4.5 GKS IMPLEMENTATIONS
0149 DMMIS Process/Procedures
0146 Core Solutions
0142 http://power.ncsa.uiuc.edu/Links/news/printers
0132 Printing in the EISL
0132 Laser Printers
0125 Cyber Zine --- Summer Edition 1994 Articles
0117 http://hpfrs6.physik.uni-freiburg.de/html/printer.html
0117 Printer Status on surf.cs.washington.edu
0113 http://smithers.gsfc.nasa.gov/Anonymous-Access/TCP-IP_on_Tektronics_Phaser_480
0112 Document TBA950117000
0111 LANÀÇ ÀâÁ¡
0107 http://xanadu.mgh.harvard.edu/Manual/peripherals
0104 Oceanography Printers

Notice the number beside each line in the display. The search engine makes an effort to help you locate a specific document that best matches your search. A 1000 means that the document should be a close match; a number lower than 1000 indicates a lower probability that this is the information you want. This score is based on where the term you entered was found within a document and other factors. For example, if the word you are seeking is in the title, there is a greater likelihood of a positive match than if the word is located only in the body of the document. Also, a higher score is assigned to a document that includes the most occurrences of the word you are searching for.

Notice the message at the top of the Search Results screen. This tells you who sponsors the WebCrawler search tool. The WebCrawler is not free, the message declares, then points you to information about the companies that are sponsoring the project.

Hmm. An interesting concept. Provide a very necessary and useful service, then promote your company, product, or service to those who use it. This is, in fact, typical of the history of the Internet. In the days when everything on the Internet was free, including access, you were expected to give something when you got something. This is how useful program utilities, technical documents, and other helpful Internet features got there and were shared among users.

Now that the Internet is moving toward commercialization, some of this convention may be passing, but not entirely. Here's another example. If you go to **http://crusher.net/education/Sea World/homepage.html**, you'll see the Sea World home page, shown in Figure 4.28.

FIGURE 4.28 Sea World Net page

Animal Information Data Base

Based on a long-term commitment to education, Sea World and Busch Gardens strive to provide an enthusiastic, imaginative, and intellectually stimulating atmosphere to help students reach their academic potential. Specifically our goals are...

- To instill in students of all ages an appreciation for science and a respect for all living creatures and natural environments.
- To conserve our valuable natural resources by increasing awareness of the interrelationships of humans and the environment.
- To increase students' basic competencies in science and other disciplines.
- To provide an educational resource for the entire community.

From here you can access—in addition to information about Sea World attractions—detailed information about a variety of sea animals. This Animal Information Data Base is based on Sea World research and provides a level of professional data that is difficult to find. You can use this information for research at no charge. But while you are there, you surely will read about the Sea World attractions, special events, prices, and schedules. Sea World is advertising, but they offer you something in return—a reason to visit their advertising page in the first place.

This may sound foreign, but it is not unlike magazine, newspaper, or television advertising. You view these ads as a coincidental part of reading articles or watching entertainment shows. It is a logical exchange: the sponsor pays for the material you read or watch, and all they ask in return is a chance to show you something about their company or product. The difference is that, in theory at least, articles and ideas presented in a magazine are free from influence by the sponsors who advertise in the publication. Likewise, television stations and networks are supposed to present news and documentaries in an environment that is free from advertiser bias.

After more than 20 years as a broadcast and print journalist, I believe that this separation may be mostly true, but it is certainly not flawless. Neither is the information you find on the World Wide Web completely objective. As with any research endeavor, view what you find with a critical eye and strive for multiple sources to validate your information.

I provide additional details on the World Wide Web and available software to help you access it in Chapter 5.

OTHER NETWORK TOOLS AND TECHNIQUES

I couldn't possibly tell you about every Internet utility. I've mentioned the major ones earlier in this chapter. In this section I will briefly introduce you to a few more tools you can use to help you in your Internet travels.

whois Information Tool

whois is another Internet database, and is also an application that helps you to search this database. This file stores a list of Internet users compiled and maintained by the DDN Network Information Center (NIC) at **nic.ddn.mil**—that's where the data is located. The client software that lets you access the information usually is stored on your local machine or on your Internet service provider's machine.

So when you type a command such as:

```
whois Tango
```

you access the client program whois on your local machine and tell it to send a request for information about users with the last name Tango to the **nic.ddn.mil** server. If your machine has the proper whois software client, you will get a screen display like the one in Figure 4.29. (I have substituted made-up information in this example.)

FIGURE 4.29

Typical whois Search Results (Tango)

```
Whois: Tango
Tango, Likado A. (LAT28)ltango@PICA.ARMY.MIL
   Army Armament Research Development
   and Engineering Center, Armament Munitions and Chemical Command
   Attn: SMCAR-ISE, Tango B/5031
   Picatinny Arsenal, NJ 07806-5001
   (201) 555-1212/6054 (DSN) 880-1212/6054
```

Note that you may get an error message instead of the answer you expect when you try to use whois. That's because some local sites have not updated the whois client software since the site where the information is stored was changed. This change occurred when the ARPAnet was retired. If your whois client software still tries to connect to the old ARPAnet host, you get an error message similar to the one in Figure 4.30.

FIGURE 4.30

whois Wrong Host Error Message

```
> whois tango

Putt's Law:
Technology is dominated by two types of people:
Those who understand what they do not manage.
Those who manage what they do not understand.
---------------------------------------------------------
Hi!  You have attempted to contact a whois server at SRI-NIC.ARPA.
Your WHOIS client program is either extremely old or your software
vendor is really out of it.  Please complain to them.
To contact the current DDN NIC WHOIS server, it will be
necessary to either:

a) Use a command-line option to tell your WHOIS client
   to connect to a different host (NIC.DDN.MIL),

b) Or, recompile WHOIS with the CORRECT name for the DDN NIC,
   NIC.DDN.MIL, in place of the ancient SRI-NIC.ARPA.

For further information about the DDN NIC, please contact the new
contractor, GSI, at 1-800-365-3642.  Thank You.
---------------------------------------------------------
[caw 91/09/24]
```

If this occurs, you may not be able to use your local whois client software (you may be able to enter a command line option to point the client to the proper location—contact your service provider), but you can still use whois by using Telnet to get to the database site. Enter this command at your service provider prompt:

```
telnet rs.internic.net
```

You should see a screen similar to the one in Figure 4.31.

FIGURE 4.31

nic.ddn.mil whois Log in Prompt

```
> telnet rs.internic.net
Trying 198.41.0.5 ...
Connected to rs.internic.net.
Escape character is '^]'.


SunOS UNIX (rs) (ttyp4)

*************************************************************************
* -- InterNIC Registration Services Center  --
*
* For gopher, type:                  GOPHER <return>
* For wais, type:                    WAIS <search string> <return>
* For the *original* whois type:     WHOIS [search string] <return>
* For the X.500 whois DUA, type:     X500WHOIS <return>
* For registration status:           STATUS <ticket number> <return>
*
* For user assistance call (800)444-4345|(619)455-4600 or (703)742-4777
* Please report system problems to ACTION@rs.internic.net
*************************************************************************
Please be advised that the InterNIC Registration host contains INTERNET
Domains, IP Network Numbers, ASNs, and Points of Contacts ONLY. Please
refer to rfc1400.txt for details (available via anonymous ftp at
either nic.ddn.mil [/rfc/rfc1400.txt] or ftp.rs.internic.net
[/policy/rfc1400.txt]).
Cmdinter Ver 1.3 Tue Aug 31 02:12:50 1993 EST
     [vt100] InterNIC >
```

Type **whois** at the prompt. You will be connected to a whois client at the remote host with the prompt **whois:**. From there you can enter names of Internet users to get more information about them.

The whois database doesn't track every Internet user. It only has about 70,000 to 100,000 entries for people who work on the Internet, maintaining it and configuring it. You may also find there the names of people conducting research about networking through Internet resources.

If you don't have access to Telnet and your local **whois** command isn't working properly, you can submit your request via email. To do this, send an email message to **mail service@nic.ddn.mil** and enter your **whois** command in the **Subject:** field of the message header. If you were looking for someone named Tango, for example, you would enter **whois Tango** in the **Subject:** field of your mail software. You won't get an immediate response this way, of course, but after the mail process has had time to work, you will receive an email message with the results of your query.

There are a couple more whois concepts worth mentioning. First of all, I have shown query examples that have only one result. You ask for a name and you get a single response with information about that individual. There may be times when you enter a name and get a list of several names with only minimal information. When this happens, issue a new query and enter the last name, a comma, and the first name from the list to get detailed information about a specific individual.

Also, there is information in the whois database besides just the name data I have demonstrated. You can search the whois files for information about networks or domains on the Internet. The process for finding this information is the same as when you are searching for a name, except that you enter the network entity you want to find. Also, you have to Telnet to a different location.

Suppose I wanted to know more about ORNL, which stands for the Oak Ridge National Laboratory, a government research and manufacturing facility at Oak Ridge, TN. I would enter a whois query such as:

```
whois Oak Ridge National Lab
```

The whois server returns a list like the one in Figure 4.32.

FIGURE 4.32
whois Search for Oak Ridge National Lab

```
Whois: Oak Ridge National Lab
Oak Ridge National Lab (NET-ORNL-NETB2)
   Oak Ridge, TN 37831

   Netname: ORNL-NETB2
   Netnumber: 134.167.0.0

   Coordinator:
      Maxwell, Don  (DM257)  MII@ORNL.GOV
      (615) 576-4182

   Domain System inverse mapping provided by:

   DNS-EAST.ES.NET                134.55.6.130
   MSR.EPM.ORNL.GOV               128.219.8.1
   NS1.LANL.GOV                   128.165.4.4

   Record last updated on 30-Jun-93.
```

You could try conducting a search for ORNL (or whatever abbreviation you know that the target entity uses), and you may or may not get a response. I entered **whois ORNL** and didn't find anything, so I tried **Oak Ridge National Lab** and got better results. Sometimes you get different results. I tried a **whois University of Tennessee** search and got about 70 networks listed in several cities across Tennessee.

Remember to turn on capture or logging software when you start searching with whois or any other tool. That way, when the information scrolls up the screen, you are capturing it in a file that you can review later with a text editor.

Here's an interesting search to try: **whois Whitehouse**. Try that and see what you get.

Finger

Finger is another information facility that is probably on your local system. It is used to display user information similar to whois, except that you have to know who is on a specific system for it to work. If you issue the finger command at your service provider prompt and follow it with the name of a user, you will get information displayed about that user.

For example, try using the finger command with your own login ID, like this:

```
finger tbadgett
```

You should get a display similar to the one in Figure 4.33.

FIGURE 4.33

Sample finger Display

```
> finger tbadgett
Login name: tbadgett  In real life: Tom  Badgett
Directory: /home/tbadgett           Shell: /usr/local/bin/tcsh
On since Aug 26 00:10:54 on ttyp0 from MARTHA.UTCC.UTK.
Mail last read Thu Aug 26 00:15:01 1993
No Plan.
```

If you issue the finger command without an argument, you will see a list of users currently on the system. However, you can use finger with users who are not currently logged on. If you want to see who has been using the system, try this command:

```
last -25
```

That will show you the login names and addresses of the last 25 logins. From that list you can pick a name and use finger to get more information. Finger should work with either the login name, first name, or last name of the person you're interested in. In fact, you can enter just about any information from the person's record and get a full display.

In addition, you can use finger across the network to get information about users on other systems, assuming you know enough about them for finger to locate the record. Simply include the destination system as part of the finger command:

```
finger tbadgett@usit.net
```

This may not always work, however, because individual systems may disable finger for security reasons. If you use the command I just showed you to finger a user at The WELL, for example (**finger tbadgett@well.sf.ca.us**), you will see a message such as:

```
Due to security and privacy considerations, the
WELL currently does not honor incoming finger
requests.
```

Other systems may say simply, **Connection refused**.

If it works, finger can provide an additional level of detailed information about the users with whom you interact on the Internet.

QUICK UNIX REFERENCE

Throughout your travels on the Internet, you will encounter UNIX command lines. UNIX is a rich operating system that handles the housekeeping chores on many of the hosts you use on the Internet. Appendix A is an annotated reference to UNIX commands (not all of them, just a select few). Here's a table (Table 4.2) that shows you the basic commands and what they do. They'll help you with a lot of what you need to navigate on the Internet. For more information on these commands, turn to Appendix A. In this table, items in angle brackets represent arguments that are added to the basic command.

TABLE 4.2

UNIX Command Summary

Command	Function
Bye	Logoff or cancel connection
cat <filename>	catenate file (display file)
cd <directoryname>	change directory to directoryname
cp <file1> <file2>	copy file1 file2
Ctrl-C	cancel process
Ctrl-D	terminate input
Ctrl-Z	suspend process
date	display current system date
ed <filename>	edit specified file
kill <project id>	kill specified process
Logout	terminate connection
ls	list files
mail address	send or read UNIX mail
man command	display command description
mkdir <directoryname>	make directory directoryname
ps	process status
pwd	working directory name
rm <file>	remove file
rx	receive XMODEM
rz	receive ZMODEM
sx	send XMODEM
sz	send ZMODEM
send <address>	send text to address
tar <-cf file.tar> <directory>	tape archive. Combine directory into single file.tar
w	(w)ho. Display user id and current activity
whereis <filename>	show location of filename
who	display user id and info

WHAT YOU LEARNED

The tools and utilities I have talked about in this chapter aren't the only ones that are available on the Internet, but they're enough for you to start finding your way around. As you travel, follow your fingertips, keep your eyes open, and make use of what else you find. Remember, I have touched on Archie, Gopher, and WAIS—software tools that help you locate other information on the Internet. I have shown you how to locate these facilities and how to use them to find what you need.

In the next chapter I'll spend some more time on Internet tools and facilities, showing how to locate these software utilities, and providing some information on configuring and using them. In particular, I'll show you details on several popular applications for navigating the Internet. You'll learn how to configure programs such as MacTCP, InterSLIP, Procomm Plus for PC users, and Trumpet Winsock as well as Netscape and NCSA Mosaic.

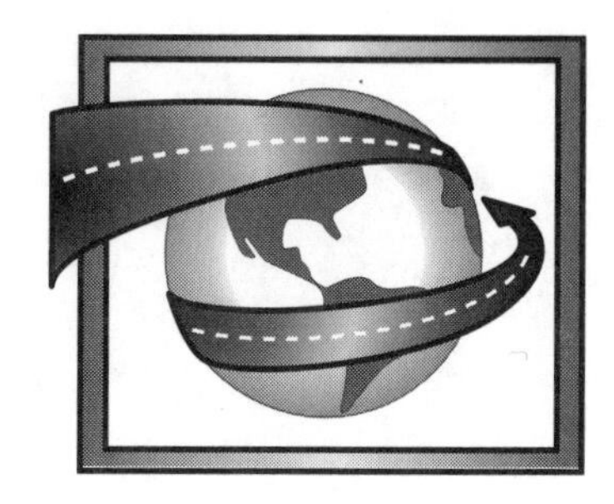

Chapter 5

Configurations for Internet Travel—Step-by-Step

The Internet today has risen above its early beginnings to provide an exciting, multimedia highway that can thrill travelers with text intermingled with color graphics, motion video, and sound. The World Wide Web (WWW) is becoming the route of choice to the Internet's wealth of information and fun. In this chapter I will show you in detail how to use a range of Internet applications including terminal emulation, SLIP connections for getting into the WorldWide Web, and the most popular Web browsers. Among the applications I'll introduce in this chapter are:

- NCSA Mosaic (Macintosh and PC)
- Netscape (Macintosh and PC)
- Chameleon (PC)

- Internet in a Box (PC)
- Trumpet Winsock/TCPMAN (PC)
- Eudora (Macintosh and PC)
- InterSLIP (Macintosh)
- MacTCP (Macintosh)
- Microsoft Windows Terminal (PC)
- DataStorm's Procomm (PC)
- ZTerm

Many of these applications change the way most of us navigate the net. These tools, designed to run on a PC or Macintosh, provide graphical applications, mouse support, color, sound and more.

Of course, some of this software is rather complex, and a complete discussion of it within a survey book such as this one is out of the question. And, there are more popular software packages than I can possibly find room for in a single chapter of one book. These limitations notwithstanding, in the following pages I will provide enough detail on many popular Internet navigational tools for you to be reasonably familiar with them if you try to use them with your local service provider's host.

TERMINAL EMULATION AND COMMUNICATIONS

One of the simplest and most common ways of accessing the Internet is through a conventional communications software package. This software enables your computer to communicate with a modem to send information over a dial-up telephone line.

This software turns your computer into a 'dumb' terminal, providing an interface with a remote computer where the processing actually takes place. When you type on the keyboard, data is sent out the computers serial port or through an internal modem, and over the telephone line link. Information that comes from the remote computer is displayed on your computer screen as if it were coming from your computer.

In addition to providing communications services, software of this type also enables your computer to emulate (act like) specific terminal hardware. Communications software may be capable of emulating many terminal types, but the most common emulation for Internet access is Digital Equipment Corporation VT-100 terminal emulation. You can use emulation for any terminal that includes VT-100 as a subset of the terminal being emulated, so emulators for VT-220, VT-320, and other terminals should work satisfactorily with an access provider that uses VT-100 emulation.

Where do you find terminal emulation and communications software? Nearly everywhere. When you bought a modem you probably also received some type of communications software as part of the package.

You can download shareware communications software from a number of sources but, of course, to be able to do that you need some type of communications software. If you have Microsoft Windows, you can use the Windows Terminal communications package. Actually, this is a fully functional utility, although its lack of a few desirable features keeps some people from making Terminal their primary, and only, communications software choice. In the next section I'll show you how to access and configure Windows Terminal for use on the Internet.

Windows Terminal

Windows Terminal is included with the other Windows utilities—Paintbrush, Write, Notepad—as a way of rounding out the operating environment package.

Terminal is communications software that allows your computer to send keyboard commands and receive video display information from remote computers through a modem or direct serial link. It is one of the dozens of popular and readily available communications software packages available for PC communications.

As with the other utilities, Terminal does not include all of the features you will find in a standalone, commercial package, but it is quite serviceable. For example, Terminal doesn't support the ZMODEM file transfer protocol. You don't have to have ZMODEM, of course, but it is one of the fastest and most functional of the current offerings. Also, Terminal lacks a dialing directory, which is a feature that lets you pre-program several host telephone numbers and configuration data so you can dial these hosts by selecting from a list.

Terminal does support Kermit and XMODEM, other popular transfer protocols. And, you can type in one phone number that you can use to connect to your favorite Internet access provider.

The Terminal default configuration assumes you will use XMODEM protocol and VT-100 terminal emulation. However, to be successful with a variety of Internet service providers and hosts, you should consider making a few changes. I'll summarize those in the following steps.

1. From the Terminal Settings menu choose **Binary Transfers**. Click on the **Kermit** button on the next dialog.
2. Click on **OK** to close this dialog box. Now your Terminal System is set for Kermit transfers, a protocol almost certain to be available on any Internet host machine you use.
3. Click on **Settings** and choose **Terminal Preferences**.
4. Uncheck the **Use Function, Arrow and Ctrl Keys for Windows** check box by clicking on the box. (This is the last line on the dialog box.) This change makes your cursor keys operate properly during VT-100 emulation.
5. Click on **OK** to accept these changes.
6. Click on **Settings** and choose **Communications**.
7. Specify the proper communications parameters for your hardware. The defaults on this screen usually are correct, except that you should turn off XON/XOFF flow control and choose **Hardware Flow Control**. This provides the surest and fastest connection, but make sure you are using a modem cable with enough connections to support hardware flow control. Some modem cables have only three wires con-

nected; this will not support hardware flow control. If in doubt, check with your dealer.

NOTE

Connector on this dialog box means the port to which your modem is attached. This usually will be COM2: or COM4:

8. Click on **OK** to accept these changes.
9. Click on **Phone Number** and enter the phone number of your local access provider.
10. Change the 30 in the **Timeout if not connected** field of this dialog to **60**. This gives you 60 seconds instead of 30 seconds to get a connection if the host you call is a little slow in finishing the modem connection after the phone answers.
11. Click on **OK** to close the Phone dialog box.
12. Click on **File** and choose **Save As...**
13. Type a file name that you can remember easily, and press **Enter**. This stores the settings you have just entered in a named file that Terminal can access during startup.

Next time you use Terminal, use **File Open** and specify the file name you used to save the configuration information. This will reload the configuration information so you don't have to enter it again.

TRAVEL TIP

You can exit Terminal now and use File Properties from the Program Manager menu to add the configuration file name to the end of the Command Line field. Your command line should read like this: terminal.exe configname.trm. Now when you load Terminal the configuration file will be loaded automatically.

You are now ready to use Terminal to contact your Internet service provider. Simply click on **Phone** on the main menu, then choose **Dial**. Terminal will automatically dial the access number you entered on the configuration screen earlier. When the host answers, type your **user ID** and **password**, and you are logged on.

Downloading a File with Terminal

To use Kermit to download a file, type **Kermit** at the service provider prompt. The host should display the **Kermit>** prompt. If this is a binary file (one that contains anything other than plain text, such as a word processor file or a spreadsheet), then issue this configuration command at the **Kermit>** prompt:

```
set file type binary
```

This will tell Kermit that you want to download a non-text file. Now, type **send <filename>**, and press the **Enter** or **Return** key. Kermit will start trying to send the specified file to your computer. You may see random characters on your screen after the Kermit prompt.

Now, click on **Transfers** on the Terminal main menu and choose **Receive Binary File** to display a typical Windows file management dialog box. Specify a path and a file name for the incoming file and click on **OK**. Terminal opens a status line at the bottom of the screen to show the progress of the transfer.

Uploading a File with Terminal

To upload a file from your computer to the host, the process is almost the same. Once you have launched Kermit and set the file type to **binary** (if you are transferring a binary file), type **receive** at the **Kermit>** prompt. Kermit will prompt you to return to your local system and issue the **send** command in Kermit.

Binary files are those created by most word processors, spreadsheet programs, database programs and other applications, as well as any program file. Even though the file you want to send appears to be text inside the application that created it, if you look at it in DOS (on a PC) you will see lots of strange characters and symbols. A text file is one that can be read with the DOS Type command, for example.

Click on **Transfers** on the Terminal menu and choose **Send Binary File** to display a Windows file management dialog box. Specify the path and file name of the file you want to send to the host. Again, Terminal will open a status display at the bottom of the screen so you can track the progress of the transfer.

Procomm (PC)

DataStorm's Procomm series is among the most popular communications packages available for the PC. It started as shareware, and was frequently downloaded from bulletin boards and other online services. As its popularity grew, the company developed documentation, added features, and offered the product in a commercial version for sale. The shareware version continues to be shared among online enthusiasts, but the DOS- and Windows-based versions of Procomm also do very well.

One reason is the excellent terminal emulation provided by Procomm software. When you choose a VT-series terminal from the Procomm configuration screen, for example, that's what you get. Another reason is Procomm's support for a wide range of file transfer protocols. And, Procomm —shareware, commercial, DOS, or Windows—offers a clean, uncluttered screen that is easy to learn and to use. Besides, Procomm just seems to work. I, myself, have used the shareware and commercial versions for years and find that Procomm frequently works when other products don't. See Figure 5.1 for a sample Procomm screen.

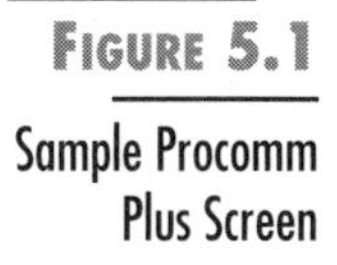

FIGURE 5.1

Sample Procomm Plus Screen

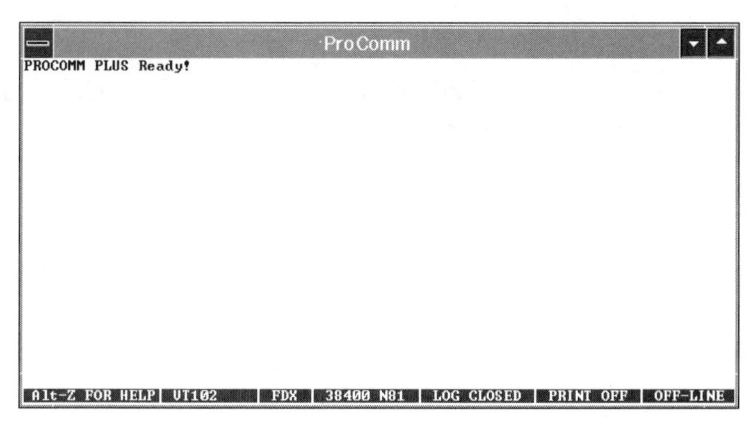

For the most part, Procomm probably is configured to work with your hardware out of the box. However, this product also contains a number of useful configuration features that let you customize it for use with just about any computer/modem combination. You can view the configuration (setup) main menu by pressing the **Alt+S** keystroke combination if you are using the DOS version of Procomm (see Figure 5.2).

FIGURE 5.2

Procomm Setup Menu Screen

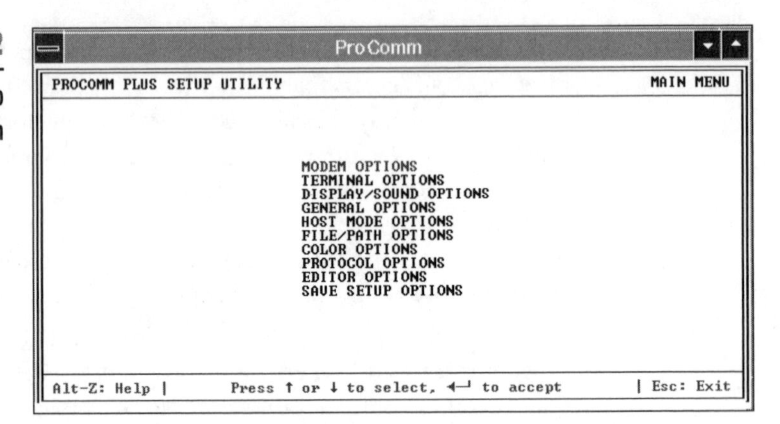

You can choose from this menu list by using the cursor keys to move up and down the list. If you are using the Windows version of Procomm, select from the Windows menu to manipulate the program.

The DOS and Windows versions of Procomm are significantly different in the way they operate, but the end result is very similar. Also, there are several versions of this software in common use. If the screens you see when you use Procomm don't look just like the ones in this book, it just means you are using a different version of the software.

To set terminal emulation, for example, choose **Terminal Options** from the main setup menu. This displays the Terminal Setup screen shown in Figure 5.3.

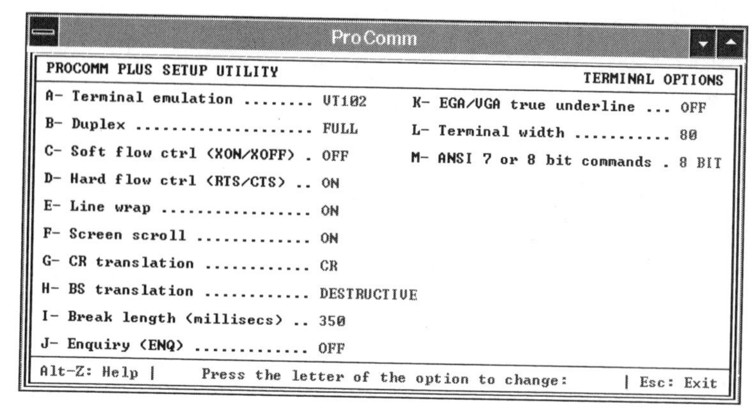

FIGURE 5.3 Procomm Plus for DOS Terminal Setup Screen

The default terminal type is probably ANSI; for most Internet access you should specify a VT-type terminal. You can see from Figure 5.3 that I have set my Procomm in this example to VT-102, a good choice for using most Internet services in text terminal mode.

To change any item on a Procomm menu, press the letter beside the item you want to change, enter the new value, and press **Enter**. This changes the value and returns you to the setup screen. To exit one of the setup screens, press **Esc**.

Choose **Save** from a setup menu to retain any new settings for the next session; press **Esc** without saving first to keep the changes only during the current session.

Procomm also has other pop-up screens that help you set the modem port you want to use, the number of data bits, baud rate, and so on. Display a general communications setting screen by pressing **Alt+P** (see Figure 5.4).

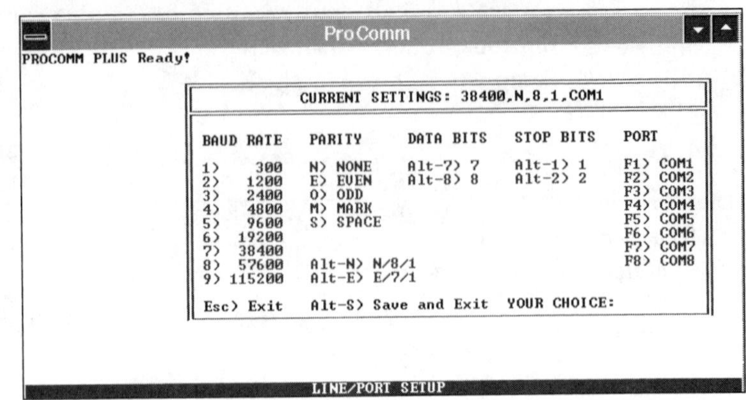

FIGURE 5.4 Procomm Plus for DOS Communications Settings Screen

Once you have set the terminal type, baud rate, modem port, and data bits, the rest of Procomm should work with almost any hardware configuration. You can use any of the other Procomm menus to make additional configuration changes if you wish.

For most online services—and particularly Internet service providers—you will want to set your communications software for 8 data bits, no parity, and one stop bit. This is sometimes called an 8N1 setting. Baud rate is the speed of the communications. If you have a 14.4K baud modem, for example, you should set your communications software for a speed of at least 19.2K baud. This allows modem compression protocols to improve actual communications throughput.

Downloading a File with Procomm

Procomm supports a wide variety of file transfer protocols. To use one of them to download a file, start the download process on the host, then press **Page Down** to display the protocol screen shown in Figure 5.5.

FIGURE 5.5

Procomm Plus for DOS File Transfer Protocol Screen

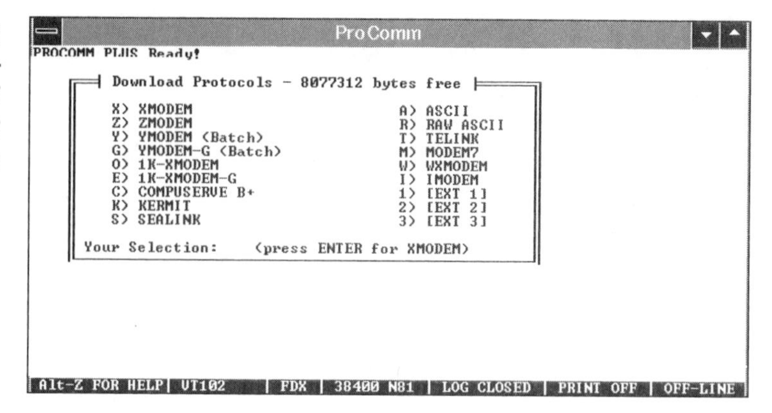

If you're using Procomm for BBS access, you may use several of these protocols, but when accessing the Internet you'll most likely use ZMODEM or Kermit.

With most ZMODEM protocols, the receive portion of the link is launched automatically. In other words, when you start ZMODEM on the host, Procomm will open a file transfer window automatically and start the file transfer. (See Figure 5.6).

FIGURE 5.6

Procomm for DOS ZMODEM File Transfer Dialog Box

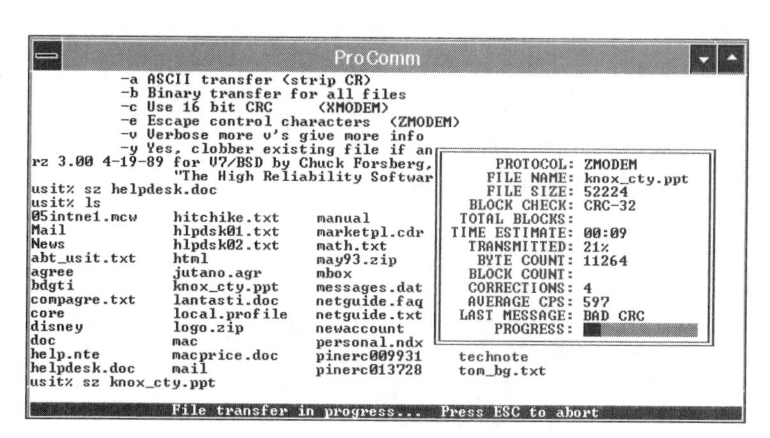

The same feature works with Kermit with most Kermit hosts, so that you don't need to do anything except start the transfer on the host to complete it on your PC.

Unlike Windows Terminal, discussed earlier, Procomm automatically downloads files into the preset download directory. If you don't know where to find your downloaded files, use File/Path Options menu from the setup menu to display the file/path options screen. This screen shows the default download path. That's where you'll find downloaded files.

If you want to start the download process yourself, without Procomm launching Kermit automatically, disable the automatic download feature by displaying the Protocol Options menu and specifying **Auto Downloading Off** on the appropriate protocol screen. This will let you specify a different file name from the originating file.

Uploading a File with Procomm

Uploading a file with Procomm is very similar to the download process. In this case, you start the receive portion of the link on the host by typing **receive** at the Kermit prompt, or by using the **rz** command to start the ZMODEM transfer.

Remember that with Kermit you must specify whether you want to receive a binary or text file.

Then press **Page Up** on the PC keyboard to display the File Transfer Protocol screen. Choose the appropriate protocol, then type the path and file name in the file name dialog box. Procomm starts the transfer and displays the programs in a window similar to the download dialog box.

ZTerm (Macintosh)

ZTerm is to the Macintosh what Procomm Plus is to the PC world. ZTerm is a popular and capable shareware communications and terminal emulator package for the Mac. It is a typical online tool that supports common file transfer protocols such as ZMODEM, XMODEM and YMODEM, and provides ANSI-BBS and VT-100 terminal emulation.

ZTerm is available from many Internet service providers for download and evaluation. If you decide to keep and use the product, then you owe a registration fee of $30 for registration alone, or $40 for registration and a disk.

After copying the ZTerm application from a floppy and downloading it directly into the folder where you wish to use it, you will need to conduct at least some configuration operations to get ready to use it.

The items in the top part of the Settings menu let you configure options for the currently selected service; the items in the bottom part of the menu let you configure global options for using ZTerm. From this section you can set modem preferences, for example, including the desired initialization string. You can specify such general preferences as display font and download text type. You can also set the default download folder for information downloaded from an online service, and you can choose color support if you have a color monitor.

For each service you want to use, including your local Internet service, it is simplest to add a service to the ZTerm directory. In general, here's how to add a service:

1. From the Dial menu, select **Directory.**
2. Click on the **New** button.
3. Enter the name for the new service
4. Enter the dialin phone number for the service.
5. Specify a communications data rate for this service. In general, you should specify the highest terminal rate your modem supports in this field. A value of 38,400 is probably a good choice for 14.4 Kbaud modems and above.
6. Choose **8 data bits**, **no parity** and **one stop bit**. This is the most common setting for Internet service providers. Choose something different only if you know for certain that your provider users something different.

7. Choose **hardware handshaking,** the most efficient setting for most modern modems. If you use this option, however, make sure you have a complete modem cable, one that supports hardware handshaking.
8. Click on **OK** to close the current dialog and display the dialing directory. The new entry should appear in the dialing list.
9. Select the new entry and click on the Terminal button to display the **Terminal** Settings Dialog.
10. Choose VT-100 terminal emulation and click on **OK.**
11. Click on the **Set** button to load the settings for the new service and display them in the Settings window.
12. Close the Directory window.
13. From the Settings menu, choose **Transfer Options.**
14. Choose the file transfer protocol. ZMODEM is probably the best choice for Internet service. You can also adjust the configuration of the ZMODEM service in ZTerm if you find it necessary, but the defaults are probably satisfactory.
15. Click on **OK** to save the current settings.

Once you have configured a new service, you can dial it to login by choosing the service name from the Dial menu, or by highlighting the service name in the Dialing Directory window and then clicking on the **Dial** button.

Downloading Files with ZTerm

Most Internet service providers support ZMODEM file transfer protocol and, if it is available, this is the one you should use. ZMODEM has at least two advantages in ZTerm over other protocol options. For one thing, ZTerm's ZMODEM protocol will launch automatically when the host starts the transfer. In addition, ZMODEM is generally faster and more reliable than other available options.

To download a file with ZMODEM protocol using a command line, type **sz** filename, where filename is the name of the file. (If you're not in the same directory as the file you wish to download, you'll have to specify the full pathname as well as the filename.) A progress gauge will be displayed, showing you the status of the download. When complete, the file can be found in the location you specified in the Receive Folder... option of the Settings menu.

If your service provider does not supply a command line interface, consult their instructions for starting file transfers.

To download a file with a different protocol, enter the command to the host machine to begin downloading the file. Then, select the **Receive Files** sub-menu item in the File menu, and choose the protocol. The file will be downloaded as described above.

If you are using XMODEM or another protocol that doesn't launch automatically on ZTerm, you must start the transfer on ZTerm after you have started the download on the host. Do this by pulling down the File menu and choosing the protocol you are using from the Receive files sub menu.

Uploading Files with ZTerm

In general, the procedure to upload a file is similar to the procedure to download a file. To upload a file using the ZMODEM protocol, type **rz** at the command line. You should see a prompt like "rz ready. To begin transfer, type "sz file ..." to your modem program." Select **Send ZModem...** from the File menu. A regular Macintosh dialog box will be displayed. Locate and select the files you wish to send. Once a file is selected, the transfer will begin.

To upload a file using a different protocol, issue the receive command for that protocol. Then, select the **Send Files** sub-menu item from the File menu and choose the protocol you're using. After you select a protocol, the dialog box described above will be displayed.

If your service provider does not supply a command line interface, consult their instructions for starting file transfers.

Evaluating Communications Software

Obviously, there are numerous other communications software offerings that you may acquire as part of a modem or computer purchase, or that you choose because of the specific features they offer. Most of today's offerings will do the basic job of providing a text screen in which you can navigate menus, enter UNIX commands, and transfer files.

There are a few things to watch out for, however. For one thing, be aware that not all communications software does a credible job of terminal emulation. Most packages perform adequately in ANSI or TTY format, but when they are called to emulate a VT-series terminal they don't perform as well. This can mean that the screen isn't always formatted properly, that the cursor keys may not work as you expect, or that other problems surface.

Sometimes you can solve these problems by creating a new session profile and specifying new settings for terminal emulation. Sometimes, even after you have changed terminal emulation, the program doesn't operate as you expect. You can try exiting the software, then launching it again. Sometimes software loads configuration information when it starts, then neglects to load it again when changes are made.

You can find a wide variety of workable terminal emulation and communications software for all computer platforms. If you don't like the way the software you have operates, or if it performs poorly, don't get stuck with it. Ask your service provider what software they recommend, query fellow users on the system through email or newsgroups, and study advertisements and catalogues to determine what options are available to you.

TCP (Networking) Software

Communications software such as Procomm or ZTerm normally is used to connect to a host with a text-based link. Through terminal emulation your computer is turned into a dumb terminal. You use the keyboard and display as a window into the host. The computing is done on the host.

An alternative to dialup, 'dumb' terminal connections is to make your desktop computer part of a remote network. This type of Internet connection has several advantages over a terminal connection. For one thing, when you connect to the Internet via a network link, your computer has its own Internet address. That means you can FTP files directly to your machine instead of going to a host first. It also means that other Internet users can send information directly to your machine. And—perhaps the most desirable reason of all—a network connection lets you use many popular graphical browsers for the World Wide Web, electronic mail and news.

If you want to make your computer part of a remote network—including the Internet—you need a network connection to a host. This connection is conducted through TCP/IP (transmission control protocol/Internet protocol) in the UNIX and Internet environment. When you connect your computer to a host using TCP/IP over a dial-up link, you may be using SLIP (serial line Internet Protocol) or PPP (point to point protocol) software to control the link.

There are a number of dial-up TCP software options. As with communications software, there are too many for me to discuss them all. I will show you the basics of a few common offerings. With the information in the following sections you should be able to configure one of these packages for use with your Internet host, or, at the very least, to gather enough data to help you ask the right questions to get things working properly.

Before You Begin

Whatever type of TCP software you are using, there are certain facts you will need before you can configure it successfully. This information, such as your assigned IP address, should be supplied by your service provider when you sign up for your account. If not, you should ask for this data. A list of fundamental information you will need is shown in Table 5.1. The examples shown are for illustration only. You must secure the correct data for your account from your service provider.

TABLE 5.1
Basic TCP/IP Configuration Information

Required Data	Example
Personal IP Address	199.1.48.3
Network Mask	255.255.255.0
Default Gateway	199.1.48.64
Domain Name Server (DNS)	199.1.48.2
SMTP (Mail) Server use.usit.net	199.1.48.3 or
NNTP News Server news.usit.net	199.1.48.11or
POP Mail Server:	199.1.48.3
Gopher Server:	199.1.48.3
SMTP Mail Server:	199.1.48.3
Domain Name:	usit.net
Your Email Address:	UserID@usit.net
MTU (Max. transfer unit size):	1006
Your Domain Name:	userid.ppp.usit.net

You may not need all of this data for every setup, and you may find that your service provider and your software use different names for some of these same terms. Once you have this information, it becomes relatively easy to configure your TCP software.

Trumpet Winsock (PC)

The Trumpet Winsock series for the PC is one of the most popular of all TCP software offerings for the IBM PC platform. It is a readily available shareware utility that you can download from your service provider's host computer. If they don't have it, ask them to get it, or ask them where you can get it. Trumpet Winsock was written by Peter R. Tattam.

Trumpet Winsock is composed of three major components:

- **WINSOCK.DLL** is a TCP driver that provides the real functionality of this package. WINSOCK.DLL is a file that resides in your Windows directory, where it can be called as necessary to provide the required network data exchange.
- **TCPMAN.EXE** is an executable front end for the TCP drivers. TCPMAN is the user interface to the TCP link. You use TCPMAN to dial the modem and to display the response of your Internet host computer after the connection is made.
- **SCRIPT FILES** are standard text files that automate the dialing and hang-up process. You can bypass these scripts by dialing and hanging up the phone manually, but these scripts make the process a lot easier. The scripts included with TCPMAN can be customized for your host, phone number, and account.

Configuring TCPMAN

To view the TCPMAN Setup dialog box, double-click on the TCPMAN icon in Program Manager to launch the program and display the main TCPMAN screen. Now display the TCPMAN Setup dialog box by clicking on **File** and choosing **Setup** from the pull-down menu. You will see a configuration screen like the one in Figure 5.7.

FIGURE 5.7
TCPMAN Setup Dialog Box

Notice that the title of this dialog box is Network Configuration. Let's look at its pertinent fields.

At the top of this dialog box is the **IP address** field. This holds the numerical identifier for your computer. At U.S. Internet, your personal IP address probably will begin with **199.1**. These numbers identify the major network of which U.S. Internet—and your computer—are a part. The last two numbers in this set further identify the network subset and your individual machine. So, you may have an IP address that ends in **60.254**, as in the example. In this case your machine is number **254** in subnet **60**.

The **Netmask** value is tied to the class of network used by your provider. In most cases this will be a class C network, so the netmask value will be **255.255.255.0**.

The **Name server** field on this dialog box holds the machine identifier (IP Address) for the name server. The Internet consists of millions of computers, each one with its own name and IP address. A list of these machines that shows their names and addresses must be maintained at some location. Name servers are located in many places around the Internet. Most service providers, including U.S. Internet, maintain a name server at the host location. The names and addresses of the provider's client machines are stored on this name server, and so are the names and addresses of many other machines across the Internet.

However, with millions of machines in use at any one time, it would be impossible and impractical for any one name server to store all of the names. Therefore, a single name server maintains a cache of the most frequently asked for addresses, along with some of the most recently asked for addresses. When an application asks a name server for an address, the server first looks to its local cache, then searches a lookup table for the appropriate secondary location for certain types of addresses.

From there, servers in multiple locations may be searched to arrive at the ultimate destination.

NOTE

It is always a good idea to specify your local name server when configuring software. The machines you are most likely to access probably are stored there, for one thing, and you will get a faster response from a local name server than if your application has to search across the Internet for the proper machine address.

As your service provider adds new machines, they are added to the name server. As other machines are added in other locations, name servers across the Internet automatically exchange this information so that all of the servers remain up to date. Every address of every machine is not stored on every name server, but information on where to get the proper addresses should always be available.

You can either enter the machine name for the domain name server, or use the IP address. Your service provider should provide this information to you when you create your account.

The **Domain Suffix** is the name of the Internet domain from which you are getting your service. For U.S. Internet, for example, the domain suffix is **usit.net**.

The **Default Gateway** holds the IP address of the computer or router to which your computer connects on its way to the Internet. This number varies depending on your information provider, which location you are using, and so on. For example, the default gateway for U.S. Internet's Knoxville host is **199.1.48.64**, whereas the U.S. Internet Nashville host is **199.1.54.16**.

The **Packet vector** is the network interrupt used on a local area network link. As a SLIP user (networking over a dial-up telephone line, remember) you will set this value to **zero**. If you are using an Ethernet connection, you'll probably set this value to **60** (or whatever your packet driver software is set to use).

The **MTU** field (Maximum Transfer Units) specifies the maximum number of **bytes** (sometimes called **octets** in networking terminology) that can be transferred at one time. This value varies according to the type of network being used, but for most Internet SLIP or PPP connections the appropriate value is **1006**. If you are using TCPMAN/Winsock over a local area network, you'll probably use a value of **1500**.

The **TCP RWIN** value is set for **4096** and defines the configuration for the reply window. The reply window setting is used for host/client confirmation interaction. A setting of 4096 means one computer can send 4096 bytes before expecting a reply. This setting is a good general purpose setting that allows reply and confirmation, but it doesn't require continuous responses, thereby improving throughput. This 4096 setting is the maximum available with the current standard, but there is talk in the industry of increasing this maximum.

The **TCP MSS** field sets the Maximum Segment Size that can be exchanged between your computer and the Internet. In TCP/IP networking, a segment is the basic unit of data transfer between two machines. The maximum segment size is established so that two machines agree in advance on the maximum size of the segments they are willing to handle.

The **Demand Load Timeout** specifies how many seconds TCPMAN will wait to establish a connection before it times out and disconnects.

The **TCP RTO MAX** value should be **60**, for most installations. This is a response time out value, which is the time one machine waits for confirmation from a remote machine. A shorter value could cause unnecessary timeouts; a very large value could mean unnecessary delays.

At the bottom of this dialog box are settings that specify how the SLIP connection will be managed. Internal SLIP or Internal PPP are checked to indicate the type of network connection. Internal SLIP is probably checked in your default setup values. If you want to try PPP instead, click on the PPP box. If your service provider supports PPP, you can compare the two protocols. You may have to check with your service provider on configuration specifics.

As this book is written, the Trumpet Winsock PPP utility is not as stable and functional as it should be. Until a new version that does a better job of PPP support is available, you should stick with SLIP when you use this package.

The **SLIP Port** value specifies which port your modem is using. The number **1** in this field means your system is using COM1:, for example, whereas a **2** in this field means COM2: is in use, and so on.

The **Baud Rate** field specifies the communications rate to be used between your computer and the modem. It is a good idea to set the baud rate higher than your modem is capable of to achieve maximum transfer rates. Most modern modems support data compression. If you send and receive data from your computer at a rate faster than the design speed of your modem, then your modem and the host modem can negotiate for compression protocol. For example, a 14.4 Kbps modem can achieve transfer rates of 19.2 Kbps or greater under ideal line conditions and when hooked up to a host modem that supports compatible compression.

To achieve the highest modem-to-modem throughput, you should let the modems themselves decide how much data to send and how fast. This is called hardware handshake. The **Hardware Handshake** check box should be enabled on your TCPMAN setup dialog box.

Hardware handshaking requires a modem cable designed to support hardware handshaking. If you have problems you probably are using a modem cable that does not include enough wires. Buy a new cable.

Just as you can use modem-to-modem compression to improve data throughput, the SLIP connection itself can include compression for faster communications. If your host supports compressed SLIP, then make sure the **Van Jacobson CSLIP compression** check box is enabled.

The **Online Status Detection** group specifies how TCP-MAN will determine whether or not your modem is connected to the phone line. For best results you should ensure that **DCD** (Data Carrier Detect) **check** is enabled.

If you make any changes to information on this Setup dialog box, then click on **OK.** The setup values will be saved and TCP-MAN will warn you that you must restart the program for the changes to take effect.

You will get this warning even if you didn't make any changes to the Setup dialog box. If you made no changes, then you don't need to restart TCPMAN. However, if there is any doubt, restart the software.

The File Menu

Although TCPMAN will be almost fully automatic for most users, the standard, Windows-type menu lets you control some TCPMAN features when the need arises.

There are five options on the TCPMAN File menu. The first choice, **Setup**, is discussed in the previous section.

File Register

The second choice is **Register**, which displays the dialog box shown in Figure 5.8.

FIGURE 5.8

TCPMAN File Register Dialog Box

Remember that TCPMAN is a shareware product. You are free to use it for evaluation, but if you decide to keep TCPMAN you should register it with the writer and pay the modest registration fee. Writing and distributing software such as this requires a lot of time and dedication. If you use it you should pay for it.

To register your copy of TCPMAN, type the name under which you want to register the product in the **Registration Name** field of this dialog box.

File Firewall Setup

In computer parlance, a Firewall is a method of isolating one computer or computer system from other systems. Firewalls are established to enhance security on one or more machines.

By default, no Firewall is established in TCPMAN. The Firewall Setup dialog box shown in Figure 5.9 is available with TCPMAN, but you'll need help and cooperation from your service provider to make this work.

FIGURE 5.9

TCPMAN Firewall Setup Dialog Box

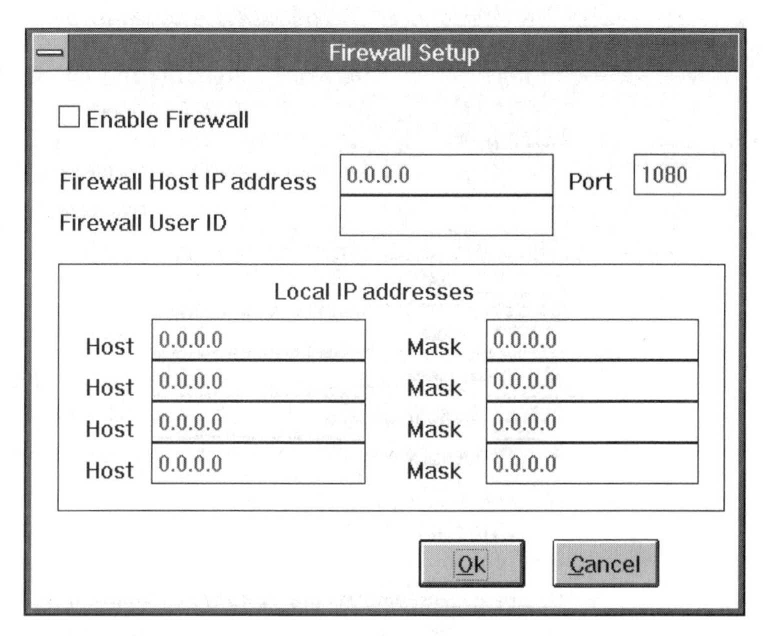

Click on the **Enable Firewall** check box to enable the Firewall, then fill in the required information on this dialog box.

File PPP Options

If you are using PPP (Point to Point Protocol) instead of SLIP, you may want to fill in some of the options on the PPP Authentication Options dialog box, shown in Figure 5.10.

FIGURE 5.10

TCPMAN PPP Authentication Options Dialog Box

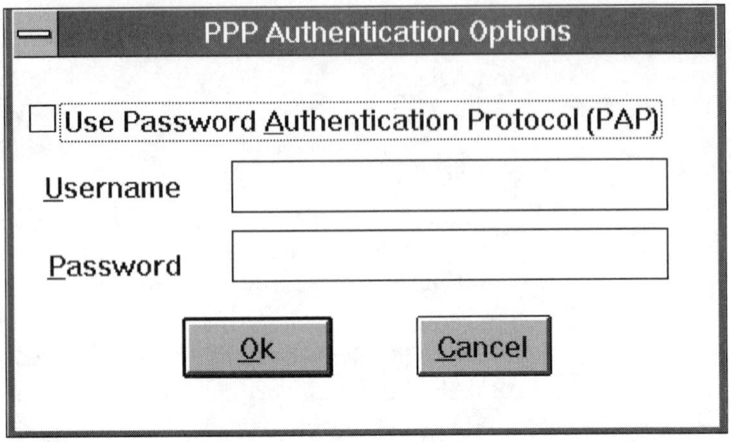

Specify whether you want to use **PAP** (Password Authentication Protocol), then enter your **Username** and **Password** before clicking on **OK** to close this dialog box and complete the PPP configuration. Whether to use PAP and what to put in the PAP field is dependent on your service provider. As with many configuration settings in online communications software, setting up TCPMAN will require information and help from your service provider.

File Exit

As with other Windows products, click on the **Exit** menu item under File (or press **x** with the File menu displayed) to close TCPMAN.

Before exiting TCPMAN, you should use the **Dialer Bye** command to run the script that closes the SLIP connection.

Sometimes when you are attempting to close TCPMAN you may get an error message saying that the program is still busy dialing. This may or may not be true. In any case, when you get this message, press the **ESC** key, then re-issue the **File Exit** command. The program should close normally at this point.

The Edit Menu

The TCPMAN Edit menu is a simple one, with only two choices, **Copy** and **Clear**.

Edit Copy

The **Copy** menu choice works as you might expect. It copies any text selected in the main TCPMAN window to the Clipboard. From the Clipboard you can paste this information into another Windows-compliant application, such as the text editor inside your mail reader. You probably won't want to do this, but you could to help track problems or to share system responses with someone else who is helping you debug your system.

Edit Clear

Use the **Clear** command on the TCPMAN Edit menu to erase the text from the TCPMAN terminal window. The Clear command removes any script, host prompt, or user typing that may be on this screen.

The Special Menu

The Special menu contains two choices, **Info** and **Kill Socket**.

Special Info

Use the **Info** menu choice to display information on socket use and socket availability.

Special Kill Socket

The **Kill Socket** command is used to disable one or more TCP socket connections. A socket is simply the logical port used for the current application that is running over the TCP network link. You may want to purposefully kill a socket if an application goes awry and you want to shut it off.

The Trace Menu

The choices from the Trace menu are used to debug or fine-tune your dial-up IP connection. These are toggles, either **on** or **off**. When you choose one of the trace items, a check mark is placed beside that entry on the Trace menu. With one or more trace items enabled, the results of the trace are displayed in the TCP-MAN window as the program runs.

When you select one of the items on the Trace menu, it may appear as if nothing has happened. However, if you click on the Trace menu again, you will see that a check mark has been placed beside the chosen item.

You will use one or more items on the Trace menu to debug your TCP connection. If you don't know what these various terms mean, then you'll need help from your service provider. Indeed, you aren't likely to need these trace utilities, particularly with a telephone line connection.

The Dialer Menu

Use the Dialer menu to start the login or bye scripts, to set some program options, and to edit the scripts. Also, in the current version of TCPMAN, this menu is misspelled dialler.

Dialer Login

Choosing this menu item causes the **login.cmd** script to execute. This text file controls the dialing and login process in TCPMAN. When this script finishes, TCPMAN should report "SLIP Enabled," which is your cue to shrink the TCPMAN application window to an icon and to get on with using one or more utilities such as Mosaic or FTP.

TCPMAN is usually downloaded with a script of some kind included in the archive. Some service providers create a custom script to make it even easier to log in. However, the basic script should get you online.

If you want to stop the script before dialing and login are complete, press the ESC key. This should halt the script and cause TCPMAN to report "Script Aborted." Then, depending on the state of your modem and where in the script you pressed ESC, you may see a message that says "SLIP ENABLED," or a message that says "SLIP DISABLED." In all likelihood you do not have a valid SLIP connection, no matter what the screen says. If you have an external modem, see if the OH (off hook) light is lit. If so, you may, indeed, be online; if not, you definitely are not. You can cancel the connection by pressing ESC again, then clicking on Dialer and choosing Bye from this menu. This will execute the hang-up script and should disconnect your modem if it is connected to a host.

Dialer Bye

This menu choice executes a second script, **bye.cmd**, which places your modem in command mode by sending three closely spaced plus signs (+++), then issuing the hang-up command **ATH0**.

You can use the **bye.cmd** to disconnect from a host at any time. However, there may be times when the command doesn't execute successfully. If this happens, try pressing **ESC** once or twice before issuing the bye command again. Eventually you should be able to gain control of the program and cause it to disconnect from the host, hanging up your modem.

Dialer Other

The **Other** menu choice on the Dialer menu lets you choose another script file to execute. The login.cmd and bye.cmd scripts appear on the Dialer menu, but you can load and execute any script file with the **Other** menu choice.

You might want to design a script to log in to an alternate host, for example. If this host is one you don't use often, you won't want it in the standard login.cmd position, but you may want to have access to it for occasional use.

Dialer Manual login

Using manual login is another way to attach to an occasional host, or to eliminate configuration problems as a cause of login difficulties.

When you choose this menu item, TCPMAN displays this message:

```
Manually dialing.
AFTER LOGGING IN, TYPE THE <ESC> KEY TO RETURN TO
NORMAL SLIP PROCESSING.
SLIP DISABLED
```

If you have selected PPP instead of SLIP, the message is slightly different:

```
AFTER LOGGING IN, TYPE THE <ESC> KEY TO RETURN TO
NORMAL SLIP PROCESSING.
PPP DISABLED
```

A blinking cursor is then positioned on the next line of the display. Now you can interact directly with your modem by typing **AT** commands to reset or configure the modem and to issue dialing commands.

NOTE

If you attempt to type modem commands and get no response, the SLIP port specified on the TCPMAN Setup dialog box may be incorrect, TCPMAN may be busy doing something else, or there may be another problem with your modem. Make sure the modem is connected and turned on, ensure that no other program such as a FAX receive utility is running, and confirm correct modem configuration. If you are sure the SLIP port is correct and that nothing else is wrong, try pressing ESC, then issue the Dialer Bye command to make sure the modem is on hook and ready to receive commands.

Generally you should reset the modem first, either by returning the configuration to factory defaults or by recalling the user-specified settings stored in non-volatile RAM.

To return to factory defaults, type **at&f** and press **Enter**. You should see OK on the screen. This recalls a series of factory settings that determine how the modem functions. These factory settings should be correct for most installations. However, you may have stored special settings into the modem's non-volatile RAM. If so, you can recall them by typing **atz** and pressing **Enter**. Again, the modem should respond with OK.

Now you can dial the host telephone number by entering **atdt** followed by the phone number. If the line you are using has call waiting, precede the number with ***70**, to disable this feature during the current call. If you are calling from inside a business where you must dial **9** for an outside line, then place a 9 and a **comma** before the number. If you need both of these dialing additions, make sure to enter the **9**, first to secure an outside line before trying to disable call waiting.

When the host answers, log in as you would for any manual session. You probably will be asked for a user ID and a password, and then you may be given a menu choice for starting a SLIP session.

When the SLIP connection is established remember to press **ESC. If you don't press ESC the SLIP connection will not work!**

Dialer Edit Scripts

The **Edit Scripts** selection from the Dialer menu displays all of the files that end in **.cmd** in the same directory in which TCP-MAN is installed. By default there are only three: **login.cmd**, **bye.cmd** and **Setup.cmd**. You can load one of these files into the Windows Notepad editor to make changes if you wish. After you have made any necessary changes, remember to use **File Save** from the Notepad menu to save the changed version of the file before exiting the editor.

You may also want to use this facility to create a new script for a secondary host. To do this, load **login.cmd**, make any changes required for the new host, and use **File Save As...** to save the file under another name. You can then use the new script to log in to another host with the **Dialer Other** menu choice.

You don't have to use a script at all, of course. You can dial manually as I described in the previous section. But a script makes things a lot easier. It stores the modem initialization string, the telephone number for your host, your userid, and, if you wish, your password. Once the script is properly configured, you can log on to your Internet service provider host by simply choosing **login.cmd** from the Dialer menu.

Particularly if you are using version 2.0B of the TCPMAN program, the supplied script should be all you need. It asks you for the host phone number, your user ID, and your password the first time you use it. Thereafter, it remembers this data to log you on automatically.

If you think you need to modify your login script, contact a representative of your service provider for help.

Dialer Options

Use the **Dialer Options** menu choice to display the Dialer Options dialog box shown in Figure 5.11.

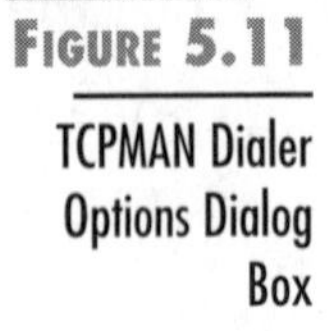

FIGURE 5.11

TCPMAN Dialer Options Dialog Box

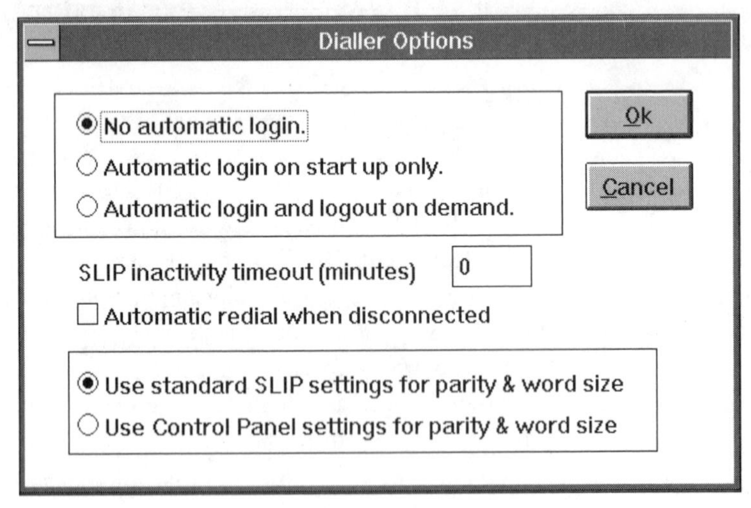

This dialog box lets you specify several options about the way TCPMAN handles your SLIP connection.

For example, the first option group lets you decide how TCPMAN will connect to the host. One possible setting is for **Automatic login on start up only**. That means that when you start TCPMAN or an application that requires a SLIP connection, the login.cmd script is executed automatically to establish a connection.

If you enable **No automatic login** instead, then when TCPMAN loads you must use the **Dialer Login**, **Dialer Manual Login**, or **Dialer Other** menu choices to establish a connection. If you are using more than one host, you may want to set **No automatic login** so you can specify the host you want to use.

Remember, however, that your user ID and IP address are unique to each host. If you are using a second host, you must edit the Setup dialog box to reflect your IP address and other configuration values before you can establish a successful connection.

If you enable **Automatic login and logout on demand,** then each time you select a program that requires the SLIP link, TCPMAN will dial the host and establish a connection. Then when you exit that program, the SLIP link will be disabled. You will get better response from your SLIP applications if you leave the setting at the default. However, if you habitually use only a single program at a time—you check your mail and logoff, for example—then you may want to set TCPMAN to disconnect when each program is halted.

The **SLIP inactivity timeout** setting in the middle of the dialog box specifies how long TCPMAN will remain connected to the host during times of inactivity over the link. The default is 5 minutes, which means that if you establish a connection, then walk away from your computer for 5 minutes, TCPMAN will break the link. Note that most host machines also have a timeout limit after which your SLIP link will be disconnected. Check with your information provider about this time limit.

The next field tells TCPMAN to redial automatically if the SLIP connection is broken. With this setting enabled you will get the highest up time. However, it may sometimes go against your desire to have TCPMAN disconnect when each application is closed.

The final option group specifies how TCPMAN communicates with the host. The most common setting is standard SLIP settings. If, on the advice of your service provider, you want to change this to something else, choose the second option, then enter the proper settings in the Windows Control Panel.

When the settings you want are correct, click on **OK** to close this dialog box and return to TCPMAN. You will have to restart the program for the changed settings to take effect.

The Help Menu

The basic TCPMAN Help menu simply tells you about the program: a copyright notice, who wrote it, and the dates of the copyright. The U.S. Internet version of the program includes full onscreen help. It is structured, like most Windows-compliant software, with a help index and the ability to search for help topics.

Chameleon (PC)

NetManage produces an Internet package for PCs called Chameleon (call 800-558-7656 for information). This commercial offering includes TCP software as well as net browsing and other utilities. You can purchase Chameleon in at least two versions: a full commercial suite that may cost hundreds of dollars, and a sampler version that is bundled with books (such as *Mosaic Users Guide* or *World Wide Web Bible* by MIS:Press.) and other online products. Either way, you'll need to install the TCP software and configure it for your local Internet service provider.

Chameleon includes a setup/install routine similar to those supplied with other Windows products. The install process is fairly straightforward, as long as you have some key information about your hardware configuration and the configuration of the machine at your Internet service provider. I'll show you a brief overview of installing and using Chameleon in this section, but since this is a commercial package, you can contact your supplier or technical support at NetManage if you have difficulty in getting this program to work properly for you.

Installing and Configuring Chameleon

Before you begin installing the commercial or sampler versions of Chameleon, you should make a copy of your install disks. Make sure you have the serial number and key, supplied with the software documentation, available during the install process.

Chameleon is a Microsoft Windows product, so you should start Windows before trying to install the software. Place the first diskette in the install set into a floppy drive and use the Program Manager **File Run** command sequence to display the Windows Run dialog box. Type **a:setup** (or **b:setup** if you placed the install disk in the b: drive) and click on **OK**.

The Setup program will copy files from the distribution disks, create a Program Manager application group, and install icons in this group window. Just follow the instructions to complete the install process.

When all of the files have been copied, click on the **Chameleon** group in the Program Manager to make it the current group, then double-click on the **Start the Custom—Connect Here** program. The dialog box in Figure 5.12 will be displayed.

FIGURE 5.12
Chameleon Custom Dialog Box

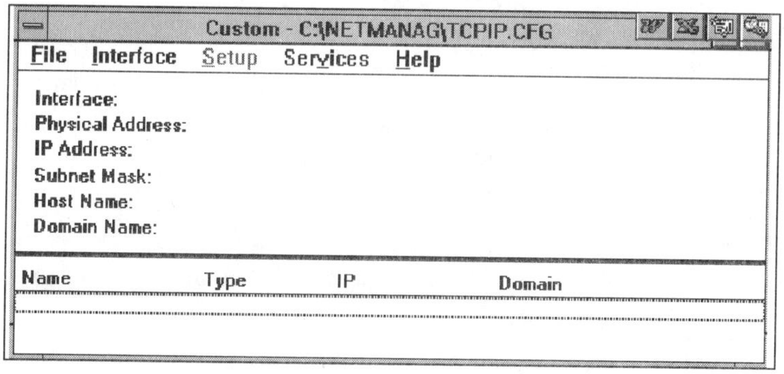

Now use the menus on this dialog box to change the following settings:

1. Select the **Interface** and choose **Add** from the pop-up menu. This works like all Windows programs. You click on a main menu and other choices are presented to you. Click on the

Type field and press the **down arrow** until you see the type of connection you want to establish. You'll need to check with your access provider for the proper setting on this dialog box. Click on OK to accept this setting.

2. Open the **Setup** menu and choose **IP Address**. Enter your assigned IP address. Note that there are two types of IP assignments, manual and dynamic. For manual IP addressing, you will have an assigned IP address. With dynamic addressing, you will be assigned a new address each time you log on. The IP address you type here will look something like 199.1.48.48.

It is very important to type the IP address you were assigned in this field. An incorrect address will mean your TCP connection won't work.

3. Open the **Setup** menu and choose **Hostname**. Enter your user name in all lowercase characters. Your user name can be up to 8 characters, but it must be the name assigned by your Internet service provider.
4. Choose **Domain Name** from the **Setup** menu. Enter the domain name assigned by your Internet service provider. This could be a variation of the host's domain, or it could be a custom name assigned to you or to your company. Unless you have registered a unique domain name, as when you want to receive mail addressed to your company, the domain name you type here probably will be the domain of your Internet service provider.
5. Again, from the **Setup** menu, choose **Port**. Specify 8 data bits, No parity, 1 Stop Bit, Hardware Flow Control (or the setting specified by your service provider). Choose the COM port your modem is using, and specify the communication

speed you want to use. This should be 38400 for any modem capable of 9600 baud or faster. Setting a speed faster than the modem's specifications lets your modem and the host modem use internal compression, When two modems communicate using compression they are capable of a faster throughput than the modem's ratings. This setting specifies how fast your computer will talk to your modem. Your modem and the host modem will negotiate to decide how fast they can actually talk. For older modems, however, you probably will have to specify a slower speed, because many older modems aren't capable of terminal speeds above 9600 baud or so. Click on **OK** when these settings have been made.

6. Choose **Modem** from the **Setup** menu and select your modem brand. Click on **OK**.
7. Open the **Setup** menu and choose **Dial**. Enter the phone number you will use to dial into your service provider's host. Remember to add **9,** in front of the number if you must dial 9 to get an outside line. Add ***70,** in front of the phone number if you are using a line that has call waiting.
8. Choose **Login** from the **Setup** menu and enter your **User name** and **Password**. In the **Command:** field, enter whatever command is required to choose a SLIP connection after you have logged into your host. With some hosts you will enter the word **SLIP** in this field. With others you may enter a numerical menu choice. Check with your service provider to find out what you should enter in this field. Click on OK.
9. Next, open the **Services** menu and choose **Domain Servers**. Enter the IP address of the domain name server used by your service provider. If you don't know what this is, contact your service provider for the proper address. Of course you could enter the domain name server on another host (such as 199.1.48.2 for the U.S. Internet server, for example), but this will slow down your access considerably. Click on **OK**. Your screen should now look similar to Figure 5.13.

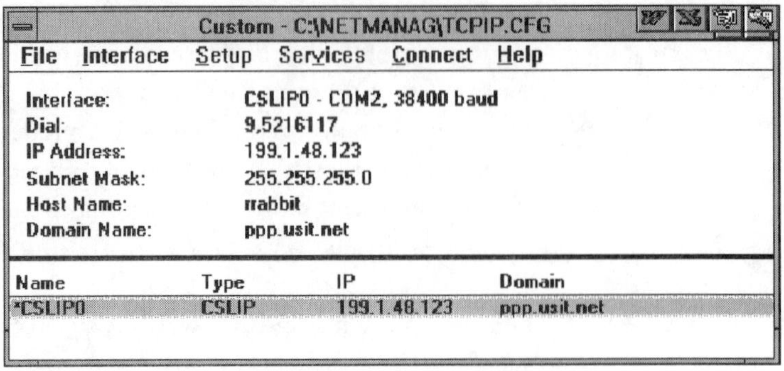

FIGURE 5.13

Completed Chameleon Custom Dialog Box

Custom - C:\NETMANAG\TCPIP.CFG

File Interface Setup Services Connect Help

Interface: CSLIP0 - COM2, 38400 baud
Dial: 9,5216117
IP Address: 199.1.48.123
Subnet Mask: 255.255.255.0
Host Name: rrabbit
Domain Name: ppp.usit.net

Name	Type	IP	Domain
*CSLIP0	CSLIP	199.1.48.123	ppp.usit.net

10. Open the **File** menu and choose **Save**. Then open the **File** menu and choose **Exit**.

The next part of the configuration is a little trickier and will require some input from the technical personnel at your service provider. You must now edit the Chameleon login script to match the commands expected by your host.

Select the Accessories Window in the Program Manager and double-click **NotePad** to open the Notepad editor. Select **File** and choose **Open**. Select the directory where you installed Chameleon (**C:\NETMANAG** by default) and type the file name **SLIP.INI.** Click on **OK**. This will display the file that holds Chameleon scripts and other configuration information.

Locate the entry that corresponds to the type of connection you specified earlier during setup. If you specified CSLIP, for example, find the line that says [CSLIP0]. This is the line you will edit to make it match what your service provider host requires for a successful login. Depending on how your host machine is configured, the default Chameleon script may work properly. Chances are, however, that you will need to make some changes. For example, here is a script that will work with U.S. Internet's host machine:

```
SCRIPT=name: $u$r word: $p$r -n $6 Choic $c$r Your $- -I
```

This may look a little strange, but it is easy enough to interpret once you understand how Chameleon uses this information.

The [CSLIP0] above this script simply identifies the script you will use. This is a title that corresponds with the type specification entered during setup.

The **SCRIPT=** tells Chameleon that what follows is a login script.

The **name:** entry is the first string (series of characters) that Chameleon will look for after the host answers. With U.S. Internet, the first prompt is for **Annex Username:**. Therefore if you tell Chameleon to look for name:, it will be able to interpret the first prompt. Again, try a manual login or contact your service provider for information on the prompt sequence during login.

The next entries in the script are variables, which are letters that stand for information you have entered previously. The **$u** tells Chameleon to insert the user name you entered as part of the configuration process (u stands for username, and the dollar sign identifies the following character as a script variable.). The **$r** says to add a carriage return. This is the same as if you typed the user name and then pressed the **Enter** key if you were logging in manually.

Next, the script tells Chameleon to look for **word:** That's because at U.S. Internet, the next prompt after username is **Annex Password:**. Telling Chameleon to look for **word:** will capture the last part of this prompt.

The following entry, **pr**, says to output the password variable you specified earlier and to follow this entry with a carriage return. Again, this is as if you had typed the password on the keyboard, then pressed the **Enter** key.

The script then tells Chameleon that there is some information coming from the host that can be ignored. The **-n** entry says to skip some data without trying to act on it. The **$6** says it will take about six seconds for this information to pass by. In other words, ignore anything coming from the host for the next six seconds. This is fairly common with Internet hosts, because the service provider frequently displays promotional information, menus, and other data that you don't want Chameleon to attempt to process.

The next part of the script tells Chameleon to look for the prompt that will start the SLIP connection. At the U.S. Internet host, the user is presented with a menu, and the prompt **Your Choice?** is displayed. If you were logging in manually, you would simply choose the menu item and press **Enter**. Here, the script tells Chameleon to look for the string **Choic,** to output the command variable (**$c**) entered during configuration, and to follow this entry with a carriage return (**$r**).

Finally, this script accepts the output of the host SLIP routine and displays your IP address as the SLIP connection is enabled.

Obviously, you will have to modify this script to match what your host expects to see. But by studying the information here, you should be able to understand at least the concept of a login script. Read the script section of your Chameleon documentation for additional information on script variables and commands.

This completes the modification of the login script, so use **File Save** from the Notepad menu to save the script. Then use **File Exit** to close Notepad. You are now ready to use Chameleon.

Connecting with Internet Chameleon

After the Chameleon configuration is complete, you can use this TCP utility to make a connection to your Internet service provider host. Here are the basic steps for making a Chameleon connection to an Internet host:

1. Open the Program Manager.
2. Open the Internet Chameleon Group in the Program Manager.
3. Open **Custom Connect**.
4. Select **Connect**.
5. Wait until the Log box says something like: **Your Address...**, then click the **Close** button on the Log Box.
6. Hold down **ALT** and press **TAB** until you see the Program Manager Icon. You are now ready to use the applications shown in the Internet Chameleon group.

Disconnecting with Internet Chameleon

Once you have connected to a host computer with Chameleon (or any other TCP software), you will leave the link up while you use Mosaic, Eudora, or other online applications. When you are finished using your Internet link, it is time to close the Chameleon TCP link. Here's how:

1. Make sure all Internet applications are closed.
2. Hold down **Ctrl** and press **Esc**.
3. Double-click on the line that says something like: **Custom - C:\NETMANAGE\.....**
4. Click on the **Disconnect** button in the window that is displayed.
5. Open the **File** menu and choose **Exit**.

Configuring the NetManage Applications

The Chameleon suite comes with more than just a TCP utility. You also get a number of online utilities that you can use to browse the WWW. Remember, you must open a SLIP or PPP connection before continuing here. If you are not connected, the following steps won't work as advertised!

Gopher

Before you use the Chameleon Gopher, conduct these configuration steps:

1. Choose **Gopher** from the Program Manager.
2. Open the **Item** menu and choose **Add Gopher Server.**
3. Fill in the form: *Name Displayed:* **<Your host name>.**
4. Fill in *Host Name*: **gopher.<your domain suffix>.**
5. Click on the **OK** button.
6. Open the **File** menu and choose **Save.**

An icon for the Name you specified appears in the Windows dialog box. You can launch the Gopher by double-clicking on the icon.

Mail

To use Chameleon Mail, conduct the following configuration steps:

1. Start the Mail program by double-clicking on **Mail** in the Internet Chameleon Group in the Program Manager.
2. Open the **Settings** menu and choose **Preferences**.
3. Click on the **Advanced** button.
4. Type: ***username*@domain.name**
5. Click on the **OK** button. *Username* is replaced with your own username.
6. Again, click on the **OK** button.
7. Open the Settings menu. Choose **Network**, then choose **Mail Gateway**.
8. Type: **smtp.domain.name**.
9. Click on the **OK** button.
10. Choose **Network** from the Settings menu, then choose **Mail Server**.
11. Fill out the form:

```
Host: pop.domain.name
User: your username as assigned by your service provider
Password: Your password
```

12. Click on **OK**. Note that the Directory field stays BLANK.
13. Choose **File Save**, then **File Exit**.

NewtNews

To configure the Chameleon newsreader utility, do the following:

1. Double-click on the **NewtNews** icon in the Internet Chameleon Group in the Program Manager.

2. Choose **Connect.**
3. Enter the hostname: **<Your Service Provider's News Machine>**.
4. Tell the program to fetch the list of newsgroups. There are over 11,000 groups; this may take quite some time.

WebSurfer

To configure the Chameleon WebSurfer graphical WWW interface, do the following:

1. Double-click on the **WebSurfer** icon in the Internet Chameleon Group in the Program Manager.
2. In the Startup Document URL, enter the WWW page you want to use as the default starting page. For example, enter **http://www.usit.net/navigate** to choose the U.S. Internet navigator page.

A URL is a Universal Resource Locater; it is a way of addressing a specific location to view a WWW page.

3. Click on **OK**.
4. Choose **Save** from the **File** menu.
5. Choose **Exit** from the File menu.

MacTCP and InterSLIP (MAC)

If you're using a Macintosh computer for Internet access, you'll need MacTCP to establish the network connection. If you're using System 7.5 or later, MacTCP is included with your system software. Users of earlier versions of the Macintosh operating system will have to purchase MacTCP software. It is readily available from Apple retail stores and is bundled with software included with a number of books.

Once you have MacTCP installed (just insert the diskette and drag the disk icon onto your system folder), you are ready to configure the software so it will work with your Internet service provider.

Configuring MacTCP

1. Locate the MacTCP icon in the Control Panels Window and double-click on the MacTCP icon. You should see a dialog box similar to Figure 5.14.

FIGURE 5.14

MacTCP Opening Setup Dialog Box

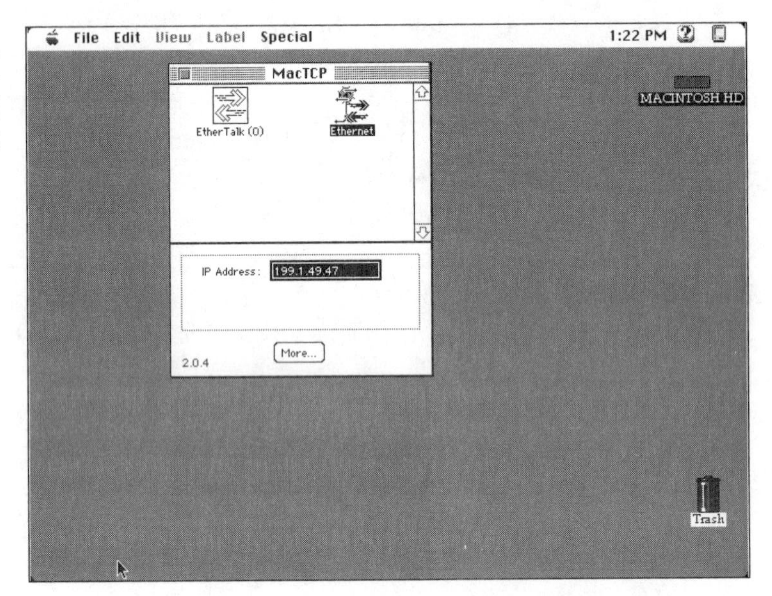

2. Enter your assigned IP address in the **IP Address** field of this dialog box. To do this, move the mouse pointer into the field and click the mouse button. This will place the insertion point in the field. Now type the assigned number.
3. When you are sure your IP address is correctly entered, click on the **More...** button to display the configuration dialog box shown in Figure 5.15.

FIGURE 5.15
MacTCP Second Configuration Dialog Box

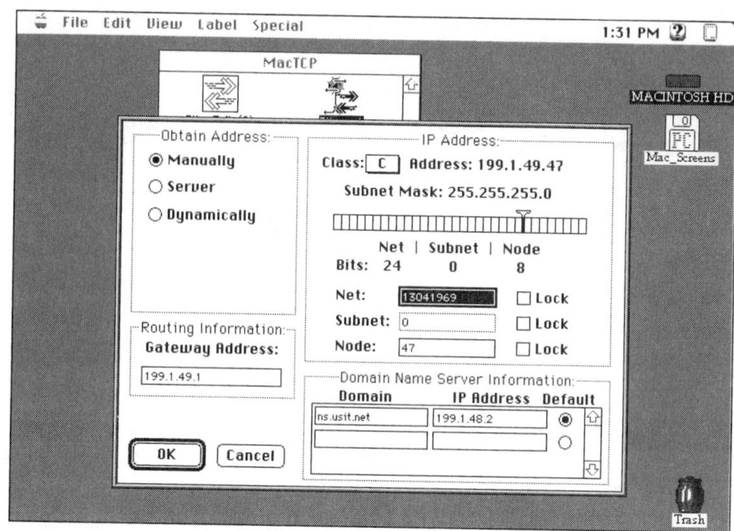

4. In the Obtain Address group, click on the button beside the type of IP addressing your host uses. If you have been assigned a unique IP address for your machine, you should click on **Manually**. If your service uses Server or Dynamic IP address assignment, then click on the proper alternate choice.
5. Specify a **Gateway Address**. This is the IP address of the machine that serves as your entryway into the host provider's network. For a dial-up link this is probably a communications server; for network access this is a bridge or a computer that is serving as a bridge. From the end user standpoint you don't really care. Just find out from your service provider what address you should put in this field.
6. Choose the network Class according to the specifications from your service provider. This is probably a class C, but find out the correct setting. The remainder of the IP address group was set automatically when you entered your IP address on the previous dialog box.
7. Set the Domain Name Server Information in the final group on this dialog box. In the **Domain** field enter the name for this server; in the IP Address field enter the **IP address** for

this server. You can choose a secondary name server as well. Be sure to specify which server should be the default server.

8. When all of the settings are complete, click on **OK** to close this dialog box and complete the configuration.

Connecting with MacTCP

As with other TCP software, you need a front end to use with MacTCP. There are a number of connectivity products you can use with MacTCP. I'll show you one popular one here, Intercon's InterSLIP. You can use the settings in this example to help you configure whatever dialer front end you are using.

To configure and connect with InterSLIP:

1. Locate the InterSLIP folder on your hard disk. Open it to display the window box shown in Figure 5.16. Your window may not look precisely like this one. It depends on what else you have placed into the InterSLIP folder.

FIGURE 5.16
InterSLIP Folder Window

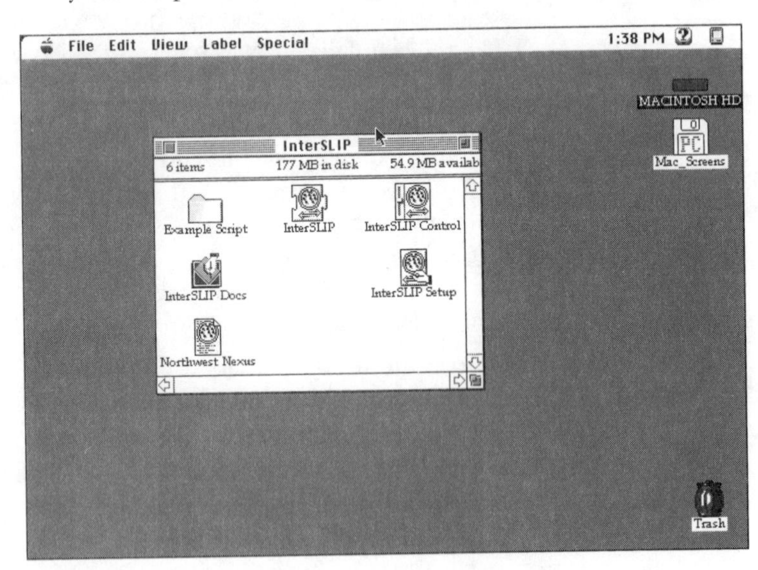

2. Double-click on the **InterSLIP setup** icon to display the Setup dialog box shown in Figure 5.17.

   When you first open this dialog box the central window may be blank. This area holds the configurations you have created.

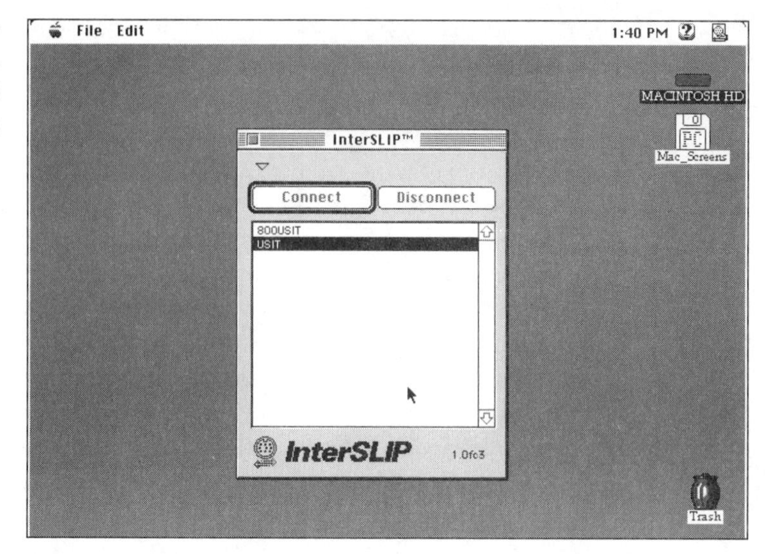

FIGURE 5.17

InterSLIP Setup Dialog Box

3. Create a new configuration by selecting **File** and choosing **New**.
4. Enter a name for the new configuration and click on **OK**. You will be returned to the Setup dialog box. This time, the new configuration name appears in the window.
5. Double-click on the name for the new configuration to open the Configuration dialog box shown in Figure 5.18.

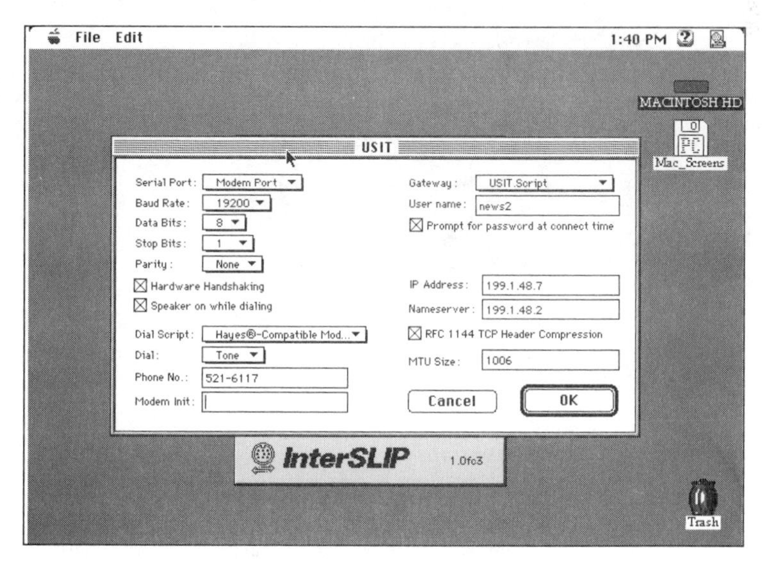

FIGURE 5.18

InterSLIP Configuration Dialog Box

Your settings may be slightly different from those shown in Figure 5.18, but except for the Phone Number, IP addresses, User name, and Gateway, these settings should work for you.

6. You may want to enter a string to initialize your modem in the **Modem Init:** field. Keep this string relatively simple unless you encounter problems connecting with your host. Try **AT&F** as the first string. This simply resets your modem to factory configurations. If you have problems establishing or maintaining a connection, try adding **&C1&D2** to the string. Finally, you can disable error correction and compression if you continue to have connection problems. Check your modem manual to find out how to do this. Your service provider probably can recommend an initialization string for your particular modem.
7. The **Gateway** should be the name of the script you will use to conduct the dialing and login process. An InterSLIP script is written in a Connection Control Language supported by InterSLIP and stored in the Gateway Scripts folder in the InterSLIP folder. A sample script is shown below. You can use this fairly simple—and obvious—script as a starting place for your own script.

```
@originate
note "waiting for prompt"
matchclr
matchstr 1 1 "username"
matchread 50
note "no username prompt"
jump 99
@label 1
note "sending username"
write "place your userid within this space fol-
lowed by \13"  i.e. "jones\13"
matchclr
matchstr 1 2 "password"
matchread 50
note "No Password prompt"
```

```
jump 99
@label 2
note "Sending password"
write "place your password within this space fol-
lowed by \13"  i.e. "fiDo\13"
matchclr
matchstr 1 4 "Choi"       ;Looking for 'Choice ?'
                          ;prompt. Place your
                          ;provider's correct
                                ;prompt
for switching to SLIP here.
matchread 120
jump 99
@label 4
note "Requesting SLIP"
write "3\13" ;Menu choice 3. Place your
                    ;provider's correct 'switch to
                    ;SLIP' command here
matchclr
matchstr 1 5 "SLIP"
matchread 120
note "Cannot invoke SLIP mode"
jump 99
@label 5
matchclr
setip "199.1.xx.yy"  ;Assigned IP address here
setmtu "1006"
exit 0
@hangup
exit 0
@label 99
exit 10
```

This script is designed to work with the U.S. Internet host. With only slight changes it should work with any service provider's host. If you study the sample carefully it should be obvious what it is doing. The script waits for a username and password prompt, sends these values, then selects a SLIP connection from the host menu.

Instead of choosing '3' from a menu, your host may require that you enter the word 'SLIP' to choose a SLIP connection. Once you understand the concept of a simple script it should be fairly easy for you to modify this one for your host.

8. If you want to enter your password each time you log on, then click in the box beside the **Prompt for password at connect time**. The password field disappears. Otherwise, enter your password in the **Password** field. This makes for a convenient login, but remember that if you write a script that includes your password, then anyone who uses your computer can log in to your account.
9. The **IP Address** field holds the address of your computer. This is the unique address that was assigned to you when you established your account. If you selected dynamic IP addressing in the TCP setup screen, then leave this field blank or place **0.0.0.0** in it.
10. The **Nameserver** field holds the IP address for your primary name server.
11. If your host supports SLIP compression (most do), click on the box beside the **RFC** prompt on this dialog box.
12. Finally, set the MTU (Maximum Transfer Unit) size. The value **1006** is probably appropriate for a dial-up connection.
13. Click on **OK** to close this dialog box.
14. Now, to connect with this setup and the included script, select the configuration name on the InterSLIP Setup dialog box and click on **Connect**. The script should dial the number automatically and complete the login for you.

Once the connection is made, you can launch one of the many Internet utility programs available to help you browse the Web.

WORLD WIDE WEB BROWSERS

The Internet has a rich history of development and use by experienced computer users who, themselves, were part of the design and development process. These users have traditionally accessed the Internet over a local area network, many of them using text-based terminals capable only of presenting text menus and scrolling screens.

Today, however, Internet users range from elementary school children to business owners, to doctors, lawyers, engineers, and others who view the computer and Internet access as tools. Whereas early users likely were computer users first and Internet users second, today's new crop of Internet users views the Internet as the end goal; the computer itself may not even be of particular interest to them. This change means that the interface into the Internet must change. Macintosh and Microsoft Windows interfaces are evolving to make the Internet—and all of its information—available to people who couldn't or wouldn't access it before.

These evolving graphical interfaces provide point-and-click access to World Wide Web facilities, as well as to other Internet data available through newsgroups, gophers, and mail. In particular, the structure of the World Wide Web makes it easy to access specific information through URL (Universal Resource Locater) addresses. By entering an address for a specific page—such as the home page for IBM Corporation, for example—you can read about the company and its products. A typical World Wide Web address begins with http://, indicating a hypertext protocol. The next part of the address can be about anything, but by convention, most addresses today include www as the next part of the address. Then the name of the company who owns the page or who is promoting the page comes next, including an extension that indicates the type of company. This can be .com, for example, meaning that this page is sponsored by a commercial entity, or .edu for education, and so on. Finally, a specific path and file name can follow the company specification, if you want.

So, IBM's net page address, for example, is:

```
http://www.ibm.com
```

When you enter that address in a URL field of Netscape, Mosaic or Lynx, you will see IBM's opening page.

Once you get into a starting page, you can jump to other pages related to the starting page by clicking on colored text or a linked graphic. These hyperlinks are really pointers to other parts of the current page or to secondary pages. When you click on a hyperlink, the application retrieves the page located at the linked address.

These graphical interfaces also offer multimedia options. For example, you can click on an icon linked to a sound file that automatically downloads to your desktop and plays through a sound card. Or, you can click on an icon or hypertext link and download a motion video file. These capabilities are bringing an entirely new personality to the Internet, making it easier to use, exciting and more functional.

Individual companies are writing custom net browsers and selling them as part of their online service offering, or are marketing them as separate products for use through any Internet access provider. In fact, the market is becoming so diverse I can't possibly cover everything available today. In the following sections I will briefly describe some of the more popular graphical user interfaces for Internet access. Check with your local provider for details on these and other software options as you plan your Internet travel.

NCSA Mosaic

Mosaic may well be the most talked-about and most familiar of Internet utility software, simply because it was the first graphical World Wide Web browser. It created a lot of excitement when it first hit the net. Netscape (see the discussion of Netscape in the next section) and many other graphical browsers are available now, but Mosaic was the earliest and is still heavily used.

Mosaic was designed and created by the Software Development Group at the National Center for Supercomputing Applications (NCSA), a nationally-funded research foundation located at the University of Illinois at Urbana-Champaign (UIUC). The NCSA was established in February of 1985 and opened its doors to service the national research community in January of 1986.

Configuring NCSA Mosaic

Mosaic is a freeware product that you download either from your service provider host or directly from the NCSA. It displays graphics images in a hypertext format so you can browse the WWW by clicking your mouse on text or on graphics prompts.

NOTE

Download Mosaic with FTP by connecting to ftp.ncsa.uiuc.edu, if Mosaic is not available on your local host. Once you are connected with an FTP client, browse the available directories to locate PC or Macintosh versions of Mosaic as well as documentation on the product.

Mosaic is usually stored on a host as a compressed archive file. After downloading it, you use a software utility to expand the file. Mosaic is available for PC and Macintosh computers.

No installation is required for Mosaic. However, when you use the PC version you must upgrade Windows to 32-bit operation. You can do this by downloading a file from your service provider host. This file is probably called something like **win32s115a.zip**. To install this Windows enhancement, unzip the file with the -d switch (**pkunzip -d win32s115a**) to create two subdirectories, **Disk1** and **Disk2**. From the Program Manager screen, select **File** and choose **Run**. Specify **Setup** from the **Disk1** directory. Thirty-two bit Windows will be installed automatically.

As soon as you decompress the Mosaic file and install it in a Windows applications group or a Macintosh folder, you are ready to use it. You must first establish a connection with your host machine, using a utility such as TCPMAN or MacTCP. Then, when you launch Mosaic, the default net page is displayed.

Unless you change the default, you will see the screen shown in Figure 5.19 when Mosaic is first loaded.

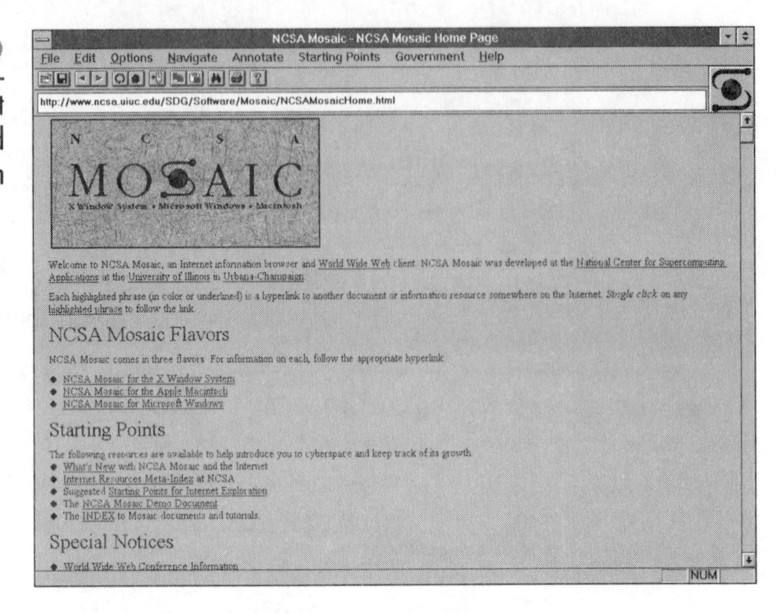

FIGURE 5.19

Mosaic Default Home Page and Opening Screen

This is the NCSA 'Home Page' at **http://www.ncsa.uiuc.edu/SDG/Software/Mosaic/NCSAMosaicHome.html.** This address is typical of page specifications on the WWW. **http** stands for Hypertext transfer protocol and begins all WWW addresses. Although older addresses may not include the WWW specification at the beginning, the trend is to use WWW at the beginning of all WWW addresses.

The rest of the address specifies the host, host machine, directory, and file that you want to load and display. As you read about the WWW and other aspects of the Internet, you will likely uncover many WWW addresses in this format. When you want to display the information at a specific address, simply click in the location field beneath the Mosaic menu bar and type in the full address. This address frequently is referred to as a URL, for Universal Resource Locator.

You can change the default home page display by using a text editor (such as Notepad in Windows, for example) to modify the **Mosaic.ini** file. This file is located in the directory where you decompressed the Mosaic archive, unless you have placed it in the Windows directory. You can make this specification from a menu on the Macintosh.

It is good practice to move this file into your Windows directory. Do this from DOS by making the Mosaic directory current, then typing move mosaic.ini \windows.

The first part of **Mosaic.ini** looks like this:

```
[Main]
E-mail="put_your_email@here"
Autoload Home Page=yes
Home Page=http://www.ncsa.uiuc.edu/SDG/Software/Mosaic/NCSAMosaicHome.html
Help Page=http://www.ncsa.uiuc.edu/SDG/Software/WinMosaic/Docs/WMosTOC.html
FAQ Page=http://www.ncsa.uiuc.edu/SDG/Software/WinMosaic/FAQ.html
Bug list=http://www.ncsa.uiuc.edu/SDG/Software/WinMosaic/Bugs.html
Feature Page=http://www.ncsa.uiuc.edu/SDG/Software/WinMosaic/Features.html
```

At the **E-mail**= entry, type your email address, replacing the **put_your_email@here** place holder text. Notice that the file also specifies that the home page will be loaded automatically. You can have Mosaic open with a blank screen by changing **Autoload Home Page=yes** to **Autoload Home Page=no**. And, you can change the default home page by changing the address after the **Home Page=** prompt on the next line. For example, if you change the ncsa address to **http://www.usit.net/navigate,** you will see the U.S. Internet navigation page when you open Mosaic. Your Internet service provider may have a custom opening page of its own that you want to substitute for the ncsa entry.

Configuring the Mac version of Mosaic is different from this Windows description. Check with your service provider if you need help. The operation of Mosaic on a Mac is virtually the same as on a PC.

Once Mosaic has displayed the opening page, you can click on any of the hypertext on the screen to jump off to other parts of the WWW. Hypertext entries are indicated by a different color—usually blue or red, but you can configure this to your own taste—and are usually underlined. In addition, graphics images, including photographs, may be set up as hypertext links to other WWW documents or to other portions of the currently-displayed document. Clicking on any hypertext link will display the page that is connected to that link.

A complete description of how to use Mosaic is beyond the scope of this book, but I'll show you a few things you might want to try in the next section. You can download a fairly complete user's manual for Mosaic directly from NCSA. From the Starting Points menu on the main menu bar, choose **Windows Mosaic Home Page**. From there you can follow directions for reading or downloading a user's guide. Bryan Pfaffenberger's *Mosaic User's Guide* by MIS:Press is also a good resource.

Using NCSA Mosaic

For the most part, you can follow your fingers (or mouse) and just click on hypertext entries to browse the WWW with Mosaic. Refer to specific locations in Chapter 8, and go to any of them by entering the WWW address in the location field at the top of the screen or by using the **File Open Location** menu sequence.

In addition, you can save a location you find for future reference by clicking on the **Navigate** menu on the main Mosaic menu bar and choosing **Edit Menu...** . The dialog box shown in Figure 5.20 will be displayed.

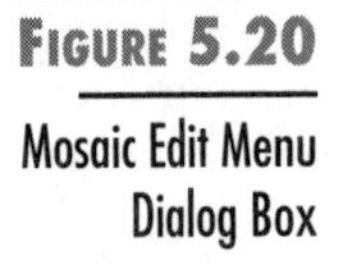

FIGURE 5.20

Mosaic Edit Menu Dialog Box

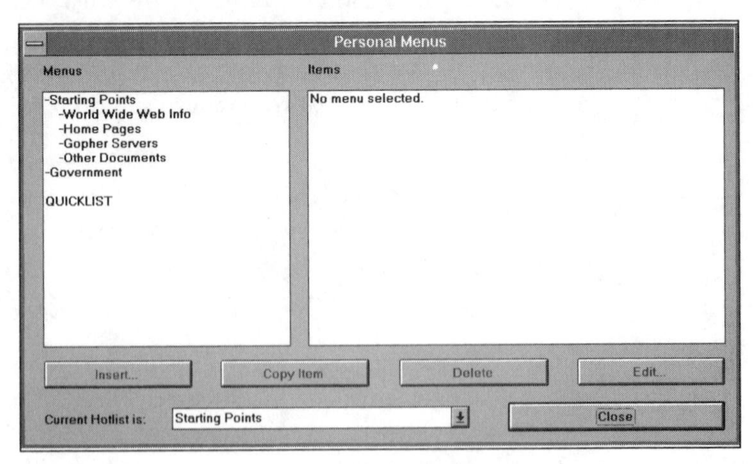

You can click on the **Insert** button to place the http address of the current Mosaic page into the menu. Choose which menu you want this entry to belong to by selecting the menu entry first. Notice that the default Mosaic menu structure includes a **Starting Points** entry that contains a number of interesting WWW locations that you may want to visit. You can add to this menu or create new menu entries of your own with the **Edit Menu...** command.

If you see a page that you want to print, use **File Print...** to send the current page to your local printer (the printer connected to your desktop computer).

In addition, you can view the source code for a particular Mosaic page by clicking on **Document Source.** Mosaic will open a window that shows the text, configuration commands, calls for graphics images, and so on, that make up the markup language that builds WWW pages.

You can save pages to disk as you display them by clicking on **Options** and then choosing **Load to Disk**. Now, each time a new WWW page is displayed, Mosaic will ask for a path and file name. The page will be stored to disk as it is displayed. You will also need to choose this option when you select a page to download. Some pages prompt you, for example, to **click here to download**. Nothing will be downloaded when you click unless you first specify **Load to Disk**.

In addition to reading the documentation mentioned earlier in this chapter, you can best learn to use Mosaic by using it. Mosaic is easy to understand and to use once you get it installed and display your first page.

Netscape

Netscape, like Mosaic, is a World Wide Web browser with a graphical user interface. Netscape had its beginnings in NCSA Mosaic. The programming team that developed Mosaic also designed and produced Netscape. Because Mosaic came first and was used by many online users for some time, the developers of Netscape had the advantage of all of this real-life research.

Netscape is produced by Netscape Communications Corporation. You can request more information about the product or place an order for the licensed version by sending email to **sales@mcom.com.** Note the address. Mcom stands for Mosaic Communications Corporation, but the company changed the name to Netscape to match the name of their WWW navigator and also to avoid conflicts with the University of Illinois.

Netscape was distributed initially as beta software available for downloading and testing. When version 1.0, the commercial version, was ready, it was offered for free download for educators and for sale to the rest of us. You can inquire about current pricing and availability through the email address shown above.

Like Mosaic, Netscape is available for a number of platforms. You can install Netscape on a PC compatible platform, on a Macintosh running System 7 or later, and on a variety of X Window platforms. A native PowerPC version of Netscape for the Macintosh was being developed as this book was written.

Netscape Advantages

The Netscape design offers several advantages over NCSA Mosaic. For example, the html (markup language) standard Netscape supports is enhanced, offering features such as graphic image centering on an html page. When Netscape downloads a graphic image, it begins painting most images immediately interleaving graphic lines to build the image. With Mosaic you see a count of bytes being downloaded, but you don't see any part of the picture until all of it is downloaded. In Netscape you can watch images appear before your eyes, sketchy and with little detail at first, then with increasing clarity as each line is added.

Netscape includes some built-in URL to help you answer questions about the product, search the Internet for specific information, and more. Access these extra features by clicking on one of the buttons under the location field on the main Netscape screen. You can take a guided tour of Netscape and its features, choose the **What's New** button for late breaking announcements and news, view frequently asked questions (and answers), search the net for a specific topic, as well as click on net directory and newsgroup buttons for even more Internet information.

Netscape also supports direct access to FTP hosts, gophers, news, and email. Mosaic supports many of these features as well, but Netscape does it better, in my opinion. Among Netscape improvements is a more versatile bookmark system that lets you add the current page to a list of pages you can return to at any time. You can even export your bookmark list to an html page so that you can access frequently-visited sites from the main Netscape screen.

Configuring Netscape

As with Mosaic, Netscape requires very little configuration to work with a properly-configured SLIP or PPP connection. However, Netscape includes configuration options that let you customize the way Netscape operates. For example, you can pull down the **Options** menu and choose **Preferences** to display the Preferences dialog box in Figure 5.21.

FIGURE 5.21
Netscape Preferences Dialog Box

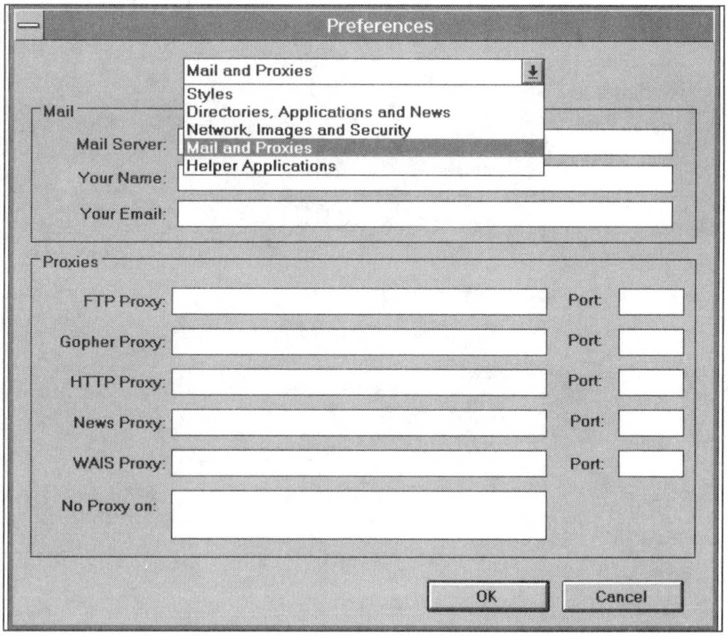

Use this dialog box to specify the news host you want to use with Netscape, to establish email settings, and so on. The specific fields available on this dialog box change according to the choice you make in the pull-down list at the top of the dialog box.

You may also want to modify the **Netscape.ini** file to control some operational features. For example, at the top of the **.ini** file is the default home page loaded when Netscape starts. You can change this to a home page of your choice by editing the file with any ASCII editor. With the latest versions of Netscape, you can change most of these settings from the Preferences dialog box as well.

Using Netscape

You use Netscape almost like Mosaic. First, you must establish a TCP network connection with Winsock or MacTCP. Once the SLIP or PPP connection is established, you are ready to launch Netscape.

By default, Netscape displays the MCOM home page, shown in Figure 5.22. That's the first thing you'll see when you load Netscape unless you have modified the default by editing the **Netscape.ini** file.

FIGURE 5.22

MCOM Netscape Home Page

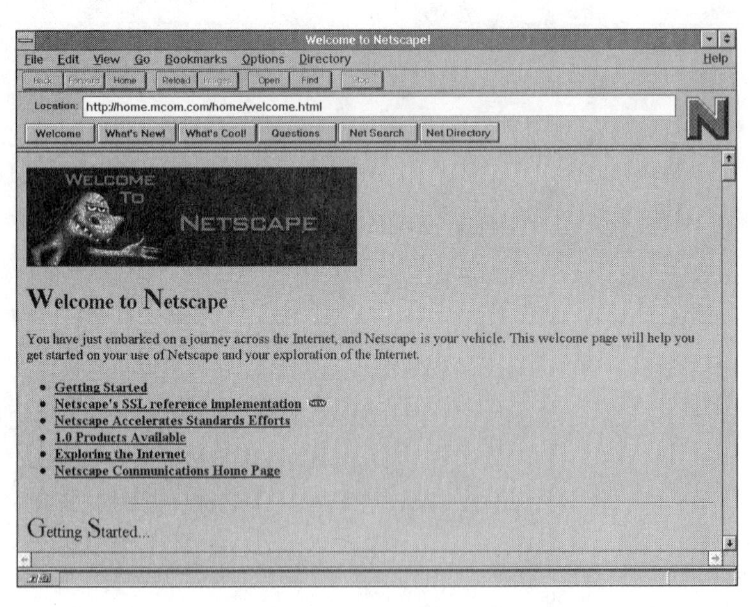

Whatever net page you set as the default, you can jump directly to any address you want by clicking in the **Location**: field under the toolbar on the main Netscape screen. Erase the current address shown and type the URL you want to display.

You can also jump to an FTP location by entering an FTP address in the **Location:** field. Click in the field, erase the address already there, and type **ftp://** plus an FTP address. For example, to display files and directories available at the Oak software archives, enter the following on the **Location:** line of Netscape:

```
ftp://oak.oakland.edu
```

Netscape makes the connection, logs you in as an anonymous FTP attachment, and displays the files and directories in the default FTP directory on the host.

In the same way, you can attach to a remote host gopher. Again, click in the **Location:** field, erase whatever address is displayed, and enter **gopher://** plus a valid gopher address. The host's main gopher screen will be displayed, and you can use your mouse to step through the gopher menus.

To add the current net page (or home page) to a bookmark, click on the **Bookmarks** menu in the Netscape menu bar and choose **Add Bookmark**. The description and html address for the current page will be added to the current bookmark list.

You can view the bookmarks you've established by clicking on **Bookmarks** and choosing **View Bookmarks**. This produces the dialog box shown in Figure 5.23.

Move any bookmark entry on the list up or down by highlighting the entry you want to move and then clicking on the **Up** or **Down** button at the bottom of the dialog box.

FIGURE 5.23

Netscape View Bookmarks Dialog Box

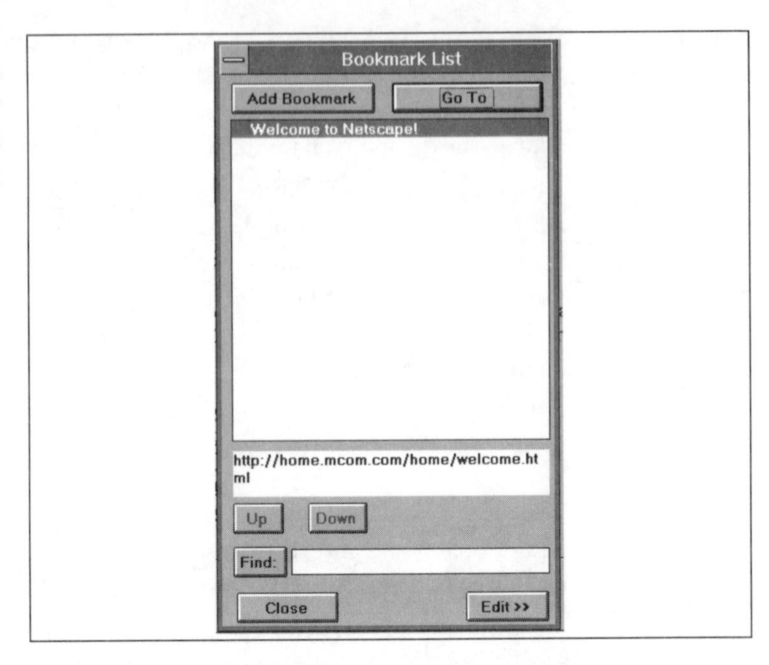

You can expand this display by clicking on the **Edit>>** button to produce the display in Figure 5.24.

FIGURE 5.24

Netscape Edit Bookmark List Dialog Box

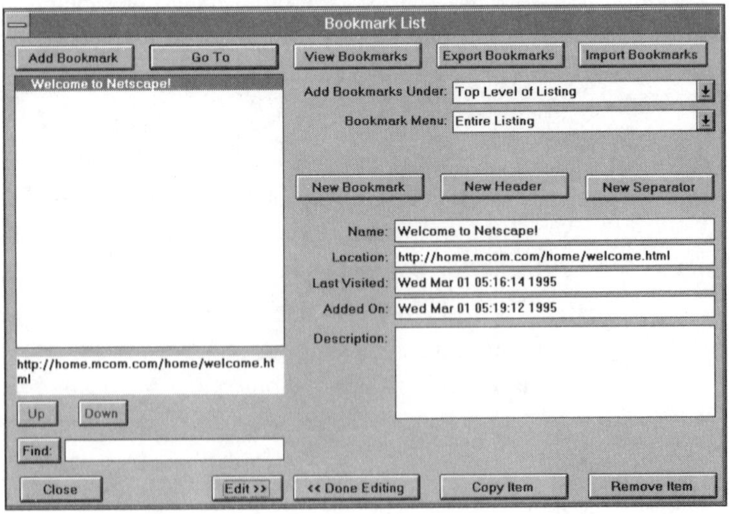

From this dialog box you can add a new header or group title, insert a separator line between bookmark entries, or copy a bookmark so you can place an entry under two categories.

To add a new bookmark category, click on the New Header button. Netscape puts a New Header title in the Name field of this dialog box. Now you can edit the New Header place holder name to say what you want it to. Use a header to separate bookmark entries, grouping them by topic.

You can also use this dialog box to export a bookmark list to a URL, or to import bookmarks. Simply click on the **Export Bookmarks** or **Import Bookmarks** buttons at the top of the edit side of this dialog box.

Other Browsers

Although NCSA Mosaic is the oldest—and original—World Wide Web browser, new commercial offerings are coming on the market all the time. There are browsers included with Internet in a Box, Chameleon, and other integrated packages such as SuperHighway Access for Windows from Frontier Technologies Corporation.

You can start your Internet browsing with Mosaic or Netscape, which are classics that are available for downloading from almost every Internet service provider. Then you should haunt the newsgroups, read the industry journals, and ask your fellow Internet travelers about the newest and latest offerings.

At the present, this market is far from stable and there are no clear, standardized leaders. Actually, it is an exciting time in the development of Internet access software. We all have a chance to evaluate and study the various offerings and to vote for the winners by our purchase and use of these products.

GRAPHICAL INTERNET APPLICATIONS

Obviously, browsing the World Wide Web and sending electronic mail aren't the only activities for Internet travelers. You'll want to read USENET newsgroup postings, transfer files, and Telnet into text-based services as well. Just as it is impossible to discuss all of the WWW browser software offerings, I can't possibly show you all of the other Internet applications you can find, download, purchase, or use. But there are a few popular and classic offerings that you'll likely encounter and may want to use. I'll offer a brief description of some of these in this section. Consider this introduction just a starting point for your exploration and investigation. Bryan Pfaffenberger's book, *World Wide Web Bible* is an excellent source for learning more about the Web.

Trumpet News (PC)

USENET news is among the most popular activities on the Internet. By browsing the topic listings, then reading selected articles posted by people from all over the world, you can research a project, get help for a tough programming or business problem, learn to cook a special recipe, exchange political views, rent a vacation condo, buy a bicycle, and more.

There are a number of software products available to help you access these discussion groups, but among the more common for PC-based SLIP and PPP users is the Trumpet News reader, written by Peter Tattam. You can download this shareware software package from most Internet service providers. It usually is stored as a PKZIP archive under the file name **wtwsk10a.zip**. (You may find other names and different versions of this archive. Ask your service provider.) Use FTP to download the file to your host or directly to your desktop if you have already installed a SLIP/PPP FTP client (see the discussion of **ws_ftp** below).

When you unzip the file and install it in Windows, you can launch Trumpet News to see the startup screen shown in Figure 5.25. The executable file should be **ws_wsk.exe**.

FIGURE 5.25

Initial Trumpet News Reader Screen

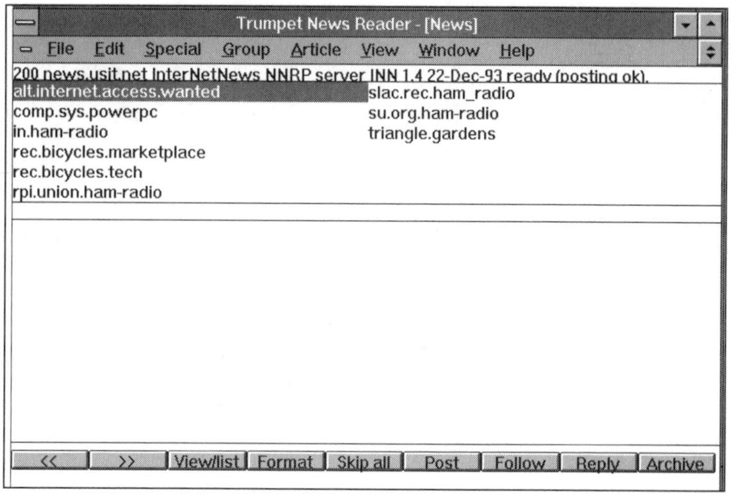

Before you can use the Trumpet reader, you'll need to configure it for your account and your service provider. To do this, click on the **File** menu and choose **Setup**. You will see the dialog box shown in Figure 5.26.

FIGURE 5.26

Trumpet News Setup Dialog Box

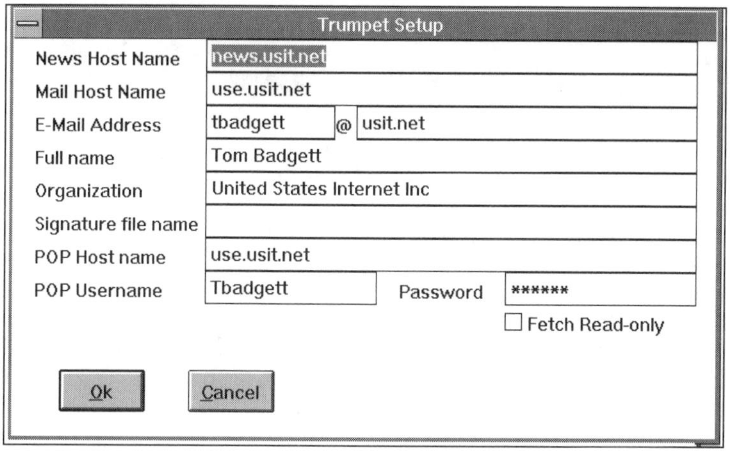

These values should be easy to fill in. If you have problems configuring the software, contact your service provider. The **News Host Name** is the name of the computer you will use to access USENET news. This may be your provider's main host, or it may be a separate computer dedicated to storing and maintaining news.

The **Mail Host Name** is the name of the computer at your provider's location that manages mail. Again, these two may be the same, or they may be separate machines, depending on how your provider has configured its service.

The **E-Mail Address** fields hold your user ID and your domain name, which is the string you use to receive your email.

On the **Full name** field, enter the name you want to appear in the name field of any news postings or email messages you send through Trumpet.

Your organization name goes on the **Organization** line of this setup dialog box. This can be the name of your service provider, or the name of your company or other entity you wish to identify during news postings.

If you have a Signature file, which is a file that is automatically attached to your email messages, enter the name of this file on the **Signature file name** field of this dialog box.

The **POP Host name** is the name of the machine that manages your email account. You can get this name from your service provider.

The **POP Username** is the name of the holder of the email account. This should be your user ID.

Finally, the **Password** field holds your account password—the one you use to log on to your service provider account.

When all of the fields are filled in, click on **OK** to store the configuration.

Next, use **File Network Setup** to display the setup dialog box shown in Figure 5.27.

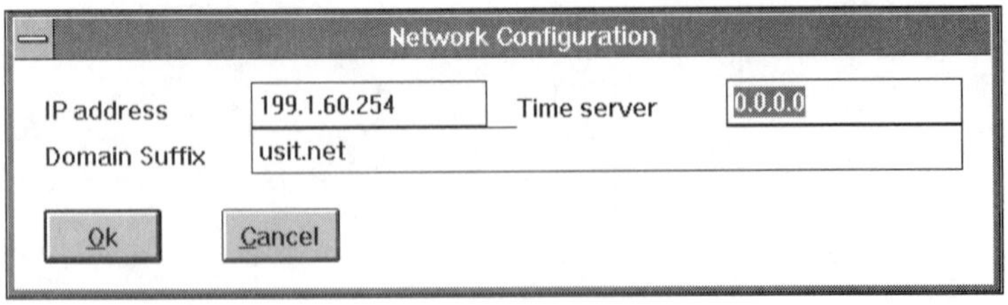

FIGURE 5.27

Trumpet News Network Setup Dialog Box

Enter the **Domain Suffix** in the last field of this dialog box and click on **OK**. You can't change the **IP address** field, and you need not make any entry in the **Time server** field of this dialog box.

Now to use the Trumpet News reader, click on the **Group** menu and choose **Subscribe** to display the dialog box shown in Figure 5.28.

Remember, you must start your TCP software first to establish a SLIP or PPP connection to a host before you can use the Trumpet news reader.

FIGURE 5.28

Trumpet News Group Subscribe Dialog Box

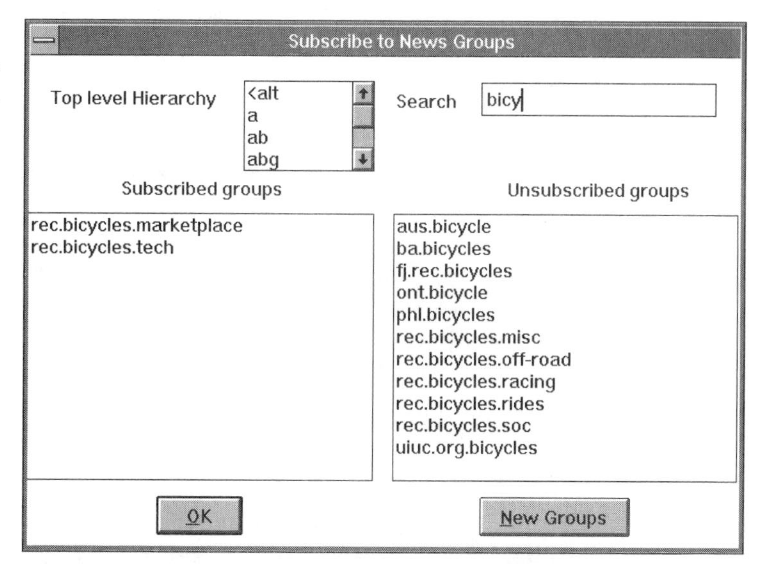

Enter the first part of a topic in the **Search** field. Trumpet will scan available groups to display a list of news groups that contain the string you entered. As you type more information, the program narrows the search. If the Unsubscribed area of this dialog is blank, it means no groups that match your search string were found.

To subscribe to one of the groups in the Unsubscribed groups list, click on the name. The group will be moved into the Subscribed groups column. This is a toggle. If you double-click, the selected group will move into the Subscribed area, then back to the Unsubscribed area.

After you have selected all of the groups you want during this session, click on **OK**. To read information from one of the subscribed groups, double-click on a group name at the top of the Trumpet News Reader screen. Use the buttons at the bottom of the screen to manipulate the news articles, respond to an article, send mail to an author, and so on.

When you use **File Exit** to close the news reader, the groups you have subscribed to are retained for the next session.

WinQVT (PC)

Even amid the real time, online graphics world of the World Wide Web, there are times when you need to establish a simple, text-based connection to a remote host. You may want to visit IRC for online chats, access a host menu, run a UNIX utility, write a program, or conduct any number of other activities that are best handled from a text-based terminal.

That's where Windows utilities like WinQVT can help. WinQVT is a popular utility that includes a Telnet or terminal client as well as support for FTP and mail. Most users of SLIP or PPP services prefer other mail and FTP software, but the WinQVT terminal package is quite serviceable.

Download the WinQVT archive. It is probably named something like **winqvt395.ZIP**, depending on where you find it and which version you are using. Uncompress it into its own directory and install an icon for it in a Windows Program Manager group.

You have to make a couple of modifications to the **qvtnet.ini** file that supports this program. Unfortunately, there is presently no automatic install utility that handles this task for you. Use

Notepad or another ASCII editor to load the **qvtnet.ini** file, located in the same directory as the WinQVT archive.

At the beginning of this initialization file are prompts for your host name, IP address, and Net Mask values (see Figure 5.29).

FIGURE 5.29

qvtnet.ini File Fragment

```
;--------------------------------------------------------------------------
;
;        QVTNET.INI
;
;        Global configuration file for WinQVT/Net
;
;--------------------------------------------------------------------------

[net]
;--------------------------------------------------------------------------
;
;        Network Information
;
;--------------------------------------------------------------------------
;
; name
;
; Your PC's host name
;
name=star.usit.net

;
; ip
;
; Your PC's IP address
; Use the format 'nnn.nnn.nnn.nnn'
;
ip=199.1.48.9
```

The host name is the name of your computer, not the name of your service provider's host. You may have to contact your service provider for the name of your machine. It may be a custom name if you have registered your own domain, or it may be a generic name assigned to all SLIP/PPP users by your service provider. Your IP address is the unique numerical identification assigned to you when you opened your SLIP/PPP account, and the net mask depends on the type of network you are using. For a Class C network, for example, the net mask is 255.255.255.0.

When you have configured the **qvtnet.ini** file, you are ready to launch the WinQVT executable, **wnqvtwsk.exe**. This produces the display shown in Figure 5.30.

FIGURE 5.30

WinQVT Main Screen

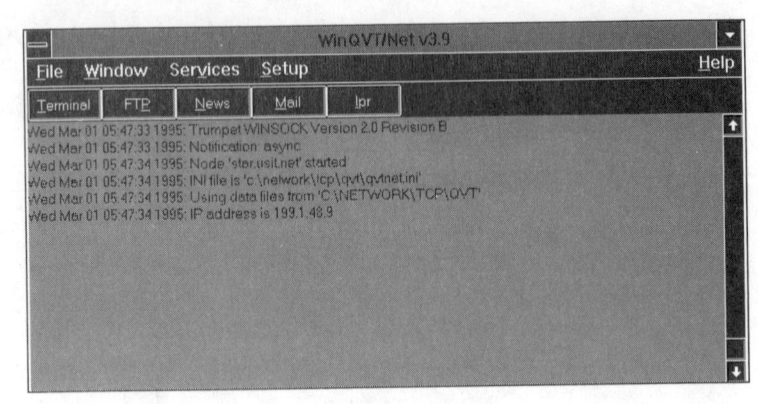

To launch a terminal (Telnet) session, click on **Terminal** to display the prompt shown in Figure 5.31.

FIGURE 5.31

WinQVT Terminal ID Dialog Box

Start Terminal Session
Host Name or IP Address:
use.usit.net
Configuration:
default
telnet
rlogin
Username:
IP Port:
23
Ok
Cancel

Type the name of the machine, including the domain, to which you want to connect. For example, to Telnet to the U.S. Internet main host, enter **use.usit.net** at the prompt.

When you click on **OK**, you will be attached to the specified host, which will then prompt you for a user ID and password. If you have a valid account on this machine, you can log in and begin using the system.

WS_FTP (PC)

FTP, or File Transfer Protocol, is an easy way to transfer information from a remote machine to your service provider's host, or, with a SLIP/PPP connection, directly to your desktop. One of the more popular FTP software packages is WS_FTP, a very functional, easy-to-use utility that you can download from a number of Internet hosts, probably including your service provider's machine.

The archive is **WS_FTP.ZIP.** Download it using a terminal package and a file transfer protocol such as ZMODEM or Kermit. Copy the archive into a directory and use PKUNZIP to expand the archive files. Install **WS_FTP.EXE** in a Program Manager group, and launch the program after establishing a SLIP/ppp connection. You will see a screen similar to the one in Figure 5.32.

FIGURE 5.32 WS_FTP OPENING SCREEN

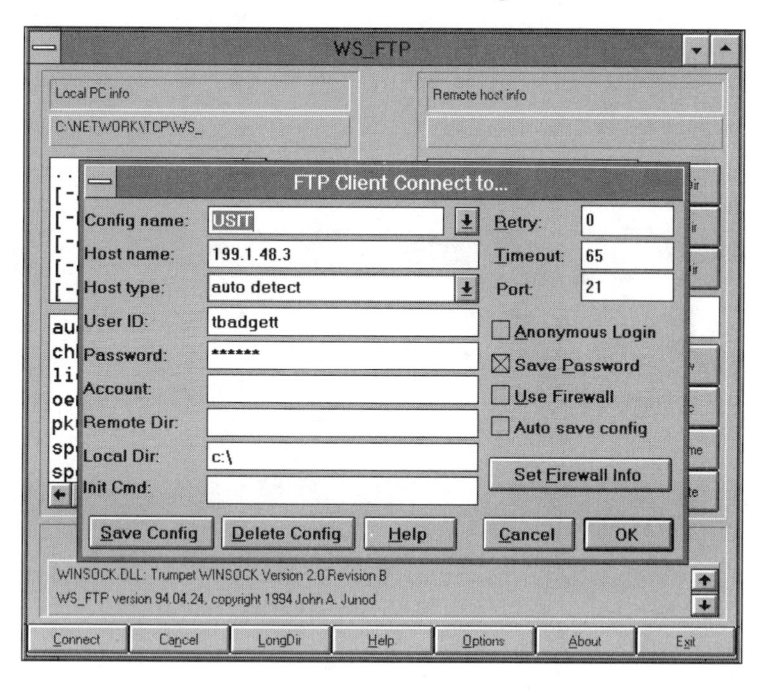

Usually you will see a default host in the Connect dialog box. You can use the pull-down list to view all of the host sites stored with the package, and you can add a host of your own. Simply click in the **Config name:** field and type a description of the host to which you want to attach. Then enter the host IP address or machine name in the **Host name:** field. To log in anonymously, click on the **Anonymous Login** check box. The program automatically enters your email address in the **Password:** field.

You can save this and other configurations by clicking on **Save Config** at the bottom of the dialog box. To start the login process, click on **OK**.

When you log into a host anonymously, you are usually logged into the host's FTP directory. It will appear to be the root, but it is probably the first directory within a public FTP area. If you have an account on the host and log in as yourself, you will be placed in your own home directory. The files to which you have access when you log in as yourself will be different than when you log in anonymously, even on the same host.

After the logon process is complete, you will see the split screen shown in Figure 5.33.

FIGURE 5.33

WS_FTP Split Screen Display

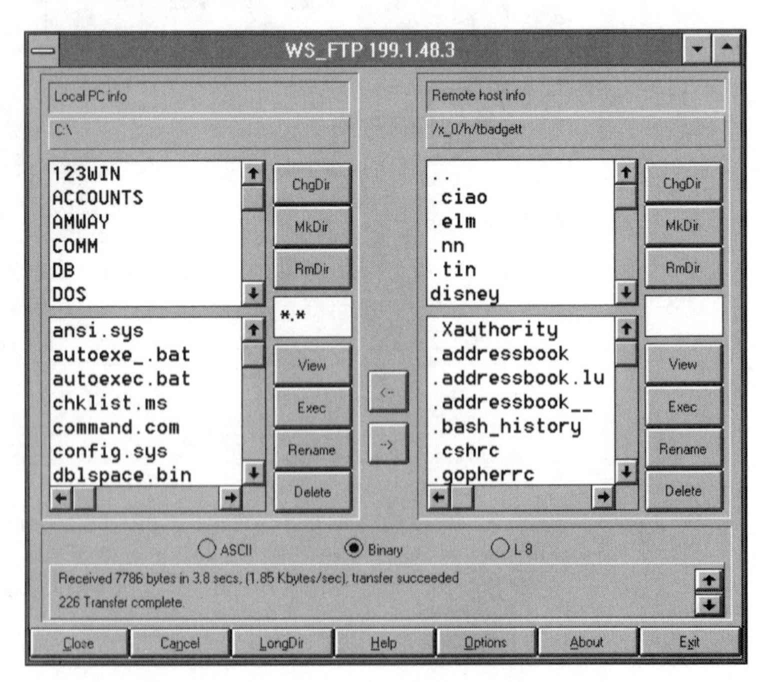

On the right of the display is the host directory and files; on the left is your local directory and files. You can change directories on the host or local desktop machine by clicking on the desired directory or by clicking on the **Chgdir** button and entering the path.

To download a file from the host, select the local directory you want to hold the file. Click on the remote file to select it, and then click on the **left arrow**. WS_FTP will open a box showing the progress of the transfer, and the file will be copied into your local directory.

Assuming you have write rights to the remote directory—as when you log in as yourself and are using your home directory on the host—you also can upload files from your desktop to the host. Simply highlight the file on the left side of the display, select the destination directory on the right side of the screen, and then click on the **right arrow**.

This utility is one of the easiest and most useful programs you will encounter for use with your SLIP/PPP account. Remember to save the configuration descriptions of new sites you visit so you can pull down the list and select a previous site to visit again.

WHAT YOU LEARNED

I've covered a lot of ground in this chapter, and yet we have only scratched the surface of online utilities you may encounter as you travel the Internet.

I have shown you how to establish a TCP connection with some of the more common SLIP/PPP utilities for the PC and Macintosh, and I have introduced you to Mosaic, Netscape, Eudora, and some other common Internet tools. The more you travel around the Internet, ask questions and try different sites and programs, the more you will learn about what is available and what you can do online. The key is to keep exploring and experimenting. Who knows what you might encounter?

In the next chapter, I'll show you what is happening on the commercial side of the Internet by introducing you to some business activities. I'll display some interesting WWW sites and discuss how you can get your business on the Internet.

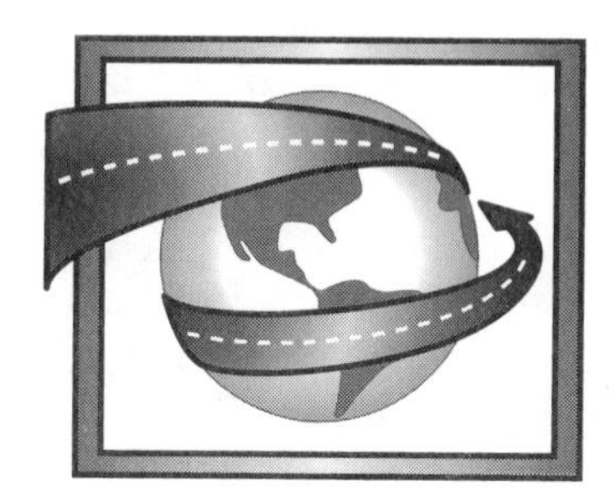

Chapter 6

THE INTERNET AND BUSINESS

Until a few years ago, most of the Internet was funded through the National Science Foundation and other government agencies. However, the NSF has announced plans to remove all public funding by the end of 1995. Unfortunately, a facility that millions of users have become accustomed to accessing for little or no expense is now going to cost money to use. Yet as public funding declines, businesses of every kind and description are moving into the Internet world and providing upbeat design, innovative features, heavy promotion, increased numbers of users, hardware innovations, improved user interfaces, and more.

With the commercialization of the Internet come changes in the medium itself, in image, in features, and in the type of people who use the net. The news media has become interested in the Internet's technology and its possibilities. Their heavy promotion and coverage of Internet activities is itself part of the change, enticing businesses and users to try them.

In this chapter I will address the following

- Businesses activity on the Internet.
- How you can use the Internet to promote your business or product.
- How you can get your business on the Internet.

ADVERTISING AND PROMOTION ON THE INTERNET

Will Henderson, CEO at U.S. Internet, Inc., describes the Internet as "the first new advertising medium since the advent of television in the mid-1950's." In fact, you could look at the communications aspects of the Internet as experimental, frustrating, unsettled... and exciting!

The changes in funding and posturing that I have already discussed are partly responsible for this frenetic view of the Internet. Some advertising agencies are flocking to the Internet with vigor, touting it as an exciting opportunity. Other advertising experts claim that Internet advertising isn't cost effective because nobody really buys anything on the Internet, and that advertising on the Internet is too new and unstructured.

Both of these views probably are valid, but my experience favors those who are embracing Internet advertising. The medium is experimental, to be sure, but look for online advertising, promotion, and selling to progress faster than television and to affect us just as significantly.

For one thing, Internet advertising and promotion is starting with a built-in global audience of around 40 million people in 159 countries. The broad nature of the user base offers both opportunity and challenge. It offers opportunity because an audience of 40 million people is a substantial advertising base, especially when you can target your approach according to areas of interest and background. At the same time, it is challenging because of the different cultures, interests, and backgrounds.

Moreover, the medium itself is new for advertising, promotion, and sales activities.

I'll leave these cultural and technical issues to other experts. In this chapter I'll show you what is already being done and describe how you can participate, if you decide to do so. If you'd like to see what one company is doing to get businesses online, check out the net page at **http://www.commerce.com.**

Advertising Examples

What kind of advertising is already being done on the Internet? Almost anything you see on television or in the newspaper you are likely to see on the Internet, but with a different approach. For one thing, there are more image ads in which a company says "here is who we are and what we do" rather than shouting "buy our product." You will find advertising that provides much more detail about companies and products than is common in conventional media. In general, Internet advertising is more like a giant catalog than like television or newspaper promotion. And because the medium is computer based, you have a broader range of options for finding particular information or products.

For example, suppose you are trying to buy a new computer printer. You may know the basic features you want. You may even narrow down the choice to one or two brands and models. But you probably want additional information about the printer and the company that sells it. Many products such as this are sold through distributors, so you have to find a distributor who has the information you need. This doesn't always work, because the distributor may not have the level of detailed technical information you want.

You can call the manufacturer if you can find a valid number. Sometimes, especially with large companies that are composed of many divisions, it can be surprisingly difficult to locate a telephone number for sales and technical information. Luckily, with the current promotional trends on the Internet, chances are excellent that you can jump directly to a Web page that has the information you need.

WWW Addresses

Suppose in this example that you have narrowed your printer search to models from Hewlett-Packard and Lexmark. To get in-depth information on a wide range of printer models from these two companies, turn to the WWW and a browser such as Netscape.

Once Netscape (or Mosaic or whatever browser you prefer) is loaded, enter a trial address for Hewlett-Packard on the address line:

```
http://www.hewlett-packard.com
```

You will see a message such as "Unable to locate host." Does that mean Hewlett-Packard doesn't have an information page on the WWW? Not at all. Just use your imagination to try another address. The Hewlett-Packard company frequently uses the H-P or HP logo, so try again:

```
http://www.hp.com
```

When you enter this address, you will see the opening screen shown in Figure 6.1.

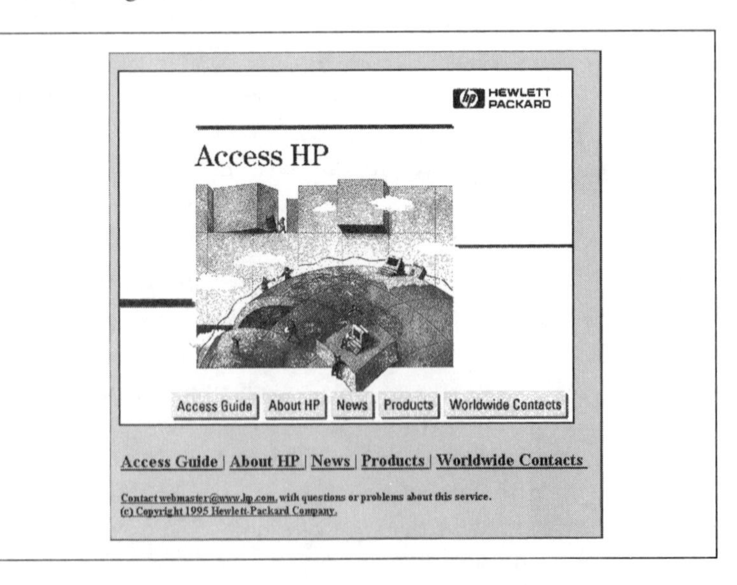

FIGURE 6.1
Hewlett-Packard opening WWW screen

This is an excellent example of how trends toward addressing standardization on the World Wide Web are making it easier to locate specific information. Such guessing of a company address won't always work, of course, and you may have to turn to a WWW search engine. But it only takes a few seconds to try a few obvious company addresses. If it works you've saved time and effort. If it doesn't you can always search the Web. You can learn more about WWW search engines in Chapter 4.

If you click on the **Products** button on this page, you'll see the screen shown in Figure 6.2.

FIGURE 6.2
HP Product WWW page

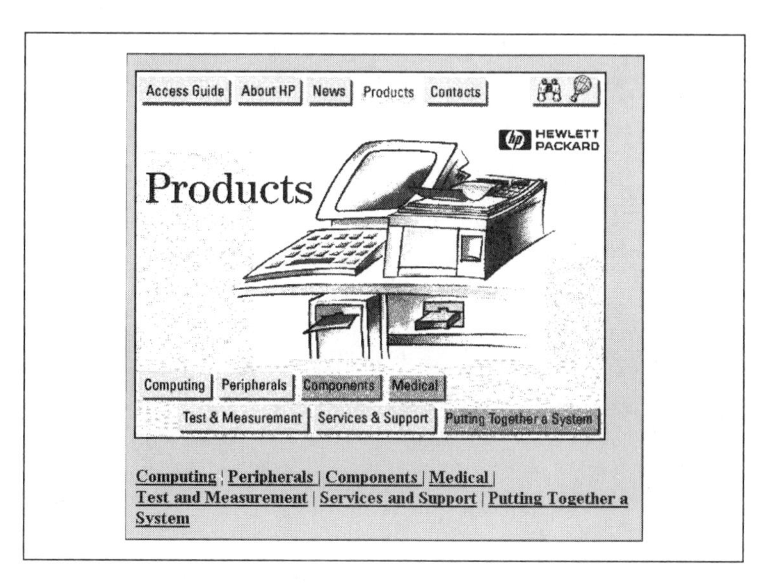

From here you can locate specific printer models and browse as much information as you want. You can also print individual pages to aid your research.

Now on to Lexmark. Enter this address on the Netscape location line:

```
http://www.lexmark.com
```

You will see the opening screen shown in Figure 6.3.

FIGURE 6.3

Lexmark opening WWW screen

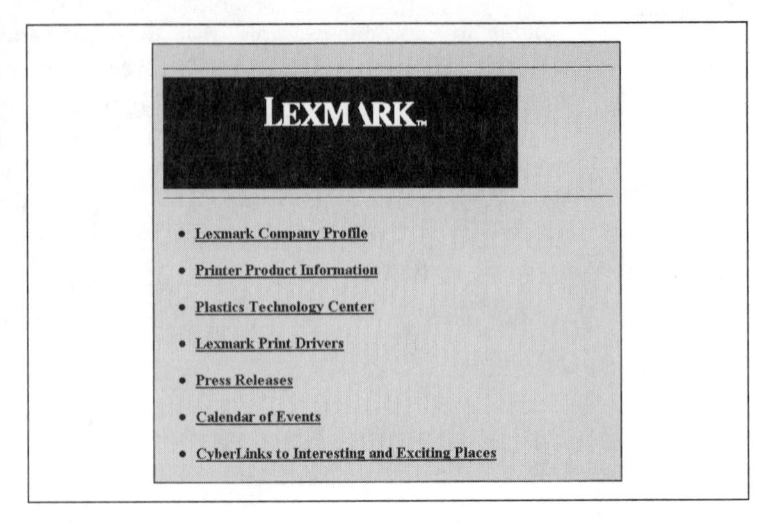

Again, you can choose the product information screen and view or print detailed information about specific printer models.

My own experience in conducting this type of search, I was able to locate more technical data on the Web than either my distributor or the manufacturer could supply, at least within a reasonable time. In fact, I discovered features about some of the printers—including options and additional models—that neither the distributor nor the manufacturer's sales representative mentioned.

In addition, I found a series of press releases that showed when the printer models I was researching were released and when updates were announced for them. Moreover, I located company sales data that showed the general success of the printer line over the past year. In short, I found data within a few minutes on the Web that otherwise would have required several long distance phone calls and perhaps half a day to secure, if indeed I could have found some of it at all.

Now, back to our search for printer information. You can find out more about printers by selecting one of the items on the hit list. Back up to select another found document by clicking on the **Back** key on the toolbar. When you locate information you want to keep, place it on your bookmark or menu, or print the document.

You are building a catalog of pages that eventually will lead you to the specific information you want. In the printer example I've used here, it is fairly easy to locate the major corporate players in this market because they have adhered to WWW addressing conventions, and because their information appears in searchable databases that you can access from within a Web browser.

With other topics, there are additional important steps in conducting your research, either because you are looking for a more general topic than a single corporate entity, or because the companies involved don't have their own easily recognizable home page addresses.

How else might you locate specific commercial information on the Internet? You could try USENET newsgroups. Although smart advertisers use newsgroups cautiously, there is a rising trend toward pointing to advertising and promotional pages within newsgroups.

Use your favorite news reader to search for topics that might support your research, then read comments to look for pointers to advertising or promotional articles. You will find that a newsgroup rarely includes direct advertising (although this happens occasionally and will likely increase in frequency with the ongoing change in Internet demographics. However, there are frequently articles that describe a commercial home page you can access for information about a specific area of interest.

Increasingly, there are WWW pages that collect data from within specific areas. For example the City Pages, is a collection of net pages that describe individual city facilities and services. Figure 6.4 shows the opening screen of the City Pages.

FIGURE 6.4

Opening screen of City Pages

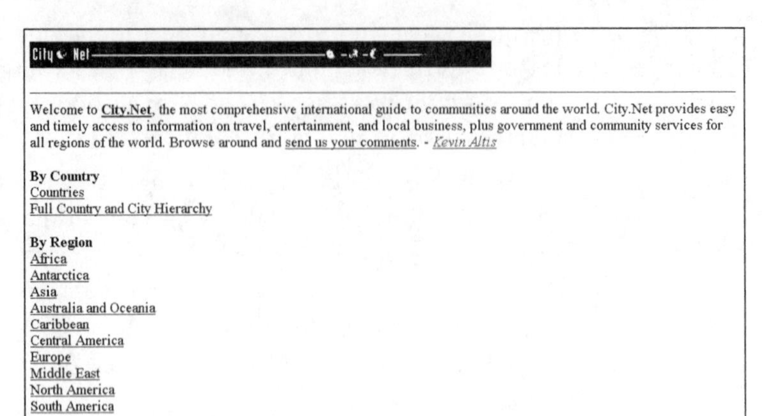

This page demonstrates two important Internet trends. First: companies, organizations, and even individuals are working to collect related net pages so you can locate specific information. Second: cities, counties, states, and Federal government agencies are reaching out to individual citizens through the Internet. Governmental pages help you learn about a geographic area—everything from climate and recreation to job opportunities, demographics, subway routes and schedules.

This, too, is a form of advertising. Although a number of these "public" pages are presented free of charge by a supportive company or institution, advertising agencies and information service providers are increasingly working with governmental agencies to produce these promotional pages for a fee. And, because it is good government to support local business, these pages frequently include pointers to promotional pages from area businesses. Therefore, if you are interested in general business within a geographic area, one place to look is on the governmental promotional pages for that location.

NOTE

A number of public and business net page locations are provided in Chapter 8.

Another resource is Gophers. You can access Gophers from a WWW browser by entering an address on the Location or URL line, or you can use a Gopher client such as hgopher to access a specific Gopher server. From a WWW browser, you would enter an address such as **gopher://.address.gopher.here**. You can Telnet to a host and type Gopher at the system prompt to launch the local gopher server, or you can use the desktop Gopher client to attach to a specific host. Once you have attached to a Gopher server, you can use Veronica or another Gopher search utility to look for specific companies or topics.

A good place to start is the Gopher server supported by your Internet service provider. Remember, Gopher is a menu utility that lets you browse topics by following various menu trees. Figure 6.5 shows a typical Gopher screen that contains business information you may want to view.

FIGURE 6.5

Typical commercial Gopher page

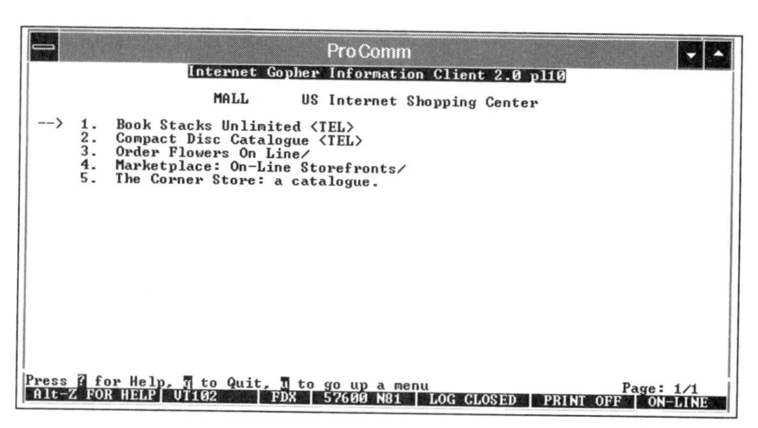

In summary, use one of the following methods to find commercial information about a particular company or that company's product:

- Try entering a direct address in a World Wide Web browser such as Netscape or Mosaic. Try the generic address **http://www.companyname.com**. If that doesn't work, try to think of variations on the company name, such as a recognized company abbreviation.

- Use WebCrawler or another search engine to look for the company name or product type. These searchers are getting more sophisticated all the time, so your chances of finding the information you seek are strong. However, as I demonstrated, you also will find a lot of references that have nothing to do with the primary topic.
- Through search engines or lists, locate a summary page or a collection of pages that display a menu or graphics list from which you can select company net pages.
- Use Gopher to browse by topic or location, or use Gopher search tools to find information by topic or company.

How to Advertise

Given the present state of Internet advertising and marketing, you probably shouldn't try to go it alone where promoting your company or product is concerned. Contact a knowledgeable advertising agency or service provider who can show you how to design promotional material for this new medium and can help you to promote the material itself.

As I mentioned, the transition of the original Internet to a commercial concern is by no means complete. This means you have a tremendous opportunity to reach an untapped market. It also means there is great potential for offending the established user base, who are not accustomed to and may, in fact, have fought the move to a commercial Internet.

If you are insensitive to this mood by posting to the wrong newsgroups, for example, you may generate more negative feedback for your company or product than positive promotion. That could mean that all of your effort and money is wasted, and you may find yourself spending money to counteract the negative image your advertising created.

This problem is not as serious as it may sound, but unless you have experience with this medium, ask an experienced and professional service provider or advertising agency to do it for you.

Your Own Domain Name

When you use the Internet through a service provider, your personal and corporate identity are tied to that provider. If your provider is registered on the Internet as **provider.com**, for example, you email is sent to **yourid@provider.com**. You might establish a user id that incorporates your company name, such as **mycompany@provider.com**, but the major entity remains the company that is providing you service.

If you are serious about your Internet use, you may want to register your own domain name to make it appear that you have a direct Internet connection. Check with your service provider for information. Most providers will help you pick a name and register it with the proper agency so you can send and receive mail and post WWW pages under your own company Internet domain name.

When you register your own domain, your email address changes from **yourid@provider.com** to **yourid@mycompany.com**, or a similar address, depending on the type of entity you are trying to promote. Registering a domain isn't difficult, but it can take a couple of weeks depending on the workload at Internic, the agency that maintains these registrations. Because your service provider must write a request, send it to Internic, follow up, resubmit a name if the one you chose is taken, then program their server to manage the new name, you will be charged a fee for registering your own domain name. The amount depends on the provider, but the best information I can find as this book is written shows that the cost ranges from a low of about $30 to a high of about $200. In addition to the original fee, some providers also ask a monthly maintenance fee to keep your name on their server. As long as the fee isn't too great—$5.00 to $15.00, typically—then it is worth the price. This fee pays the provider to create and maintain the programs required to route your email to and from your domain.

Functionally, nothing really changes when you register your own domain, assuming you don't change your level of service. If you have been using the Internet through a provider's shell or dial-up account you will continue to do so, but you can now advertise your email address as the one that contains your company name. In addition, when you send mail, your return address will show up as the one with your company name. In reality, your mail is still sent and received through your provider's physical host. Logically, however, information comes and goes from your company domain.

There may be another reason for registering your own domain. You may want to set up a local area network (LAN) within your company to provide Internet service to all LAN users and have your email routed to a local mail host. You can talk to your provider technical or sales staff about how to set this up. Suffice it to say that you can do this, and there are several levels of service of this type. You could set up a LAN with a continuous Internet connection, for example, or with a dialup ISDN link that would provide high bandwidth but a connection only when you decided to dialup the host. And, you can have this sort of locally distributed mail with a modem and gateway software that shares the modem with all LAN users, if you want. The difference us that you can't support multiple users (at least not very many) on line at once, and the link you use to transfer your mail is relatively slow.

As you begin working on advertising material for the Internet, you will encounter a number of tools that can help you design and prepare promotional pages. Again, particularly in the beginning, you should work through a knowledgeable provider or advertising agency.

There are a number of online resources you can study to learn how WWW pages are designed, for example, and you can even find software that will help you build your own promotional pages.

You can start looking for information online. Try a WebCrawler search for **html**, for example. This will uncover more than 8,000 sources that you can access by simply clicking on the entry in a list. Use your favorite Web browser to conduct this search. Some of these sources aren't what you're looking for at all. They are simply html pages about anything and everything. But you will find some useful information.

For example, the introduction to the World Wide Web at **http://fox.cs.vt.edu/WWWintro.html** includes many interesting sites. Among them is the Beginner's Guide to html at **http://www.ncsa.uiuc.edu/demoweb/html-primer.html**. This is a wonderful starting place for users who want to find out about the Web in general and the hypertext markup language in particular.

From this resource, you may find your way to **http://info.cern.ch/hypertext/WWW/status.html**. This page includes information about hypertext editors and other software tools you will need to create your own web pages.

Designing and creating Web pages is beyond the scope of this book, but by studying some of these resources you can learn a lot about the process. In addition, you will need the cooperation of a service provider. You will need space to store your Web pages and you will need read and write privileges to certain directories to provide other users access to the pages you produce. In general, you will create a simple file in a directory specified by your service provider. This file will point to (reference) a directory and file in your home directory or another location that you can control with read and write access rights.

Cautions and Caveats

As I have mentioned, the Internet is in transition. You can find and post commercial information on the Internet, but there are some limitations that you should be aware of. Many of these problems and shortcomings will go away soon, however, so stay in touch with your advertising agency or service provider.

When it comes to marketing on the Internet, one of the most serious shortcomings is the inability to transfer money securely. Although some vendors are providing interactive catalogues or order forms, complete with space for your credit card number, the majority of Internet marketers are not yet accepting credit card information over the Internet.

The problem, of course, is the possibility of someone intercepting credit card information. The common browsers—Netscape, Mosaic, etc.—are not particularly secure. As you can imagine, this is an important issue and work is going on to correct this shortcoming. Netscape, for example, has a secure server that supposedly can manage credit card or other financial transfers without danger of loss.

Other companies are approaching the problem in another way. In fact, the research that is continuing in this area may result in a different way of doing business—a change in the way we transfer money from one person to another.

You can get current information on this topic by searching for **credit card** through a Web searcher. My search for credit card using WebCrawler during the preparation of this book, resulted in 631 hits. Among them are:

```
http://www.capital1.com/CapitalOne/c1-home.html
http://kbt.com/cardservice/
http://www.firstunion.com/conref.html
http://digicash.support.nl/publish/sciam.html
http://cyberzine.org/html/Credit/morganpage.html
```

You can conduct a search of your own, or try jumping directly to these pages.

PUTTING YOUR BUSINESS ON THE INTERNET

In addition to promoting your business or product by placing net pages on the Internet, you will want to provide Internet access for your employees. Especially if you are advertising on the Internet, it makes sense for you to have access to the medium you are using.

There are a number of ways to achieve this. Which method you use depends on what facilities, if any, you can locate through a local service provider, how much money you want to spend, how many people need simultaneous access, and what you will do with the Internet once you have access to it.

Online Options

As I have discussed previously, you have several low-end options for providing Internet access for your company. Most service providers offer what is called a dial-up or shell account. This is a text-based interface using terminal emulation communications software. Depending on your service provider offerings, this may give you a menu for navigation, or it may offer only a UNIX system prompt.

If you get a menu with your access, it should be fairly easy to train new people to use electronic mail and to access the research facilities the Internet offers. If the shell account does not offer a menu, training is more involved and it is more difficult to use the Internet. However, once on a shell account, users can learn fairly quickly how to access a basic Gopher, even if it is not located at your local provider's machine. From there, the basic Internet access is with a menu. Figure 6.6 shows a menu from U.S. Internet's shell account.

FIGURE 6.6

Main U.S. Internet menu

```
               U n i t e d   S t a t e s   I n t e r n e t
            Your Connection to the Information Superhighway!
   Questions? Call us!! (800)218-USIT  24 hours a day, 7 days a week!

 *** THE NEW USIT FOR WINDOWS SOFTWARE IS HERE *** See the <USIT> menu ***
  If your version of USIT for Windows is older than 1R4.2B please upgrade

  <Mail>        The Electronic Mail Menu
  <Info>        The Internet Information Sources Menu
  <Chat>        The Internet Chat Menu
  <Games>       The Games Menu
  <FTP_Menu>    The FTP Menu
  <Files>       The Files Menu
  <Fingerm>     The 'Finger' Menu
  <Telnets>     The Telnet Menu
  <Other>       Other Things To Do Menu
  <News>        The Electronic News Menu
  <BDGTI>       The Big Dummy's Guide To Internet
  <NEW>         What is New at the USIT Systems?
  <COPYRIGHT>   Copyright Notices <PLEASE READ!>
  <USIT>        The US Internet Software and Information Menu

      %%% Comments or suggestions? Please mail helpdesk@usit.net %%%
   Ciao!        <ARROWS> move  u up menu  m main menu  q quit  ? help
t-Z FOR HELP| VT102      | FDX | 57600 N81 | LOG CLOSED | PRINT OFF | ON-LINE
```

If you select shell access, you won't be able to see the graphics and color that make Internet promotion and advertising so attractive. Especially if you are promoting your own company or service on the World Wide Web, you will want to be able to view your own pages and those of similar or competitive entities.

For this level of access you need some type of network access to the Internet. For individual access this means a SLIP or PPP account. With SLIP and PPP, remember, your computer is assigned a network address (an IP number); while you are logged onto a host, your machine is part of the Internet.

Accessing the Internet through SLIP or PPP requires several software components. You need some kind of TCP/IP (Transmission Control Protocol/Internet Protocol) and dial-up IP software, and you need one or more software utilities—such as Mosaic or Netscape—to run over this serial network link. Refer to Chapter 5 for additional information on specific products for accessing the Internet with a SLIP or PPP account.

For comparison of a WWW connection with a text based connection, see Figure 6.7, U.S. Internet's WWW navigational page. This is accessible through your favorite graphical viewer.

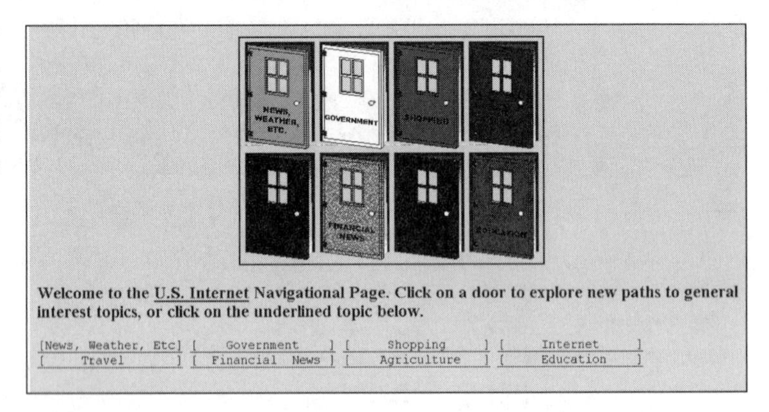

NEWS, WEATHER, ETC.
GOVERNMENT
FINANCIAL NEWS
Welcome to the U.S. Internet Navigational Page. Click on a door to explore new paths to general interest topics, or click on the underlined topic below.
[News, Weather, Etc] [Government] [Shopping] [Internet]
[Travel] [Financial News] [Agriculture] [Education]

FIGURE 6.7 U.S. Internet Navigational page

Individual SLIP, PPP, or shell accounts work fine when the number of people accessing the Internet from your company is relatively small, when the volume of data you will transfer is low, and when you don't need full-time, continuous access to the Internet.

When you need to provide Internet access for more than six or eight people (the exact number depends on several factors, including the number of modems you already own and the type and cost of individual accounts available through your service provider), you should investigate the possibility of network access through a bridge and a high speed, dedicated line.

Microsoft Network

Among the information providers who are offering access to the Internet is Microsoft Corporation with its Microsoft Network. Microsoft is not currently serving as a full service Internet provider with its network, rather it is initially establishing a large, BBS-type service similar to CompuServe or America Online from which you can have limited Internet access. Graphical access software is included with Windows 95.

When you install Windows 95 you have the option of installing the Microsoft Network access software, along with Microsoft Exchange, which is an email and data exchange utility that lets you send and receive mail and files with CompuServe, Internet and other online users. You'll need to use the Custom Install option.

As this book is written, Microsoft promises to expand their Internet services beyond the initial email and Usenet news offering. In fact, the Beta version of Windows 95 and Microsoft Network provides read-only access to Usenet news, so you can't post information to the news groups. And, while the range of promised services is broad and information in the Microsoft Network user interface indicates an impressive array of options, the beta offering is somewhat limited.

Among the most impressive aspects of this initial offering is the user interface itself, which includes an easy-to-use, automatic registration facility and automatic software upgrades. The first time you use Microsoft Network you are asked to fill out a form that includes your chosen online ID, password, credit card billing number, and so on. Then the software dials an 800 number to make the initial contact. During this first login, the program determines which version of the software you are using and offers to upgrade the software if a later version is available. In addition, your dialing directory is updated to include local access numbers, when they are available.

Microsoft has done a good job of designing an interface that includes an open design that is easy to understand and to use. Which makes the wait for images easy. This interface is comfortable for even new online users with features such as interleaved graphics download which makes the wait for images easy. In addition, the software is integrated with existing Microsoft products. Microsoft Word, at least, is linked to the Microsoft Network interface so that when you choose information files online, the data is downloaded and inserted automatically into Microsoft Word. This gives you a good online interface that features full document formatting including multiple fonts, color and so on. However, the files are transferred in rich text format (rtf), so you could use them with any word processor that supports rtf files.

The news reader also is a good design. Icons are used to help you select the general topic you want to review, then a directory-tree-style display lets you step into groups to choose specific information to read.

The largest area of Microsoft Network, however, is not the Internet or Usenet news. It is the service's own BBS-style discussion groups, malls and mail. The future of Microsoft Network's Internet presence depends on future services and pricing, neither of which has been announced as this book is written.

LANs and the Internet

Many—probably most—companies with more than a few employees who use computers have some form of Local Area Network, or LAN. By connecting individual computers to a network, users can exchange local email, share printers and disk drives, back up critical information to a single tape drive, and so on. Today's network can even provide shared access to CD-ROM drives.

Suppose you want all or most of the users of the LAN to also have access to the Internet. You could supply each user with a modem and a dedicated telephone line for dial-up access, of course, but this bypasses the benefits of the existing network and can be relatively expensive.

A better choice is to attach a gateway server of some type to the network and provide Internet access for all members of the LAN through the gateway. Your LAN software, or an optional software addition to your LAN software, may provide this type of support directly. You would install a computer on the network and attach a modem to this computer. The modem is attached to a dedicated telephone line for dialing the Internet service provider.

This solution is a step above individual modems on each desk in that you save money on modems and you don't have as many upgrade and configuration problems. The shortcoming to this approach is that a modem connection limits your bandwidth. Depending on your software, you may be able to support two to four people on a 28.8 Kbps modem across a network, but response will be very slow.

A step above this LAN-to-modem connection is a networked ISDN (Integrated Services Digital Network) connection. ISDN offers connections at up to 128 Kbps—enough bandwidth to really support a network of users. You can order dial-up ISDN, which is a connection that is up only when you need it. You can also order a dedicated ISDN link, which is always up and provides Internet access to anyone anytime. In some parts of the country, the local telephone companies are pushing ISDN service through reduced or no installation fees and very low line charges.

An ISDN link for your LAN involves installing a networked bridge that is connected to the ISDN line. You must pay the local line charges for the ISDN line that connects your office to the local telephone company office.

Depending on your service provider, you may also have to pay for the provider's ISDN line to support your dedicated service. ISDN line charges vary widely, from about $27 per month in parts of Tennessee to more than $150 a month in other areas. However, I expect prices to level off and become reasonable nearly everywhere.

Likewise, the cost of full-featured ISDN bridges should get much better than it is now. Presently bridge prices range from about $400 to around $2,000. Bridges at the low end of the price scale are little more than high speed modems. They may plug into a PC or Macintosh expansion slot and provide a data-only, 64 Kbps link to your host. At the high end is an external bridge with built-in Ethernet interface, standard telephone interface, and support for 128 Kbps data transfer. With a bridge in this class, you can plug your computer or computer network into the Ethernet interface, an ISDN line into the ISDN jack, and a telephone or fax machine into the included modular jack. Now you can connect to the Internet at 128 Kbps, using both halves of the ISDN link. However, if you need to send or receive a fax, the bridge moves all of your data transfer onto one ISDN channel and supports the phone or fax on the other half of the link.

In addition to line charges and equipment costs, you must pay your service provider for Internet access. ISDN Internet access prices are far from settled. As this book is written, you can find ISDN access for as little as $30 per month for dial-up connections, and for as much as $600 for full time access. A wide range of prices and services is available in between. Because ISDN service is changing so rapidly, you should contact your local telephone company and your Internet service provider for the latest information on ISDN Internet access.

Of course, with a lot of users on a LAN, even a 128 Kbps ISDN link won't be fast enough. You'll need to step up to a T1 connection. This high speed digital link transfers data at the rate of 1.54 Mbps and is the fastest, most reasonably priced option for Internet connection today. You will need an interface for the T1 line at your end and, depending on how your service provider is set up, you may have to purchase a similar interface at the other end.

The hardware for Internet access may run $2,000 to $3,000, and the monthly charge for the T1 link will range from a few hundred to a few thousand dollars a month, depending on how far you are from your host location. In addition to the hardware and line charges, you will pay a separate fee for the Internet access. The amount you pay for T1 Internet access depends on your service provider, but expect to pay hundreds or even thousands of dollars for full-time T1 access.

GOING IT ALONE—BECOMING YOUR OWN INTERNET SERVICE PROVIDER

If, after considering all of the commercial options for Internet access, you decide to become your own Internet service provider, then think again. Even with reduced costs for hardware and communications access, supporting your own Internet link is not a trivial or inexpensive task. However, for a large number of users who need full-time access, this may be your best choice.

The object of this book is not to show you how to set up a full Internet node. However, I will point up a few basic issues to give you a starting place for your own investigation.

Hardware Considerations

In addition to local networking and computer hardware, you need interface hardware to a high speed communications line such as a T1.

NOTE

Some companies establish a full-time Internet connection over a 56 Kbps line. This may work for some applications, but if you are going to the expense and effort to establish your own Internet presence, make the installation complete. Use a T1 connection.

You will use this T1 link to attach to a national backbone carrier such as Sprint or MCI. Their backbone will, in turn, attach to an Internet node. Depending on your location, you will pay $2,000 to $6,000 per month for this network connection.

You'll also need a local server. This can be a high-end PC, but a UNIX-based workstation is more practical. By far the most popular Internet workstation is a Sun SparcStation, but workstations from HP, DEC, and other manufacturers also are used as Internet servers. Depending on the workload and storage requirements you will extract from this server, you will pay from $15,000 to $40,000 for this computer and its associated hardware.

Software and Administration Considerations

The UNIX operating system itself provides much of the software you need for basic Internet service. This is a multi-user, multitasking operating system designed for the networking environment. However, there are configuration, security, and other considerations that must be addressed. You will need someone with a good deal of experience in networking who can also create custom code and configurations when necessary. Managing an Internet node will require at least one full-time system administrator—maybe more, depending on your usage—and some additional network support people. How large a staff you will need depends on the number of people who will be accessing the Internet through your node, the level of technical expertise among the users, and so on.

In short, if you are considering a custom Internet link for your company, you have considerable investigation and study to do. You can probably secure the help of a local service provider, and representatives from Sprint and MCI will gladly counsel you on establishing a full-time, dedicated Internet link.

WHAT YOU LEARNED

In this chapter, I have shown you some of what is happening on the commercial side of the Internet, and have opened the door for you to learn how to put your own business or product on the Internet. As a starting point, I listed a number of World Wide Web pages you might use to learn more about advertising and selling on the Internet.

I briefly discussed how to put your company and your company's people on the Internet. The basic path to the Internet is the same for a company as for an individual. However, when the usage or the numbers climb, you may be in line for alternative, high speed access methods.

In the next chapter I'll introduce online talk, and will describe how you can use the Internet for direct, global communications that cost a fraction of conventional methods.

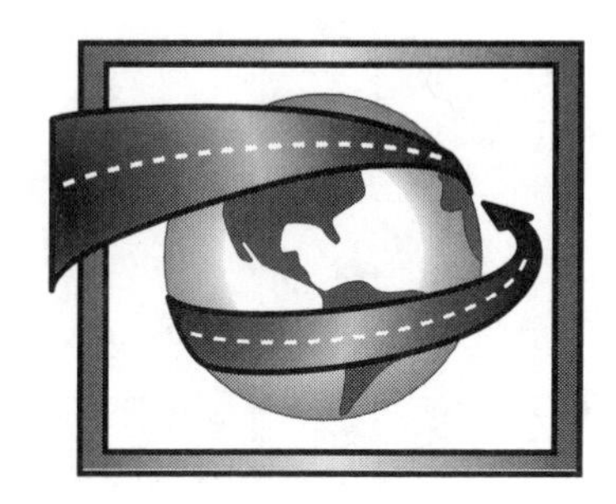

Chapter 7

Reaching Out: Talking and Listening

The excitement of an electronic journey often sparks from encounters with fellow travelers. Talking, sharing, arguing, and playing games are common community bonds on the Internet. In this chapter you will learn how to talk more directly across the Internet. You don't have to send someone an email message and then wait for them to check a mailbox before they respond. You can use commands such as talk and send to exchange messages right now. Also, an Internet-wide feature called Internet Relay Chat lets you start or join discussion groups with an unlimited number of other Internet users. We'll show you how to use these commands and more in this chapter. Among the topics we'll cover are:

- Using Talk
- Using IRC (Internet Relay Chat)
- Using CU See Me Video Conferencing
- Using Internet Phone Audio Communications
- Internet etiquette
- Showing emotions
- Exploring games

TALKING ON THE INTERNET

Most of what we have talked about so far in terms of getting information across the Internet involves locating and downloading files, displaying World Wide Web pages for study and research, and using store and forward electronic mail. When you use electronic mail, you type a letter and send it to someone to read whenever they get around to checking their mailbox. There are ways to converse in real time with the people you find on the Internet. We'll explore two of those methods, talk and IRC, in this section. Talk is a text-based (terminal) application that runs on the host to allow you to converse in real time with other users who are online at the same time as you. IRC (Internet Relay Chat) is also a text-based application, which works either with a dumb terminal or desktop clients (such as Windows or a Macintosh) that run over a SLIP or network connection. IRC is a realtime talk application, which provides access to multiple users all over the world simultaneously.

Using Talk

One of the quickest and simplest ways of conveying information to someone who is online with you at a local host is with the **talk** command. If you know that someone you want to talk with is logged on, simply issue the command:

```
talk username
```

To find out who is on the system, use the **who** command or simply **w**. These two commands display a list of current users. The **w** command adds information about what each user is doing, such as using mail, using IRC, and so on. Figure 7.1 shows results for a typical **who** command, and Figure 7.2 shows results for the **w** command on the same system. Remember, you can use **who** to display more detailed information about a specific user if you need to:

```
who tbadgett
```

Once you have determined that the person you want to contact is on the system, use **talk** to display a split screen like the one in Figure 7.3.

FIGURE 7.1

Typical who command

```
pollard  ttypc  Sep  2 13:05   (PERSIL.SLIP.UTK.)
leon     ttype  Sep  2 13:00   (DCA2.UTK.EDU)
operator ttypf  Aug 30 16:15   (OPLOCAL3.UTCC.UT)
harp     ttyq0  Sep  1 10:35   (MAGIC.UTCC.UTK.E)
jepeway  ttyq1  Sep  2 09:05   (lemon.cs:0.0)
sunil    ttyq2  Sep  2 09:37   (polysun.engr.utk)
mkovarik ttyq3  Sep  2 10:55   (SLEEMAN.UTCC.UTK)
kovarik  ttyq4  Sep  2 10:42   (SLEEMAN.UTCC.UTK)
rell     ttyq5  Sep  2 13:06   (DCA2.UTK.EDU)
hamed    ttyq6  Sep  2 10:19   (VISION9.ENGR.UTK)
snyder   ttyq9  Aug 30 09:21   (voodoo.utcc.utk.)
snyder   ttyqa  Aug 30 10:42   (voodoo.utcc.utk.)
springer ttyqc  Sep  2 11:26   (ENTROPY.UTCC.UTK)
bagri    ttyqe  Sep  2 09:36   (MIRAGE.UTCC.UTK.)
bagri    ttyqf  Sep  2 09:36   (MIRAGE.UTCC.UTK.)
bagri    ttyr0  Sep  2 09:36   (MIRAGE.UTCC.UTK.)
mcconnel ttyr1  Sep  2 11:16   (MACSTAT2.UTCC.UT)
eljazzar ttyr8  Sep  2 11:03   (saturn.utcc.utk.)
bill     ttyr9  Sep  2 11:48   (UX.UTCC.UTK.EDU)
root     ttyra  Aug 31 12:05   (r1w2.pub:0.0)
harp     ttyrd  Sep  2 12:07   (MAGIC.UTCC.UTK.E)
root     ttyre  Aug 31 12:05   (r1w2.pub:0.0)
ximing   ttys8  Sep  1 12:15   (UTKVX1.UTK.EDU)
```

FIGURE 7.2

Typical w command

```
chung    ttypc     1:07pm                           -csh
leon     ttype     1:00pm                           vi .mailrc
operator ttypf    Mon 4pm 3days                     -csh
harp     ttyq0    Wed10am 23:45       6             vi .twmrc
jepeway  ttyq1     9:05am  4:02       9        9    xterm -T
Uther -name Uther -e lo
sunil    ttyq2     9:37am     6       8        2    -sh
mkovarik ttyq3    10:55am    12      39             -csh
kovarik  ttyq4    10:42am     5       4             -csh
rell     ttyq5     1:06pm                           w
hamed    ttyq6    10:19am  1:31                     -csh
snyder   ttyq9    Mon 9am    33                     -sh
snyder   ttyqa    Mon10am    34      36             -sh
springer ttyqc    11:26am     4       6             rn
bagri    ttyqe     9:36am  3:31                     -sh
bagri    ttyqf     9:36am    51                     -sh
bagri    ttyr0     9:36am  1:49                     telnet utkvx3
mcconnel ttyr1    11:16am             7        6    rn
eljazzar ttyr8    11:03am    40                     -sh
bill     ttyr9    11:48am  1:06      12             -csh
root     ttyra    Tue12pm 2days                     -sh
harp     ttyrd    12:07pm  1:00                     -sh
root     ttyre    Tue12pm 2days                     -sh
ximing   ttys8    Wed12pm 22:19       2             -csh
```

FIGURE 7.3

Split talk screen

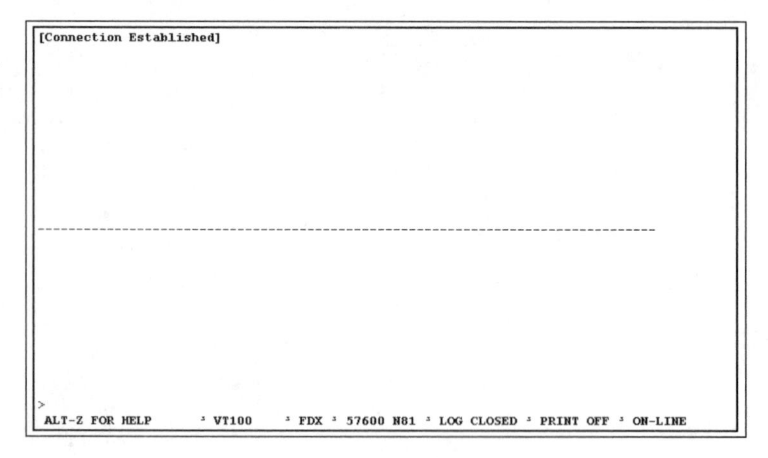

Of course you may not see this screen, even if the person you want to reach is online. That's because you can configure your account to reject such requests to talk, or the other person may be busy and simply choose not to respond. But when the connection is established, anything you type appears at the top of the split screen, and whatever the other person types appears at the bottom of the screen. This is a two-way link, so you both can type at the same time. It is a useful way to share a quick bit of information with someone else online with you, or to ask someone a quick question.

A similar command is **write**. This is a one-way link that lets you send a sentence to a specific user. To use **write**, type the following at the system prompt:

```
write username
```

The cursor moves down one line and waits for you to type the text. You can enter one or more lines, pressing **Enter** at the end of each line. When you have entered the last line, enter a **period** (.) by itself at the beginning of the last line, and the text will be sent to the specified user.

Write and **talk** are both useful ways to exchange information quickly with another user online. However, you should remember that the other person is logged into the Internet system for a reason. They may be downloading files, conducting research, or already talking with someone else.

TRAVEL TIP

__Write__ and __talk__ can be intrusive, so use these commands with people you know already. Even with people you know it is sometimes preferable to send them email first. If they are online, chances are they will check their mail within the next few minutes, so you can tell them you'd like to talk and let them contact you.

Using IRC (Internet Relay Chat)

When you want to go beyond talking briefly with a single user, you might want to try *IRC*, the *Internet Relay Chat*. This is a varied real-time conference system that lets you talk with as many people as you like, grouped together on *channels* by topic. Many users liken IRC to online CB, and that's not a bad analogy. If you've ever used Citizen's Band (CB) radio, you know that there are 40 radio channels accessible through a two-way radio.

Although any channel can be used to discuss any topic, by convention certain channels are used for specific purposes. Channel 9 is considered an emergency channel, for example, and there are other channels that are frequented by long-haul truck drivers. There is a channel to begin a conversation, but you are expected to move to another channel to continue your talk.

The IRC is, in some ways, similar. However, instead of 40 channels, there are usually around 2,000 or more. This is a dynamic number that changes depending on who is online and what they wish to discuss. However, channels are named and you can find channels dedicated to specific topics.

IRC Text Clients on the Host

Accessing IRC is a little like getting to Archie or Gopher. You probably have a local command file that will attach you to a preselected IRC server when you type the command **irc** at your service provider system prompt. Or, the following command sequence may work on your system:

```
irc nickname server
```

The nickname is the name you wish to use while on IRC. Many users simply use their own login name, in which case you can omit the nickname designation. However, if you would like others online to see you as "brighteyes," "hiker," "captncook," or another "handle," then specify it here. The server in this command is one of the active IRC servers. In fact, your service provider may have a command established to contact a default server so that all you need to do is type **irc** on the command line, or select **IRC** from a menu. Contact your service provider for the precise procedure for getting access to IRC.

Once on IRC, you will be presented with a split screen. There is only one line and a status bar at the bottom of the screen, and the top part of the screen is blank (see Figure 7.4).

FIGURE 7.4
IRC startup screen

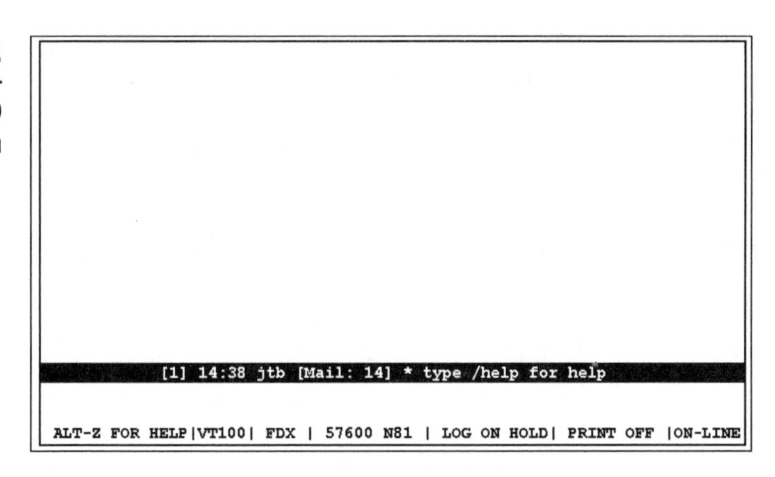

From this screen you can join a channel in progress or start your own conversation.

To find out what commands are available (and they vary slightly from server to server), type a forward slash and help: **/help**. You should see a screen similar to the one in Figure 7.5.

FIGURE 7.5
Sample IRC help screen

```
-help_US- *** HELP choices:
-help_US- !             @             ADMIN         ALIAS         ASSIGN
-help_US- AWAY          BASICS        BIND          BYE           CD
-help_US- CHANNEL       CLEAR         COMMANDS      COMMENT       CONNECT
-help_US- CTCP          DATE          DCC           DEOP          DESCRIBE
-help_US- DIE           DIGRAPH       DMSG          DQUERY        ECHO
-help_US- ENCRYPT       ETIQUETTE     EVAL          EXEC          EXIT
-help_US- EXPRESSIONS   FLUSH         FOREACH       HELP          HISTORY
-help_US- IF            IGNORE        INFO          INTRO         INVITE
-help_US- IRCII         JOIN          KICK          KILL          LASTLOG
-help_US- LEAVE         LINKS         LIST          LOAD          LUSERS
-help_US- ME            MENUS         MLOAD         MODE          MOTD
-help_US- MSG           NAMES         NEWS          NEWUSER       NICK
-help_US- NOTE          NOTICE        NOTIFY        ON            OPER
-help_US- PART          QUERY         QUIT          QUOTE         REDIRECT
-help_US- REHASH        RESTART       RULES         SAVE          SAY
-help_US- SEND          SERVER        SET           SIGNOFF       SLEEP
-help_US- SQUIT         STATS         SUMMON        TIME          TOPIC
-help_US- TRACE         TYPE          USERS         VERSION       WAIT
-help_US- WALLOPS       WHICH         WHILE         WHO           WHOIS
-help_US- WHOWAS        WINDOW        XECHO
      47 jtb [Mail: 14] * type /help for help

 ALT-Z FOR HELP| VT100| FDX |57600 N81| LOG OPEN | PRINT OFF | ON-LINE
```

From here the best way to find out about using IRC is to use the available help topics. Try **/help etiquette**, for example, to view a file that tells you some of the conventions of using IRC. Try **/help newuser** or **/help basics** for more information on getting started.

You can find out what topics are currently being discussed and how many users are working on each topic with the **list** command:

```
/list
```

This will produce a list similar to the one in Figure 7.6, except that it will be much longer. In fact, there may be two thousand or more conversations going on at any one time. You may be able to use **Ctrl+s** to stop the display and **Ctrl+q** to resume the display if you need time to read a screen. You also can turn on screen capture in your communications software to capture the list to disk. Then you can print it or study it in a word processor.

FIGURE 7.6

Partial IRC channel list

```
*** Channel    Users  Topic
    *** #pulse      4      Hey Ladies....I'm HERE!!!!!!
    *** #zircon     1
    *** #queen2     2
    *** #malacca    1
    *** #Randomnes  1      OD on BCNU -- September 6!!!
    *** #singapore  2
    *** #gbm        1      GAY_BLACK_MEN
    *** #buaya      2
    *** #omni       3
    *** #ffi        1
    *** #jen]       2
    *** #Roma       1      yes folks....that's Italian for Rome
    *** Prv         1
    *** #sexx       2
    *** Prv         2
    *** #desdemona  1
    *** #Talk       15     Stop messing with the channel!
    *** #wolvesden  1
    *** #mod        1
    *** #BoyScout   1
    *** #Sauna      1      Huh, heat ..
    *** Prv         2
    *** #Higgins    1
```

Another way to limit the length of the list is to specify how many users you'd like to see on any channel listed. If you enter the list command with a number switch, you will limit the list. The command **/list -10**, for example, lists only channels that have 10 or more users currently online. Be aware that some of the conversations that take place on IRC are strictly adult.

When you identify a conversation youÕd like to join from the list, you can type the following:

```
/join channelname
```

Your name is then added to those on that channel. Note that channels usually carry alphabetic names, such as #vine, #hamradio, or #bicycles. The pound sign (#) must be the first character in the name, but other than that requirement, a session can be named almost anything.

If you don't see a channel name that appeals to you, create your own by using **/join** and a name that does not already exist. Just be sure to place the pound sign at the beginning of the name. Before you create your own channel, try the **list** command. Notice that some channels have a description or comment beside them. After you create your own channel, you can add comments with the **/topic** command:

```
/topic      <--Wherein we discuss the weather
```

Then when anyone uses **/list**, your channel is displayed with this topic beside it:

```
#Wx   <--Wherein we discuss the weather
```

When you use the **/join** command, the others on the channel will see a message:

```
Tom has joined Channel #Bicycle
```

This lets everyone on the channel know you're there. Depending on who else is in the group, you may get a series of hellos from people welcoming you, or you may feel invisible. If no one talks to you for several minutes, you might try saying something to one of the other participants.

Select the name or nickname of the person you want to reach and type a message that begins with the name:

```
Curly: I'm really interested in the trip you mentioned.
Tell me more.
```

Without knowing who this person is, it is impossible to predict the response. You may get something like:

```
Who are you?
```

At that point, respond with some information about yourself, such as your real name (if you are using a nickname and don't mind sharing your real name with the channel) and perhaps your city. Each participant's nickname is displayed at the beginning of the line, but unless someone goes out of the way to find out more, that's all anyone knows.

If no one responds to you at this point, you can figure you have just joined a tightly closed clique. You might as well use **/leave channel** (where channel is the name of the channel you just joined) to back out of that conversation and move on somewhere else. In the unlikely event that you get an abusive message when you log on (**Get out of here! Who do you think you are?**), simply type **/leave channel** and don't go back. You gain nothing in arguing with boorish, inconsiderate people. When you're ready to leave IRC entirely, use **/quit** on the command line to return to your local host.

What about using some of the IRC commands after you get linked up with someone on a channel? Maybe you'd like to find out if there is anyone on IRC from Canada. Use the **/who** command with some additional information:

```
/who *.ca
```

You'll get a list of users currently logged on to any channel with **.ca** as the last entry in their user ID. This is the international abbreviation for Canada.

To find out who is on your channel, use **/who** with the channel name:

```
/who #tea
```

You'll get a display that shows you the real names, host names, and other information about everyone currently logged on to the channel #tea.

Suppose you suspect that someone you know is on IRC somewhere, but you don't know where. You can use **/who** to find out. Just join a channel (some **/who** features don't work if you're not on a channel), then use **/who** with the name of the person you're looking for. The display will show you that person's name and which channel he or she is currently on.

When you join an IRC channel, you are identified by the nickname you used to log on to IRC. You can change this with the **/nick** command:

```
/nick tomtom
```

IRC displays a message like: **Tom is now known as tomtom**.

Graphical Clients on Your Desktop

In addition to running an IRC client on your service provider's host machine, you can run an IRC program on your desktop if you have a network connection to the Internet. Remember, by network connection I mean that you are accessing the Internet over a Local Area Network to a local host that is in turn connected to the Internet, or you are using a SLIP or PPP connection.

Among the popular graphical IRC clients is WSIRC, written by Caesar M. Samsi. It is available for download from most service provider hosts. Look for the archive file **WSIRC14B.ZIP** (or something similar—versions change) for the PC. You must expand the storage archive and install the program on your desktop. First copy the **WSIRC14B.ZIP** file to a directory by itself. Then use PKUNZIP to expand it. Finally, in the Windows Program Manager, install an icon for the executable file by selecting **File** and choosing **New**. Specify the program Item, then choose the file **WSIRC.EXE** from the directory where you stored the files.

Now you can run the client from within the Program Manager. The program first will ask for a host name. You should check with your service provider for an appropriate address to insert in this dialog box. However, here is one that can get you started: **cs-pub.bu.edu**.

Once you enter the host information, you can launch the program. It produces the display shown in Figure 7.7. At the bottom of the screen is the familiar split-screen IRC display, but at the top is a Windows-compliant menu and icon bar. The help files with this product are excellent. Click on **Help** and read or print the information you need to get the most out of this client.

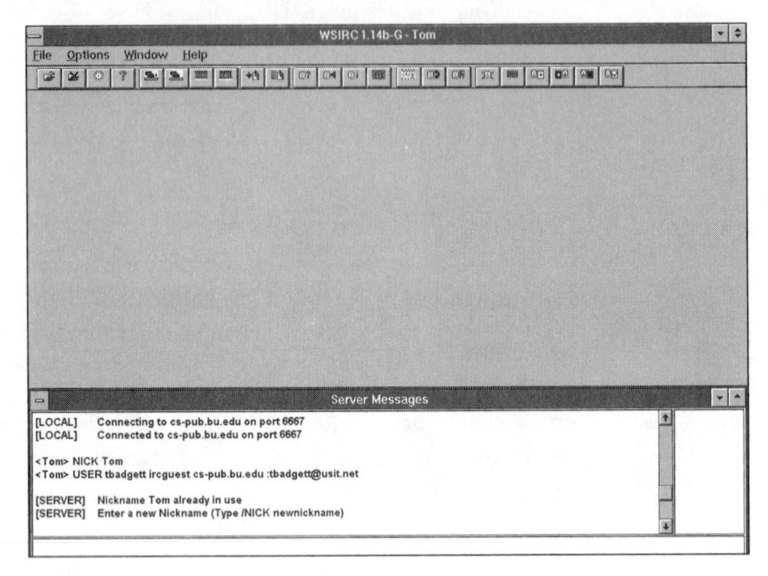

FIGURE 7.7
WSIRC opening screen

Learning your way around IRC is a lot like learning another language, finding your way around a new town, or playing blindman's buff. But there's also nothing like it. Get on, browse around, use help as often as you need, and ask questions of those you meet. Soon you'll be a veteran traveler whose IRC passport is full of stamps and whose memories are sharp and fresh. Enjoy!

MULTIMEDIA CONVERSATIONS ON THE INTERNET

It was only a matter of time. Put up a reasonably fast global network, make it available to the general public at a reasonable price through a network of service providers, and soon new applications will be developed. That's what has happened with the Internet. The traditional text-based Internet already is giving way to graphical access through the World Wide Web. Now, through the innovation of multimedia desktop computers and innovative software, you can talk through your computer, over the Internet, to other computer users anywhere in the world. In addition, with very little additional hardware and some software, you can add motion video for an impressive, low-cost video conferencing option.

The audio communications tool most widely distributed as this book is written is InternetPhone and the most popular video conferencing tool is C U See Me. I'll discuss these products briefly in the next section, but this is only the beginning. Keep your eyes—and your mind—open. We are destined to see even more innovative Internet communications tools as wider bandwidth options such as ISDN and fiber-optic connections become more common and more reasonably priced.

Using InternetPhone

InternetPhone, from Vocaltec, Inc., is a software application that uses a PC's sound card (Sound Blaster, for example) to process audio from a microphone and send it over the Internet connection. A similar sound card on the other end of the link converts the digitized audio for processing through the sound card to a set of speakers or ear phones.

As this book is written, InternetPhone is available for download from **ftp.vocaltec.com** or through the WWW at **http://www.vocaltec.com**. Registering the software costs $99.00. You can evaluate the product without registering it, but you will be limited to a 60-second talk time before you must exit the program and restart it. You can do this as often as you want, but obviously, to be useful, the program must be registered so you can obtain the key to remove this restriction. Figure 7.8 shows a typical InternetPhone screen.

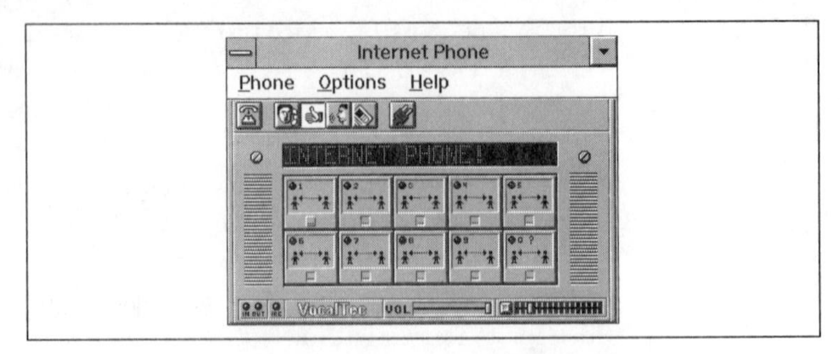

FIGURE 7.8 Typical InternetPhone screen

This product—and others like it—is changing so rapidly that it is difficult to provide firm specifications. In general, however, InternetPhone works in the following way. After the software is installed, you can connect over the Internet to another computer running InternetPhone. Then, like a two-way radio, you can click on a **push to talk** button and talk through your sound card to the remote machine. When you are finished, you release the **push to talk** button to listen to the response.

Sound quality is reasonably good and conference call and duplex (without push to talk) versions are in the works. In addition, similar products from other vendors are being designed and will be on the market soon.

The best way to get more information about InternetPhone is to download the evaluation version, install it, read the help files, and try it out.

Using C U See Me

If hearing the person on the other side of the connection isn't good enough for you, consider video conferencing. A shareware product called C U See Me, available for PC and Macintosh computers, lets you use a computer with a sound card and a video card attached through an Internet reflector to see and talk with other users who also are using the same reflector.

If you have a Mac AV or a PC with a sound card and a video card such as the Video Blaster, you can attach a simple camera such as a surveillance camera or a home-style camcorder to your computer, launch the software, and talk in real time with users anywhere in the world.

You can have up to eight screens active at one time, but you get better response if you keep the number of active windows to a minimum. Figure 7.9 shows a typical C U See Me video screen.

FIGURE 7.9

Typical C U See Me video screen

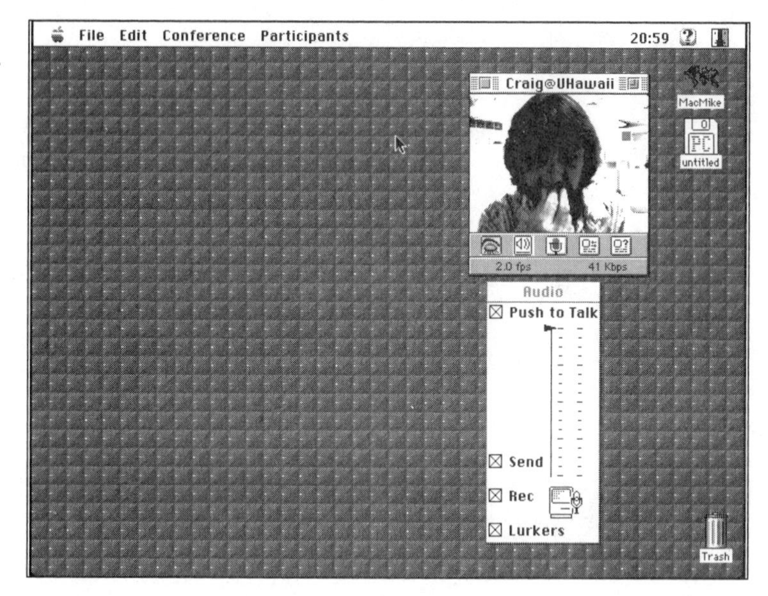

You won't see full-motion video on this link. The software is capable of about 15 frames per second, which is about half the 30 frames per second required for natural, full-motion video. But for most video conferencing applications, where one or more persons sit at a desk in front of the computer-based camera, very little motion is going on in the first place. When someone does move, you'll notice a jerky motion—more jerky at some times than at others—but once you get used to it, the effect is quite acceptable.

Just as you learn your way around the WWW by browsing with Netscape or Mosaic, you soon will learn which sites you prefer to use. A popular site is **reflector.cit.cornell.edu (192.35.82.96)** at Cornell University. You can nearly always find some kind of video activity there. Other public sites include:

```
nysernet.org (192.77.173.2)
isis.dccs.upenn.edu (130.91.72.36)
hilda.ncsc.org (128.109.178.103)
gatekeeper.imagen.com (161.33.3.1)
skyhawk.gte.com (132.197.10.74)
norm.itn.med.umich.edu (141.214.20.107)
fenris.dhhalden.no (158.36.33.3)
sunten.wiezmann.ac.il (132.76.64.143)
```

As you use C U See Me, ask the people you meet about other sites. You'll also find useful information about this application in newsgroups where people use the keyboard to talk about C U See Me.

Even if you don't have a sound card, you can still use a video card and a camera for video conferencing. The software supports typing text from the keyboard. The text appears at the bottom of your open window on the remote computer. You can then listen to audio from the remote user, if available, or watch as they respond to your comments with the keyboard. Either way, you can see the other user in real time as you communicate.

INTERNET CULTURE

Whenever any group gathers, whether you realize it consciously or not, there is an underlying culture that most people observe—a set of rules or guidelines of language, behavior, and common history. As you move from one group to another—from family to work to school and so on—the culture changes. You have a different relationship with members of your family during breakfast than you do with your coworkers at the office. There's also a difference between the relationship among you and your coworkers and between you and the boss.

The same is true as you travel the Internet. In general, you should approach the people and groups you meet on the Internet as you would coworkers in your office. The relationship will be semi-formal and generally relaxed. As you spend more time on conferences and talking within groups, you will find a few individuals or groups with whom you are more comfortable.

It has been said many times, but I'll say it again here: don't get lulled into a false sense of detachment as you exchange electronic mail or live conversations. I see a lot of messages cross the Internet in conferences and other public places where it is obvious that a couple of individuals have a history of disagreement. Their written tone is inappropriate, their language harsh. It is impolite to impose this kind of personal conflict on the others who share the conference.

Also, even as you get to know one or more individuals better than others, maintain a sense of restraint and propriety. Until you know who you really are talking with, there's no way to know who is on the other end of the wire.

Who is Internet?

The Internet is composed of companies, groups, and individuals from virtually all walks of life. The sameness of the text-based screen strips away the size of the office, the cut of the suit, the glitter of the diamonds, and the shape of the bike. I've talked to company presidents, government officials, college students, teachers, housewives, and elementary school kids.

What comes through is the knowledge each individual brings to the keyboard, a sense of helpfulness, a willingness to share, a tolerance for and acceptance of those who know less or whose lifestyle may be different.

The point is, don't ever assume anything about another Internet user. Just as you would when meeting someone in person for the first time, maintain a courteous, open demeanor as you get to know each other.

Internet Etiquette (Netiquette)

Etiquette in any social situation is a varied and personal call. What is appropriate for one group or pair of individuals may be unsuitable for someone else. My best advice is to try to match your language and tone to that of the others with whom you relate on the Internet. And, trite as it may seem, the golden rule—treat others like you want to be treated—is hard to beat as a general operating principle.

Language

I've mentioned earlier in this book that there are occasions on the Internet when language becomes raw. It depends on your background and orientation, of course, but I don't believe it is necessary or appropriate to sprinkle your Internet conversation with four letter words, personal or racial slurs, or any other language that might be offensive to the person you are talking with or to anyone else who may view the message.

You will see some of this on the Internet, unfortunately. When it occurs it is best ignored. Calling attention to someone else's inappropriate behavior won't usually gain you anything and may in fact cause another inappropriate barrage.

Such comments on the Internet are called flames and the person who acts this way is sometimes called a flamer.

Joining Conversations

Conferences and IRC conversations are generally open so that anyone can wander through the electronic room where they are taking place and listen in or comment. Just as you would slowly approach two people standing together talking, you should develop the habit of making yourself known if you want to join a discussion, and then wait to be recognized.

In addition, make sure you are up to speed on what is being discussed and who is taking part in the conversation before you jump in. As I've said, it is sometimes easy to let the electronic medium isolate you from the people on the other end of the link to the point that normal social conventions you follow automatically in person get sidestepped. Just be aware that this is a possibility and move slowly. You'll be glad you paused to review what you said before you send that email message. It takes only a moment, and it can save face if you tend to react too quickly.

Introductions

As a participant in an existing conversation or conference, you can do your part to make new people feel welcome (if they are!) by doing what you would do in person: introduce people to each other.

Suppose you're on an IRC channel and see a message like:

```
Blondie has joined Channel: #vine
```

If you know who Blondie is (a friend, perhaps, or someone you met on another conference), then you can mention to others on the conference or IRC channel who Blondie is, how you know this person, and any special interests she may have. This helps others understand who they are talking to.

Of course, you should make sure this is the same "Blondie" you know. Anyone can choose to use any nickname, as long as it is not already in use.

Showing Emotions

As we have said, the text-oriented screen tends to cause some isolation among Internet users. It is easy for conversations to become rather staid. Over the years, conventions have evolved for showing emotions that can spice up your conversation and help others understand your current state of mind.

Probably the most common symbol for showing emotions that you're likely to see is the smiley face:

```
:)
```

Sometimes you get a variation on the basic face:

```
:-)
```

Or a winking smiley face:

```
;-)
```

Or one with glasses:

```
8-)
```

Then of course, when things aren't going too well, or if the topic is a sad one (such as "I have a dental appointment after school"):

```
:(
or
:-(
```

By convention, these *emoticons* are also used:

```
(@@) you're kidding
:-1  smirk
:-D  said with a smile
```

You may see others. Different groups use different symbols. Use your imagination, squint a little, and you'll be able to understand what is being said.

You can also specify emotions by spelling out a word. Usually you surround the emotion with asterisks:

```
*grins*
*sigh*
*poor me*
*giggle*
```

You get the idea. As you are talking, or within email messages, you can tell the other person what you are feeling with one or two word statements like this surrounded with asterisks.

You can also explain actions, either to be funny or to describe what is happening on your end. Suppose you just spilled a coke on your keyboard:

```
***ACTION: Clumsily Tom knocks over the glass.
```

Or someone on your link says something that makes you happy ("I'm sending you a report that will answer all those questions and more."):

```
***ACTION: Tom stands up, jumps up and down, shouts!
```

As you get more experience with real-time links you will become creative in expressing yourself. It adds life to the conversation and makes you and the people you meet more relaxed. Just remember the first rule we mentioned earlier—be polite, reasonably reserved, and slow to jump in. Once you have gotten "in" with a group, however, be yourself, say what you feel, and show what you feel. It's fun!

However, one word of caution. You should get to know the group with which you are interacting before you use these emoticons too freely. Some groups think of these additions to your text as childish and look down on those who use them. This is a narrow view, in my opinion, but as in any other interpersonal relationship, you will get along better with fellow Internet travelers if you try to adhere to the conventions of the group.

Games

Just traveling around the Internet is fun, even if all you do is poke around looking at conversations and finding files. However, there are other things you can do besides talk with other travelers. There are interactive games you can play by yourself or with others.

What would traveling be like without games? Your family vacation is headed for problems if there aren't enough games in the back seat to keep the kids happy in the car. Your Internet travels also lack something if you don't investigate the games you can find there. I can't possibly show you where all the games on the Internet are, but I can point you in the right direction. Here's one way to start researching Internet games on your own with Archie.

At your local host, execute the Archie client, if you have access to one. (If you don't know what this means, reread the discussion of Archie in Chapter 4.) If you don't have a client, Telnet to one of the available Archie sites. Once you are in Archie (or the client), issue this command:

prog game

You should get a familiar Archie list of hosts, directories, and files similar to Figure 7.10.

FIGURE 7.10

Portion of Archie PROG game search results

```
>prog game
Processing Case Insensitive Substring Search for 'game'

Host iamsun.unibe.ch

Location: /
      DIRECTORY drwxrwxr-x        512  Aug 24 1992  games

Host hpcsos.col.hp.com

Location: /mirrors/.scsi5/386BSD/0.1-ports
      DIRECTORY drwxr-xr-x       1024  Jun 16 02:16  games
Location: /mirrors/.scsi5/hp95lx
      DIRECTORY drwxr-xr-x       1024  Aug 30 01:36  games

Host inf.informatik.uni-stuttgart.de

Location: /pub/archive/comp.sources/amiga
      DIRECTORY drwxr-xr-x        512  Mar 30 11:02  games
Location: /pub/archive/comp.sources
      DIRECTORY drwxrwxr-x       4608  Sep  1 00:04  games

Host irisa.irisa.fr

Location: /pub
      DIRECTORY drwxr-xr-x        512  Jul  2 15:49  games

Host grasp1.univ-lyon1.fr

Location: /pub/faq-by-newsgroup/rec/rec.games.empire
    DIRECTORY drwxrwxr-x        512  Aug  6 23:20  games
Location: /pub/faq-by-newsgroup/rec/rec.games.frp.announce
      DIRECTORY drwxrwxr-x        512  Feb  7 00:00  games
```

The listing in Figure 7.10 is a partial one. Notice how many of the directories in the list have the name **games**. There's no real way to know exactly what is in there, but the parent directories (the ones above the games directories) give you some hints. Notice the series of directories at the **grasp1.univ-lyon1.fr** host, for example. (This domain name indicates that the host is in France at the University of Lyon.) There are several game directories that have **/pub/faq-by-newsgroup/rec** as the parent. You can guess that the directories under this parent will deal with recreation topics (**rec**), and that they include newsgroups and will deal with frequently asked questions (**faq**) stored in a public directory (**pub**).

If you FTP to this site, then change to one of the game directories under this parent, you can use **ls** to see what is there. Here's the complete process from your local host. Enter these commands and you should get the results we show. Remember to turn on screen capture or a log file within your communications package to save information to disk. (We have eliminated some of the login banners for clarity.)

```
> telnet archie.sura.net
login: qarchie
>prog game
Processing Case Insensitive Substring Search for 'game'
```

This will produce the listing shown in Figure 7.10. When the listing is complete, exit Archie by typing **quit** at the prompt:

```
> quit
```

Now you are back at your local host and you are ready to use FTP to get some of the information you've found. Try any directory you like, but here's one sample series of commands that will show you how to explore these game directories on your own:

```
> ftp graspl.univ-lyon1.fr
Name (graspl.univ-lyon1.fr:tbadgett): anonymous
331 Guest login ok, send your complete email
address as password.
Password:
```

At the **Password:** prompt, enter your complete mailing address. The system will display the **ftp>** prompt and wait for your command. Enter the following:

```
ftp> cd /pub/faq-by-
newsgroup/rec/rec.games.netrek/games
250 CWD command successful.
```

```
ftp> ls
200 PORT command successful.
150 Opening ASCII mode data connection for file list.
netrek
226 Transfer complete.
8 bytes received in 3e-06 seconds (2.6e+03 Kbytes/s)
ftp> cd netrek
250 CWD command successful.
ftp> ls
200 PORT command successful.
150 Opening ASCII mode data connection for file list.
faq
server-list
ftp-list
226 Transfer complete.
28 bytes received in 0.02 seconds (1.4 Kbytes/s)
ftp> get faq
200 PORT command successful.
150 Opening ASCII mode data connection for faq (17844
bytes).
226 Transfer complete.
local: faq remote: faq
18279 bytes received in 1.8 seconds (9.8 Kbytes/s)
```

Now you have the file **faq** on your local host. This file is a text file that includes the answers to many questions about the networked game Netrek, which is played by teams of players simultaneously. Follow the same procedure to get the remaining files in this directory, and you have the basis for learning about playing an interactive, multiuser Star Trek–type game over the Internet. When you have all the files you want from this server, type **close** to stay in FTP but disconnect from the Univ-Lyon1 host. Now you can use the **open** command to attach to another FTP site and browse for more files or games. If you are through with FTP, type **quit** to return to your local host.

There are many other networked and single-user games you can play on your PC, Amiga, or Macintosh. Simply use FTP to get to the listed site, use **cd** to change to the directory that contains the information you want, then use **get** to copy the files from the remote host to your local host. If you want to get the games over to your own desktop Macintosh or PC, use Kermit, ZMODEM, or another protocol. See the discussion of protocol transfers in Chapter 3.

To find out more about Internet game playing, get onto IRC (see the discussion earlier in this chapter) and look for a discussion group about games or entertainment. Join the conference and ask a lot of questions. With few exceptions, the people on the Internet are more than willing to help you find what you're looking for. And, of course, you can use USENET newsgroups to find a lot of game information. Just browse the newsgroups list for games, or for the specific game you're interested in discussing.

If you look around you'll find servers for popular board games such as chess, bridge, go, backgammon, and maybe Scrabble. Use Gopher or Archie to scan the network for games or game topics that interest you. See the Recreation section in Chapter 8 for a listing of other games available on the Internet.

WHAT YOU LEARNED

I have discussed how to talk to other users directly, either by using **talk** or **write** for one-on-one communications, or by using IRC for general discussion with many users. Then I introduced you to C U See Me, an interactive video conferencing application, and InternetPhone, a way to talk, using your own voice, to users anywhere in the world.

These facilities are useful additions to the general network features of email and file storage. They bring the Internet alive, making it full of people with feelings, skills, and interests that match your own or that lead you into entirely new directions. These facilities, like most of what you'll find on the Internet, are best learned with hands-on practice. That should be your next step after studying this lesson: get on the Internet and try talking to someone or joining an IRC channel. This is how you find your way through new territory.

In the next chapter I will show you some specific places to look for interesting conversations or files to read. Chapter 8 will serve as an ongoing reference as you use the Internet to search for specific information. You can also use the reference information in Chapter 8 to get you started with your Internet travels.

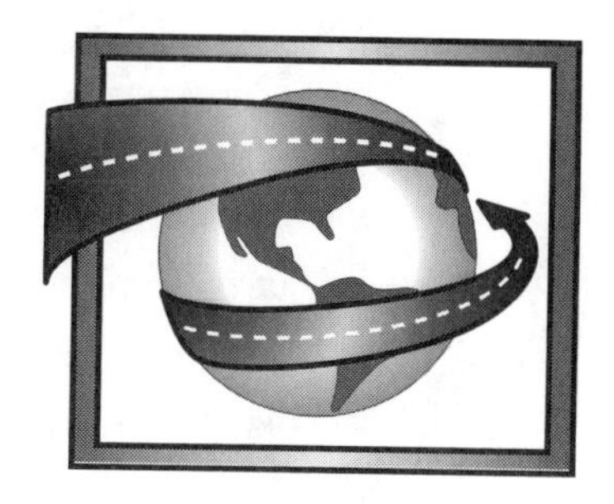

Chapter 8

Collecting Souvenirs on the Internet

As you roam the Internet you will find reference files, graphics images, sound files, names and addresses, and other items of interest. In addition, you can start with an idea of something you'd like to find or learn, then go to the Internet to search it out.

This chapter can serve as a reference of interesting, educational, and commercial items you might want to look for on the Internet. Pick some items at random and practice your searching skills, then refer back to this chapter later as you think of specific areas you want to research or learn.

In this chapter I will list and describe many of the souvenirs and treasures I have found on the Internet as a way of helping you find your own collectables. I can't possibly show you everything that's out there—and my treasures may be your junk—but from the descriptions and road maps you can get into areas you might not have found alone.

I have organized information into groups analogous to the USENET newsgroups I described earlier—with some poetic license. You will find Internet resources grouped under these headings:

- Computers
- Science and Other Technology
- Recreation
- Commerce and Business
- Religion
- Education
- Government
- Reference
- Books and More
- Art
- Miscellaneous Resources

I have included one or more subgroups within some of these broad areas. The groups and subgroups are set up as table of contents entries, so you can turn back to the table of contents for a quick outline-type summary of what you might find in this chapter. In addition, the index lists most of the items you'll find here by topic and description. And, of course, you can just turn through the pages and see what names, headings, or descriptions capture your attention.

Some of the entries will show you simply where to find the information on the Internet. With other entries I'll provide descriptions depending on the information I have and, frankly, on my level of interest in the topic. Most of the resources I mention are accessible via FTP or by sending an email message asking for more information. Others are reached with Telnet. For example, there is a mail server on **rtfm.mit.edu**. You can address this server as **mail-server@rtfm.mit.edu**. For details on how to operate this server, send a message to that address with the word "help" in the BODY of the message.

You'll find some references to FTP sites that you also can reach with a news reader such as Trumpet News (if you have a

SLIP connection or another IP connection) or tin (for terminal access). These are entries with newsgroup references, or with file names such as **alt.society**. If you are comfortable with one of the available news readers, just go to a news server and search for the topic I mention. That's a better way of following a specific topic. On the other hand, the reference I give will get you started with a topic, and show you how to locate specific files on the Internet.

In addition, I'll show many World Wide Web listings in the form of a URL with perhaps some additional text describing the site. As I have said before, you may be able to find a WWW reference to a topic I list in another format by using a WebCrawler or by entering a host name as an http address. That's part of the Internet experience: experimentation to find what you want.

Use this listing as you would any telephone directory or catalog, remembering that things on the Internet change rapidly. If I tell you how to find something and you can't locate it where I said, you can assume that it has been removed or moved. If it has been removed, there's not much you can do. If, on the other hand, it has been moved, you might look around and find it. I have discovered, for example, that as the number of files in a particular area gets larger, system managers frequently create another subdirectory for that group of files.

So, if I tell you that a series of files on baboon feeding habits is at a certain host in the subdirectory **/pub/sci/animal** and you can't find them there, try another directory. It might be that the diversity of the animal directory grew to the point that a separate directory was created for baboons. Use **ls** to see what files are there, then try **cd** to change to the baboons directory if it is listed. Then your files would be in the directory **/pub/sci/animal/baboons**.

With most systems, when you enter via FTP you have a fair amount of freedom to move among directories and look for entries. Before you leave where you are, use **pwd** to list the current directory. That will help you return to the location later if you discover that what you want is in this directory after all.

If, after trying all this, the files you thought should be there can't be found, you might as well go on to another topic. In all likelihood the files have been moved to another system or deleted.

I also urge you to try Gopher, Archie, and other tools you'll find along the way. Browsing the Internet is like looking up something in an encyclopedia. You start out looking for one thing and end up finding something else as well.

Because you most likely are dealing with UNIX-based systems as you travel the Internet, remember that what you enter at any prompt is probably case sensitive. If I tell you to look for something in the **/pub/libraries/INFO.net/Files** directory, for example, you must enter the path exactly as indicated, using the same upper and lower case combinations. Otherwise, you probably will get an error message indicating that no such file or directory exists.

The directories and resources I list are only a small portion of what any listed server has available. Once you have connected to an FTP site to download one specific file, look around and see what else is there. Chances are that there are lots of additional offerings you might want in addition to the one listed.

INTERNET TOOLS: A REFRESHER

I've already shown you how to use Archie, Gopher, and WAIS to locate information on the Internet, and I've discussed FTP as a way to download that data. For full details on these topics, refer to Chapter 4. In Chapter 5 you can learn about Netscape, Mosaic and other World Wide Web tools for navigating the Internet. Here I will present a quick reference to finding an information searching server.

Archie Reference

Archie is a facility for searching Internet archives for files that contain words or characters you specify. It is a way of finding all files that deal with a specific topic.

You usually access Archie through a local client that attaches to a remote server. To get to your client, try one of the following commands: **Archie**, **QArchie**, or **XArchie**. If none of these work, contact your service provider to see if there is another

Archie command that you should use. If not, you can access an Archie server directly via Telnet. The syntax is **telnet ArchieServerName**, where ArchieServerName is the address of an Archie server. Choose one of the servers listed in Chapter 4.

When you have established a connection to an Archie server, either via Telnet or through a local client, use **prog text** to find a topic, where text is a one-word topic you'd like to find. This will locate the names of files that include the text you specified. You can narrow the search by adding additional parameters to the search line, as I showed in Chapter 4.

If you don't find what you want by searching for file names, try the **whatis** command, which searches a database of topics instead of file names. For example, a file named **elemedu** may contain information about elementary education, but if you conduct an Archie file search for **education** or **elementary**, you won't find it. The subject database will list this file along with the topics it contains.

Gopher Reference

The Gopher utility presents a menu-driven interface that lets you browse for topics. Like Archie, Gopher is accessed through a local client that attaches to a remote server (in most cases). The command **gopher** (or **xgopher**) at your local prompt should get you online with a Gopher server. If not, contact your service provider.

You can use Gopher itself to find out more details about Gopher. For example, if you launch Gopher at **gopher.tc.umn.edu** (University of Minnesota—a popular Gopher server), you can select "All the Gopher Servers in the World/" under "Other Gopher and Information Servers/" from the main menu. This will lead you down a winding path of server site and Gopher information.

You can also FTP information about Gopher by using the following commands:

```
ftp rtfm.mit.edu
cd /pub/usenet/news.answers
get gopher-faq
```

WAIS Reference

WAIS (Wide Area Information Servers) is another searching tool. WAIS—pronounced "ways"—provides a searchable user interface like Archie. Try **wais** or **swais** at your system prompt to access a local client that will attach automatically to one of the available WAIS servers. If that doesn't work, use Archie and **prog wais** to help you locate a WAIS server by finding systems that have files having something to do with WAIS. Then you can use Telnet to attach to WAIS.

FTP Reference

When you find a file with Archie, you have to use FTP to get it to your system where you can read it. You may also use FTP with Gopher and WAIS, or you may be able to download files directly inside these utilities.

To use FTP, first identify the host name where the information you want to access is located. Then use this command:

```
ftp hostname
```

When the host answers and displays a **name**: prompt, type **anonymous** or **ftp** (these terms are synonymous). Use your full electronic mailing address (email address) as the password. You should see a prompt such as:

```
ftp>
```

Now you can set the current directory with the **cd** command, and list the files and subdirectories in this current directory with **ls**. Use **get** to copy a file or files from the remote machine to the home directory on your machine.

Remember that FTP can transfer files in ASCII (text) or binary format, but that the default format is ASCII. Before you transfer a program file or any file with a **.Z**, **.ZIP**, or **.GZ** extension, type **binary** at the FTP prompt. This will change the ASCII default to binary, ensuring a reliable file transfer. If you fail to do this, compressed files will transfer as text, and you won't be able to uncompress them once you have them copied.

INTERNET REFERENCE GUIDE

In this section I'll show you a sampling of information available on the Internet, organized by major topics. Practice using Archie, Gopher, WAIS, and FTP with the files and addresses I provide here. Then you can go out on your own looking for topics I didn't include for you.

Computers

It is appropriate that the network that ties together so many different computer systems would provide a lot of information about the technology it serves. From computer games and technology to software, security, and networking data, you can find a lot of information about computers on the Internet.

Computer Security

```
ftp cert.sei.cmu.edu
cd /pub
```

Use **dir** or **ls** to locate a variety of files and directories. You can find information from CERT, the Computer Emergency Response Team, a federally-funded group that works in the field of computer and network security.

Computer Ethics

```
ftp ftp.unm.edu
cd /ethics
```

Use **ls** or **dir** to find a variety of files that deal with computer use and ethics. The data includes a bibliography of Canadian and U.S. articles, the Bitnet abuse policy, and information on laws that cover computer crime.

Free Computer Software

```
ftp prep.ai.mit.edu
cd /pub/gnu
```

This directory contains a number of public software offerings, primarily for UNIX platforms. This software is offered under the umbrella of the Free Software Foundation (FSF), an organization that creates and distributes software without fee or license restrictions.

Get the file COPYING for information on the "general public license," under which this software is distributed.

You can get more information by sending email to **gnu@prep.ai.mit.edu**.

MS-DOS Archive

If you are into studying MS-DOS machines and learning what others are saying about MS-DOS and doing with it, send an email message to **listserv@TACOM-EMH1.Army.Mil.** Place the command **subscribe msdos-ann** in the body of the message. This will get you on the MS-DOS mailing list. If you want to turn off your subscription, send an email message to **listserv@TACOM-EMH1.Army.Mil** and include the message **unsubscribe msdos-ann**.

KnowBot

As you roam the Internet you'll encounter interesting characters with "bot" in their names, or who introduce themselves as something bot. These are software "robots" that are written to perform a variety of information services, such as automatically logging onto a service, searching for certain strings of characters and providing a pre-programmed response, and other jobs.

One interesting bot is the KnowBot Information Service. It is really a database of Internet services, hosts, and users that you can search for data. Here's how to get to it:

```
telnet regulus.cs.bucknell.edu 185
```

You don't have to log on; you are attached automatically to the KnowBot server.

TRAVEL TIP

The number after this Telnet command (185 in this case) is a port number. This is a way of entering a remote host in a special way, triggering onsite software to handle the logon. Usually when you Telnet to a specific port number, the remote host will log you on automatically and launch a specific utility or service. In this case, it is the KnowBot service.

Figure 8.1 shows the opening screen, while Figure 8.2 lists available commands on this service.

FIGURE 8.1

Opening KnowBot screen

```
usit% telnet regulus.cs.bucknell.edu 185
Trying 134.82.20.31 ...
Connected to regulus.cs.bucknell.edu.
Escape character is '^]'.
Knowbot Information Service (V1.0). Copyright CNRI 1990. All Rights Reserved.
Try ? or man for help.
> █
```

Type **man** at the KnowBot prompt to display a manual entry telling you how to issue commands and find the data you want to locate.

FIGURE 8.2

Available KnowBot commands

```
Queries must be longer than one character, must start with an alphabetic
character, and cannot be a common word such as netaddress, whois or finger.

Commands are:
-------------
service  service@host [service@host ...]
services
org      organization
country  country
echo     [on|off]
ident    service-specific-identifier
print
query    username
username (where ``username'' is the name
         to be searched for
help, ?  print this summary
man      print manual page entry
quit
exit
>
```

Sound Files

Look for an increasing number of picture, sound, and motion video files on the Internet. These are just a portion of what's out there. Download these **.au**, **.WAV**, **.MID,** and other sound files for use directly on a Sun or compatible workstation, a PC, or a Macintosh. To play some files on a PC or anything else, you may need to convert them. A program called SOX will convert **.au** files. Get it in the **/pub/sounds/SoundConversion** directory at the FTP site **ftp.luth.se**. Get the file appropriate for your system. **sox7dos.zip**, for example, is the current MS-DOS version. Be sure to get **sox.doc** for information on using the programs as well.

Here are a few representative sounds you can find out there. If you're using MS Windows you can use SOX to convert to **.WAV** format, then use these sounds in your Windows programs, including Media Player. You can use the **.au** files directly on your Sun workstation.

```
ftp sunsite.unc.edu
cd /pub/multimedia/sun-sounds/startrek
get energy_loss.au
ftp ftp.cica.indiana.edu
cd /pub/pc/win3/sounds
```

You'll find a variety of sound files in this directory. Use **get** to download them to your local host. Just make sure you set the file type to binary as described earlier before starting the download.

```
ftp sunsite.unc.edu
cd /pub/multimedia/chinese-music
ftp ftp.luth.se
cd /pub/sounds/songs
```

Use **ls** at both of these sites for a list of available sound files.

Network Information

As you might expect, you can use the resources of the Internet to learn about the Internet and other network resources. For example, suppose you want to send email to someone on FIDOnet, but you don't know their address. Use the **fidonet-nodelist** entry in WAIS to search for the name, then get the list.

Here are some other network information resources you can access on the Internet.

```
ftp ftp.msstate.edu
cd /pub/docs
get internetwork-mail-guide
```

This is an online mail guide to help you use the mail facilities of the Internet, particularly internetwork mailing. Also try **get finding-addresses** for additional information.

```
ftp nic.ddn.mil
cd /rfc
```

Use **dir** to list the files there, a series of RFCs (request for comments). These are files that describe how the Internet works, how to use it, and what its future might be. You'll find files in various formats here, from text to PostScript. This is a large directory with well over 1,300 files. Obviously, this is a dynamic resource that changes as new comments are added. The files are named with numbers, so there's no way to know from the file name what the topic of the file might be.

You can get a clue to what's here with the **fyi-by-title.txt** file and the **fyi-index.txt** file. Use **get** to download them to your system, then use **!cat** to view them, or exit to your local host and use more or an editor to look at them.

```
ftp boulder.colorado.edu
cd /pub/news-talk
get What_is_Usenet?
```

This is a file that gives you some insight into USENET (as the title suggests). It is a good place to start understanding this sometimes slippery world. Also, there are a number of other USENET-related files in this subdirectory.

Freenets

A freenet actually is somewhat of a misnomer. These public Internet access points aren't necessarily free, but they certainly can provide very low-cost access to the Internet or to some Internet facilities such as email and USENET news. The majority of freenets are configured alike, using the "city" metaphor—Look for interesting or useful information according to its location within the city. In general, you Telnet to a freenet, login as guest or visitor, and you have access to the services of the freenet and to the Internet. For general freenet information, send email to **bbslist@aug3.augsburg.edu.** Just a mail message is all that is required; no subject or body necessary. This will get you three very interesting lists.

To try a freenet, use this command:

```
telnet freenet-in-a.cwru.edu
```

This connects you to the Cleveland Freenet. You will get an opening screen where you can just follow directions. As with many freenets, there is a maximum number of users. If the system is full, you will receive a message telling you to try again later.

Heartland Free-Net

```
Peoria - 674-1100  Bloomington-Normal - 438-2300
telnet heartland.bradley.edu
login: bbguest
Press enter at the password prompt.
```

This is a freenet funded by a variety of private and public sponsors, including Caterpillar, Inc., Illinois State University, Peoria Journal Star, Illinois Bell, and others.

Through this system you can browse as a visitor, or access more facilities as a registered user. Either way, there's no charge, except that out-of-state residents must pay a $5.00 registration fee. Among the features of this freenet are:

1. Send and receive electronic mail from other Registered Users.
2. Link to Other Selected Computer Systems on the Internet.
3. Pose anonymous questions to experts in a field within the Free-net system to which you may not normally have access.
4. Exchange ideas with other users in the Public Forum or in any of the Open Discussion Areas of the Free-net.

Youngstown Freenet

```
telnet yfn2.ysu.edu
login: visitor
```

As a guest you can browse the freenet and read messages. However, to post any messages of your own, you'll need to register. The system is offered at no charge under the sponsorship of the St. Elizabeth Hospital Medical Center and Youngstown State University. After a brief opening message, you'll see the main menu screen shown in Figure 8.3.

FIGURE 8.3

Main Youngstown Freenet menu screen

```
<<< Main Menu >>>
  1 Administration
  2 Post Office
  3 The Public Square
  4 The Communications Center
  5 The Animal Hospital
  6 The Business & Industrial Park
  7 The Computer Center
  8 The Courthouse
  9 The Government Center
 10 The Hospital
 11 Library Systems
 12 The House of Worship
 13 The Human Services Building
 14 The Teleport
 15 Television & Radio Stations
 16 The USA/Today Headline News
 17 Youngstown State University
 18 Academy One
 19 NPTN Special Projects
-----------------------------------------------------
h=Help, x=Exit YFN, "go help"=extended help

Your Choice ==> █
```

National Capital Freenet

```
telnet freenet.carleton.ca
login: guest
```

The main National Capital Freenet menu screen is shown in Figure 8.4.

FIGURE 8.4

National Capital Freenet main menu screen

```
          <<< The National Capital FreeNet -- Main Menu >>>

  1 About The National Capital FreeNet...
  2 Administration...
  3 Post Office...
  4 Public Discussion...
  5 Social Services, Health, & Environment Centre...
  6 Community Associations...
  7 The Government Centre...
  8 Science, Engineering and Technology Centre...
  9 Schools, Colleges and Universities...
 10 The Newsstand...
 11 Libraries...
 12 Special Interest Groups...
 13 Communications Centre...
 14 Professional Associations...
 15 Help Desk...
 16 Menu principal français...
 17 Make a donation to keep FreeNet free
-----------------------------------------------------
h=Help, x=Exit FreeNet, p=previous, u=up, m=main
Your Choice ==> █
```

Victoria Freenet

```
telnet freenet.victoria.bc.ca
login: guest
```

The main Victoria Freenet screen is shown in Figure 8.5.

FIGURE 8.5

Main Victoria Freenet screen

```
Welcome to the VICTORIA FREE-NET
*** MAIN MENU ***
==> go main
  1 Victoria Free-Net Headquarters (Register Here)
  2 Commerce Building
  3 Douglas & Yates ... the Hangout!
  4 Government Building
  5 House of Worship
  6 Library and Information Services
  7 Local/Global Community Centre
  8 Medical Centre
  9 Post Office
 10 Schoolhouse
 11 Science and Environment Centre
 12 Performing Arts Centre
 13 Special Interest Groups (SIGs)
 14 Help Desk
 15 What's New on the Victoria Free-Net
 16 Fundraising (Get your Personalized Account Application form here!)
 17 Canadian Federal Budget Information (bilingual access) <Web>
--------------------------------------------------------------------------
h=Help, x=Exit Free-Net, m=Main Menu, p=Previous Menu, "go help"=Extended Help
Your Choice ==> █
```

Tallahassee Freenet

```
telnet freenet.scri.fsu.edu
login: visitor
```

This freenet is sponsored by a number of public and private institutions, including IBM, DEC, the City of Tallahassee, Florida State University, and Apalachee Federation of Jewish Charities. This information is shown in the opening screen (Figure 8.6).

FIGURE 8.6

Opening Tallahassee Freenet screen

```
                    Welcome to Tallahassee Free-Net

Sponsored by:                                   Equipment Donated by:
  City of Tallahassee                             Apple Library of Tomorrow
  Florida State University                        Digital Equipment Corporation
  Leon County                                     IBM
  LeRoy Collins Leon County Public Library        Sun MicroSystems
  Supercomputer Computations Research             Unisys Corporation
      Institute (SCRI)                            Xyplex

                  With additional support provided by:
  Apalachee Federation of Jewish Charities        Apogee Systems
  Broad and Cassel                                Centel/Sprint
  Computer 101 Inc.                               Leon County Schools
  Telebit                                         Williams, Cox, Weidner & Cox
```

The main menu for this system is shown in Figure 8.7.

FIGURE 8.7

Main Tallahassee Freenet menu screen

```
TALLAHASSEE FREE-NET MAIN MENU

 1. NOTICE TO USERS OUTSIDE FL, GA, & AL WHO REGISTERED BEFORE 2/6/95
 2. All About Free-Net (Registration, Help, & Overview)
 3. Mail Service for Registered Users
 4. Social Services and Organizations
 5. Business & Professional Center
 6. Medical & Health Services
 7. Agriculture Center
 8. Government Complex
 9. Education Complex
10. Religion Center
11. Science and Technology Center
12. Home and Garden Center
13. Library Complex
14. Community Center
15. Disabilities Information
16. Additional Internet & Local Services

(h) help  (x) Exit   Type "notes" for information
Your Choice:
```

SCIENCE AND OTHER TECHNOLOGY

Weather

WWW Weather Reference

There are plenty of weather references on the World Wide Web. One place to start searching the Web for weather information is the U.S. Internet weather reference page:

```
http://www.usit.net/np/misc/weather.html
```

Use the references here to research weather or to find other WWW weather-related services.

Weather Service

```
telnet downwind.sprl.umich.edu 3000
```

This service offers city and state weather forecasts, ski conditions, earthquake reports, and other weather information. You are logged on automatically (without a user name or password) to the University of Michigan WEATHER UNDERGROUND. At the first prompt you can enter the three-digit identifier for your location (these are FAA and Weather Service identifiers that usually are related to the local weather station or airport). You will see a weather summary like the one in Figure 8.8.

FIGURE 8.8
Sample weather report

```
Weather Conditions at 11 AM EST on 22 MAR 95 for Knoxville, TN.
Temp(F)    Humidity(%)    Wind(mph)    Pressure(in)    Weather
=====================================================================
  70          52%           SSW at 9       29.74       Mostly Cloudy


236
FOUS1 KTYS 221603 COR
LFPTYS
TNZ036-069-071-222215-

KNOXVILLE AND VICINITY FORECAST
NATIONAL WEATHER SERVICE KNOXVILLE TN
1015 AM EST WED MAR 22 1995

.THIS AFTERNOON...PARTLY CLOUDY AND WARM. HIGH IN THE UPPER 70S.
SOUTHWEST WIND 10 TO 15 MPH.

.TONIGHT...MOSTLY CLOUDY WITH A 40 PERCENT CHANCE OF THUNDERSTORMS. LOW IN THE
MID 50S. WEST WIND 5 TO 10 MPH...BUT STRONGER IN OR NEAR THUNDERSTORMS.

.THURSDAY...PARTLY SUNNY. HIGH IN THE MID 70S. WIND BECOMING NORTHWEST
   Press Return to continue, M to return to menu, X to exit: █
```

The service is menu driven after that. You can display the three-digit city codes to help you find yours. You can print climatic data for a selected city, and so on.

Weather Maps

Weather information is a natural for the Internet. There are a number of university and national weather service sites that can give you a forecast for your local area, a national weather summary, satellite maps that are only hours or minutes old, weather theory, and more. As with other Internet resources, you can conduct a Veronica or Archie search or use a WebCrawler to help you find weather-related data.

Here are a few places to start:

`http://www.usit/net/np/misc/weather`

This is a pointer page that leads you to a number of regional and national weather information pages. Among them is a NOAA (National Oceanographic and Atmospheric Administration) page with satellite images at:

```
http://hpcc1.hpcc.noaa.gov/nws/6panel.html
```

Another site that offers hyperlinks to weather-related information is this page at the University Corporation for Atmospheric Research:

```
http://http.ucar.edu/WeatherInfo.html
```

More weathermaps? Try:

```
http://rs560.cl.msu.edu:80/weather/
```

Energy Reference

A good place to start for Internet Energy information is the Department of Energy. You can read the DOE home page at:

```
http://www.doe.gov/
```

This page will lead you to other DOE and government resources. For an excellent list of energy-related resources, try this virtual library page:

```
http://solstice.crest.org/online/virtual-library
/VLib-energy.html
```

This site is rich in governmental, association, educational, and commercial energy-related references. They include the Real Goods page from the people who design and sell energy-related products, and the Energy Federation page, a non-profit organization that supports contractors and others in energy-related information.

Here are some other energy-related sites:

```
ftp ftp.std.com
cd /obi/Economics/energy
get energy.zip
ftp cobalt.cco.caltech.edu
cd /pub/bjmccall/Clint.pos
get energy.txt
ftp ftp.cs.colorado.edu
cd /pub/cs/distribs/energy-shootout
Use ls to view file and directory names.
ftp sunsite.unc.edu
cd /pub/academic/environment/alternative-energy
```

Use **ls** to view file names and directories. A number of interesting files are available here.

```
cd /pub/academic/geography
```

Read the INDEX file for information about what's in this directory.

Observatory Data

You can access some U.S. Naval Observatory files via the Internet. The information is varied, from gps (Global Positioning System) to LORAN navigation data. Not only can you access the standard time services, but you can also learn a lot about the Observatory. Here's how to get there:

```
ftp tycho.usno.navy.mil
cd /pub
```

Then use **ls** (or **dir**) to list the files and directories there. For the most part the file names are obvious. You can use **cd** to move into any directory that promises to deliver information you might be interested in.

Space

NASA SpaceLink

```
telnet spacelink.msfc.nasa.gov
```

SpaceLink is a space-related information database provided by the educational affairs division of NASA and operated by the Marshall Space Flight Center. You'll be given a one-screen introduction to this service, then prompted for a user name. Enter the user name you normally use online, then a password. On your first visit you will be asked some additional questions for registration. After that, just use the same name and password for direct access. This is a menu-driven system that is easy to use.

The same information is also available through the World Wide Web. Use a WWW browser to reach **http://spacelink.msfc.nasa.gov**. This screen looks like the sample in Figure 8.9.

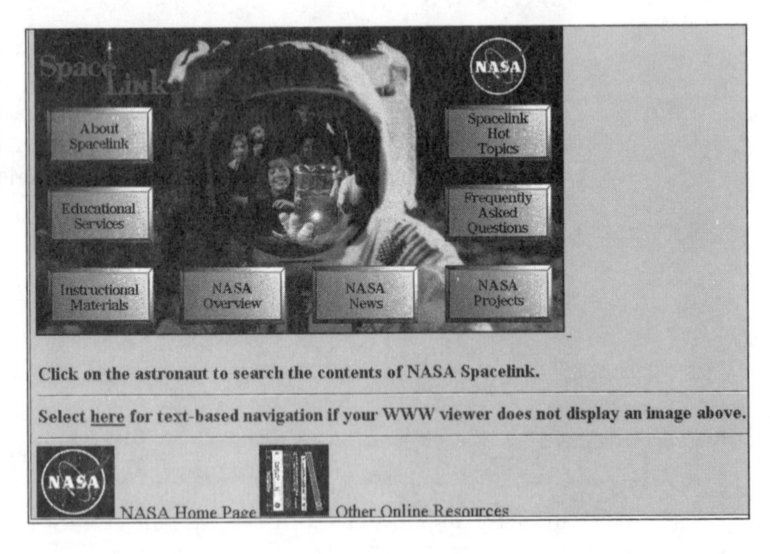

FIGURE 8.9 WWW NASA SpaceLink opening screen

This is an interesting resource for anyone who wants to keep up with the shuttle launch schedule, research space topics, or learn more about NASA.

NASA News

```
Finger nasanews@space.mit.edu
```

Turn on a log file or screen capture before issuing this command. Once the finger command attaches to the host, you'll get several screens of data that scroll by. This is a daily bulletin that varies in length and changes topics according to what is current. This material reads like a press release or a newspaper or wire story. It is interesting, timely, and gives you the feeling of keeping up with the space program in a direct way.

NASA Lunar and Planetary Institute

```
http://cass.jsc.nasa.gov/lpi.html
```

Look for the Lunar & Planetary Information Bulletin. Also, you can access a bibliographic database of planetary information. This is a research service from NASA and is targeted at researchers in the field. However, as a teacher or student, you may find some of the information here of interest. Figure 8.10 shows the LPI opening screen.

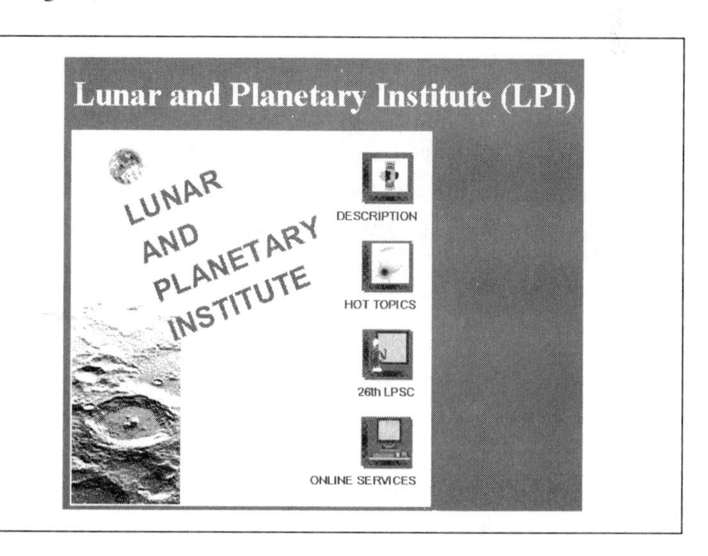

FIGURE 8.10
NASA Lunar and Planetary Institute main screen

NASA Extragalactic Database

```
telnet ned.ipac.caltech.edu
Login: ned
```

This is a database of astronomical facts and figures, plus a bibliography of astronomical publications. You'll be advised about an X-Windows-based graphical user interface, and will need to decide whether you want results emailed to you. Then you will see the main NED screen shown in Figure 8.11.

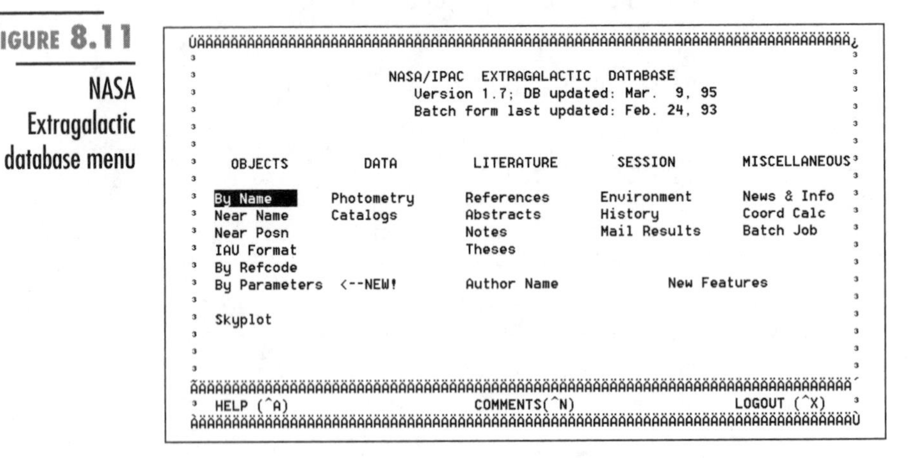

FIGURE 8.11 NASA Extragalactic database menu

The database, according to a NASA notice on one of the opening screens, "is an on-going effort, funded by NASA to make available over computer networks the rapidly accumulating literature on EXTRAGALACTIC objects."

You can use the database to search for bibliographic references associated with extragalactic objects, abstracts of recent journal articles, and published notes.

Hubble Telescope Information

```
ftp stsci.edu
```

This resource contains several directories with information about the Hubble space telescope experiment. You can find instrument reports, FAQ lists, plans for the future, software, and more.

Use **ls** or **dir** to view the files and directories in the default directory, then use **cd** to change to a directory that looks interesting to you. Remember, the FTP **get** command copies specified files to your local host.

Shuttle and Satellite Images

```
ftp ames.arc.nasa.gov
cd /pub/GIF
```

Use **ls** or **dir** to view available images. You should be able to download these images for use in word processors and other applications that support graphics. There are other directories on this host that contain useful information and images. Try:

```
cd /pub/SPACE/GIF
cd /pub/space/CDROM
telnet sanddunes.scd.ucar.edu
```

You'll need login information and a password to access this facility. You can probably get authorized. Simply email **kelley@sanddunes.scd.ucar.edu** and request information on accessing this host.

```
ftp pioneer.unm.edu
cd /pub/info
```

Download **beginner.info** first with the **get** command. Then use **!cat beginner.info** while still at the FTP prompt to view the file. This will give you valuable help in finding and using data on this host.

```
ftp irisl.ucis.dal.ca
cd /pub/GIF
```

This system affords only restricted use. Access is available only between 1700 and 2000 Eastern time.

NASAServers

Want to know where NASA maintains servers on the network? That information is available through WAIS. Look for **NASA-directory-of-servers**.

Technology

Earthquake Information

Just in case you'd like to know current earthquake information (location, time, magnitude of recent quakes), here's how to find it:

```
finger quake@geophys.washington.edu
```

This is an immediate-response list that scrolls up your screen. Turn on screen capture or be prepared to press **Ctrl-S** and **Ctrl-Q** to stop and start the display.

From a World Wide Web browser, select **http://www.geophys.washington.edu**. Figure 8.12 shows a portion of the information you get from this resource.

FIGURE 8.12

WWW screen at geophys. washington

```
 `http://www.geophys.washington.edu/'
DATE-TIME is in Universal Time (UTC) which is PST + 8 hours. Magnitudes are
reported as local magnitude (Ml).  QUAL is location quality A-good, D-poor,
Z-from automatic system and may be in error.
 DATE-(UTC)-TIME   LAT(N) LON(W)   DEP  MAG QUAL COMMENTS
yy/mm/dd hh:mm:ss   deg.   deg.    km   Ml
95/01/31 22:46:46  47.03N 119.93W   0.0 2.0  C    9.8 km NNE of Vantage
95/01/31 23:51:20  49.03N 122.75W  10.0 2.3  A   23.8 km ESE of Vancouver,BC
95/02/02 09:13:52  49.05N 122.75W  10.0 2.0  B   23.9 km ESE of Vancouver,BC
95/02/06 11:45:59  47.71N 122.28W  22.7 2.4  A    8.4 km  NW of Kirkland, Wa
95/02/07 23:24:22  47.73N 122.28W  22.9 2.2  A    8.9 km  NW of Kirkland, Wa
95/02/08 09:10:27  45.11N 122.70W  31.7 3.6  C FELT  12.0 km   E of Woodburn, O
95/02/10 11:17:36  47.71N 122.28W  23.7 2.9  A    8.8 km  NW of Kirkland, Wa
95/02/13 01:05:33  45.56N 122.88W  22.8 2.2  B   21.1 km WNW of Portland, OR
95/02/23 02:21:54  48.53N 123.43W  29.3 2.2  B   14.3 km NNW of Victoria,BC
95/02/24 06:35:28  47.60N 121.78W   3.7 2.0  C    8.6 km  NE of Fall City
95/02/24 13:21:28  47.55N 122.03W   9.7 2.2  B   11.3 km   W of Fall City
95/03/02 02:38:23  48.58N 123.00W  14.2 2.2  B   31.8 km  NE of Victoria,BC
95/03/02 17:26:24  47.61N 121.98W  17.2 2.0  B    6.7 km WSW of Carnation, Wa
95/03/09 07:22:36  47.18N 120.95W   1.6 3.0  C   38.1 km  NW of Ellensburg
95/03/09 09:08:40  47.21N 119.85W   8.0 2.2  B   30.6 km NNE of Vantage
95/03/13 04:51:34  44.61N 122.78W  25.9 2.7  B FELT  40.8 km SSE of Salem, OR
```

Technical Reports

```
ftp daneel.rdt.monash.edu.au
cd /pub/techreports/reports
```

Use **ls** or **dir** to view the files there. This directory is a repository of technical information from private companies and universities about a broad range of topics. Among the findings here are bibliographies that refer you to published articles about a variety of technical topics.

Miscellaneous

Network Addresses

A WAIS resource will help you locate very specific addresses. Look for **biologists-addresses** (**net.bio.net**) on the main WAIS topic list. You can search this database. If you want to browse through the list, enter a period or any other general key word and you will be shown the catalog for that section.

You can get biologists' addresses and other information from this host via FTP.

```
ftp net.bio.net
cd /pub/BIOSCI
```

Use **ls** (**dir**) to view available files and directories. Since the topics are varied just browse around and locate files you'd like to see.

For more general address information, search the FAQ in the newsgroup **news.answers**, or from **rtfm.mit.edu**. In addition, some Gopher sites include a search tool to scan USENET news articles for specified names or user IDS. You can find it under tools or search on some systems.

As you search the Internet for specific people, don't overlook the online telephone directories available from many university Gophers. Narrow down your search by geographical location, choose a Gopher in the proper locale, then look for specific institutions that might contain the name you seek.

Biological and Medical Gophers

Look for a list of Internet medical resources available via Gophers at **gopher.dartmouth.edu**. Similar information is available on the World Wide Web at:

```
http://www.dhmc.dartmouth.edu/
```

A sample screen is shown in Figure 8.13.

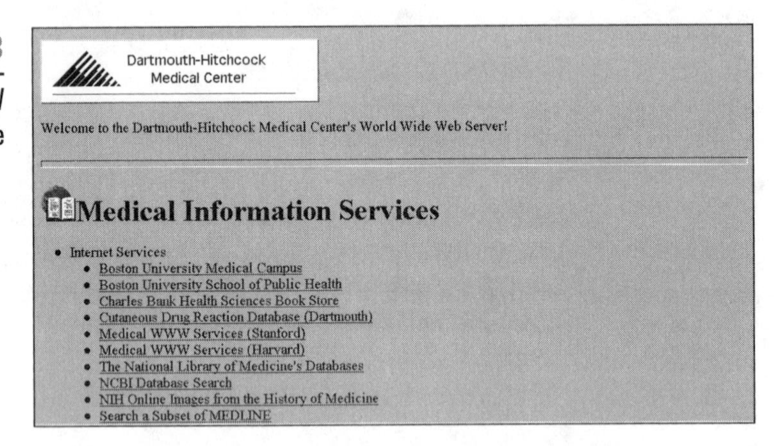

FIGURE 8.13 Dartmouth WWW page

You can search for specific information at FTP sites. Suppose you are interested in information on cholesterol, for example. Try this site and, while you're there, look for other medical and health-related information:

```
ftp flubber.cs.umd.edu
cd /other/tms/veg
get PCRM.cholesterol
```

Also in this directory are many other files that deal with nutrition. The directory looks like the one in Figure 8.14.

FIGURE 8.14

Directory from flubber.cs. umd.edu

```
-rw-r--r--  1 483        9109 Feb 24  1993 PCRM.cholesterol
-rw-r--r--  1 483        6186 Feb 24  1993 PCRM.dairy
-rw-r--r--  1 483        5317 Oct  6  1992 PCRM.diabetes
-rw-r--r--  1 483        3446 Oct  6  1992 PCRM.hypoglycemia
-rw-r--r--  1 483        6348 Oct  2  1992 PCRM.milk.press-release
-rw-r--r--  1 483        4816 Oct 19  1992 PCRM.protein
-rw-r--r--  1 483       10848 Oct 19  1992 PCRM.veg.food
-rw-r--r--  1 483        4419 Oct  6  1992 PCRM.weight
-rw-r--r--  1 483        4382 Feb 24  1993 Xian.veg
-rw-r--r--  1 483       18968 Oct  6  1992 animal.ingredients
-rw-r--r--  1 483        2741 Sep 25  1992 beef
-rw-r--r--  1 483        8570 Sep 25  1992 brethren
-rw-r--r--  1 483        6529 Feb 24  1993 comstock
-rw-r--r--  1 483       21131 Feb 24  1993 fat.land
-rw-rw-r--  1 483       28243 Jan 20 20:47 leather.faq
-rw-r--r--  1 483        4452 Sep 25  1992 osteoporosis
-rw-r--r--  1 483        4689 Feb 24  1993 self.sufficiency
-rw-r--r--  1 483        3631 Feb 24  1993 singer
-rw-r--r--  1 483        4436 Feb 24  1993 son.sue
-rw-r--r--  1 483       10148 Oct 14  1992 viva
226 Transfer complete.
remote: -la
2413 bytes received in 1.5 seconds (1.5 Kbytes/s)
ftp> █
```

For some general information, get **FAQ.rec.food.veg**.

You can access a broad selection of medical information from a variety of Internet Gophers. You can either browse your favorite Gopher (slow and uncertain), or you can use a direct Gopher command at your service provider's system prompt, as I show below:

Anesthesiology Gopher

```
gopher eja.anes.hscsyr.edu
```

Offers lots of medical info, archives, and positions.

Biology Gophers

```
gopher fragrans.riken.go.jp
gopher dna.cedb.uwf.edu
gopher life.anu.edu.au
```

Offers access to biological sciences information.

CancerNets

```
gopher gopher.nih.gov
```

Health & Clinical Information/

```
gopher gan.ncc.go.jp
```

Genomic Databases

```
gopher gopher.hgmp.mrc.ac.uk
```

Healthline Information Database

```
gopher selway.umt.edu 700
```

Offers drug and alcohol info, sexuality/AIDS info, and more.

Nursing Gopher

```
gopher nightingale.con.utk.edu
```

Offers nursing information on research, practice, education, publications, etc.

Cryonics

```
ftp rtfm.mit.edu
Directory: /pub/usenet-by-group/sci.cryonics
```

Use **ls (dir)** to look for a variety of interesting files on this interesting—and controversial—topic. Cryonics is the science and study of freezing the body of a person who has just died in the hope that it can be preserved until a cure for the illness that caused death can be found.

RECREATION

Recreation Database

```
ftp ftp.cs.dal.ca
cd /comp.archives
```

Use **ls** to show the available directories under this one. This is a gold mine of useful files and pointers to other information. Data is stored by topic, and the number of files is large. You might want to turn on a log file (screen capture) and issue several **ls** commands:

```
ls rec.*
ls rec.arts*
ls rec.aviation*
ls rec.bicycles*
ls rec.food*
ls rec.games*
ls rec.music*
ls rec.radio.amateur*
ls alt.*
ls comp.*
ls soc.*
```

Once you have identified a directory you want to explore, use **cd dirname** to make that directory current, then use **ls** again to view the names of the available files or directories. If you're not sure which names are files and which are directories, use **dir** and note the first character in the file description at the left of the display. If it is a **d**, then the name at the end of that line represents a directory. And, as I mentioned at the beginning of this chapter, information such as this is also available from a news server via a news reader such as Trumpet or tin.

Movies

```
ftp ftp.univ-lyon1.fr
cd /pub/faq-by-
newsgroup/rec/rec.arts.movies/movies
get faq
Get trivia-faq
```

These files give you information on a broad set of movie topics. You'll also get pointers toward other files that might be of interest. These files are configured as a series of common questions and trivia about movies of all kinds. For example, "who was the voice of Jessica Rabbit in the film *Who Framed Roger Rabbit*," or "when is George Lucas going to make more Star Wars films?" Whether you're a dedicated movie fan who studies every new film and star or just someone who likes to watch movies, you'll find some interesting facts and figures here.

Games

Information about games on the Internet is available from a variety of sources. For a WWW jumping off place for games, you can try the Fun&Games reference at:

```
http://www.usit.net/np/misc/Fun&Games.html
```

For game-related files, a good place to start (as always) is Archie. Log on to an Archie server through your local client, and search for games (**prog games**). You'll get a fairly long list of directories named **games**. Try some of these and you'll find FAQ files about a variety of game topics. Some of the files in the Archie list will be grouped by topic, so you can locate video game FAQs or pinball FAQs, and so on. As with nearly anything on the Internet, the key to finding what you want (or to serendipitously finding something you didn't know about) is to poke around, ask questions, and see what you can find.

You'll uncover at least three types of game information on the Internet:

1. PC, Macintosh, and other microcomputer games you can download and play on your own machine.
2. Interactive, networked games that you play with many users simultaneously across the Internet.
3. Text files that contain game hints, conversations about games, and directories for locating games.

As with other topics in this chapter, consider using a WebCrawler, Veronica, or another search tool to help you find topics of interest. You can also access summary pages with lists of topics, such as this one:

```
http://www.yahoo.com/Entertainment/games
```

In this section I will list a few of the game resources you can find on the Internet, just to get you started.

Flight Simulators

```
ftp cs.dal.ca
cd /comp.archives/rec.aviation.simulators
```

Use **ls** to view available files. Also, search any FTP site for the directory **news.answers** (probably under the **/pub** directory) for FAQs about flight simulators and a variety of other game topics.

Pinball

There is a surprising amount of interest on the Internet in discussing pinball—both electronic, computer-based versions, and the old, klunky machines once so popular in diners and clubs. If you're interested in learning more about pinball, do an Archie search for **pinball** as a place to start. Also, you can try these files:

```
ftp ftp.univ-lyon1.fr
cd /pub/faq-by-
newsgroup/rec/rec.games.pinball/games
get part1
get part2
```

Not only will you get an interesting discussion of pinball, but you'll also get a list of current pinball magazines and newsletters. You can email Andy Oakland, who maintains this monthly posting, at **sao@athena.mit.edu**, for additional information.

Taking Care of Business

```
ftp potemkin.cs.pdx.edu
cd /pub/frp/stories/business
```

Use **ls** to view file names. This is a series of compressed files about business. Get the **business.intro.Z** file first. Use **uncompress** on your UNIX host to expand it, and then use **cat** or **more** to view it. This is a very specialized, text-based role playing game. I'll say no more, but you might find the exchanges interesting.

Star Trek

I started working with computers in about 1975—first Digital Equipment Corporation PDP-11-series minicomputers, then a variety of microcomputers. This was long before the IBM PC was designed and before Apple had a popular machine. But nearly every computer in those days had some form of Star Trek game. This was in the days of text-based displays, remember. There were almost no graphics applications, and certainly no real-time, flight-simulator-type, joystick controlled games.

Star Trek certainly would have been an excellent graphics game, but those early versions were played with Xs, plus signs, and some text hints. And you know what? Some twenty years later, Star Trek—not shoot-em-up color graphics versions, but the old text games—are still popular on UNIX machines and across the Internet.

There are several places to look for Trek games. The first place may be on your local host. From your home directory, try **cd/usr/games**. You should see a list of several game files, including one called **trek**. Type **trek** with the games directory selected, and see what happens. You will be asked for game length and skill level. Answer **s** for short and **n** for novice (unless you want something else), then supply a password at the prompt. You are asked for a command. That's all—a simple **Command:** prompt and you're into the game. You can enter a question mark to get a list of possible commands, similar to the list in Figure 8.15.

FIGURE 8.15

Trek help list

```
Trek73 Commands:
Code        Command                          Code        Command

  1:     Fire phasers                      : 17:   * Damage report
  2:     Fire photon torpedoes             : 18:     Scan enemy
  3:     Lock phasers onto target          : 19:     Alter power distribution
  4:     Lock tubes onto target            : 20:     Jettison engineering
  5:     Manually rotate phasers           : 21:     Detonate engineering
  6:     Manually rotate tubes             : 22:     Alter firing parameters
  7:   * Phaser status                     : 23:     Attempt defenseless ruse
  8:   * Tube status                       : 24:     Attempt corbomite bluff(s)
  9:     Load/unload torpedo tubes         : 25:     Surrender
 10:     Launch antimatter probe           : 26:     Ask enemy to surrender
 11:     Probe control                     : 27:     Initiate self-destruct
 12:   * Position report                   : 28:     Abort self-destruct
 13:   * Position display                  : 29:   * Survivors report
 14:     Pursue an enemy vessel            : 30:   * Print version number
 15:     Elude an enemy vessel             : 31:   * Saves game
 16:     Change course and speed           : 32:   * Reprints above list

 * does not use a turn

jones: Code [1-32] _
```

You can find out the status of your game by typing **status** at the **Command**: prompt. Your screen should look something like the one in Figure 8.16.

FIGURE 8.16

Typical text-based Trek screen

```
 <Long John Dilithium frng phasers>
hit 27 on Potempkin's shield 4
   tube 4 damaged
:: torp 10 ::
hit 29 on Potempkin's shield 4
hit 42 on Long John Dilithium's shield 4
hit on torpedo 13
:: torp 13 ::
hit 22 on Long John Dilithium's shield 4
 <Long John Dilithium frng phasers>
hit 28 on Potempkin's shield 3
   tube 2 damaged
   tube 1 damaged
   phaser 4 damaged
   Probe launcher damaged.
   Warp Drive damaged.
 <Long John Dilithium frng phasers>
hit 30 on Potempkin's shield 3
   Probe launcher damaged.
Message to the Federation:  This is Commander
   Pharoah of the Orion Pirates.  We have defeated
   the Potempkin and are departing the quadrant.

jones: Code [1-32]
```

I've shown you an example from the file **trek73**. You may find other files and other game versions on your local host. You can spend some time with this local game to get an idea of how Trek is played, then you can branch out and look for network versions. Where do you look? Try:

```
ftp ftp.csua..berkeley.edu
cd /pub/netrek
get netrekFAQ
get netrekFTP
get netreklist
```

The **netrekFAQ** and **netrekFTP** files are particularly useful for beginning Netrek players. Download them and study them. Try some of the sources listed for more information. At some point, you will be ready to try your hand at the game yourself. These files will give you answers to a lot of questions about Netrek, the networked version of Star Trek, and will also show you where you can find Netrek servers. To access a network game, Telnet to one of the listed servers (be sure to include the port number).

MUD

The MUD game, available in many varieties on many hosts, is a multiuser role playing game like Dungeons and Dragons. MUD stands for multiuser dimensions or multiuser dungeons. One place to find a version is on your local host. Again, try the **/usr/games** directory. There may be a version of MUD there, and that's a good place for some hands-on experience. Also, you can ask other users on your system about using the local MUD and about finding a popular MUD server.

You can get information about MUD servers with an Archie search. Log on to an Archie server and issue a **prog mud** search. Here's one resource:

```
ftp ftp netcom.com
cd /pub/pdh/lpmud
get mudlist
```

This will show you a very long list of MUD servers, places you might be able to find out more about MUD, and where you might play the game.

If you're familiar with Dungeons and Dragons, you have an idea of how MUD works. There can be many variations of the game, each with a different set of characters, and different worlds or scenes. Once you join a MUD game, you are a character in a MUD dimension and can interact with other characters in that dimension.

Usually there is a quest to solve or another adventure. The players who solve the quest become wizards who often get the ability to program part of the game. They just take a room or other place and start programming from there. They may make a new exit to the East or West, add a teleporter—you name it. When you go into their part of the game, they can have their own programs there that do what they want. Suppose you are playing a Startrek MUD and end up in an area that is a holo-deck. When you are a wizard you can change the holo-deck to whatever you want. The fun is that you become a part of the creation of the game. For others who are not on that level, the fun is playing a game that people you know made, and seeing their creativity.

Each MUD server has different help files and different forms of the game. If you'd like to try one MUD, try this:

```
telnet almong.enmu.edu 1066
```

This is a MUD game that helps you learn about MUD games. Like many MUD games, it attracts a wide variety of players and personalities. You are liable to see anything, so adults should monitor how children use MUD and other interactive games and conversations. Experiment to find a MUD that you enjoy.

You log on automatically and will be asked for a name. You can either continue an existing character or create a new one. If you haven't logged on to this particular MUD server before, you'll need to create a character. The MUD playing screen is made up of prompts and a blank line at the bottom of the screen. You enter commands on this blank line. Type **create character-name** to create a new identity on this MUD. Next you'll get a screen welcoming you to the MUD. The system knows you are a new player and steps you through several screens of information where you describe your character any way you like.

When the questions are over, you are sent into one of the "rooms" where other players are passing information back and forth, asking questions, and moving through the game. The opening screen from this MUD is shown in Figure 8.17.

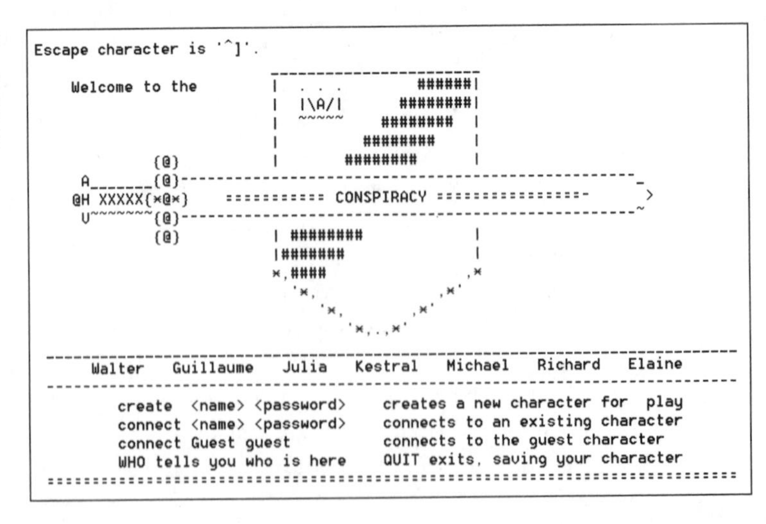

FIGURE 8.17 MUD opening screen

You can return to your "home" room and QUIT the game at any time. Follow the instructions and move around until you've had enough, then move on.

Other Role Playing

MUD isn't the only role-playing activity you can find on the Internet. Keep your eyes open as you browse IRC and conferences. Also, you can try some of the BBS sources listed through Gopher. From the main Gopher menu, choose **Fun & Games**, then select **games/Fantasy Role-Playing Games**, then **BBSes** from the next menu. You can get a list of active BBSes that conduct role-playing.

Hobbies

If you think about it a moment, you realize that the folk, like you, who use the Internet have a wide range of interests. It is only natural, then, that a lot of discussions, files, and articles you will come across on the Internet have to do with hobbies of one kind or another. I'll list some sample hobby-related files in this section.

For example, are you a cook? Do you like to get recipes from other cooks? You can browse any Gopher, or you can conduct a Veronica search for a particular topic of interest. And, with the growth of the World Wide Web, some of the best references are likely to show up on WebCrawler searches.

Aviation

The field of aviation is changing rapidly. It is more difficult than ever to keep up with technology and regulations, but some of the information on the Internet can help. I predict that as more pilots and others interested in the field access the Internet, this area of online data will grow apace.

Flying is a popular recreation/hobby topic on the Internet. You can find someone to talk to you about it on IRC or on conferences. There are some interesting files you can check out as well. Here are some samples:

```
ftp sol.cs.ruu.nl
cd /pub/AIRCRFT-IMAGES
```

Use **ls** or **dir** to view the available files. You'll see a series of **.jpg**-format graphics images of a variety of aircraft, from a MiG-29 to a Tiger Moth.

NASA also has some interesting images on a WWW site:

```
http://ails.arc.nasa.gov/cgi-bin/catalog/archive
```

Figure 8.18 is a typical image from this page.

FIGURE 8.18

Typical NASA aircraft/shuttle image

Bicycling

```
ftp ftp.uni-paderborn.de
cd /doc/FAQ/news.answers
```

Use **ls** to display available files (there are five files as this book is written, named **bicycle-faq/part1–bicycle-faq/part5**). Use **get** to download the ones you want.

The **/doc/FAQ/news.answers** directory is rich in frequently-asked question files and directories. Once you get to this FTP site, study it carefully. Use **ls** to display the contents of **/doc/FAQ** for more bicycle information.

To begin a WWW search for bicycling, use your WWW browser to contact this page of listings:

```
http://www.yahoo.com/Entertainment/Sports/Cycling/
```

From there you can jump to a variety of bicycling sites, including the following:

Technology:

```
http://uni.uiuc.edu/~dtucker/product.html
```

Organizations:

```
gopher:://cycling.org/11/org
```

Ham Radio

Amateur radio operators, or hams, have been on the leading edge of communications technology for nearly three-quarters of a century. These private citizens have spent their own money, time, and expertise to develop communications hardware and procedures for personal communications, emergency services, and research. The ham community has launched over a dozen satellites, for example, and there are radio servers that "talk" TCP/IP and can access Internet addresses. You'll find ham radio talk and information in many Internet locations. Here are some to try:

```
ftp oak.oakland.edu
cd /pub/hamradio
```

Use **dir** or **ls** to view the files and subdirectories there. You'll find information about amateur testing, organizations, using computers with radio, radio TCP/IP, and more.

Try this URL: **http://www.acs.oakland.edu/barc.html**

Ham Radio Callbook

```
telnet callsign.cs.buffalo.edu 2000
```

You are logged on automatically and receive a double chevron prompt: >>. Type **help** at the prompt for information on searching the database. Basically, this is an electronic version of a licensed amateur radio operators' call book. You can search by call sign, city, surname, zip code, and other criteria. A sample record is shown in Figure 8.19 (the actual information was changed for this example):

FIGURE 8.19 Sample callbook entry

```
     help [command]              - get help on command
     info                        - get info about server
     more rows                   - set number of terminal rows
     name [filters] surname      - lookup last name
     quit                        - exit the server
     set name|data|raw|addr      - set the display mode
     zip [filters] zipcode       - lookup zip code

Available regular expression filters:
     -c   filter by callsign
     -f   filter by first name
     -l   filter by last name
     -a   filter by street address
     -z   filter by zip code
     -t   filter by town
     -s   filter by state (or province)

For information on regular expressions:
     help regexp
>> call k8ao
Call-Sign: K8AO                         Class: EXTRA
Real Name: JOHN T BADGETT               Birthday: SEP 14, 1944
Mailing Address: 7004 FAIRVIEW RD, CORRYTON, TN  37721
Valid From: AUG 23, 1988                To: AUG 23, 1998
>> _
```

The American Radio Relay League is the premier source of information about the state of ham radio, about current happenings, and about laws and technology. ARRL has moved with current technology to support the hams they serve. The organization operates radio packet stations, publishes **QST**, a monthly journal, and is active on the Internet. The ARRL Internet postings are a good place to start if you need information on ham radio.

Study the ARRL from the World Wide Web, too. Try:

```
http://www.acs.oakland.edu/barc/arrl.html.
```

The opening screen for the ARRL WWW page is shown in Figure 8.20.

FIGURE 8.20

ARRL opening screen on WWW

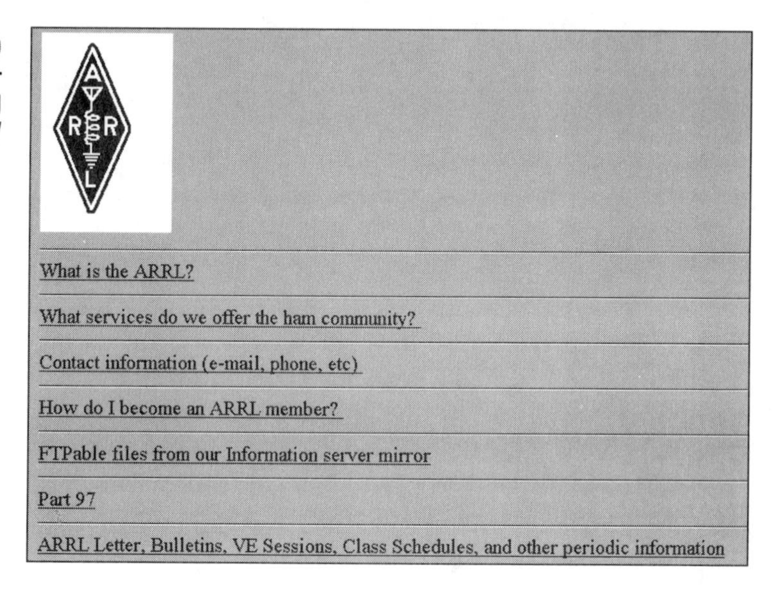

In addition, you can FTP to **oak.oakland.edu** and check the files in the directory:

```
/pub/hamradio/arrl/infoserver
```

This directory holds sample files available from ARRL, including the ones shown in Figure 8.21.

FIGURE 8.21 ARRL available file list

Current directory is /pub/hamradio/arrl/infoserver

Up to higher level directory

File	Size	Date	Type
bbsfiles/		Sun Mar 19 08:08:00 1995	Directory
bibs/		Sun Mar 19 08:08:00 1995	Directory
circ/		Sun Mar 19 08:08:00 1995	Directory
clubs/		Sun Mar 19 08:08:00 1995	Directory
digests/		Sun Mar 19 08:08:00 1995	Directory
ead/		Sun Mar 19 08:08:00 1995	Directory
evp/		Sun Mar 19 08:08:00 1995	Directory
faqs/		Sun Mar 19 08:08:00 1995	Directory
fsd/		Sun Mar 19 08:08:00 1995	Directory
help.txt	5 Kb	Fri Nov 11 15:28:00 1994	Plain text
hq-email.txt	13 Kb	Tue Mar 07 16:42:00 1995	Plain text
index.txt	34 Kb	Thu Mar 09 16:25:00 1995	Plain text
info.txt	2 Kb	Mon Feb 06 14:40:00 1995	Plain text
letter/		Sun Mar 19 08:08:00 1995	Directory
msd/		Sun Mar 19 08:08:00 1995	Directory
new.txt	19 Kb	Thu Nov 17 15:42:00 1994	Plain text
oldfile.txt	43 Kb	Mon Feb 06 14:42:00 1995	Plain text
qex/		Sun Mar 19 08:08:00 1995	Directory
qst/		Sun Mar 19 08:08:00 1995	Directory
realarrl.txt	3 Kb	Wed Mar 02 00:00:00 1994	Plain text
rib/		Sun Mar 19 08:08:00 1995	Directory
subscrib.txt	717 bytes	Mon Feb 06 14:40:00 1995	Plain text

As I have mentioned, there are other locations for information on ham radio as well. A rich resource is the new group postings (some of which are available from ARRL archives as well). Start by searching these directories on any newsgroup server:

```
rec.radio.amateur
digital.misc
rec.radio.info
rec.answers
news.answers
```

These directories and associated ham radio information should be available on the following FTP sites:

```
ftp.cs.buffalo.edu
rtfm.mit.edu (pub/usenet/news.answers directory)
```

SCUBA

SCUBA activities are among the rapidly growing leisure time activities at seashore locations and inland as well. It is natural that Internet travelers would share what they know about this fascinating topic. Here are some SCUBA references I came across. You can find your own with an Archie search, by using Gopher, or by simply posting questions on bulletin boards and conferences.

```
ftp ames.arc.nasa.gov
cd /pub/SCUBA
```

Use **dir** or **ls** to list the files available in this directory. This is a rich repository of comments and personal experiences, from diving reports on specific locations to schedules and suggestions. These are mostly text files which you can access easily.

One file you might enjoy seeing, if you're a Macintosh user, is **dive-log-15.hqx**. Download it and see what you have.

```
ftp sol.cs.ruu.nl
cd /pub/NEWS.ANSWERS
get scuba-faq
```

This is just one of hundreds of FAQ files in this directory. Use **get** to copy the file to your local host. Then you can use **cat** to look at it or use a protocol to download it to your own system.

Astronomy

Whether as a hobby or a profession, the field of astronomy is a fascinating topic. You'll find discussions and references of one kind or another on this topic if you use Internet resources to scope it out. As with other specialized topics of this sort, the best advice is to use Archie, Gopher, and WAIS for generalized searches to get you started. Then access some or all of the sites you locate. From these first contacts, you will get other information that will send you in different directions. I'll list a resource here to get you started.

```
ftp ftp.std.com
cd /pub/astronomy
```

Use **dir** or **ls** to view available files. These are mostly program files designed to help in astronomy activities. For example, you can find a file that shows librations (oscillations) of the moon, and a C program that computes ephemerides of sun, moon, planets, comets, and stars.

Other Recreation

Collecting

```
ftp ftp.univ-lyon1.fr
cd /pub/usenet-stats/groups/rec
get rec.antiques
```

Electrical Information

```
ftp ftp.uni-paderborn.de
cd /doc/FAQ/misc.answers
get electrical-wiring.gz
cd /doc/FAQ/misc.consumers.house
get electrical_Wiring_FAQ.gz
get rec.woodworking_Electric_Motors_Frequently_asked_ Questions.gz
```

Bulletin Boards

SpaceMetBBS

```
telnet spacemet.phast.umass.edu
```

Simply press **Enter** when you are connected. No logon is required except that you will be asked for your first and last names. You can enter **GUEST** to tour the facility with limited access. The initial screen is shown in Figure 8.22.

FIGURE 8.22

Initial SpaceMet BBS screen

```
MAXIMUS v2.01
      @@@@@                                    @@   @@           @@
     @@   @@                                   @@@ @@@           @@
     @@       @@ @@@   @@@@@    @@@@@   @@@@@  @@@@@@@  @@@@@   @@@@@@
      @@@@@    @@  @@     @@   @@      @@   @@ @@ @ @@ @@   @@   @@
          @@   @@  @@  @@@@@   @@      @@@@@@@ @@    @@ @@@@@@@   @@
     @@   @@   @@@@@  @@  @@   @@      @@      @@    @@ @@        @@  @@
      @@@@@    @@      @@@@@@   @@@@@   @@@@@  @@    @@  @@@@@     @@@@
              @@@@@

Welcome to SpaceMet Internet, brought to you by
   Department of Physics and Astronomy, University of Massachusetts, Amherst
   Five Colleges, Inc., National Science Foundation and MassNet
==============================================================
DEDICATED TO SERVING MASSACHUSETTS K-12 TEACHERS AND STUDENTS
==============================================================
SYSOP (SYStem OPerator): Helen Sternheim  (413) 545-3697, 545-1908

New Users:  Enter your REAL FIRST AND LAST NAMES to apply for a full access
    account.  Enter GUEST (first name) and leave the last name blank to
    just look around with limited access.

What is your name: █
```

This is a BBS dedicated to space information and targeted at the science educator. It offers help with curriculum planning, plus information on NASA plans and schedules. After you complete registration, you will see a screen similar to the one in Figure 8.23.

FIGURE 8.23

BULLETIN MENU from SpaceMet

```
This is the BULLETIN MENU
 (to return here later, enter B in Main Menu)

Select one of these:
   U) USA Today News
   W) UMassK12 Internet BBS Workshops 10/21, 11/2, 11/16, 11/30
   5) Five College/WMass Public School Partnership Events
   F) Five College Calendar of Events
   D) 5C/5E 1993-1994 Meeting Schedule
   A)ppeal for SpaceMet Monetary Contributions
   C)urrent workshops, courses, lectures, etc.
   R)edisplay Bulletin Menu
   Q)uit (go to the Main Menu)



Select (R=Redisplay Bulletin Menu, Q=Go to Main Menu):





 ALT-Z FOR HELP|VT100 | FDX | 57600 N81 |LOG CLOSED|PRINT OFF | ON-LINE
```

ISCA BBS

```
telnet bbs.isca.uiowa.edu
Login: New to open a new account; Guest to look around
```

This is certainly among the largest BBS systems on the Internet. You may find as many as 300 participants at any given time. You can find somebody on here to talk about almost anything.

For a list that contains many interesting and unusual BBS services available through the Internet, send an email message to **bbslist@aug3.augsburg.edu**. You don't need to include a subject or any message in the body. In return, you'll receive three useful lists of resources.

PRISM BBS

```
telnet bbs.fdu.edu
Login: bbs
```

This is a general purpose BBS with a room motif. You will be asked to enter a handle to use on the system, then some real information about yourself. After that, you are presented with a command-oriented BBS for messages and discussions. Different activities and topics are covered in different rooms. Which rooms are available is dynamic, but you can get a list of current rooms, as shown in Figure 8.24.

FIGURE 8.24

Typical room list in PRISM BBS

```
Ground Floor:The End> Known Rooms

Rooms on this floor with new messages:
  The End>  Open Discussion>  New Users>  PrismBBS Help>  Suggestion
Box>
  Hand Me the Flyswatter>

No unseen messages in:
  Mail>

Other floors with new messages:
  Arts & Entertainment:(19/19)  Silly Stuff:(19/19)  Fun and
Games:(11/11)
  Physical:(15/16)  Metaphysical:(10/10)  Science & Technology:(10/10)
  Breaking News:(2/2)  Discussions:(14/18)  Emotions:(7/7)
  Education:(9/9)  Business:(4/4)  NetLife:(7/7)  Music:(13/13)
  New Jersey:(1/1)  Computing:(15/16)

Uneventful floors:
  Arts & Entertainment:  Silly Stuff:  Fun and Games:  Physical:
  Metaphysical:  Science & Technology:  Breaking News:  Discussions:
  Emotions:  Education:  Business:  NetLife:  Music:  New Jersey:
Computing:



Ground Floor:The End>
ALT-Z FOR HELP|VT100|FDX | 57600 E71 | LOG CLOSED | PRINT OFF | ON-LINE
```

Searching for a BBS

Want to find additional BBS information? Turn to the World Wide Web and the Yahoo index. Use your WWW browser to reach:

```
http://www.yahoo.com
```

Then click on the **Search** button on the first screen. Enter **bbs** in the search field, click on **Search** again, and you will get the screen shown in Figure 8.25.

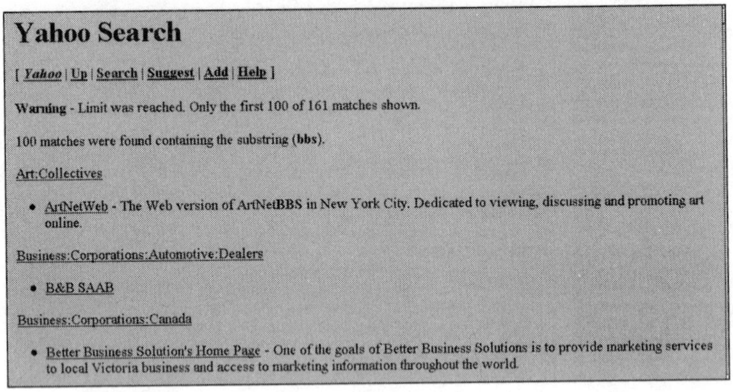

FIGURE 8.25

Yahoo BBS search results

Yahoo Search

[Yahoo | Up | Search | Suggest | Add | Help]

Warning - Limit was reached. Only the first 100 of 161 matches shown.

100 matches were found containing the substring (**bbs**).

Art:Collectives

- ArtNetWeb - The Web version of ArtNetBBS in New York City. Dedicated to viewing, discussing and promoting art online.

Business:Corporations:Automotive:Dealers

- B&B SAAB

Business:Corporations:Canada

- Better Business Solution's Home Page - One of the goals of Better Business Solutions is to provide marketing services to local Victoria business and access to marketing information throughout the world.

Travel

There are a number of travel resources on the Internet. A search with Veronica, Archie, or a WebCrawler will turn up many. Here's a starting point:

```
http://www.digimark.net/rec-travel
```

or

```
http://www.stolaf.edu
```

You can search a WebCrawler, and you can start looking for travel topics at:

```
http://www.yahoo.com/Entertainment/travel.
```

COMMERCE AND BUSINESS

Internet Business Journal

A relatively new effort that may generate real interest across the Internet is the *Internet Business Journal.* This is an electronic publication, targeted at an international business audience, which deals with topics about the Internet business community. You can find it through Gopher (depending on your Gopher server and client). Look under Electronic Information or a similar title. For information about access, email Editor-in-Chief Christopher Locke at **chris@avalanche.com**, or write Avalanche Development, 947 Walnut Street, Boulder, CO 80302, 303-449-5032.

Agriculture

Agriculture is, of course, big business. Increasingly, those involved in agribusiness are using computers and the Internet to stay in touch with each other and to stay up to date.

This reference is at Iowa State University. It gives you access to general database resources, particularly books and periodicals with plenty of information about agriculture.

```
telnet isn.iastate.edu (129.186.99.8)
```

At the **DIAL**: prompt, enter **scholar**. Press **Return** at the **Enter terminal type: (default=VT100)** or enter the terminal type if different from VT100. At the **Command**: prompt, enter **scholar** again. At the **Database Selection**: prompt, type **ICAT**. You will see the prompt screen shown in Figure 8.26.

FIGURE 8.26

Scholar's ICAT database screen

```
                    WELCOME TO SCHOLAR'S ICAT DATABASE

ICAT contains records for library materials cataloged since 1978, and all
cataloged serials. Pre-1978 books are continually being added to the database.

     To search for:          Use command:             Example:
       keywords                   k             k lasers           <ENTER>
       titles                     t             t war and peace    <ENTER>
       authors                    a             a bronte c         <ENTER>
       subjects                   s             s acid rain        <ENTER>
       call numbers               c             c jc571z45x 1990   <ENTER>

For more information on SEARCHING, press <ENTER>.
For INFORMATION about the Library, type exp info and press <ENTER>.
For DATABASE SELECTION menu, type cho and press <ENTER>.
------------------------------------------------ + Page 1 of 4 ------------
                   Enter search command                 <F8>  FORward page
                   NEWs


NEXT COMMAND:
ALT-Z FOR HELP  | VT100   | FDX | 57600 N81 | LOG CLOSED | PRINT OFF | ON-LINE
```

Agriculture FTP

```
ftp sunsite.unc.edu
cd /pub/academic/agriculture
```

Use **ls** or **dir** to display resources, and then **cd** to change directories.

Livestock reports, market prices

```
telnet psupen.psu.edu
```

At the **Username**: prompt, enter the two-digit abbreviation for your state. This gives you access to PENpages (College of Agricultural Sciences at The Pennsylvania State University), and to TEACHER*PAGES (The Pennsylvania Department of Education). The system is entirely menu-driven and provides a number of search and database services that you may find useful. For example, in PENpages, you can access the International Food & Nutrition Database, files on Small and Part-Time Farming, information on the National Family Database and the 4-H Development Database, and more. A PENpages menu screen is shown in Figure 8.27.

FIGURE 8.27

PENpages menu screen

```
                         *** PENpages Main Menu ***

PENpages User Information             Databases
----------------------------          ------------------------------------------
  1..How to Use PENpages                5..International Food & Nutrition Database
  2..Recent Changes                     6..Information on:
  3..Recent Changes - Market News           MAPP - National Family Database
  4..PENpages Announcements                 Senior Series
                                            The 4-H Youth Development Database

National & International News and Information
--------------------------------------------------------------------------------
  7..Ag*SAT                            13..PDA Ag & Weather Statistics
  8..Colorado                          14..PA Calendars & Events
  9..Rutgers, New Jersey               15..PA Market News
 10..West Virginia University          16..PA News & Newsletters
 11..USDA                              17..PA Drought Information
 12..Small & Part-Time Farming         18..PSU College of AG Information

                        * To EXIT press Control-E *
              * <PF1> then 7 to go to a known page number *

        C h o i c e :
ALT-Z FOR HELP | VT100  | FDX | 57600 N81 | LOG CLOSED | PRINT OFF | ON-LINE
```

USDA files available through this system include the Farm Broadcasters Letter, Market Reports, News Releases, and so on.

When you select TEACHER*PAGES, you can access a WHAT'S HERE menu like the one in Figure 8.28.

FIGURE 8.28

TEACHER*PAGES WHAT'S HERE menu

```
==============================
  WHAT'S HERE AND HOW TO USE IT
==============================

1...Welcome to TEACHER*PAGES!
2...Hardware and Software Selection for TEACHER*PAGES
3...Configuring Your Equipment for TEACHER*PAGES
4...TEACHER*PAGES Public Access Locations and Telephone Numbers
5...How to Use Keyword Search
6...TEACHER*PAGES Command Reference
7...TEACHER*PAGES Quick Command Reference

                 TO EXIT
            PRESS <CONTROL>E

    C h o i c e :
ALT-Z FOR HELP|VT100 | FDX | 57600 N81 |LOG CLOSED | PRINT OFF | ON-LINE
```

TEACHER*PAGES is a full-text information database of interest to teachers. New data is added daily and is available for viewing and downloading without a subscription fee. Data is accessed primarily through keyword search.

Big Sky Telegraph

```
Telnet 192.231.192.1 or bigsky.bigsky.dillon.mt.us
Dial direct:406-683-7680 (300/1200 bps)
     406-683-7685 or 406-683-7686 (2400 bps)
     406-683-7880 (9600 bps)
Type hrn at login.
```

The Headwaters Regional Network (hrn) is a commercial and educational service (see separate listing under Education) that provides conferencing, Internet access, and other services. In all, there are five online services under the Big Sky Telegraph umbrella:

- System One: Type **bbs** for rural education and the online class.
- System Two: Type **hrn** for rural economic development and community services.
- System Three: Type **wmc** for Istern Montana College campus activities, clubs, and classes.
- System Four: Type **gold** for rural peer counseling.
- System Five: The AKCS professional computer conferencing global system connected to USENET, BITNET, Internet, and FIDOnet. This is for subscribers only.

Shopping and Advertising

With the growth of the World Wide Web, we're seeing more and more true commerce in the form of shopping and advertising on the Internet. If you use a WebCrawler to look for shopping, mall, or other commercial topics, you'll find a lot to look at. You can check out a list page such as Yahoo at **http://akebono.stanford.edu/yahoo**. In this section I'll share a random selection of URLs for you to try on your own.

As part of this movement, we're seeing a number of "malls" or commercial lists that point to commercial online resources. And, we're seeing companies managing their own malls, of sorts.

Online Malls

MecklerWeb

This general purpose shopping and reference site on the World Wide Web will get you started in online malls:

```
http://www.mecklerweb.com/
```

This includes shopping, news, tutorials, and other online resources.

The Internet Shopkeeper

Try this site for a look at an expanding mall:

```
http://www.ip.net/shops.html
```

Downtown Anywhere

The Main Street page offers another type of shopping experience:

```
http://www.awa.com
```

CyberMont

Vermont's own Cyber mall is another choice:

```
http://cybermalls.com/cymont/cymonmal.htm
```

Hall of Malls

For a list of mall sites, check out:

```
http://nsns.com/MouseTracks/HallofMalls.html
```

Imagemaker's Gifts for Dog Lovers

Just goes to show you: anything is possible on the WWW. Try

```
http://www.onramp.net/imagemaker
```

for a complete catalog of doggie items.

RELIGION

Religious information on the Internet is varied. Look for specific topics, or search in general areas to find what you want.

```
ftp cs.dal.ca
cd /comp.archives
```

Use **ls** to view available directories. Among the ones you'll find are:

```
soc.religion.christian
soc.religion.islam
ftp ftp.std.com
cd /obi/Quotes
get religion
ftp ftp.uni-paderborn.de
cd /doc/FAQ/soc.religion.quaker
get soc.religion.quaker_Answers_to_Frequently_Asked_ Questions.gz
```

Use any news reader to locate the newsgroup:

```
alt.religion.scientology
```

For an unusual twist to WWW topics, check out the Digital Priest at:

```
http://anther.learning.cs.cmu.edu/priest.html
```

EDUCATION

One useful aspect of the Internet is the amount of educational and reference material you can find there. Colleges and universities, government agencies, students, writers—lots of Internet users—place information files where you can find them. Some of these files are personal research projects—information that is gathered by an individual who has an interest in a particular area. This includes Internet references that show you where to find games or other information. Universities, through their researchers, place files on the Internet that discuss an aspect of their studies or that list resources in a particular field.

As you browse the Internet, you'll find data that fits right into something you're working on now, and you'll locate files that are serendipitous, happenstance findings that you download and read simply because they are interesting. Use this information as a place to start your own research.

Distance Learning

Among the more popular trends in education is distance learning. People are busy today—they move around and work long hours. It is important for institutions of higher learning to respond to individual needs for instruction. One way to do this is with television classes, and online instruction. The facilities of the Internet are an obvious tool for this type of instruction.

Here is one place to learn about distance learning on the Internet:

```
ftp acsvax.open.ac.uk
```

At the Login prompt, enter **ftp**, and use **ftp** at the Password prompt as well. Once you are logged onto the system, type: **get icdlinfo**. This file will give you background and current information on the Commonwealth of Learning information services at the British Open University.

National Education BBS

This is one of several bulletin board services you can find that support educators through discussions, suggestions, training, and so on. To access this BBS, do the following:

```
telnet nebbs.nersc.gov
Login: new
```

The stated purpose of this BBS is "to support education by providing access to advanced computational and network resources for students in grades K through 12."

This is a command-driven system, but there are prompts and help screens to help you learn your way around. For example, the default command on the first screen is HELP, which produces the display shown in Figure 8.29.

FIGURE 8.29

Help command display in National Education BBS

```
National Education BBS                          Current Board = 'general'
Enter Command: Help

HELP SCREEN
(I)nfo          Get Version and Copyright Information
(B)oards        List boards on system
(C)ount         Count posts by board
(D)ist          Distributed Processing menu
(S)elect        Select current board
(R)ead          Enter multifunction Read Menu
(T)alk          Enter Talk Menu (Talk, Chat, Query, User List)
(G)oodbye       Leave This BBS
(H)elp          Get this Help Screen

ALT-Z FOR HELP |VT100|FDX|57600 N81|LOG CLOSED|PRINT OFF | ON-LINE
```

This system is divided into "boards" for different topics. When you issue the Boards command by typing **B** at the prompt, you will see a list similar to the one in Figure 8.30.

FIGURE 8.30

Boards list on NEBBS

```
National Education BBS                          Current Board = 'general'
Enter Command: Select

List of Boards (* = zapped board)
 Name                     Title
 Announcements          Official NESP / BBS Information
 General                Main BBS Board - General Use
 Network                Network Information - Sites, Archives & Services
 Libris                 Library and Information Science
 Math                   Mathematics Discussion Board
 Science                General and Interdisciplinary Science
 Physics                Physics and Computational Physics
 Programming            General Computer programming
 Macintosh              Discussion of Macintosh computers and programming
 PC                     PC and Compatable computers
 Politics               Political Issues of the Day
 Poetry                 Sharing and discussing Poetry
 Philosophy             Philosophical Discussion
 Sysop                  Messages to the system operator
 Chemistry              Computational Chemistry

ALT-Z FOR HELP| VT100 | FDX | 57600 N81|LOG CLOSED | PRINT OFF | ON-LINE
```

Educational Software

You can get a list of educational software, plus a number of additonal resources here:

```
http://www.csu.edu.au/education/library.html
```

Literature

Literature Lists

```
ftp nic.cic.net
cd /pub/nircomm/gopher/e-serials/alphabetic/m/mim
get README.literature.list.Z
```

Literature Reviews

```
ftp ski.utah.edu
cd /net
get literature_reviews
```

Online Literature

```
ftp top.magnus.acs.ohio-state.edu
cd /pub/library/books
```

Use **ls** to view available files in this directory.

There are other interesting online literature offerings. Use Gopher and access **Libraries** from the main menu, then choose **Electronic Books**. From there you can read literature including *Alice in Wonderland*, the *CIA World Factbook*, the *Bible*, *Moby Dick*, and lots more. You won't find everything you might ever want to search from the world of literature, of course, but there certainly is an interesting cross section of information here.

Libraries

Basic Library Information

You can use Gopher to find out how to access card catalogs from a number of colleges and universities around the country. From the main menu, choose **Libraries**, then choose **Library Catalogs** via Telnet. You'll get a menu of available card catalogs.

In addition, you can retrieve a list of useful library information via FTP:

```
ftp ftp.utdallas.edu
cd /pub/staff/billy/libguide
```

Use **dir** or **ls** to view available files. The list is separated by country. To get information about available online libraries in America, for example, get **libraries.america**. For Asian libraries, get **libraries.asia**. Figure 8.31 shows a sample entry from these files.

FIGURE 8.31

Sample entry from Libraries Asia

```
                        Bond University

Location:  Gold Coast, Queensland, Australia
Catalog: URICA

To access:

1.    Type TELNET LIBRARY.BU.OZ.AU.
2.    At the login prompt, type opac.

To exit, type OFF on main menu

Contact:
   Joanna Richardson
   <richardj@surf.sics.bu.oz.au>
   075 95 1401
IP address:  131.244.7.7


                      Charles Sturt University

Location: Bathurst and Wagga, New South Wales Australia
Catal
 ALT-Z FOR HELP| VT100 | FDX| 57600 N81| LOG CLOSED| PRINT OFF | ON-LINE
```

ERIC (Educational Resources Information Center) has been around university libraries for a long time. It is a database of educational articles, abstracts, and summaries of doctoral dissertations, master's theses, and other research and publications. It is a source of published and unpublished information that is excellent because it comes from front line researchers and is usually very current. One source for ERIC information is this one, on the WWW:

```
http://www.ericse.ohio-state.edu
```

Figure 8.32 shows the opening screen of this Eric reference.

FIGURE 8.32

Opening ERIC WWW page

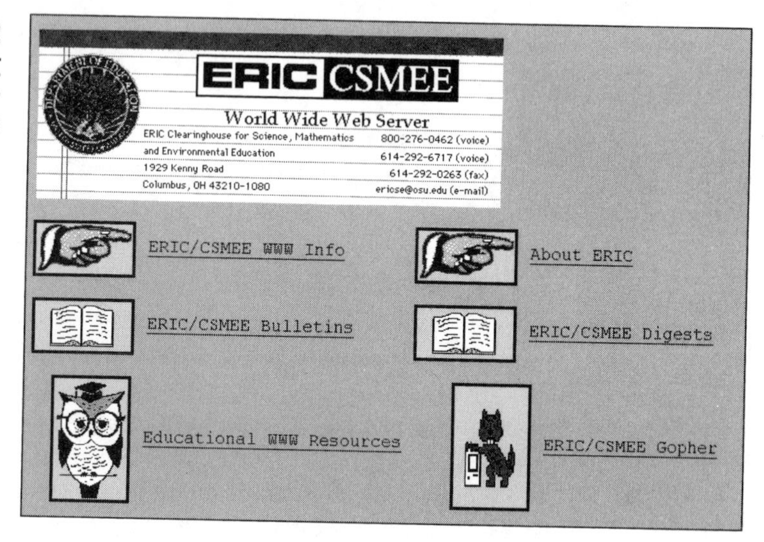

Law Library

This is one more of the almost unbelievable assets you can reach online through the Internet. You'll have more luck accessing this system after hours, as during regular business times you frequently get "Sorry load too great" messages and are disconnected.

```
To access the Liberty legal system:
telnet liberty.uc.wlu.edu
```

Log in as **lawlib** and enter **lawlib** as the password. You will be presented with a welcome screen and instructions.

```
ftp sulaw.law.su.oz.au
cd /pub/law
```

Use **dir** or **ls** to view available files and directories. You can find laws for each state, computer law information, and more. Most of these files have been compressed with COMPRESS (.Z extension) or combined with tar. You'll have to uncompress them and separate them before you can access the information.

```
ftp ftp.cwru.edu
cd /hermes
```

Use **ls** or **dir** to find out what files and directories are available. Among the reference material you should find here are ASCII files of U.S. Supreme Court rulings. You can also download WordPerfect and Xywrite versions of these files. Download the Index, INFO, and README files to get more information about this repository.

Periodicals

You can find listings of periodicals as well as online material by searching the Internet. Use Gopher to find online magazines. Try Archie (**prog periodical**) and see what you find. Here are some sample references:

```
ftp ftp.std.com
cd /periodicals
```

Use **dir** or **ls** to view the additional directories. You can look at the Network-World or Middlesex-News directories, for example, to find various articles and news.

USA Today

You can get to *USA Today*, headline news, and other online references through some freenets. Try:

```
telnet hela.INS.CWRU.Edu
log in as visitor.
```

This is a busy freenet system. If you get a busy message, try the Youngstown freenet listed below.

```
telnet yfn.ysu.edu
log in as visitor.
```

This is the Youngstown Free-Net, provided free of charge by St. Elizabeth Hospital Medical Center and Youngstown State University. This is a menu-driven system that includes entries for administration, business & industrial, The Government Center, etc. This is typical of freenets, which frequently are set up as small towns, with different types of information and services set up in different "rooms" or areas that can be chosen from a menu. Figure 8.33 shows one selection from the YFN main menu..

FIGURE 8.33

YFN main menu screen

```
<<< USA-Today Headline News >>>

  1 About the Electronic News Center
  2 Headline News Summary
  3 Weather
  4 Sports
  5 Money
  6 Life
------------------------------------------------
h=Help, x=Exit YFN, "go help"=extended help

Your Choice ==> █
```

Notice that this menu includes the USA Today and Headline News. This area is further divided into snapshots, sports, and other areas which, again, you can access via the menu.

Ziff-Davis Publishing

Ziff-Davis Publishing is responsible for *PC Magazine*, *PC Week,* and a bookshelf full of other periodicals related to the computer industry. You can access the Ziff-Davis home page, and jump from there to many of these publications online, from the WWW home page at:

```
http://www.ziff.com
```

Journalist Files & Resources

The Internet is a rich resource for journalists. Any of the resources mentioned elsewhere could serve as a starting point for article or book research. So, it is natural that journalists gather on the Internet to support each other in their efforts. Here's an excellent resource that points you toward dozens of mailing lists, discussion groups, and databases of interest specifically to journalists. Send an email message to **verbwork@access.digex.net** and ask for the Journalism List.

You'll receive a long list of resources; you'll have to investigate them on your own to determine whether they are what you need. To join any of the discussion groups that use listserv, send email to **listserv@domain**, where domain is the address provided in the list you are sent. In the body of the email message, say **sub listname** followed by your first name and last name. Your actual mail list will be provided in the header of the email message. For Internet mailing lists, send email to **listname-request@domain,** and in the text, type **sub firstname lastname**.

Internet References

You'll find a number of rather good online publications about the Internet as you browse around. Most of them are available in multiple locations. Among the earliest is Zen and the Art of the Internet. It is somewhat outdated but it is still an easy to read, well-done book. Look for it in several forms: PostScript, ASCII, and more. Here's one place to get it:

```
ftp ftp.cs.widener.edu
cd pub/zen
get README
```

Use **!cat README** to scan this file for additional information. There are several versions of this Internet guide in the directory. One quick and easy way to get a copy of the guide is to get **zen-1.0.PS**. This is a PostScript version of the file. Simply send it to a PostScript printer using the appropriate command for your computer system. The guide will print with page formatting and be ready for hole punching and inserting in a three-ring binder.

"Kids" General

These listings contain files of general interest to or about kids. FTP to the specified site, change to the listed directory (**cd directoryname**), and get the file shown. Use **ls** to display a list of available files in the listed directory.

```
Host: ftp.uni-paderborn.de
Directory: /doc/FAQ/misc.answers
```

Use **ls *kids*** to list files with kids in the title.

```
Directory: /doc/FAQ/misc.kids
File: Welcome_to_Misc.kids_FAQ_File_Index_(Updated_12_8_94).gz
Directory: /doc/FAQ/news.answers
```

Use **ls *kids*** to list files with kids in the title.

```
Host: cs.dal.ca
Directory: /comp.archives/alt.missing-kids
```

You can find some kid-oriented material in various places on the WWW, of course. Here's one:

```
http://www.manytmedia.com/show-n-tell/
```

Sharing Educational Resources

Big Sky Telegraph

```
Telnet 192.231.192.1 or bigsky.bigsky.dillon.mt.us
Dial direct:       406-683-7680 (300/1200 bps)
     406-683-7685 or 406-683-7686 (2400 bps)
     406-683-7880 (9600 bps)
Type bbs at login.
```

Big Sky Telegraph is a consortium of educators interested in sharing resources and information about computers and online education. The group claims to have more than 600 lesson plans online. It solicits lesson plans, ideas, and other resources from the education community for K–12 age groups. Among the resources you can get online is a course titled "Microcomputer Telecommunications," which covers the basics of telecomputing and modem use for connection to any of 60,000+ systems for users on a limited budget. A number of other online classes—some that qualify for teacher re-certification—are available through BST. A companion commercial service is available. (Log in as **hrn** instead of **bbs** for a look at the commercial offerings.)

```
Questions? Contact:
franko@bigsky.dillon.mt.us
Frank Odasz, Director of BST
Western Montana College
710 S. Atlantic
Dillon, MT 59725
Voice: 406-683-7338
Fax: 406-683-7493
Modem: 406-683-7680
Operation Uplink
ftp ftp.OpUp.Org
cd /pub/library/Opup
get edu.networking
```

This file provides a basic introduction to online education. The offerings in this directory will grow rapidly, so check frequently. Operation Uplink is an innovative elementary and secondary educational program run within Knoxville, TN, public schools, but operated with teachers and professionals from around the world. Funding for the program is mostly private.

Operation Uplink uses computers—and particularly the Internet—to link youngsters with other students and with adults in a sharing, learning environment. You can usually find V_Kids (a multi-user UNIX machine that puts up to 13 kids on the Internet at once) on IRC in #vine or #UpLink channels. Questions? email **Towne@OpUp.Org**.

GOVERNMENT

National Science Foundation

The National Science Foundation is among the founders of the Internet as we know it today. It should not be surprising, then, that you can access NSF information via the Internet. Here's how:

```
> telnet stis.nsf.gov
Login: Public
```

You will see a welcoming screen, then a login prompt. Enter **new** if you've never accessed this facility before. Then you will be prompted for the ID you want to use on the system and you will be asked a few more questions to register with this system.

Now you can access this host to perform sophisticated text searches on NSF Publications as well as a database of award abstracts. The screen should look like the one in Figure 8.34.

FIGURE 8.34

NSF main menu screen

```
STSMAIN                              Main Menu

Use arrow keys or numbers to make a selection, and then Enter.

                   ......................................
                   .  1  Search/Browse Documents (TOPIC)  .
                   .  2  Edit User Registration           .
                   .  3  View Help Menu                   .
                   .  4  Download STIS Manual             .
                   .  5  Download Index to Files for FTP  .
                   .  6  Send a Message to STIS Operator  .
                   .  7  Exit STIS (log out)              .
                   ......................................

Enter  ?=Help  ESC

ALT-Z FOR HELP | VT100|FDX | 57600 N81|LOG CLOSED | PRINT OFF | ON-LINE
```

The search engine is TOPIC, from Verity, Inc. You can download a user's guide for TOPIC from the host, or call 202-357-5000, and request a printed copy of NSF publication NSF 91-19.

You can also access information from this host through anonymous FTP and the Internet Gopher. An even better choice is to use a WWW browser. Try the URL:

```
http://stis.nsf.gov/.
```

Federal Information Exchange

You can access the Federal Information Exchange (fedix) from a variety of sources, including Gopher. You can also get to it via Telnet or through a dial-up 800 number. For Telnet access, issue this command:

```
telnet fedix.fie.com
```

You will get a logon banner that looks something like the one shown in Figure 8.35.

FIGURE 8.35 FEDIX opening screen

```
        FFFFFFFFF EEEEEEEEE DDDDDDDD  IIIII  XXX   XXX
         FFF       EEE        DDD  DDDD  III    XXX XXX
         FFF       EEE        DDD   DDD  III     XXXXX
         FFFFFF    EEEEEEEE   DDD   DDD  III      XXX
         FFF       EEE        DDD   DDD  III     XXXXX
         FFF       EEE        DDD  DDDD  III    XXX XXX
         FFF       EEEEEEEEE DDDDDDDD  IIIII  XXX   XXX


logged in on - /dev/ttyp6
Internet

      F E D E R A L   I N F O R M A T I O N   E X C H A N G E

      555 Quince Orchard Road          dialup..: (800) 783-3349
      Suite 200                        internet: fedix.fie.com
      Gaithersburg, MD  20878          helpline: (301) 975-0103
```

As you can see, you can use the Internet or direct dial-up. The first time you access the service, log on as **NEW** and follow directions. You can use the WWW at **http://fedix.fie.com**.

What is on Fedix? A variety of federal information services, including:

1. Federal Opportunities (FEDIX)
2. Minority College & University Capability Information (MOLIS)
3. Higher Education Opportunities for Minorities & Women (HERO)

As you work through the menu system, you will learn that Fedix is "an on-line information service that links the higher education community and the federal government to facilitate research, education, and services. The system provides accurate and timely federal agency information to colleges, universities, and other research organizations."

Information from at least nine federal agencies is available online, including data from The Department of Energy (DOE), Office of Naval Research (ONR), National Aeronautics and Space Administration (NASA), Air Force Office of Scientific Research (AFOSR), and Federal Aviation Administration (FAA). They are providing comprehensive education- and research-related agency information, while the National Science Foundation (NSF), Department of Housing and Urban Development (HUD), Department of Commerce (DOC), and the U.S. Agency for International Development (AID) are providing minority information exclusively. The list is changing, so consult the online list for current availability.

U.S. Federal Register

You can find the U.S. Federal Register through some Gopher clients, and you can Telnet to **locis.loc.gov**. Now, you can use the WWW to access the Federal Register information through a new facility called Thomas.

Thomas is a part of the Library of Congress offerings. It lets you retrieve a surprising amount of information about the federal government, including the status of current legislation and a lot more. Access Thomas at:

```
http://thomas.loc.gov/
```

See Figure 8.36 for an opening Thomas page.

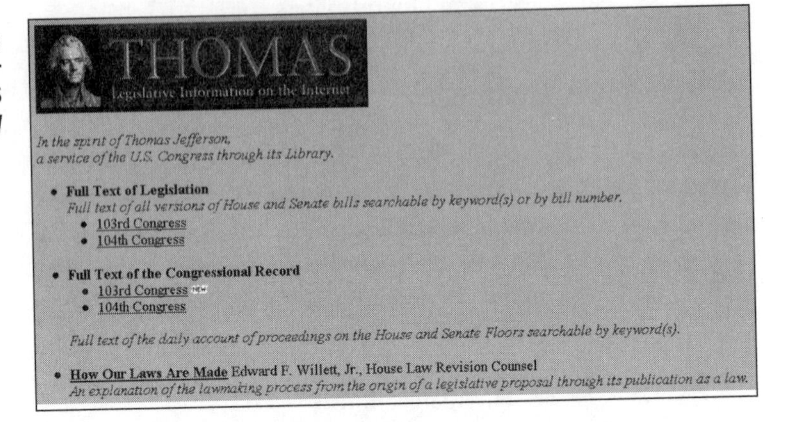

FIGURE 8.36
Opening Thomas page WWW

You can also access the Federal Register and the Commerce Business Daily over the Internet through a Gopher server. The Federal Register is at:

```
gopher.counterpoint.com:2002/11/
```

while the Commerce Business Daily menu is at:

```
gopher.counterpoint.com:2003/11/
```

Figure 8.37 shows the Commerce Business Daily screen.

The Commerce Business Daily

The Commerce Business Daily (CBD) lists notices of proposed government procurement actions, contract awards, sales of government property, and other procurement information. A new edition of the CBD is issued every business day. Each edition contains approximately 500 - 1,000 notices. Each notice appears in the CBD only once.

Help Using the Commerce Business Daily

Browse the latest issue of the Commerce Business Daily

- Supplies, Equipment and Material
- Procurement

FIGURE 8.37
Commerce Business Daily

Project Gutenberg

Through Project Gutenberg you can access the latest U.S. Census information, articles, reference material, and more. It may be on your Gopher. If it isn't, you can FTP directly to it:

```
ftp mrcnext.cso.uiuc.edu
cd etext/etext94
```

Use **dir** to list files. There is an INDEX file in each of these directories. You can use **get** to copy it to your system, then use **cat** to look at it to find out what each of these files means. Then go on to other directories:

```
cd etext/articles
cd etext92
cd etext93
```

You can find interesting books, articles, and reference material in these directories.

CIA Information

There are at least a couple of CIA resources you can locate in various places on the Internet: the *CIA World Map* and the *CIA Factbook*. If you want to see something interesting, use Archie to do a substring search for **cia**. You'll get a number of resources from the CIA.

Here's one place to get the CIA World Factbook:

```
ftp ftp.std.com
cd /obi/World.Factbook
get The.World.Factbook.1990
```

The 1994 factbook is available on the WWW at:

```
http://www.ic.gov/94fac/fb94toc.html
```

As for the *CIA World Map*, try:

```
ftp relay.cs.toronto.edu
cd /doc/geography/CIA_World_Map
```

Within this directory are a number of additional directories. Start by getting the file README. Use **!cat README** to view this file and find out what you need to do. This is actually an archive that contains map drawing programs that use the *CIA World Map* data.

Social Security Administration

Whether you're near retirement or are merely curious about what is current in the Social Security Administration, this can be an interesting resource:

```
ftp ftp.ssa.gov
cd pub
```

Use **dir** to find out what is there. It is a mixed bag. Just browse around by using **cd** and a directory name, then use **dir** to look for files and directories that make sense. One interesting resource is the **ssa.phone.book.Z** file located in the **/pub** directory. Use **get** to download this file to your local host, then use **uncompress** to unpack it. There are a number of speech files that offer some data. You can start with the **README.1st** file, or with one of the abstract files to get you underway here.

Congress

Ever wanted to contact your congressman? You can get the phone and fax information for any member of congress through WAIS. Once on WAIS, locate the **US-Congress-Phone-Fax** entry on the main list. Highlight it, press **Space**, and enter the name you are looking for. WAIS will search the database and display a list of any entries that match. Figure 8.38 shows the results of a search for duncan, congressman from Tennessee.

FIGURE 8.38

WAIS Congress search: Duncan

```
R TN Duncan Jr., John J.                1-202-225-5435  1-202-225-6440
  p st representative                     phone           fax
```

If you only know the last name of the person you're looking for, enter that and then choose the correct one from the list on the screen.

There are other reference sections you'll find close to the congressional entry. For example, there is a file for **us-judges**, and you can reference the **US-Budget-1994** or **US-Gov-Programs** sections for some interesting information. Figure 8.39 shows a sample screen from the 1993 budget file.

FIGURE 8.39

Sample screen from US-Budget-1993 file

```
Document # 44
Headline: Executive-Office-of-the-President The-Points-of-Light-Foundation
DocID: 0 391 /b/FEDERAL-PROGRAMS-BY-AGENCY-AND-ACCOUNT/Executive-Office-of-the-P
resident/The-Points-of-Light-Foundation

Document # 45
Headline: Executive-Office-of-the-President Summary
DocID: 0 679 /b/FEDERAL-PROGRAMS-BY-AGENCY-AND-ACCOUNT/Executive-Office-of-the-P
resident/Summary

Document # 46
Headline: Funds-Appropriated-to-the-President Unanticipated-Needs
DocID: 0 380 /b/FEDERAL-PROGRAMS-BY-AGENCY-AND-ACCOUNT/Funds-Appropriated-to-the
-President/Unanticipated-Needs

Document # 47
Headline: Funds-Appropriated-to-the-President Investment-in-Management-Improveme
nt
DocID: 0 338 /b/FEDERAL-PROGRAMS-BY-AGENCY-AND-ACCOUNT/Funds-Appropriated-to-the
-President/Investment-in-Management-Improvement

Document # 48
Press any key to continue, 'q' to quit.
```

You can look at political speeches through WAIS as well. Just open the main WAIS screen, then look for **clinton-speeches**, **bush-speeches**, and so on. (I found these with the **sunsite.unc.edu** WAIS client SWAIS.) You can FTP to this information as well:

```
ftp sunsite.unc.edu
cd /pub/docs/speeches
```

Use **dir** to find out what is there. The directory should look like Figure 8.40.

FIGURE 8.40

Directory at sunsite.unc.edu

```
ftp> dir
200 PORT command successful.
150 Opening ASCII mode data connection for /bin/ls.
total 52
-rwxr-xr-x  1 root     daemon       1262 Mar 18  1993 .cache
drwxr-xr-x  2 root     daemon        512 Jul  6 20:31 .cap
-rw-r--r--  1 root     daemon       3616 Aug 26  1992 ABOUT.NPTN.TXT
-rw-r--r--  1 root     daemon       2484 Aug 26  1992 CAMPAIGN.92.TXT
-rw-r--r--  1 root     daemon        613 Jan  4  1993 INDEX
-r--r--r--  1 root     daemon       5206 Oct 28  1992 INDEX.BUSH
-r--r--r--  1 root     daemon      13177 Nov  2  1992 INDEX.CLINTON
drwxr-xr-x  2 root     daemon        512 Mar  4  1993 Perot
-rw-r--r--  1 root     daemon        124 Jan  4  1993 README
drwxr-xr-x  2 root     daemon       3584 Mar 18  1993 bush.dir
-r--r--r--  1 root     daemon       3003 Oct 19  1992 cl99.txt
drwxr-xr-x  2 root     daemon        512 Mar  4  1993 clinton-positions
drwxr-xr-x  2 root     daemon       9216 Mar  4  1993 clinton.dir
drwxr-xr-x  2 root     daemon        512 Oct 21  1992 debates
drwxr-xr-x  2 root     daemon        512 Aug 26  1992 demo-conv
drwxr-xr-x  3 root     daemon        512 Jun  3 21:24 kibo-for-prez
226 Transfer complete.
1057 bytes received in 0.32 seconds (3.2 Kbytes/s)
ftp>
```

Download **INDEX** or **INDEX.CLINTON** first. That will point you in the right direction toward finding the files you want. Then use **cd clinton.dir**, for example, to access actual speeches.

Use WAIS to locate the **White-House-Papers** entry, then search for entries by keyword, or enter a space to get a directory list. You can FTP to this information as well:

```
ftp sunsite.unc.edu
cd /pub/academic/political-science/whitehouse-
papers/1995
```

Use **dir** to see how this directory is structured. You will find a separate directory for each month, then files about different topics. You can use **get** to download these files for your own reference.

Local Governments

You'll also find a lot of information from local government entities, including state government and travel agencies, cities, and more. Here are a few starting places on the WWW.

`http://www.neosoft.com/citylink`

This listing includes pointers to WWW pages in all 50 states and the District of Columbia. It includes such local information as subway schedules, where to eat, what to see and do, job information, and more.

`http://www.usit.net/sundquist`

This WWW page started as a four-week project to track the inaugural activities of Tennessee Governor-elect Sundquist early in 1995. Now that the inaugural activities are over, the pages are being expanded to include information about Tennessee government, cities, tourism, and so on.

A specific Tennessee community page, and an excellent example of the kind of joint commercial and government projects we can expect to see on the Internet, is the page for Lawrence County:

`http://www.usit.net/lawrence.html`

For information on California State government, try:

`http://www.sen.ca.gov`

And, of course, don't forget the White house server:

`http://www.whitehouse.gov`

This is a well-designed page that also includes some sound files.

REFERENCE

With the growth of the WWW and associated graphical browsers, the Web is one of the best places to start when you are doing research about a variety of topics. I'll give you a good selection of these lists or searching tools, then move on to some Internet specific locations.

Search Tools and Lists

A popular starting place is the Virtual Library:

```
http://info.cern.ch/hypertext/DataSources/bySubject/Overview.html
```

You can start here, looking for information by subject, and then follow your mouse finger almost anywhere in the world.

One of the best all around and comprehensive reference pages on the net is produced at U.S. Internet by Jack Utano, an Internet content specialist. His reference page is at:

```
http://www.usit.net/np/misc/rererence.html
```

You'll find a wide variety of reference material for Web searching and general reference on this page.

Another good starting point is the EINet Galaxy:

```
http://www.einet.net
```

Or you could try the Planet Earth Home Page:

```
http://white.nosc.mil/info_modern.html
```

As I mentioned in Chapter 6, there are a number of search engines or WebCrawlers that can be useful in finding information. The Lycos engine is one:

```
http://lycos.cs.cmu.edu
```

The WebCrawler is another:

```
http://www.biotech.washington.edu/WebCrawler/Home.html
```

Try also Yahoo, an index of Web resources:

```
http://www.yahoo.com
```

Or try Jumpstation II:

```
http://www.stir.ac.uk/jsbin/jsii
```

The Whole Internet Catalog is another good choice:

```
http://nearnet.gnn.com/wic/newrescat.toc.html
```

You could also try the World-Wide Web Worm, sometimes called WWWW:

```
http://www.cs.colorado.edu/home/mcbryan/WWWW.html
```

The RBSE URL database is a good starting place for broader or more general Web searches:

```
http://rbse.jsc.nasa.gov/eichmann/urlsearch.html
```

Not as easy to use as some, but definitely a useful resource, the CUI W3 Search Engines Page is located at:

```
http://cuiwww.unige.ch/meta-index.html
```

Library of Congress

Perhaps the ultimate reference on the WWW or anywhere is the Library of Congress. You can access the LOC in several forms on the Internet. A good starting place for learning your way around the LOC is the home page at:

```
http://lcweb.loc.gov/homepage/lchp.html
```

Access this page with your favorite WWW browser, and follow it to many interesting and informative places.

Dictionary

A rich collection of dictionary and other language-related reference material is available on the WWW at:

```
http://www.willamette.edu/~tjones/Language-Page.html
```

Thesaurus

Use a WWW browser (or a Gopher on a text system) to display the page at

```
gopher://odie.niaid.nih.gov:70/77/.thesaurus/index
```

You can use a search screen, like the one in Figure 8.41, to enter a word. When you do, the system searchs for entries and returns the display in Figure 8.42. This is the result of a search for the word **fortune**.

FIGURE 8.41

Search criteria screen in nih Thesaurus

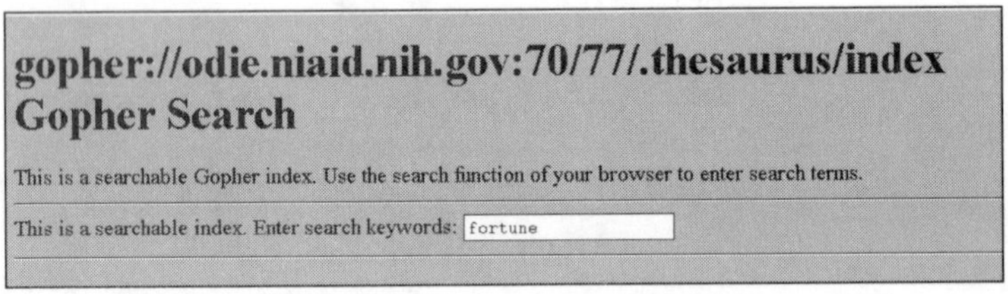

gopher://odie.niaid.nih.gov:70/77/.thesaurus/index
Gopher Search

This is a searchable Gopher index. Use the search function of your browser to enter search terms.

This is a searchable index. Enter search keywords: fortune

FIGURE 8.42

Results of search for Fortune

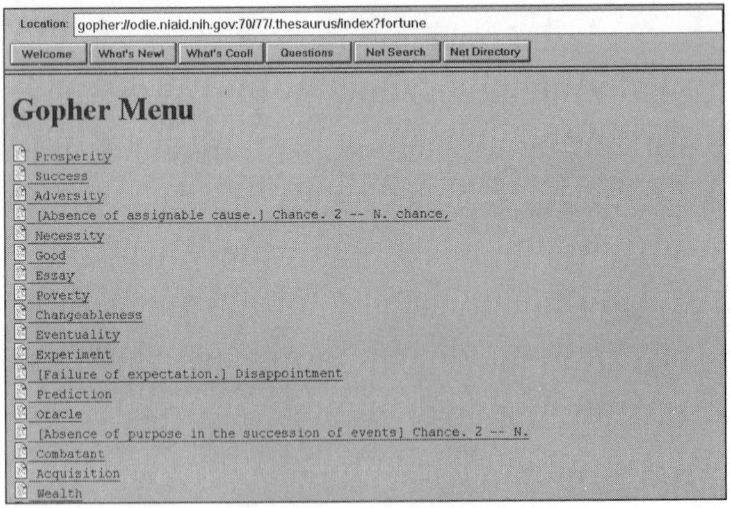

Location: gopher://odie.niaid.nih.gov:70/77/.thesaurus/index?fortune

Welcome | What's New! | What's Cool! | Questions | Net Search | Net Directory

Gopher Menu

Prosperity
Success
Adversity
[Absence of assignable cause.] Chance. 2 -- N. chance,
Necessity
Good
Essay
Poverty
Changeableness
Eventuality
Experiment
[Failure of expectation.] Disappointment
Prediction
Oracle
[Absence of purpose in the succession of events] Chance. 2 -- N.
Combatant
Acquisition
Wealth

Another forms-based searchable thesaurus is:

```
http://tuna.uchicago.edu/forms_unrest/ROGET.html
```

News WWW Page

A good place to start searching the WWW for online news resources is the e-news page created by U.S. Internet:

```
http://www.usit.net/np/misc/e-news.html
```

You will find such goodies as an Associated Press search page and other online news resources that are quite useful.

NewsHound

Another way to look at online news is to have a service search and clip articles of interest. One such service is the Mercury Center NewsHound. It searches news articles and classified ads in a range of periodicals according to your search criteria, then emails articles of interest to you. The company claims to search about 2,000 articles a day from more than 60 sources, including the *Chicago Tribune*, *Detroit Free Press*, *Associated Press*, *PR Newswire*, and more.

Search requests are sent via email to the NewsHound program. You'll get new responses returned by email every hour or so.

The service costs $9.95 per month for up to five search profiles. Get information by sending email to:

```
newshound-support@sjmercury.com.
```

UPI News (UPI Newswire)

Use Gopher to locate the **News** entry and select **UPI News**. You can view a short description of what UPI News is, and see a menu for UPI News access. You may not be able to get to some of this information (except the About UPI News Introduction) unless you are accessing the information from on the campus.

This information is provided (at least where I found it) through a site license purchased by the University of Minnesota.

UPI and other news services are offering similar licenses to colleges and universities as well as businesses which use it for research and general information. This is provided through a facility called Clarinet, a commercial information provider.

You can search the database for information by topic and receive a list of available stories, like the one shown in Figure 8.43.

FIGURE 8.43

Typical UPI news story list after search

```
Client v1.11Search Today's News: india

 -->  1.  1993/Sep/Sep 30/news/New Navy Chief takes charge in India : From: .
2.  1993/Sep/Sep 30/news/India quake toll mounts to 6,200 : From: clar.
3.  1993/Sep/Sep 30/news/India quake toll rises to 6,513 : From: clari.
4.  1993/Sep/Sep 30/news/A UPI News Update [Sep 30 8 am PDT] : From: c.
5.  1993/Sep/Sep 30/news/A UPI News Update [Sep 30 9 am PDT] : From: c.
6.  1993/Sep/Sep 30/news/A UPI News Update [Sep 30 10 am PDT] : From: .
7.  1993/Sep/Sep 30/news/A UPI News Update [Sep 30 11 am PDT] : From: .
8.  1993/Sep/Sep 30/news/A UPI News Update [Sep 30 12 pm PDT] : From: .
9.  1993/Sep/Sep 30/news/The UPI Afternoon Report [Sep 30 12 pm PDT] .
10. 1993/Sep/Sep 29/local/UPI Midwest Farm Report : From: clarinews@cl.
11. 1993/Sep/Sep 29/local/Georgia Second News In Brief [Sep 29 7 am P .
12. 1993/Sep/Sep 29/news/India sets up human rights commission : From:.
13. 1993/Sep/Sep 29/news/Inter-tribal warfare spreads in India's nort .
14. 1993/Sep/Sep 29/news/Earthquake measuring 6.4 hits southern India .
15. 1993/Sep/Sep 29/news/500 trapped under debris after quake in Indi .
16. 1993/Sep/Sep 29/news/A UPI News Update [Sep 29 8 pm PDT] : From: c.
17. 1993/Sep/Sep 29/news/A UPI News Update [Sep 29 9 pm PDT] : From: c.
18. 1993/Sep/Sep 29/news/Quakes jar western India, killing as many as .

Press ? for Help, q to Quit, u to go up a menuPage: 1/2
```

Zip Code List

This FTP site will give you an excellent reference list for U.S. zip codes:

```
ftp top.magnus.acs.ohio-state.edu
cd /pub/library/lists
get US_zip_codes
```

For users of the World Wide Web, try:

```
http://www.usps.gov/ZIP4Form.html
```

Language References

Here is a Web site for language reference that you might find interesting:

```
http://www.itp.berkeley.edu/~throne/HumanResources.html
```

This is a reference page to other WWW pages for learning languages and learning about languages.

For a link to Spanish language sites, try:

```
http://www.rcp.net.pe
```

or

```
http://gias720.dis.ulpgc.es/spain.html
```

Culture References

In addition to language, you can find references to culture, geography, and more. Here are some simple and admittedly limited examples to get you started.

A good Argentina reference is:

```
gopher.recyt.net
```

You can use your WWW browser to get there (**gopher://gopher.recyt.net** on the URL line), or use the gopher command at a UNIX prompt.

For some map references related to Latin America try:

```
http://www.lib.utexas.edu/Libs/PCL/Map_collection
/americas.html
```

See Figure 8.44 for a sample screen from this reference.

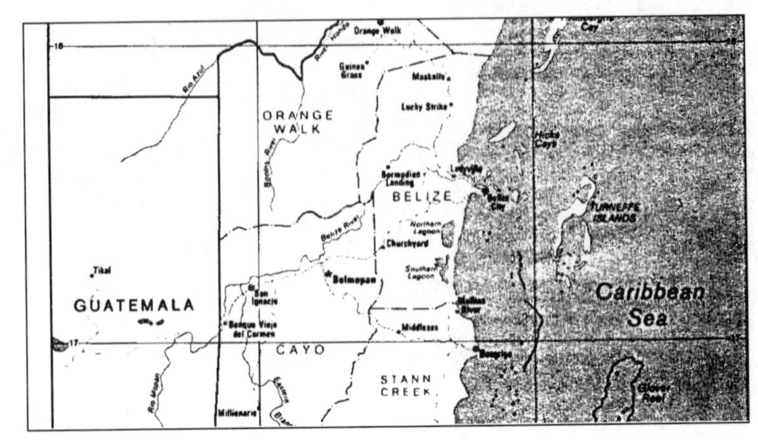

FIGURE 8.44

Sample screen from Map_Collection

BOOKS AND MORE

Books and book references are readily available on the Internet. I've shown elsewhere how to access library information and some online publications. There's more...

Bookstores

There are references on the Internet to bookstore locations, for example. Try:

```
ftp rtfm.mit.edu (18.172.1.27)
cd /pub/usenet/news.answers/books/stores/north-
american
get nyc
```

or

Send email to **mail-server@rtfm.mit.edu** with the subject line "send usenet/news.answers/books/stores/north-american/nyc", leaving the body of the message empty.

This is an annotated list of Manhattan bookstores by section of town. The author describes the store, mentions any special information that may be useful ("identify the mystery quote of the day and get an additional 20% off your purchase"), and shares personal experiences.

This is just one example. Want books in other parts of the country, mail order, or around the world? Check the list under Entertainment Books at the Yahoo site:

```
http://www.yahoo.com/
```

Dinosaurs

Popular topics come and go, but dinosaurs seem to remain high on everybody's list of interesting topics. A traditional (older) Internet site for dinosaur information is:

```
ftp wiretap.spies.com
cd /Library/Article/Misc
get dinosaur.fly
```

This is a brief discussion of which dinosaurs were able to fly.

```
ftp ftp.uni-kl.de
cd /pub0/humor/funnies
get dinosaurus.jokes.Z
```

A truly surprising site in terms of its breadth and depth is:

```
http://ucmp1.berkeley.edu/exhibittext/dinosaur.html.
```

College Lists

```
ftp ftp.denet.dk
cd /pub/wordlists/places
get Colleges.Z
```

Business Reference

For years researchers have resorted to the familiar green Thomas Register books. Now you can access at least a part of this resource online. Try:

```
http://www.thomasnet.com
```

Figure 8.45 shows the opening screen for the Thomas Register of American Manufacturers.

FIGURE 8.45 Opening screen for Thomas Register

ART

If you have even a passing interest in art, you can find some interesting resources on the Internet. One place to start is with a simple Archie search. Once you are inside Archie, use **Set Search Exact** at the prompt to narrow the search, then use **prog art** to produce a list of files with the name art. What you'll get is several pages of host and directory names. Some are obvious, and others require a little imagination or a hands-on check to find out what's really there.

A good site to browse (as opposed to searching) is:

```
http://www.yahoo.com/Art/
```

Images

For example, one listing is at

```
http://www.yahoo.com/computers/multimedia/pictures
```

The list on this World Wide Web page is shown in Figure 8.46.

FIGURE 8.46

http://www.yahoo /com/computers /multimedia /pictures WWW Page

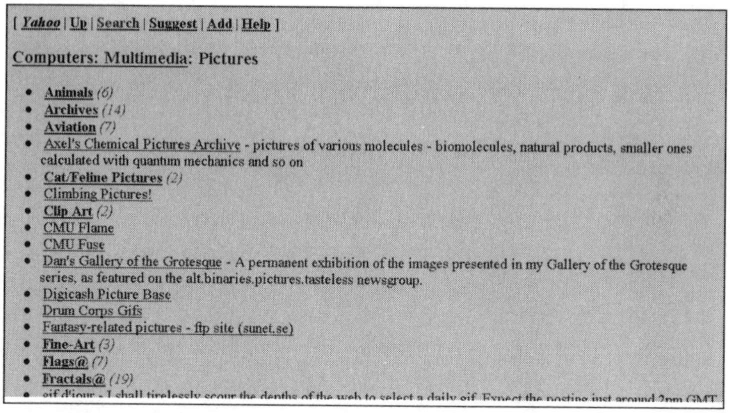

[Yahoo | Up | Search | Suggest | Add | Help]

Computers: Multimedia: Pictures

- Animals (6)
- Archives (14)
- Aviation (7)
- Axel's Chemical Pictures Archive - pictures of various molecules - biomolecules, natural products, smaller ones calculated with quantum mechanics and so on
- Cat/Feline Pictures (2)
- Climbing Pictures!
- Clip Art (2)
- CMU Flame
- CMU Fuse
- Dan's Gallery of the Grotesque - A permanent exhibition of the images presented in my Gallery of the Grotesque series, as featured on the alt.binaries.pictures.tasteless newsgroup.
- Digicash Picture Base
- Drum Corps Gifs
- Fantasy-related pictures - ftp site (sunet.se)
- Fine-Art (3)
- Flags@ (7)
- Fractals@ (19)

If you back up one directory on this host, you'll find some additional image possibilities. Simply issue the **cd ..** command and then use **dir** again. The file names that end with a forward slash (/) are directories. You can use **cd** to change into different directories, then use **ls** to find out what they contain.

Here's an interesting resource: the "Bryn-mawr-classical-review." Access it through WAIS and enter search key words. This online publication consists of articles about a number of "classical" topics, and is fully searchable.

Television

It's an age-old question that I won't try to resolve here: Is television art? Whatever the answer to that, you can find out more about current and past television programs over the Internet. Here's how:

```
ftp ftp.uu.net
cd /usenet/rec.arts.tv
```

Use **dir** to find out what's there. This is a dynamic database that comes from a variety of sources. There are data and comments here about past and present shows. You'll find both files and directories of files in this subdirectory. Many of the files are compressed those whose file names end in **.Z**.

Those topics that have grown rather large earn their own subdirectory. Simply use **cd** again to make the desired directory current, and use **dir** again to see what you have available.

For example, if you change to the **twilightzone** subdirectory, you'll find the **Vidiot** directory. Inside that directory are two more subdirectories, each with a handful of files about *Twilight Zone*. Some of these files are in PostScript format (the file names end in **.ps**), which means they will print directly on a PostScript printer.

On the World Wide Web you can find interesting television resources as well. Here are some starting points:

```
http://www.yahoo.com/Entertainment/Television
rec.arts.tv
```

Music

Under the art category you may also discover some music files and information. A Lycos search of the WWW in Netscape turned up a number of different music references. The site:

```
http://www.music.indiana.edu/misc/music_resources.
html
```

is a good starting point for further WWW music research (See Figure 8.47).

FIGURE 8.47

WWW music reference at Indiana.edu

Music Resources on the Internet

This music resource list is offered as a service of the Indiana University Music Library.

Standard Disclaimer: *Due to the fact that these services are out of our control, The IU Music Library is not reponsible for the availability or content of these links.*

To make a suggestion mail *webmaster@www.music.indiana.edu* or fill out this form.

Index

- Academic sites
- User-maintained information
- Non-academic sites
- Geographically Local Sites
- Artist-specific sites
- Other lists and indices

You'll also find music information here:

```
ftp cs.uwp.edu
cd /pub/music
```

This archive, at the University of Wisconsin-Parkside, contains a variety of music-oriented information, including data on CD collections, lyrics, guitar chords, and graphics files that contain pictures of some artists. The directories that were in this location as this book was written are shown in Figure 8.48.

FIGURE 8.48

Directories in /pub/music at host cs.uwp.edu

```
dir
200 PORT command successful.
150 Opening ASCII mode data connection for /bin/dl.
CHANGES             1126
GOPHER.README       2023
README.CORRUPT      2611
SITES               2387  Other music-related FTP archive sites
artists/               =  Artists- Archives by Artist name
classical/             =  Classical Buying Guide
composition/           -  Articles of Music Composition
database/              =  Music Database program
faqs/                  =  Frequently Asked Questions files
folk/                  =  Folk Music Files and pointers
guitar/                =  Guitar TAB files from ftp.nevada.edu
info/                  =  rec.music.info newsgroup archives
kurzweil/              =  Kurzweil K2000 Archives
lists/                 =  Mailing lists archives
lyrics/                =  Lyrics Archives
midi/                  -  Some midi files
misc/                  -  Misc files that don't fit anywhere else
pictures/              =  GIFS, JPEGs, PBMs and more.
programs/              -  Misc music-related programs for various machines
releases/              =  USA release listings (now info/releases)
reviews/               =  rec.music.reviews archives
uap/                   -  Usenet Artist Polls
226 Transfer complete.
1140 bytes received in 0.38 seconds (2.9 Kbytes/s)
ftp>
```

Simply use **cd** to change to the directory you're interested in, and use **dir** to list the available files and directories. One interesting resource here is the music database, located in the **/pub/music/database** subdirectory. First, get **README** and look at it to determine how to use the files here. Among the information is a database of over 700 CDs, plus an executable program to manage this database. You can use the Albums program to retrieve CD information by title or artist, and there is even a routine to help you determine how many songs from a given album will fit on a cassette tape. Useful stuff!

You'll also want to look at the **/pub/music/artists** subdirectory. Here you'll find 26 subdirectories, one for each letter of the alphabet. This is an interesting archive because the alphabetical subdirectories contain links to the other resources on this host. That means you can use **cd /pub/music/artists/p** and then **dir** to get a list of all artists catalogued there. Each of these subdirectories contains additional information. So, for example, if you **cd presley.elvis** and use **dir**, you'll see additional subdirectories, including **guitar**, **lyrics**, and **pictures**.

Check out the lyrics under many of the artist's directories. You'll find compressed files designed to be used in Windows (crd format) so you can create your own database of artists and lyrics.

TRAVEL TIP

*In many FTP systems, you don't need to issue the entire path command to get to a specific subdirectory. Simply use **cd presley.elvis** at any local directory (for example), and you should be transferred immediately to the specified directory without entering the entire path. This may not work on all systems.*

MISCELLANEOUS RESOURCES

Sure, I probably could have found a specific topic under which to place these resources, but it would have required a number of different resource names, and some would have had only one or two listings. Anyway, here's a list of Internet resources you can reference when you don't find what you wanted elsewhere in this resource chapter.

Here's one:

```
finger yanoff@csd4.csd.uwm.edu
```

This will tell you how to get a comprehensive list of Internet resources.

Here's a resource for a wide range of information, much of which will also show up on other systems around the Internet. Try this:

```
ftp ftp.uu.net
cd /usenet
```

In this subdirectory you'll find a number of other subdirectories, most named after the USENET recreation topics. You can see how the list looked as this book was written by studying Figure 8.49.

FIGURE 8.49

FTP directory from ftp.uu.net

```
drwxrwsr-x 528 6       archive     8192 Mar 21 10:49 control
drwxrws--x   5 0       0            512 Dec  1  1993 lost+found
-rw-r--r--   1 34      archive   773698 Mar 22 16:23 ls-lR.Z
drwxrwsr-x   2 34      archive     1024 Jul 29  1992 net.sources
drwxrwsr-x  18 27      archive      512 Jan  4 18:40 news.announce.newgroups
drwxrwsr-x 325 34      archive    12800 Mar 22 05:52 news.answers
drwxrwxr-x   2 34      archive     4608 Mar 22 04:56 news.lists
drwxr-sr-x   2 192     archive      512 Jan  8  1993 rec.arts.movies
drwxrwsr-x   5 251     archive      512 Oct 27 14:07 rec.arts.movies.reviews
drwxrwsr-x  13 192     archive      512 May 14  1993 rec.arts.startrek
drwxr-sr-x   2 192     archive     1024 Jan 25  1993 rec.arts.startrek.current
drwxr-sr-x   2 192     archive      512 Jan 25  1993 rec.arts.startrek.fandom
drwxr-sr-x   2 192     archive      512 Jan 25  1993 rec.arts.startrek.info
drwxr-sr-x   2 192     archive     1024 Jan 25  1993 rec.arts.startrek.misc
drwxr-sr-x   2 192     archive     1024 Jan 25  1993 rec.arts.startrek.tech
drwxr-sr-x  26 192     archive     5120 Jul 28  1993 rec.arts.tv
drwxrwsr-x  36 282     archive     3072 Mar 22 17:01 rec.audio.high-end
drwxr-sr-x  23 188     archive      512 Aug 11  1992 rec.food.recipes
drwxrwsr-x   2 34      archive      512 Jan 22  1994 rec.humor.funny
drwxr-sr-x   2 34      archive      512 Jul 29  1992 rec.juggling
drwxr-sr-x   6 98      archive      512 Nov  3  1993 rec.music.gaffa
drwxrwsr-x   7 34      archive      512 Jul 29  1992 uunet.tech
226 Transfer complete.
2711 bytes received in 0.58 seconds (4.6 Kbytes/s)
ftp> █
```

Publications

The *Wall Street Journal*, *USA Today*, and numerous other newspapers are either online or are experimenting with offering some online offerings. Use WAIS to search for **wall-street-journal-**

sample. Here are a few more online publication resources to get you started in this direction.

NewsHound

To try the NewsHound service (for details see the Reference section), email a request for information to **newshound-support@sjmercury.com.**

San Jose Mercury News

You can also access the *San Jose Mercury News* online at:

```
http://www.sjmercury.com
```

The New South Polar Times

Here's an interesting, if offbeat, publication, written by the staff at the Amundsen-Scott South Pole Station. Check it out at:

```
http://www.deakin.edu.au/edu/MSEE/GENII/NSPT/NSPTh
omePage.html
```

Boardwatch Magazine

Boardwatch is a print publication that covers BBSs and other online services. Catch the online version at:

```
http://www.boardwatch.com
```

Resnick's Review

For a review of 50 or so online magazines, check out the list compiled by Rosalind Resnick at:

```
http://www.gate.net/~rosalind
```

PC Week Best of the Web

PC Week Magazine publishes its pick for best Web offerings. You can judge for yourself after checking out their picks at:

```
http://www.ziff.com/~pcweek/pcwbests.html
```

Employment

There are a number of job reference files. Some are fairly localized, and others are more general. On The Well, for example, you can find conferences dedicated to job searches. Savvy employers scan these files looking for people with certain skills. You can upload a file of information about yourself and wait for the call. Here are a few job-related files to get you started.

```
ftp ftp.concert.net
cd /triangle.jobs
get INDEX
```

This directory contains a continuously updated list of files (dozens and dozens of them) listed by number and date. Use the **dir** command to get a list that shows the file date. The INDEX file will also describe these files so you can get an idea of what's there. Some are very local and time sensitive ("I need a ride to DC"). Others discuss job offerings in a variety of fields. This set of files certainly won't answer all your needs for a job, but it is another resource you can tap as you start your research.

One series of files you can find there, for example, is staff openings at the University of North Carolina. There are several files that detail opportunities, requirements, salaries, and so on. Full-time as well as part-time opportunities are posted. Jobs in one listing I saw ranged from secretarial to administrative, from carpenter and security to accounting and programming. Look for similar files on other systems as you browse through Internet facilities.

You can also use Gopher (at whatever site) to look for any entry that lists positions or campus information. Many Gopher servers are run by a university. As part of the general campus information offered by the school, there frequently will be a current job listing.

Another Gopher site:

```
una.hh.lib.umich.edu/00/inetdirsstacks/employment%3araytay.
```

In addition, you can use WAIS for job openings. Try the **AAS_jobs** listing on the main WAIS menu as a place to start. This is maintained by NASA (**ndadsb.gsfc.nasa.gov**). You can look for job opportunities with lawyers, again with WAIS. Search for the **law-employers** (**pegun.law.columbia.edu**) entry on the WAIS topic list.

Use the World Wide Web to help in your job search also. Here is a starting point:

```
http://www.espan.com
```

This is a searchable job database that also provides additional employment information.

Also try:

```
http://www.lib.umich.edu/chdocs/employment
```

WHAT YOU LEARNED

What you got from this chapter depends to some extent on how willing you were to put your hands on the keyboard and try out some of the resources I suggested. I reviewed the use of Archie, Gopher, WAIS, and FTP to help you find and access information on the Internet. Then I showed you specific examples of resources you can find within several topic areas, including Science, Recreation, Commercial and Business, Art, Education, Government, and Computers.

Use this guide as an ongoing reference to topics as you perfect your use of the Internet. But don't forget to check out the information in the appendices and glossary to help you prepare for your own journey.

Appendix A

Everything You Never Wanted to Know about UNIX

The good news about using the Internet is that most of the hardware used to manage it and connect to it runs under UNIX, an almost universal operating system with a long history that manages networking and communications very well.

The bad news about using the Internet is that most of the hardware used to manage it and connect to it runs under UNIX, a ponderous, text-based, old operating system that is not used by very many people other than system designers, engineers, and programmers (of course X-Window and other graphical user interfaces help this traditional UNIX image). For people accustomed to Macintosh or Microsoft Windows user interfaces, the dial-up, text-based user interface common in UNIX is counterintuitive, obscure, and difficult.

Luckily, with the rapid trend toward graphical browsers for the World Wide Web and more user-friendly interfaces even for traditional facilities such as Gopher, WAIS, and IRC, your need to know UNIX becomes less and less. However, there still are times when a little knowledge of the command line is useful. After all, you don't have to program in UNIX as a user of the Internet—you just have to interact with it a little. In this appendix I will show you how UNIX systems are structured, and will explain some of the more important commands and features you are likely to encounter during your Internet travels.

SIMPLE ESSENTIALS OF THE UNIX OPERATING SYSTEM

In some implementations of UNIX, up to 300 megabytes of storage space are required just to hold all the components of the operating system! One reason UNIX needs so much room is that it is rich in features. Built into the operating system are applications to conduct most of the operations you need. As a casual user of the Internet, however, you will encounter only a small portion of UNIX.

What is UNIX?

As I have said, UNIX is an operating system. If you know what that means, skip to the next section. If you don't, read on.

An operating system is the low-level software that conducts most of the housekeeping chores for a computer system. The operating system accepts input from the keyboard or mouse and sends it to applications or to other parts of the operating system. This software also is responsible for managing all output to the screen and to printers. In UNIX, the operating system also controls networking and other communications chores. The operating system manages the disk drives and other storage media, and conducts all input and output operations. In addition, an operating system must provide links to other applications, so that a spreadsheet or database program, for example, can access the screen, load and store information to disk, and print.

UNIX is a multiuser and multitasking operating system, which means it will support more than one user and more than one program at the same time. The operating system includes numerous utility programs to send and receive mail, to show you who else is on the system, and to let you talk to other users. UNIX also manages the log on and log off process and supports security features to protect the system.

As a user of a UNIX system on the Internet, it is these utility applications you are most likely to encounter, as well as disk and directory services. I will talk about some of these utilities—accessed as commands—later in this appendix.

In addition, UNIX is accessed through a shell program that provides a command line and other tools. There are many available shells. Your service provider may supply one by default and may offer one or more optional shells. In general, the commands and procedures discussed here will work with any shell; if you have questions about the shell in use at your service provider's host, contact support personnel for more information.

Typical UNIX System Design

In your journey around the Internet you are likely to encounter a wide variety of UNIX systems, from a Digital Equipment Corporation VAX, to an IBM or HP minicomputer, to a Sun workstation, to a PC running shareware UNIX. You won't always know what type of machine you are using, and it really doesn't matter. Until you get fairly deep into UNIX—enough to know the differences among different implementations—you don't need to know precisely which machine you are using. Even if you encounter an operating system with a name other than UNIX, you may, in fact, be using a flavor of UNIX. Popular implementations include A/UM, DNIX, ULTRIX, XENIX, LINUX, SCO/UNIX, AUX, and so on. Generally, if you come across something that is called *IX or *UX, it is a variety of UNIX.

Whatever the machine, however, there are general structures they have in common and which you should understand to use the Internet efficiently.

UNIX, like most operating systems, uses a series of directories and subdirectories to store information on a hard disk. If the hard disk is analogous to a filing cabinet, then the directories are the drawers in the cabinet. Inside a file drawer is a series of folders, and each folder contains one or more pieces of paper with letters, reports, and other information. On a disk, the folders are files. Each file has a name, just as you might label a folder inside a file cabinet. If your file cabinet contained a drawer for EMPLOYEES, each folder inside the drawer might be labeled with an employee name: Able, Baker, Charles, Davis, Edwards, Franklyn, and so on. In fact, you might divide each drawer into alphabetic sections, and within each alphabetic division might be several folders: Able, Allison, Ashley, Axel, Azden. If you have more than one employee named Able, you could have multiple Able folders: Able, Bob; Able, Sarah; Able, Tom.

If you can understand that filing cabinet structure, you can understand the directory structure on a UNIX disk. The disk may be divided into any number of drawers, and each drawer can hold a varied number of subdivisions and folders.

On the disk, the first directory, which represents the entire file cabinet, is called the root directory. Under the root are all the subordinate directories. Any directory that has other directories under it is usually referred to as a *parent* and the directories under the parent are called *children* or *child directories.* You may hear other names for these directories, but the concept is the same—a hierarchy of directories and files helps the system administrator and the users keep straight all the information stored on the disk.

When you log on to a UNIX server, you probably are using a default directory that carries your logon name or nickname. That directory may be located in a directory off of the root called **usr** or **user**, or it may be several directories deep. In Figure A.1 I have shown one possible directory structure. This is a much simpler structure than you are likely to encounter on most UNIX systems, but it gives you an idea of how files are arranged.

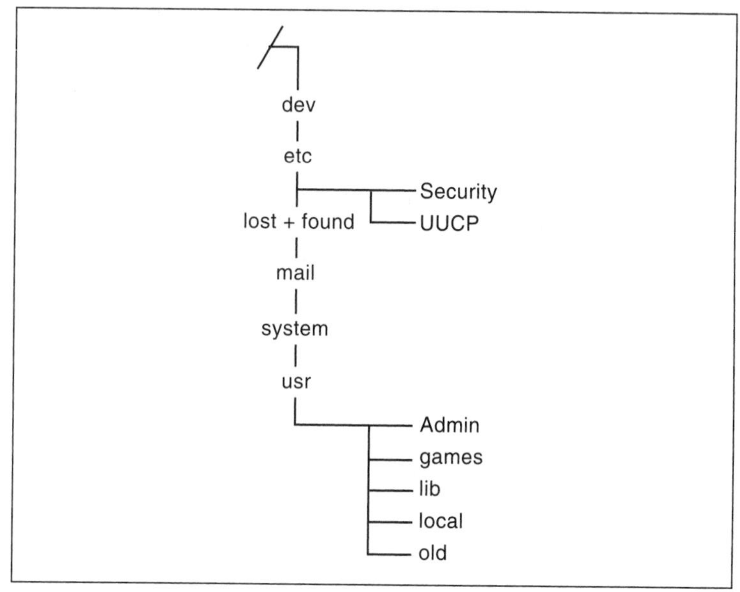

FIGURE A.1

Simplified UNIX directory structure

One job UNIX must conduct is managing security. You can imagine that with dozens or even hundreds of users accessing a system, you have to have a way to keep prying eyes and destructive fingers out of where they don't belong.

You probably have free privileges within your own directory: you can read, copy, and erase files at will. However, you may have severely limited access to the rest of the system. Sensitive files are either stored on another physical disk or on another companion system, or the files and directories you don't have rights to see or manipulate are hidden or protected.

Still, you can poke around the system to get a feel for its structure. I'll show you how to do that in the next section, where I introduce a few of the important UNIX commands for Internet travelers.

IMPORTANT UNIX COMMANDS

When you log on to a UNIX system, one of two things may happen. Either you are placed at a command line prompt, or you are placed directly into a menu-driven system. If your service provider puts you into a menu system when you log on, then your need to know very much about UNIX is diminished—until you move off of the home system and out onto the Internet. Then it would be useful if you understood a few basic commands.

If the default operating environment for you is the UNIX command line, then you will see some form of prompt and a blinking cursor. A common prompt is a greater-than symbol and a blinking underline cursor:

```
> _
```

On some systems you may get a more elaborate prompt, such as the one from The WELL:

```
OK (type a command or type  opt  for Options):
```

The WELL calls this the "OK Prompt," but obviously you are given information about what to type if you need help with the commands. In this case, if you type **opt** and press **Enter**, a short menu is displayed that shows you some of the available conference commands. What you don't know, unless you have played with the system a little, is that there is another command, **help**, that will display a much longer list of available WELL commands.

In fact, many systems offer a **help** command, so as you try to learn your way around a UNIX system, try **help** and see if you can display additional information about which commands are available to you. Remember, I said that for security reasons you may be restricted in the files and directories you can access. Likewise, some systems provide a limited command interface. They either lock out some UNIX commands, or substitute an entirely non-UNIX user interface with its own set of commands. Which you use depends on the system, so if you have problems with any of the UNIX commands I discuss here, call your service provider for help, or try to find some online assistance.

Whatever the command line prompt is, your system is not going to do anything until you issue a command. To do that, type the appropriate command and press **Enter** or **Return**. Following is a list of UNIX commands grouped by function. Find the function you need to perform, locate an appropriate command, then refer to the alphabetical listing in the next section to find out how to use it.

UNIX Commands by Function

In addition to UNIX commands, there are some keyboard conventions you should know. For example, the keyboard combinations **Ctrl-C**, **Ctrl-D**, and **Ctrl-Z** perform useful functions. See Table A.1 for a list of UNIX commands grouped by function.

- **Ctrl-C** Use this combination to halt a running process. If you are in the middle of a command operation you don't want to finish, you can press **Ctrl-C** and (usually) the process will terminate right where it is. For example, if you use the **man** command and it produces a very long list that you don't want to view, simply hold down **Ctrl** and press **C**. You should be returned to the system prompt.
- **Ctrl-D** This is an input terminator. Sometimes it functions like **Ctrl-C**, but sometimes it won't halt a process when **Ctrl-C** will. You can use **Ctrl-D** to signify that you are finished entering data in some cases, for example.
- **Ctrl-Z** You sometimes can use it like **Ctrl-C** or **Ctrl-D**, but with many processes it signifies that you want to suspend the process. If you press **Ctrl-Z** while a UNIX program is running, for example, you will get a message like "Suspended," and the program will stop. It has not gone away, but is waiting for you to start it up again. You can view all suspended jobs with the **ps** command. You can either use **kill** to end these jobs or **fg** to bring a suspended job to the foreground.

TABLE A.1

UNIX Commands grouped by function

System Commands
bye
date
logout
File & Disk Commands
cd
cp
cat
chmod
ls
more
mkdir
rm
rmdir
tar (Tape Archiver)
Process Commands
fg (foreground)
kill
ps (Process Status)
Utilities
mail
man
pwd
rx
rz
send
w
who

UNIX Commands: Alphabetical List

Obviously, these aren't all of the UNIX commands, but they are most of the ones you should need as a casual user of a UNIX system on the Internet. See especially the **man** command, which can give you more information on these and other UNIX commands whenever you need it.

Bye

Not necessarily a UNIX command, but one frequently used on UNIX systems to log off from a program or from the system. If **bye** doesn't work, try **quit**, **logout**, or **logoff**.

cat

The **cat** command, for concatenate, displays files on your terminal and also combines multiple files into a single file. Use **cat <filename>** to display a file (see also the **more** command). To combine files into a new file, use **cat file1 file2 >file3**.

cd

Change directory. Makes the specified directory the current directory. Use **cd** with a full path name:

```
cd /usr/games
```

You might want to try looking at the directory specified in this example. After changing to the games directory, type **ls** to view the files there. Most UNIX systems automatically have some games installed. They aren't exciting graphics-and-sound games, but they are traditional text-based games that have been around for a while. But you can play them!

For MS-DOS users: Notice that the directory name separator in UNIX is a forward slash, not the backward slash you're used to in DOS.

chmod

Use **chmod** to change the permissions mode of a specified file. Permissions are used to control who has rights to view, edit, execute, or modify a file. One way to set rights is with a numerical designator. This is called absolute mode and involves specifying numbers to set specific bits within a designator byte. (For more information on how this works, use the **man chmod** command or ask your service provider.) Set permissions for a specific file with **chmod nnnn <filename>**, where **nnnn** is the numeric code and **<filename>** is the actual file name. Examples of chmod rights are:

```
4000  Set user ID on execution.
20#0  Set group ID on execution if # is 7, 5, 3, or 1.
Enable mandatory locking if # is 6, 4, 2,  or 0.
This bit is ignored if the file is  a  directory; it may
be set or cleared only using the symbolic mode.
1000  Turn on sticky bit (see chmod(2)).
0400  Allow read by owner.
0200  Allow write by owner.
0100  Allow execute (search in directory) by owner.
0070  Allow read, write, and execute (search) by group.
0007  Allow read, write, and  execute (search) by others.
```

You can also use symbolic settings that use letters and symbols instead of numbers. Use the man command (**man chmod**) for more information.

cp

Copy a file or directory. To copy file1 to file2, enter the following:

```
cp file1 file2
```

This copies the contents of file1 to file2, overwriting file2 if it already exists.

date

Display the current system date. As a casual user it is unlikely that you will be able to change the date, but the command structure for doing so is:

```
date yymmddhhmm
where yy = year
mm = month
dd = day
hh = hour (24 hour format)
mm = minutes
```

Use **date** to find out what the current date and time are and to verify that the computer knows the correct date and time. This is useful when sending and receiving mail, especially if you suspect that mail is being delayed somehow.

fg

Foreground. Brings the most recently suspended process to the foreground and resumes execution. If you inadvertently suspend a process, you can resume the process with the **fg** command.

kill

Kill a process. Use **kill** if you have suspended a process with **Ctrl-Z** and don't want to restart it. You must specify the process ID to kill a process. Use the **ps** command to display a list of suspended jobs with their process IDs. Then you can kill the process with **kill id**, where **id** is the numerical ID displayed with **ps**.

logout

Terminate a current session. May be interchangeable with **bye** and **logoff**.

ls

List files. Displays files and directories in the current directory. To list files in a subordinate directory, use **ls directoryname**. You can display more information about a file by adding switches to the **ls** command. A switch is simply an argument to the basic command that causes the command to act in a different way or to provide additional information. The switch you are likely to need is **-l**, which expands the directory listing to include file or directory type, size, and more.

mail

Display any pending mail. If you add a user ID to the mail command, you are placed into an editor to type the mail message. When you have entered the last line of the mail entry, enter a **period** on a line by itself.

man

Manual. Display online help in the form of manual pages for the specified command. **man intro** provides a general introduction to the online manual. If you're not sure which command to display, use **man -k <keyword>**, where **<keyword>** is the word you want information about.

mkdir

Make directory. Creates a new subdirectory under the current directory. This is helpful if you need to store a number of different files about different topics within your home directory. For example, **mkdir games** creates a new directory called **games** in your current directory.

more

Display the contents of a text file, one screen at a time. The syntax is **more <filename>**.

ps

Process status. Use this command to secure a process ID number, which you will need to kill a suspended process.

pwd

Display the current directory. Use this command to find out what directory you are using.

rm

Remove. Use this command to remove a file or directory. For example, **rm newbooks.txt** erases the file **newbooks.txt** in the current directory.

rmdir

Works like **rm** (above) except that it removes an existing directory. The directory to be removed must contain no subdirectories or files.

rx

Receive XMODEM. Launches the XMODEM protocol application and prepares to receive a file that you want to upload from your desktop.

rz

Receive ZMODEM. Launches the ZMODEM protocol application and prepares to receive a file that you want to upload from your desktop.

talk

Lets you talk with another user. Use **talk username** to request a conversation with another user who is logged onto the same host you are using. See Chapter 7 for more information on talk.

tar

Tape archiver. A utility that groups multiple files into a single file. While conceived as a tape archiver, it also is useful for transmitting files across the Internet. When you download a game application, for example, it frequently is in tar format, which means it contains more than one file. For example, to combine the entire directory **games** into a file called **games.tar**, use this command:

```
tar -cf games.tar games
```

In this example I use two of the available switches with the tar command, **-c** and **-f**. The **-c** switch tells tar to create a new file and to start writing the files at the beginning of the tar file. The **-f** switch specifies that the next name on the command will be the name of the archive. (The **-f** switch is combined with **c** in this example. Only one switch symbol is needed.)

If you download a file called **games.tar** and you want to extract it, use the **tar** command this way:

```
tar -xf games.tar
```

Again, two switches were used with **tar**. The **-x** switch tells tar to extract the files contained in the file named after the **f** switch, which is **games.tar** in this example.

w

A variation of **who**. Displays current user IDs and information about what each user is doing.

who

Display IDs of current users and shows other information about them, including their home system or directory.

HOW TO GET MORE INFORMATION

As I said earlier, many systems include a help command that will display available commands. If so, there are probably subcommands under the main help command. (On UNIX systems the help command may result in a suggestion that you use **man**.) If you type **help** and get a screen full of available commands, you can either type one of those commands at the prompt (if it says something such as **Help on Topic?**), or you can type **help topic** at the command line, where **topic** is the command you want to know more about.

If you try help and get a bad command error, try preceding the command with an exclamation point:

```
!help
```

Some systems that use a shell of some kind to isolate the user from UNIX will send commands to UNIX if they are preceded with an exclamation.

In addition, one useful feature of UNIX is the online manual system. Most or all of the available commands should have a manual entry that you can display on your screen and capture to disk for future use. At the command prompt simply type **man command**, where **command** is the command you need help with. You should get a display of one or more pages that describe fully how the specified command works.

You could also call technical support at your service provider, or try talking to someone else on the system. Some service providers have help desk or tech support personnel online nearly all the time. Once you know who they are, you can use **talk userid** to tap them on the shoulder and ask for help.

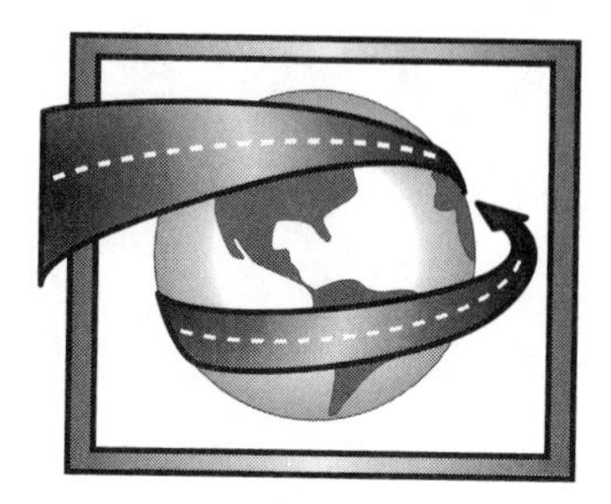

Appendix B

You Have Been Warned!

Unless you have never read a newspaper or magazine and your radio and television are permanently set to hard rock sounds instead of news, then you've heard about the threat of computer viruses. In fact, the Internet itself was infected in a serious way not long ago. I think the published scare stories about viruses make the problem seem worse than it is, but, my experience has shown that far too many computer users ignore the threat until they have experienced it.

I can tell you—from first-hand experience—that viruses can cause real damage to your computer and data. Fortunately, there are numerous software utilities to scan your system for virus infection and to remove the infection. I can't cover every aspect of viruses here, nor can I tell you about every commercial product available, but I can alert you to the threat and show you how to inspect your system and rid it of a virus should you contract one.

WHAT IS A VIRUS?

A computer *virus* is a software program that is designed to install itself on a computer, and then conduct various tasks depending on the programmer's design. The term virus describes how these programs work. They act a lot like a biological virus—such as a cold or the flu—that attaches itself to certain cells within a living organism and causes distress.

Computer viruses do the same thing. They sneak into your system as part of a file you download from a network or bulletin board, or even on a commercial disk you purchase. You can't see the virus by looking at a directory of the disk. Viruses are smart enough to hide themselves cleverly, even to the point of modifying a directory entry to show that the size of an infected file has not changed, when, in fact, it has.

If you think you can avoid a virus infection by dealing only with people or bulletin boards you know, or by carefully studying disk directories or any other kind of simplistic mumbo jumbo, you're setting yourself up for a fall. No computer system is immune, and the results of an infection can be catastrophic.

WHAT DO VIRUSES DO?

There are hundreds—even thousands—of strains of viruses. Many of them are similar, while others are frighteningly unique, so it is impossible to say with certainty exactly what a virus does. But here are some things they have done in the past:

- Reprogram the keyboard so the letters don't mean what they say.
- Freeze the computer system when certain characters are typed or when a date and time arrive.

- Play music or display a picture randomly or when certain events occur.
- Erase specific data files—or all of the files on a disk—after a pre-determined period of time or when a specific date and time arrive.
- Slowly change the size and contents of executable files until the program doesn't work because it grows too large or fails automatic error checks that the program conducts each time it executes.

Regardless of what it does, a virus is probably programmed to spread from disk to disk and from computer to computer. Once the virus program executes, it starts doing its work within the current system, but it also hides inside one or more applications. Some viruses, for example, install themselves in the boot record of your hard disk so that they reload each time the computer is started. Then every time a new program is executed, the virus code installs itself inside the executable program. If you move that program to another computer or copy it to another disk, the virus moves with it. When the program runs for the first time on a new computer, the virus checks to see if it already is running in memory. If not, it installs itself and starts the process all over again.

Some viruses are more aggressive in their attempts to expand. Once they are running, some viruses will scan the system looking for other disks or computers to infect. Suppose you are attached to a network and load a program that contains a virus. The virus infects your system, then looks for other disk drives to infect.

You can see that viruses are serious threats to your computer and its data. Even if the virus isn't designed to erase files, it can damage data by saving a piece of itself or some other code into a data file from the host application. While some viruses are benign, you still don't want one in your system. Even a virus that doesn't actually damage any files can make things work unpredictably. The key is to avoid an infection in the first place.

You can do this by never installing foreign software and by never downloading any files from a network or bulletin board. Obviously, this is not a practical solution. But you can take steps to minimize the threat and to rid your system of a virus if you do get infected.

HOW TO TELL IF YOUR SYSTEM HAS BEEN INFECTED

Because there are so many kinds of viruses, there is no set, fool-proof formula for detecting a virus. In fact, many strains show absolutely no symptoms until it is too late. They may lie dormant inside an infected program waiting for a specific date to arrive, for example. They do nothing and cause no change in system performance until that date arrives, and then they systematically erase everything on your hard drive.

So even if you don't have any virus symptoms, it is a good idea to conduct regular scans for them. Use one of the software utilities listed in the next section to keep viruses from entering your system and to conduct regular scans to make sure you don't have any hidden infections.

Beyond that, be aware of how your system performs. If a virus is alive and operating in your system, there are some things that may happen to give you a clue. For example, if you notice an unusual amount of disk activity while you are running applications, you can suspect that a virus is saving the program file to store additional code.

Notice whether the sizes of program files change or the directory date changes. Most viruses that modify the application executable file are smart enough to hide file size and date changes, but some are not. Notice whether applications seem to be running more slowly or whether you get an unusual number of errors. Are you having problems with application areas that used to run, yet nothing that you're aware of has changed? Do you see messages that you've never seen before?

Any of these events could mean a virus attack. Of course they could also mean that you are having some kind of hardware problem. The only real way to find out is with some kind of virus detection and eradication software such as the ones I list later in this appendix.

VIRUS PROTECTION

The best way to protect your system against a virus infection is never to get one in the first place. There are software packages designed to do just that. If you have DOS 6 for your PC-compatible machine, for example, there is an included utility that loads and stays RAM-resident. It constantly scans the system looking for anything unusual and will alert you in the event that a suspected virus is detected. It isn't foolproof, but it may catch a virus as it loads from an infected program before it can do any more damage.

There are similar programs for PCs, Macintoshes, and UNIX machines from a variety of vendors. Some programs will scan your system memory and all the programs on your disks to see if there are any known viruses already present. If any infections are found, these routines can either eliminate them or tell you to run another program that will take them out. After a virus has been detected and removed, you may not be able to run the infected program, however. In fact, it is always a good idea to re-install a program that has been infected by a virus.

As with data backup procedures, a good plan for virus prevention goes a long way toward protecting the integrity of your system. You should get in the habit of running a virus detection program every day when you boot your system. You should run a virus detection program on any new software you acquire, whether it is from a commercial vendor or from the Internet or another online service.

Anytime you have been online, whether or not you downloaded anything, run a virus utility before you go on with the rest of your work. All of this may seem tedious, and it is. But if you ever experience the anger, frustration, and lost time that a full-blown virus infection can cause, you'll gladly take these steps to keep from having to go through it again.

NOTE

To read more about virus threats, virus types, and virus protection, type ***virus*** *in the search field of one of the WWW search utilities such as WebCrawler. You will find many references, including places to download software to detect and kill viruses.*

VIRUS PROTECTION SOFTWARE

Since the threat of virus infection has gotten so universal, a number of companies have started selling virus detection and eradication software. If you don't already have such software, get it. In this section I show you some of the available offerings. You'll have to decide for yourself which is best for you—based on your hardware, where you live or work, what features you need, and what other applications you already are running. The first step is to contact one or more of the vendors I list and ask them for a recommendation. Then pick a package, install it, and use it.

Note that many of these packages do much more than just offer virus protection. Some are full-fledged security systems; others are part of a package of utilities and tools. Contact the vendor for complete information.

PC (MS-DOS)-Based and Microsoft Windows-Based Software

D-FENCE, SWEEP, AND VACCINE
Alternative Computer Technology, Inc.
7908 Cin-Day Rd., Ste. WB
West Chester, OH 45069
513-755-1957
FAX: 513-755-1958

INFORMATION SECURITY POLICIES MADE EASY
Baseline Software
PO Box 1219
Sausalito, CA 94966
800-829-9955; 415-332-7763
FAX: 415-332-8032

CENTRAL POINT ANTI-VIRUS (V.2.0), CENTRAL POINT ANTI-VIRUS FOR WINDOWS (V.1.4), SAFE SIX, SAFE SIX FOR WINDOWS
Central Point Software, Inc.
15220 N.W. Greenbrier Pkwy., Ste. 150
Beaverton, OR 97006
800-333-0744; 503-690-8088
Direct Sales: 800-445-4208
FAX: 503-690-8083

INOCULAN—THE NETWORK GUARDIAN, INOCULAN/PC
Cheyenne Software, Inc.
3 Expressway Plaza
Roslyn Hgts., NY 11577
800-243-9462; 516-484-5110
FAX: 516-484-3446

F-PROT PROFESSIONAL (V.2.07), FREEZE!, SECURITY GUARDIAN PLUS (V.3.65)
Command Software Systems, Inc.
1061 E. Indiantown Rd., Ste. 500
Jupiter, FL 33477
800-423-9147; 407-575-3200
FAX: 407-575-3026

DETECT PLUS (V.2.11)
Commcrypt, Inc.
10000 Virginia Manor Rd., Ste. 300
Beltsville, MD 20705
800-334-8338; 301-470-2500
Direct Sales: 800-683-1313
FAX: 301-470-2507

PC CANARY
Compass/New England
PO Box 117
Portsmouth, NH 03802
603-431-8030

VICTOR CHARLIE (VC) (V.5.0)
Computer Security Associates
738 1/2 Meeting St.
West Columbia, SC 29169
803-796-6591
FAX: 803-796-8379

PC/ASSURE (V.4.0)
Cordant, Inc.
11400 Commerce Park Dr.
Reston, VA 22091-1506
800-762-5632; 703-758-7000
FAX: 703-758-7380

SWIFT PROFESSIONAL VIRUS TERMINATOR (V.2.1), SWIFT PROFESSIONAL VIRUS TERMINATOR FOR WINDOWS (V.2.1)
Cosmi Corp.
2600 Homestead Place
Rancho Dominguez, CA 90220-5610
310-833-2000
FAX: 310-886-3500

VFIND
CyberSoft, Inc.
210 West 12th Ave.
Conshohocken, PA 19428-1464
215-825-4748
FAX: 215-825-6785

VACCINE (V.5.0), VACNET (V.5.0), VACWIN (V.5.0)
The Davidsohn Group
20 Exchange Place, 27th Fl.
New York, NY 10005
800-999-6031; 212-422-4100
Direct Sales: 212-363-3018
FAX: 212-422-1953

DATA PHYSICIAN PLUS! (V.3.1B)
Digital Dispatch, Inc.
55 Lakeland Shores Rd.
Lakeland, MN 55043
800-221-8091; 612-436-1000
FAX: 612-436-2085

PC DOCTOR
Diversified Computer Products and Services, Inc.
PO Box 579
Swampscott, MA 01907
617-592-9001

CODESAFE HD, VIRUSAFE-GOLD, VIRUSAFE-GOLD FOR WINDOWS
Eliashim Microcomputers, Inc.
520 W. Hwy. 436, Ste. 1180
Altamonte Springs, FL 32714
800-677-1587; 407-682-1587
FAX: 407-869-1409

SAFE (V.2.0), SEARCH & DESTROY FOR DOS AND WINDOWS, UNTOUCHABLE (V.1.13), UNTOUCHABLE FOR WINDOWS (V.1.12), UNTOUCHABLE NETWORK NLM (NETWARE LOADABLE MODULE) (V.1.1)
Fifth Generation Systems, Inc.
10049 N. Reiger Rd.
Baton Rouge, LA 70809-4562
800-677-1848; 504-291-7221
FAX: 504-295-3268

WATCHDOG (V.7.02), WATCHDOG VIRUS BUSTER
Fischer International Systems Corp.
PO Box 9107, 4073 Merchantile Ave.
Naples, FL 33942
800-237-4510; 800-331-2866 (FL); 813-643-1500
FAX: 813-643-3772

IBM ANTIVIRUS (V.1.0)
IBM (International Business Machines)
Old Orchard Rd.
Armonk, NY 10504
800-426-3333; 914-765-1900
Direct Sales: 800-426-2968 (IBM Direct)

COP (COMPUTER OWNER PROTECTION)
IDX Technologies, Inc.
14 Research Way
Setauket, NY 11733
800-626-6863; 516-689-9866
FAX: 516-689-1419

LANDESK VIRUS PROTECT (V.2.0), LANPROTECT (V.1.5)
Intel Corp.
(Personal Computer Enhancement Operation)
5200 N.E. Elam Young Pkwy.
Hillsboro, OR 97124
800-538-3373; 503-696-8080
FAX: 503-696-4633

VIRUSCURE PLUS (V.2.41)
International Microcomputer Software, Inc. (IMSI)
1938 Fourth St.
San Rafael, CA 94901-2682
800-833-4674; 415-454-7101
Direct Sales: 800-833-8082
FAX: 415-454-8901

VIRUS-PRO (V.3.0)
International Security Technology, Inc.
99 Park Ave., 11th Fl.
New York, NY 10016
212-557-0900
FAX: 212-808-5206

PALLADIUM
Laser Digital, Inc.
1030 E. Duane Ave., Ste. H
Sunnyvale, CA 94086
408-737-2666
FAX: 408-737-9698

VIRUS BUSTER (V.4.0), VIRUS BUSTER FOR WINDOWS
Leprechaun Software International, Ltd.
PO Box 669306
Marietta, GA 30066-0106
800-521-8849; 404-971-8900
FAX: 404-971-8828

VIRUSALERT (V.2.08)
Look Software
PO Box 1356
Ogdensburg, NY 13669
800-267-0778; 613-837-2151
FAX: 613-837-5572

INTEGRITY TOOLKIT (V.3.7.7)
Management Analytics
PO Box 1480
Hudson, OH 44236
216-655-9770
FAX: 216-655-9776

CLEAN-UP, NETSCAN, NETSHIELD (V.1.51), PRO-SCAN (V.3.0), SCAN, SCAN FOR WINDOWS, VIRUSCAN (V.1.02), VSHIELD, WSCAN FOR WINDOWS
McAfee Associates, Inc.
2710 Walsh Ave., Ste. 200
Santa Clara, CA 95051-0963
408-988-3832
FAX: 408-970-9727

NET/DACS, PC/DACS (V.3.0)
Mergent International, Inc.
70 Inwood Rd.
Rocky Hill, CT 06067
800-688-3227; 203-257-4223
FAX: 203-257-4245

FULL ARMOR (V.2.0)
Micah Development Corp.
955 Massachusetts Ave., Ste. 302
Cambridge, MA 02139
800-653-1783; 617-489-5854
FAX: 617-489-5844

BIT-LOCK
Microcomputer Applications
3167 E. Otero Circle
Littleton, CO 80122
303-770-1917
FAX: 303-770-1863

VIRUSTOP PLUS
Multix, Inc.
4203 Beltway Dr., Ste. 7
Dallas, TX 75244
214-239-4989
FAX: 214-239-6826

FS SCANMASTER, PC SCANMASTER
NetPro Computing, Inc.
8655 E. Via de Ventura, Ste. E155
Scottsdale, AZ 85258
800-998-5090; 602-998-5008
FAX: 602-998-5076

DR. SOLOMON'S ANTI-VIRUS TOOLKIT (V.6.01), DR. SOLOMON'S ANTI-VIRUS TOOLKIT FOR WINDOWS (V.6.01)
Ontrack Computer Systems, Inc.
6321 Bury Dr., Ste. 15-19
Eden Prairie, MN 55346
800-752-1333; 612-937-1107
FAX: 612-937-5815

PC PASSKEY
Optimum Electronics, Inc.
425 Washington Ave., PO Box 250
North Haven, CT 06473
203-239-6098
FAX: 203-234-9324

VIRUCIDE PLUS
Parsons Technology, Inc.
One Parsons Dr., PO Box 100
Hiawatha, IA 52233-0100
800-223-6925; 319-395-9626
FAX: 319-395-0217

DATA SECURITY PLUS (V.5.3), VIRUS PREVENTION PLUS
PC Guardian
118 Alto St.
San Rafael, CA 94901
800-288-8126; 415-459-0190
FAX: 415-459-1162

PS-LOCK, SECURE WRAP
PS Publishing, Inc.
25 S. Livingston Ave., Ste. A
Livingston, NJ 07039
800-777-2663; 201-740-1750
FAX: 201-740-9118

VI-SPY PROFESSIONAL EDITION (V.11.0)
RG Software Systems, Inc.
6900 E. Camelback Rd., Ste. 630
Scottsdale, AZ 85251
602-423-8000
FAX: 602-423-8389

DRIVE-IN ANTIVIRUS (V.2.03), VIRUSNET (V.2.06), STOPLIGHT (V.1.71)
SafetyNet, Inc.
55 Bleeker St.
Millburn, NJ 07041-1414
800-851-0188; 201-467-1024
FAX: 201-467-1611

IRONCLAD (V.2.0)
Silver Oak Systems, Inc.
8209 Cedar St.
Silver Spring, MD 20910
301-585-8641
FAX: 301-588-6484

FLU SHOT PLUS (V.1.84)
Software Concepts Design
PO Box 908
Margaretville, NY 12455
607-326-4422
FAX: 607-326-4424

PROTEC (V.4.0)
SOPHCO, Inc.
PO Box 7430
Boulder, CO 80306-7430
800-922-3001; 303-530-7759
FAX: 303-530-7745

TNT ANTIVIRUS
SST (System Security Technology, Inc.)
3310 Berwyck St.
Las Vegas, NV 89121
800-782-9110; 702-454-7855
FAX: 702-454-7700

INTEGRITY MASTER (V.1.41)
Stiller Research
2625 Ridgeway St.
Tallahassee, FL 32310-5169
800-622-2793; 904-575-7884
Direct Sales: 708-397-1221

CERTUS (V.2.11), NORTON ANTIVIRUS (V.2.1), NOVI (V.1.15)
Symantec Corp.
10201 Torre Ave.
Cupertino, CA 95014-2132
800-441-7234; 408-253-9600
FAX: 408-252-4696

ANTIVIRUSPLUS (V.4.20.09), VIRAWAY
T.C.P. Techmar Computer Products, Inc.
98-11 Queens Blvd., Ste. 2-C
Rego Park, NY 11374
800-922-0015; 718-997-6606
FAX: 718-520-0170

PC RX ANTIVIRUS (V.2.65), PC-CILLIN (V.3.65), PCOPY (V.1.0), WIN RX ANTIVIRUS (V.1.4)
Trend Micro Devices, Inc.
2421 West 205th St., Ste. D-100
Torrance, CA 90501
800-228-5651; 310-782-8190
FAX: 310-328-5892

VIR-GUARD
uti-maco Safeguard Systems, Inc.
750 Old Main St.
Rocky Hill, CT 06067
800-394-4230; 203-257-4230
FAX: 203-257-8390

FAILSAFE COMPUTER GUARDIAN
Villa Crespo Software, Inc.
1725 McGovern St.
Highland Park, IL 60035
800-521-3963; 708-433-0500
FAX: 708-433-1485

VIRUS CHECK AND CURES
Wizardworks, Inc.
5354 Parkdale Dr., Ste. 104
Minneapolis, MN 55416
800-759-5645; 612-544-8581
FAX: 612-541-4973

X-LOCK 50
X-Lock Corp.
1 Mecca Way
Norcross, GA 30093
404-564-5545
FAX: 404-564-5528

Macintosh-Based Software

FILEGUARD (V.2.75)
ASD Software, Inc.
4650 Arrow Hwy., Ste. E-6
Montclair, CA 91763
909-624-2594
FAX: 909-624-9574

INFORMATION SECURITY POLICIES MADE EASY (V.3.0)
Baseline Software
PO Box 1219
Sausalito, CA 94966
800-829-9955; 415-332-7763
FAX: 415-332-8032

ACCESS MANAGED ENVIRONMENT (V.2.1)
Casady & Greene, Inc.
22734 Portola Dr.
Salinas, CA 93908-1119
800-359-4920; 408-484-9228
FAX: 408-484-9218

CENTRAL POINT ANTI-VIRUS (V.2.0)
Central Point Software, Inc.
15220 N.W. Greenbrier Pkwy., Ste. 150
Beaverton, OR 97006
800-333-0744; 503-690-8088
Direct Sales: 800-445-4208
FAX: 503-690-8083

VFIND
CyberSoft, Inc.
210 West 12th Ave.
Conshohocken, PA 19428-1464
215-825-4748
FAX: 215-825-6785

VIREX
Datawatch Corp.
(Triangle Software Division)
3700-B Lyckan Pkwy.
Durham, NC 27707
919-490-1277
FAX: 919-490-6672

MENU MASTER MAC (V.1.4)
Electronic Learning Systems, Inc.
4131 Northwest 28th Lane, Ste. 3A
Gainesville, FL 32606-6681
800-443-7971; 904-375-0558
FAX: 904-375-5679

COP (COMPUTER OWNER PROTECTION)
IDX Technologies, Inc.
14 Research Way
Setauket, NY 11733
800-626-6863; 516-689-9866
FAX: 516-689-1419

MACSECURE (V.1.7)
Learning Performance Corp.
2850 Metro Dr., Ste. 413
Minneapolis, MN 55425-1405
800-926-3279; 612-854-2730
FAX: 612-854-8975

EMPOWER I (V.4.0.8)
Magna
332 Commercial St.
San Jose, CA 95112
408-282-0900
FAX: 408-275-9147

ANTITOXIN (V.2.1)
Mainstay
591-A Constitution Ave.
Camarillo, CA 93012
805-484-9400
FAX: 818-484-9428

SAM (SYMANTEC ANTIVIRUS FOR MACINTOSH) (V.3.5)
Symantec Corp.
10201 Torre Ave.
Cupertino, CA 95014-2132
800-441-7234; 408-253-9600
FAX: 408-252-4696

FT. KNOX (V.1.05)
Transfinite Systems Co., Inc.
PO Box N, MIT Branch PO
Cambridge, MA 02139
617-969-9570

ULTRASECURE (V.1.36)
usrEZ Software
18881 Von Karman Ave., Ste. 1270
Irvine, CA 92715
714-756-5140
FAX: 714-756-8810

UNIX-Based Software

VFIND
CyberSoft, Inc.
210 West 12th Ave.
Conshohocken, PA 19428-1464
215-825-4748
FAX: 215-825-6785

FORTRESS
Los Altos Technologies, Inc.
2111 Grant Rd., Ste. 100
Los Altos, CA 94024
800-999-UNIX; 415-988-4848
FAX: 415-988-4860

SECURITY AUDIT
SunSoft, Inc.
(subsidiary of Sun Microsystems, Inc.)
2550 Garcia Ave.
Mountain View, CA 94043-1100
800-227-9227; 415-460-3267
FAX: 415-336-0362

FORTRESS
Woodside Technologies, Inc.
474 Potrero Ave.
Sunnyvale, CA 94086-9406
408-733-9503
FAX: 408-732-7335

X-LOCK 50 .
X-Lock Corp.
1 Mecca Way
Norcross, GA 30093
404-564-5545
FAX: 404-564-5528
Tech support: 404-475-8787

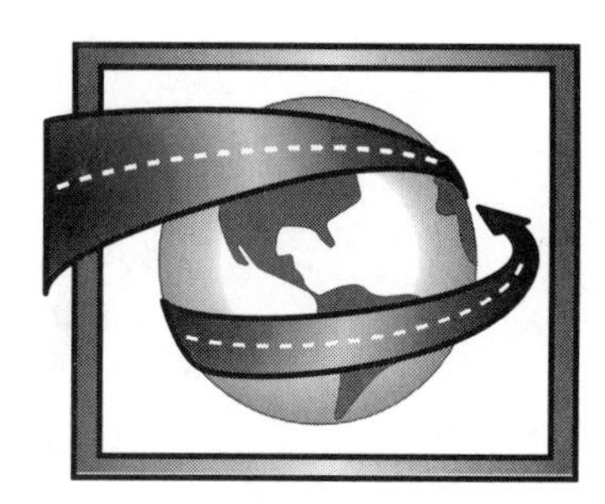

Appendix C

The Unofficial Smiley Dictionary

Wherever you go on the Internet, you will find users attempting to express emotions as they type on text-based screens. The symbols they use vary from the simple smiley face :) to much more complicated symbols such as >:-> or C=}>;*{)). The symbols used vary from place to place on the Internet, and even what these symbols mean may be different, depending on which group you frequent. Still, it is fun to play around with these "emoticons," as they are frequently called (emotional icons). Here's a portion of one list compiled by Clay Spinuzzi (spinuzzi@gab.unt.edu) Use ftp to retrieve the file EMOTICON.TXT in the directory /pub/misc at ftp.unt.edu.

:-) Your basic smiley. This smiley is used to inflect a sarcastic or joking statement since we can't hear voice inflection over Unix.

;-) Winky smiley. User just made a flirtatious and/or sarcastic remark. More of a “don’t hit me for what I just said” smiley.

:-(Frowning smiley. User did not like that last statement or is upset or depressed about something.

:-I Indifferent smiley. Better than a Frowning smiley but not quite as good as a happy smiley

:-> User just made a really biting sarcastic remark. Worse than a :-).

>:-> User just made a really devilish remark.

>;-> Winky and devil combined. A very lewd remark was just made.

(-: User is left handed

%-) User has been staring at a green screen for 15 hours straight

:*) User is drunk

::-) User wears normal glasses

:-[User is a Vampire

:-F Bucktoothed vampire with one tooth missing

:-7 User just made a wry statement

:-* User just ate something sour

:-@ User is screaming

|-I User is asleep

|-O User is yawning/snoring

:-Q User is a smoker

:-P Nyahhhh!

:-S User just made an incoherent statement

:-D User is laughing (at you!)

:-X User’s lips are sealed

:-C User is really bummed

:-/ User is skeptical

C=:-) User is a chef

:-o Uh oh!

X-(User just died

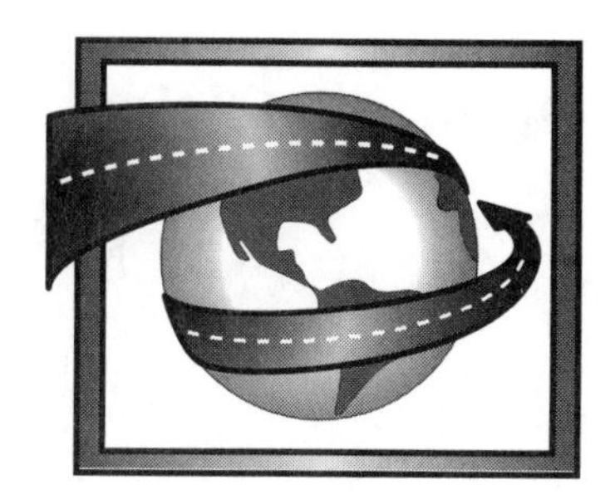

Appendix D

FILE TYPE REFERENCE

As you browse the Internet, you may find files of many different types. There may be executable program files for a particular platform, image files that require a special program to view, or files for your personal computer that have been compressed and require a special program to expand. One source for a file type reference is: **ftp nic.funet.fi**. Look for the file **README.FILETYPES** for a list of common file types used on this system. I have reproduced that list in this appendix as a place to start learning about file types on the Internet.

Below are some additional file type resources on the Internet:

```
ftp oak.oakland.edu/SimTel/msdos/README.file.formats
#http://ac.dal.ca/~dong/contents.htm
ftp fto.ripe.net/rfc/rfc959.txt
```

ABOUT FILE TYPES

Different file compression and packaging utilities are used for different platforms. These methods are often denoted in a file name by a more-or-less standardized suffix(es). In UNIX-like environments, where packaging is done with a different utility than the compression, and where name-spaces aren't limited by some artificial 8+3 rules, there may be multiple suffixes.

Sometimes you might see strange hybrids of suffixes when files are intended for use on a system that limits the number of characters that can be used in a file name and extension.

This is NOT a list of ALL file type suffixes there are—only those that are common.

TABLE D.1
File Type Reference

Suffix	Methods	Environment
.arj	ARJ compress + packing	MS-DOS
.dms	DMS-compressed Amiga floppy *disk*	Amiga
.gif	GIF-type packed (colour) image	image
.gz	GNU-Zip	UNIX
.jpeg	JPEG-compressed colour image	image
.jpg	—"—	image
.lha	LHA/LHARC compress + packing	multiple (Esp.Amiga)
.lhx	Variant of .lha	CBM C=64 ?
.lzh	LHA/LHARC compress + packing	multiple
.ps	PostScript-document (or program)	
.sea	Macintosh self-extracting archive	Mac
.tar	UNIX tar—"Tape ARchive" packaging	UNIX
.tgz	== .tar.gz (Esp. Linux)	
.Z	BSD compress	UNIX
.z	GNU-Zip (old suffix, to be phased out)	UNIX
.z	SysV pack (Huffman compression)	UNIX
.zip	(PK)ZIP compress + packing	MS-DOS
.zoo	ZOO compress + packaging	multiple

The FTP server at **ftp.funet.fi** (and some others) can unpack GNU-Zip, BSD Compress, and sysV pack files while the files are being sent to you. Any file with the name **XXX.YYY.gz** can be automatically unpacked by simply requesting file **XXX.YYY**. The file will automatically be uncompressed at the receiving end. Because the data is being expanded, the transfer time for the file will be longer than if you'd requested the compressed file.

Locations of Utilities to Handle these Formats

ARJ:

/pub/amiga/utilities/archivers/unarj-0.5.lha (Amiga binary)

/pub/msdos/starter/arj241a.exe (MS-DOS)

/pub/msdos/starter/unarj241.exe (MS-DOS)

/pub/msdos/starter/unarj221.tar.Z (UNIX)

DMS:

Amiga floppy disk compressor.

/pub/amiga/utilities/archivers/DMS-1.11.run (Amiga binary)

GIF, JPG:

Image formats, see /pub/pics/viewers/. That directory contains symbolic links to places that have programs per machine/operating system/.

GNU-Zip:

/pub/amiga/utilities/archivers/gzip-1.1.2.lha (Amiga binary)

/pub/gnu/gzip-1.2.4.msdos.exe (ready MS-DOS binary)

/pub/gnu/gzip-1.2.4.tar (Just plain TAR, SOURCE)

/pub/gnu/gzip-1.2.4.tar.gz (GNU-Zipped tar)
/pub/msdos/starter/gzip124.zip (MS-DOS-binary)
/pub/unix/386ix/Solaris.x86/gzip (binary for Solaris 2/x86)
/pub/unix/386ix/isc/arcers/gzip (binary for ISC UNIX)
/ftp/bin/gzip (binary for SPARC, SunOS4.1.x)

LZH/LHA:

/pub/amiga/utilities/archivers/LhA_e138.run (Amiga binary)
/pub/atari/arcers/lharc2.ttp (ATARI binary)
/pub/atari/arcers/lzh_201l.lzh (ATARI binary)
/pub/msdos/starter/lha213.exe (MS-DOS binary)
/pub/unix/tools/lha-lharc/lha-1.00.tar.Z (UNIX source)

SysV pack:

GNU-Zip can unpack this; otherwise just use your favorite SysVr3 machine (command: **unpack**).

PS

PostScript—document layout, etc. language. Feed to your PostScript printer.

SEA:

Macintosh self-extracting archive. Upload the file in "macbinary" mode to your Macintosh and execute it (like EXE-wrapped ZIPs et al. on MS-DOS).

TAR-unpackers:

UNIX tar-program

/pub/amiga/utilities/archivers/tar-1.1.0 (Amiga binary)
/pub/gnu/tar-1.11.2.shar.gz (sh(ar)-packed GNU-tar source)

/pub/gnu/tar-1.11.2.tar.gz (tar-packed GNU-tar source)
/pub/msdos/starter/detar11.zip (MS-DOS tar-program)
/pub/msdos/starter/tar.zip (MS-DOS tar-program)
/pub/msdos/starter/extar10.zip (MS-DOS tar-program)
/pub/msdos/starter/pdtar.zip (MS-DOS tar-program)
/pub/msdos/starter/tar4dos.zip (MS-DOS tar-program)

BSD compress:

GNU-Zip can unpack this too.

/ftp/bin/uncompress(binary for SPARC, SunOS4.1.x)
/pub/amiga/utilities/archivers/compress-4.1.lha (Amiga binary)
/pub/msdos/starter/comp430*.zip (MS-DOS compress/)
/pub/msdos/starter/decomp2.zip (uncompresses)

ZIP:

One particular format of PKZIP can be opened by the GNU-Zip (see GNU-Zip documents); however it is not a general case.

For MS-DOS there seems to be two mutually incompatible PKZIPs, more info when I know better (I am not a DOS user ...).

/pub/amiga/utilities/archivers/unzip-5.1d3.lha (Amiga binary)
/pub/atari/arcers/stzip21.lzh (ATARI binary)
/pub/msdos/starter/pkz204g.exe (MS-DOS self-extracting arch)
/pub/msdos/starter/unz50p1.exe (MS-DOS—another one)
/pub/unix/tools/zip/unzip50.tar.Z (UNIX source)

ZOO:

/pub/amiga/utilities/archivers/Zoo-2.1.lha (Amiga binary)
/pub/atari/arcers/zoo*.* (ATARI programs)
/pub/msdos/starter/zoo210.exe (MS-DOS binary)
/pub/unix/tools/zoo/zoo-2.1.tar.Z (UNIX Zoo source)

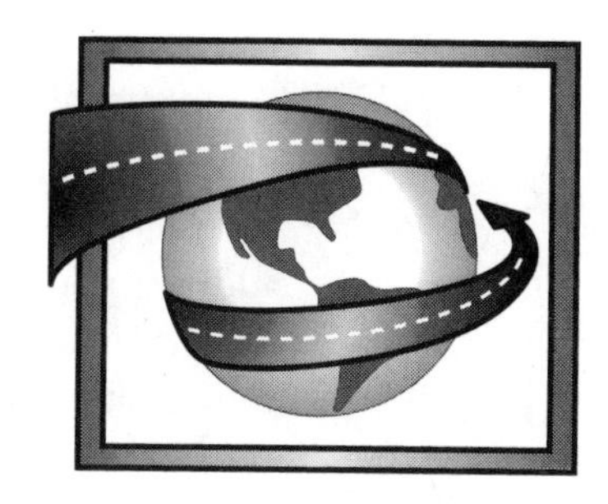

Appendix E

Internet Resources: Companies and Products to Aid Your Internet Journey

Throughout this book, I've listed resources you may want to access as part of your Internet travels. In this appendix I've listed these and others you may find useful. Please don't think this is a comprehensive or exhaustive list. The Internet and related businesses are changing so rapidly that it would be impossible to publish anything remotely resembling an all-inclusive list.

Notice, too, that because much of this information was captured online, I have shown only a company or product name and an Internet address. In fact, this is the way most of these companies are listed in their own advertisements on the net and in popular magazines. The Internet is becoming the way to contact companies about their products.

If you access information about a listed company on the Internet, you may be able to find a telephone number and an address; you may also discover that you can only use email to contact a particular company. However, the resources listed here will certainly get you started.

INTERNET SERVICE PROVIDERS

When I wrote the first edition of this book, there were only a handful of Internet service providers. It was a real chore for me to locate someone to help me get online. Today, that situation is drastically changed. Most major towns and many small communities now have Internet service providers. I will list some of the major ones here. Use this list as a starting point toward finding the resources you need in your local area.

An additional place to check is the local telephone book yellow pages. I find that more and more service providers are becoming real businesses with yellow page listings, offices, and storefronts. This was not the case in the beginning; many providers, even those serving relatively large towns, were located in basements or bedrooms.

If you have more than one provider choice in your locale, look for the company that has a 24-hour, 7-day-a-week technical support or helpdesk line. It is quite frustrating to be in the middle of configuring software or researching a topic on the net and not be able to find anyone to help you.

Look also for a full-service company. An information provider who provides only shell service, or only SLIP access, may not have the resources to support your needs as you grow. This may be less of a consideration if you are interested only in part-time, hobby-type access. But if you are looking for Internet service for your company, you want the service provider to be as professional and capable as you are.

For example, you may start out with a shell account, but as your needs grow you may need to expand to SLIP, ISDN, or even a T1 high-end link. If you start with a provider that can support this full range of services, it will be much easier to make the transition.

Also, full-service providers offer help with equipment configuration. They may even sell networking hardware such as bridges and routers, and have available personnel to conduct onsite installation and training.

The following list is only a minor fraction of what's available. For an up-to-date list of service provider resources (still not everything!), access the WebCrawler or another search engine and enter **Internet Access** as your search criteria. I did this while writing this appendix and got 6101 hits. You can also try Yahoo and look in **Business:Internet:Access Providers**.

AlterNet
UUNET Technologies, Inc.
800-258-9695
703-204-8000
info@alter.net

U.S. Internet, Inc.
127 N. Broadway
Knoxville, TN 37917
800-218-USIT (8748)
615-522-6788
info@usit.net

Internet Exchange
New York City
212-935-3322
217-322-1212

Netcom On-line Communication Services, Inc.
800-353-6600

Hooked
800-246-6533
http://www.hooked.net

PSI
800-774-0852
Interramp-info@psi.com
http://www/psi.net/interramp/

Cyberspace
515-945-7000

Prodigy Service
PO Box 8667
Gray, TN 37615-9967
800-776-3449

Delphi Internet
800-695-4005
info@delphi.com

Biddeford Internet Services
207-286-3581
Info@biddeford.com
http://www.biddeford.com/

Southeast Network Services, Inc.
http://jax.jaxnet.com/sns.commercial.html
Florida access

Microcom Internet Services
208-368-5400
sales@microcon.net
http://www.microcon.net

Internet Service Company
206-392-2897
http://www.netserve.com
Washington State access

Consolidated Access and Networks, Inc.
http://www.can.net/
Canadian access

Databank
1473 Highway 40
Lawrence, KS 66044
913-842-6699
accounts@databank.com

http://www.databank.com
CompuServe
aboyer@csi.compuserve.com
http//www.compuserve.com
800-433-0389
614-798-3356

SOFTWARE

Internet support software is a growing field. In the beginning all you really needed was a simple communications package with terminal emulation. You still need software of this type to make a shell (dial-up) connection, and there is a better selection than ever before.

However, the changing face of the Internet means you also need TCP and dial-up IP software, World Wide Web browsers, FTP clients, and so on. A number of companies are now offering suites of software to conduct these tasks. I'll list a few prominent players in this section.

PC Software

InfoMagic
PO Box 30370
Flagstaff, AZ 86003-0370
800-800-6613
602-526-9565
info@infomagic.com
CD-ROM-based software utilities, games, and reference material.

NetManage
800-558-7656
Chameleon Internet Software Suite

Cybernation
PO Box 130183
Sunrise, FL 33313
800-748-2988
TCP/IP and applications suite for Internet access.

Luckman Interactive
800-500-4411
Super Mosaic WWW Browser Software

InterCon Systems Corporation
950 Herndon Parkway
Herndon, VA 22070
703-709-5500

TCP/Connect II TCP/IP plus
Gopher, email, Telnet, and remote
SLIP/PPP Diai-in Software
ftp.intercon.com

Spry, Inc.
800-777-9638
info@spry.com
Internet in a Box
AIR Series Application Suite

Morning Star Technologies, Inc.
3518 Riverside Drive
Columbus, OH 43221-1754
800-558-7827
sales@morningstar.com
Morning Star Express Plus Internet
access suite

International Business Machines
Corporation
Personal Software Products Division

1000 N.W. 51st Street
Boca Raton, FL 33432
800-342-6672
OS/2 Warp operating system with
Internet access applications.

Microsoft Corporation
http://www.microsoft.com
Windows 95 with integrated online
support.

FTP Software, Inc.
100 Brickstone Square
Andover, MA 01810
800-863-4548
508-685-3300
info@ftp.com
http://www.ftp.com/home/explore
Internet access software suite.

Winweb WWW browser for
Windows
ftp.einet.net /einet/pc/winweb

Booklink
InternetWorks WWW browser
508-657-7000
ftp.booklink.com

ForeFront Group, Inc.
1360 Post Oak Boulevard
Suite 1660
Houston, TX 77056

800-867-1101
info@ffg.com
html authoring application.

Macintosh Software

Synergy Software
2457 Perkiomen Avenue
Reading, PA 19606
610-779-0522
maxwell@sales.synergy.com
Internet Access Suite

InterCon Systems Corporation
950 Herndon Parkway
Herndon, VA 22070
703-709-5500

TCP/Connect II TCP/IP plus
Gopher, email, Telnet, and remote
SLIP/PPP Dial-in Software
ftp.intercon.com

Morning Star Technologies, Inc.
3518 Riverside Drive
Columbus, OH 43221-1754
800-558-7827
sales@morningstar.com
Morning Star Express Plus Internet
access suite.

Samba WWW browser
ftp.w3.org /pub/www/bin/mac/old

MacWeb WWW browser
ft.einet.net /einet/mac/macweb

PUBLICATIONS

If any single part of this listing stands to become out of date quickly, it is the publications section. However, I want to list a few things here that you may find helpful as a way to get you started on your Internet research quest. The last time I checked, there were more than 200 current books in print about the Internet. I won't even try to list these. Check with your local bookstore and browse the shelves to locate what you need.

I will list in this section some monthly publications as well as some online resources you should consider as part of any research about the Internet and Internet resources. You may also see some of these listed in Chapter 8, but I wanted to group these resources where you could find them quickly.

Internet World
PO Box 713
Mount Morris, IL 61054-9965
800-573-3062
Monthly Magazine

Wired Magazine
520 Third Street, Fourth Floor
San Francisco, CA 94107
415-222-6200
editor@wired.com
info@wired.com

HotWired
http://www.hotwired.com/
online magazine

NetSurf
http://www.netsurf.com/nsd/index.html
online magazine

YPN (Your Personal Network)
800-638-1133
http://www.ypn.com/
Magazine-style guides on focused network topics. Bookstores or mail order.

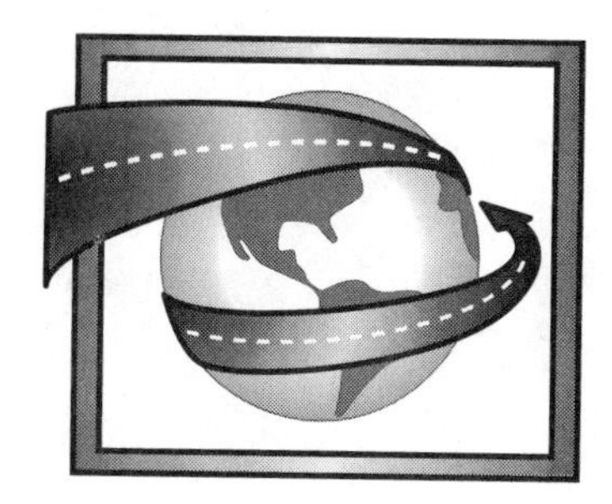

Glossary

Advanced Research Projects Agency	ARPA, the government agency initially responsible for starting the Internet.
Archie	A (mostly) universal on-line searching tool that lets you find files in archives that are available via anonymous FTP on the Internet by entering a name or description. You normally require a local client for most efficient Archie access.
ARPA	See *Advanced Research Projects Agency.*
ARPAnet	The beginnings of the Internet. ARPAnet was started by the Advanced Research Projects Agency (ARPA).
BTW	By The Way. Used as an abbreviation on email and real-time conversation links.

Chameleon	Packaged PC software that includes TCP/IP and dialup IP support, as well as graphical Internet applications.
Capture File	A file managed by your terminal emulation and communications software that stores information viewed on the screen during a communications session. There are several forms of capture file. The most common is a file that captures text as it scrolls on the screen. Another is a snapshot file—a text or graphics representation of a single computer screen display.
Channel	On IRC and other communications applications, a named area where users gather to discuss specific topics.
Client	A software application that runs on your desktop or local host machine to provide a user interface as well as to conduct some of the required processing for a data search and retrieval. There are Internet clients that link to Archie, Gopher, IRC, and other facilities.
CompuServe (CIS)	CompuServe Information Service. A commercial network that provides email, games, discussion, research, and other services. CompuServe users can access the Internet.
CompuServe Packet Network (CPN)	An international network provided and maintained by CompuServe. It was designed primarily to service CompuServe Information Service users, but it also carries traffic for other networked services, including Internet providers.

CSNET

Computer Science Network. Among the early networks that grew with the Internet.

Cu See-Me

A two-way video conferencing technology that permits desktop computer users to see and hear each other through the use of a local camera and sound card. CU See-Me works by attaching, over the Internet, to a reflector site which re-transmits the video signals of other users.

DARPA

See *Defense Advanced Research Projects Agency*

Defense Advanced Research Projects Agency

DARPA, a later version of the Advanced Research Projects Agency (ARPA). This agency also gave its name to an early version of the Internet, the DARPA Internet.

Distributed Application

A software application that runs on multiple machines in different locations. One component may be the user interface, which is run on a local machine, while a database searching component is executed on a remote computer.

Domain

A method of identifying Internet nodes with words or abbreviations instead of numbers. Domain Name Servers (DNS) maintain lists of network domains to help systems link with each other.

Download

The process of copying a file or files from a remote computer to a local one.

DNS

Domain Name Server. See *Domain*.

Email	Electronic mail. Text, graphics, sound, and photographs transmitted from one computer system to a specific user or group of users at a remote system or systems.
Electronic Mail	See *Email.*
Emoticon	A symbol used to convey emotions on a network link. Among the most popular emoticons are the smiley face :-) and the sad face :-(. Other symbols vary with the network or group.
Eudora	A graphical electronic mail interface designed for a SLIP or other network connection. Eudora is a shareware product, is available for Macintosh and PC platforms, and is among the most popular email packages for Internet use.
FAQ	Frequently Asked Questions. An abbreviation used on newsgroups, conversation links, and with file names. When researching a new topic, look for files labeled FAQ for quick introductory information.
Fiber Optic	An optical technology to carry high speed communications. Optic cable is being increasingly used for network backbone links.
File Transfer Protocol	A set of communication rules that provides for error-free transfer of files across a computer-to-computer link. FTP runs on a host computer and is used to copy files from a remote loca-

tion to the local host. When using the Internet with a SLIP or other network connection, you may run an FTP client on your desktop. Otherwise, the FTP software runs on your host machine.

file transfer protocol A computer protocol used to transfer data between machines. Common protocols include Kermit and ZMODEM.

Freenet A network service provider that offers the service as a community or free service. Freenets often are associated with libraries, universities, and other public institutions. Freenets can be accessed through the Internet and often provide access to the Internet via a local dial-up number.

FTP File Transfer Protocol.

FYI For Your Information. An email and real-time link abbreviation.

Gopher An Internet menu system used to find and access data by topic or through a pre-defined hierarchical system.

Hit In database terminology, a found record. If you search a database for files on games and you locate 23 files, your search resulted in 23 hits.

Host A computer system that accepts local and remote logins to provide some type of computer service, such as running programs, conducting database searches, communications, and network access. You use a host computer to access the Internet.

Home Page The starting page for a World Wide Web site. The Home Page is the starting address for multiple and sometimes complex pages of information. A WWW Home Page can be used like a menu or BBS, as an advertising tool, to interface with a variety of data, and so on. Home pages generally provide graphics and sometimes multimedia interfaces to information.

IMHO In My Humble Opinion. An abbreviation used on email and real-time computer links.

ISDN Integrated Services Digital Network. A method of interconnecting computers and other devices over a digital 64 Kbps or 128 Kbps link. ISDN is becoming increasingly popular for Internet connections as service providers offer dedicated and dialup ISDN links to their hosts. Although ISDN telephone service itself is relatively inexpensive, the technology still requires a relatively expensive bridge at each end of the link.

Interchange Point A network-to-network link that provides a set of services such as email to users of the linked networks.

Internet in a Box Packaged software that includes TCP/IP and dialup IP suppost, as well as graphical Internet applications.

Internet Protocol	One of the packet switching protocols that defines the Internet.
Interoperability	The ability of computer hardware and software systems from different manufacturers to work together. Interoperability takes on different forms, from complete software and hardware compatibility, to the ability simply to exchange data from specific applications.
InterSlip	A popular IP client that uses the SLIP protocol.
IP	See *Internet Protocol.*
IPHONE	A software application that permits Internet users with multimedia desktop computers and an IP connection to use voice communications in real time.
IRC	Internet Relay Chat. A real-time, channelized Internet service that allows multiple users to talk among themselves using the keyboard and screen. Whereas email is a store and forward system, IRC communications take place in real time.
Kermit	A file transfer protocol.
Listserv	An automated application that maintains mailing lists and other data. You can subscribe to a Listserv to keep abreast of specific fields or technologies.

Local Area Networks (LAN)
A grouping of local PCs and other computers that connects the machines via Ethernet or another networking protocol. A LAN lets the linked machines share files and printers, and exchange email. Many LANs include a communications gateway that allows users to communicate with dial-up services or other networks.

Log File
A form of capture file generated and managed by your communications software. A log file captures all characters and keystrokes during a communications session.

Lynx
A text-based World Wide Web Browser that can be used with text-based terminals for WWW access when a graphical system is not available. Lynx can be used with a dumb terminal or terminal emulator whereas a graphical WWW interface requires a computer with a graphical user interface, such as Microsoft Windows or a Macintosh.

MacTCP
TCP networking software designed to operate on the Apple Macintosh. MacTCP is included with the Macintosh operating system System 7.5 and later.

MCI Mail
A commercial electronic mail service from MCI. MCI Mail users can exchange mail among themselves and with Internet users.

Metropolitan Area Networks
A form of local network that connects users across a metropolitan area.

Milnet

One of the early networks that derived from the original ARPAnet.

Modem

Modulator/Demodulator. An electronic device that converts a computer's digital information into analog data for transmission across a dedicated line or dial-up link. A modem also converts the transmitted analog data back into digital information for use by the computer.

Mosaic

A graphical user interface for browsing the World Wide Web. Mosaic was designed and programmed by NCSA, the National Center for Supercomputer Applications, at the University of Illinois. It has been distributed as freeware, but now the technology has been licensed by a number of commercial companies who now sell the product under various brand names or bundled with online software packages.

Netiquette

A term to describe accepted standards of behavior on the Internet: Internet etiquette.

Netscape

A graphical user interface for browsing the World Wide Web. Netscape was designed and programmed by some of the same team members responsible for Mosaic. Netscape, however, was a commercial venture from the beginning. After initial freeware distribution of the beta versions, Netscape Communications is offering the product as commercial software.

Node A computer system that serves as a host on the Internet. A node can be a mini-computer or a mainframe, a PC, Macintosh or other personal computer configured as a host. A node is connected directly to the Internet as opposed to using Internet facilities through another machine.

NSFNET National Science Foundation Network. A network established in 1986 to tie together users with five national super-computer centers. This network is no longer in operation.

Packets Groups of data to be transmitted over a network. Packets include information for error correction in addition to the actual data being transmitted.

Peer-to-peer A computer-to-computer network relationship that makes each computer equal in power. Peer-to-peer networks allow all computers to share resources equally, rather than having a single server through which all computers on the network must work.

Pine A menu-driven UNIX mail software application. Pine is available on many Internet hosts to make sending and receiving email easier. A PC client version of Pine also is available.

PPP Point to Point Protocol. A dialup IP protocol often used instead of SLIP. In addition to better dialup IP support,

PPP also allows you to put a small network on the Internet.

Procomm A popular shareware and commercial communications software application for PCs.

Router A network facility that manages communications links.

Server Computer software that manages the major part of a software system in conjunction with a remote client application. Also, a portion of a distributed application.

Service Provider A company or other entity that provides Internet or other computer services for third parties.

Shell A user interface that provides access to an operating system or other application.

SLIP Serial Line Internet Protocol, a method for running an IP network connection over a serial line, usually through a modem over a dialup telephone link. SLIP connections are rapidly becoming the preferred method for connecting to the Internet as more and more service providers make it available. A SLIP or other network connection is required to take advantage of the graphical user interfaces to the Internet, such as Mosaic and Netscape.

Tar — A UNIX-based application that groups multiple files into a single file for transmission over a network, or between two computers through a dial-up link. This enables the transfer of a single file when multiple files are required for an application. Tar files are frequently compressed before they are transmitted.

TCP/IP — Transmission Control Protocol/Internet Protocol. Networking data transmission protocols used on the Internet.

Telix — A popular shareware software package for PC communications.

Telnet — A local software tool that lets you log on to remote computers. Telnet software knows how to convert domain names to Internet addresses and how to use those addresses to locate the target computer. Once your system is attached to the target, a normal logon sequence is initiated.

Text File — A computer file that contains only text characters, with no graphics or special symbols. A text file can be edited with most UNIX or PC editors and can be displayed on a computer screen without using a special application.

TCPMAN — Application software that provides a dialing and configuration interface to the Trumpet Winsock package.

Trumpet News — A popular shareware news client for the Microsoft Windows environment.

Trumpet Winsock A popular shareware software package for Microsoft Windows machines that handles TCP/IP and dialup IP support.

Upload The process of transmitting a local computer file up the network link to a remote computer system.

USENET A bulletin board network system used to exchange special interest information. USENET was around before the Internet, but now a lot of USENET traffic is carried over the Internet.

User Interfaces The part of the operating system or application with which the user interacts to send commands to the computer and to view the computer's response.

UUCP UNIX-to-UNIX Copy. A built-in feature of UNIX that provides users with email, news and file transfer access to the Internet.

Virus A software application designed to infect existing software and cause damage. Viruses are sometimes injected into networks and computer systems to harass the users and to damage data.

w A UNIX command that displays the user ID of everyone logged on to the local system and shows what tasks they currently are conducting. See also *who*.

WAIS Wide Area Information Servers. An Internet facility for managing and distributing a variety of data across the Internet.

who	A UNIX command that displays the ID and other information about all the users logged on to the local system, or about a specific user when a user ID is included. See also *w*.
whois	A UNIX command that displays the user ID and other information about the person whose on-line handle or nickname is supplied as an argument to the command. whois tbadgett, for example, will show registered information about user tbadgett if this user is maintained in the Internet whois server database.
Wide Area Networks	A network connecting users from many areas that (WAN) transcends cities or other geographical boundaries.
WinQVT	A shareware software application that includes Telnet, FTP, News and Mail support for SLIP or other networked Internet access.
Winsock	Windows Socket. Software that permits Microsoft Windows computers to establish TCP/IP links with the Internet.
XMODEM	A file transfer protocol.
Z	A file extension in UNIX that shows that the file with which it is associated has been compressed with the COMPRESS command (e.g. filename.Z). You must use UNCOMPRESS to expand the file before using it.
ZMODEM	A file transfer protocol. ZMODEM is among the fastest and most popular error free file transfer protocols in common use on the Internet.

INDEX

A

B

C

D

E

F

G

H

I

J

K

L

N

O

T

U

V

W

X

Z